Warman's JEWELRY

Fine & Costume Jewelry • *5th Edition*

IDENTIFICATION & PRICE GUIDE

Christie Romero

Published by

Krause Publications, a division of F+W Media, Inc.
700 East State Street • Iola, WI 54990-0001
715-445-2214 • 888-457-2873
www.krausebooks.com

To order books or other products call toll-free 1-800-258-0929
or visit us online at www.krausebooks.com.

ISBN-13: 978-1-4402-3597-9
ISBN-10: 1-4402-3597-X

Cover Design by Sharon Bartsch
Designed by Jana Tappa
Edited by Kristine Manty and Mary Sieber

Printed in China

On the cover, clockwise from upper left, all photos courtesy of Heritage Auctions, Inc.: Retro diamond, ruby, platinum, and gold earrings, round-cut rubies weighing 6.50 carats, enhanced by full and single-cut diamonds weighing 1.50 carats, set in platinum, completed by clip backs; also has matching brooch, not pictured, price for whole set: **$14,340**; ring with grayish yellowish green oval-shaped diamond measuring 10.22 x 7.43 x 3.87 mm and weighing 2.25 carats, enhanced by pink full-cut diamonds weighing a total of 0.30 carat, set in 18k pink gold, accented by full-cut diamonds weighing a total of 0.50 carat, set in 18k white gold, **$41,825**; diamond and white gold flexible cuff bracelet, full-cut diamonds weighing 22.38 carats, set in 18k white gold, 7" x 13/16", **$20,315**; azurmalachite, diamond and gold necklace, enhanced by full-cut diamonds weighing 5.75 carats, set in 18k gold, 15" x 1-1/8", **$11,352**; sapphire, ruby, emerald, diamond, and gold earrings, leaf-shaped earrings suspend detachable pendants, pear-shaped sapphires measuring 8.25 x 6.20 x 3.50 mm and 8.20 x 7 x 3.20 mm and weighing 1.40 and 1.45 carats respectively, enhanced by round-shaped sapphires weighing 1.80 carats, further enhanced by round-shaped rubies weighing 1.60 carats, accented by round-shaped emeralds weighing 0.85 carats, further accented by full-cut diamonds weighing 0.60 carat, set in textured 18k white and yellow gold, completed by clip backs, marked Buccellati, Italy, for non-pierced ears, 2-1/8" x 7/8", **$8,365**; more information on this diamond and gold starburst pendant-brooch is on P. 82; more information on this amethyst, diamond and silver-topped gold necklace is on P. 90.

On the back cover: More information about these pieces, from top right, can be found on the pages listed: garnet and silver pendant, P. 109; platinum and fancy blue diamond Tiffany ring, P. 158; emerald and diamond bracelet-necklace, P. 194.

ACKNOWLEDGMENTS

The publisher wishes to thank the following people, without whom this new edition of *Warman's Jewelry* would not be possible.

Foremost gratitude goes to the late Christie Romero, one of the top authorities on antique and period jewelry in the world, and whose work makes up the bulk of this book. The founder of the Center for Jewelry Studies and a regular appraiser on *Antiques Roadshow*, Romero is best known as a jewelry historian, consultant, gemologist and instructor of antique and period jewelry. She taught classes in Southern California for more than 20 years before her death in 2009.

Romero lectured throughout the country at seminars, meetings, conventions and special events. She was on the faculties of the annual summer conference on Antique Jewelry and Gemstones at Hofstra University in Hempstead, NY, and the Jewelry Design Department at the Fashion Institute of Design & Merchandising in downtown Los Angeles. She lectured for the American Society of Appraisers, the College for Appraisers, the Gemological Institute of America, Women's Jewelry Association, the Northwest Gemological Institute and many other groups.

The Center for Jewelry Studies, created by Romero, was dedicated to the sharing of information on the history, identification and marketing of antique, period and vintage jewelry. The Center offered quality programs designed to supplement the careers of those in jewelry-related fields – including dealers, appraisers, jewelers and gemologists – as well as enhance the enjoyment of collectors, heirs and jewelry lovers.

Romero authored three previous editions of *Warman's Jewelry*. We are proud to keep Romero's lifelong passion and scholarly work alive with this new edition.

Thank you to Pamela Y. Wiggins, who wrote the introduction to this book. Wiggins has been an avid collector of vintage costume jewelry for the past 25 years and is the co-founder of Costume Jewelry Collectors International and the Expert Guide to Antiques for About.com, where she often writes about jewelry and related topics.

Thank you also to Kathy Flood, author of *Warman's Costume Jewelry Figurals*, the fourth edition of *Warman's Jewelry*, and *Warman's Jewelry Field Guide*, 2nd edition. She is also a columnist and regular contributor to *Antique Trader* magazine. Kathy's beautiful images of jewelry are sprinkled throughout the book.

Many auctions houses provided the stunning color photos featured throughout. Those auction houses are noted in the back of the book. And last, but not least, we extend much appreciation to all collectors and dealers out there keeping the fun and fascinating hobby of jewelry collecting alive and well.

TABLE OF CONTENTS

TABLE OF CONTENTS

INTRODUCTION

WHY JEWELRY COLLECTING REMAINS SO STEADFAST

There's no question about the timeless appeal of jewelry. Even people who don't see themselves as bona fide collectors likely have a stash of jewelry they have either purchased, inherited, or received as gifts. Time passes, and suddenly it's "vintage." Some people sell it once they realize the value, others pass it on to family members, and a few become true collectors, adding to the pieces they have already accumulated over the years.

From precious metals and gemstones to trinkets of yesteryear purchased at dime stores, every piece of jewelry has a place in a collection somewhere, and each collection is as unique as the individual who puts it together. The pieces gathered together express the past in a unique way, since popular movies, celebrities and historical events are reflected in these special adornments. From antique suffragette jewelry to pieces inspired by the movie *Gone with the Wind* to sterling items made during World War II when metals were rationed, and even peace sign pendants dating to the 1960s, popular culture has always been reflected in jewelry worn around the world.

But why the buzz and interest in antique, vintage, and collectible jewelry today? Believe it or not, pop culture is still influencing the way women accessorize and, now more than ever, what individuals are inspired to collect.

"Antique" jewelry, defined as 100 years old or older by the United States Customs Service, encompasses many eras collectors find appealing. From before the Civil War, moving into the Victorian era, and during the decades when automobiles, electricity and telephones were just coming about, jewelry with great romanticism and symbolic meaning was lovingly worn. Whether a family heirloom or a treasure found at a flea market, these older pieces take their new owners back in time. Even the recent Steampunk move-ment, which combines steam-age fashion with the age-old tendency to rebel against the norm, has a new generation learning about Victorian adornment.

Fans of the *Downton Abbey* television series have admired jewelry on the show, which ranges from Victorian to Edwardian and Art Deco styles, and they're inspired to own similar looks. Movies like *The Great Gatsby* and shows like *Boardwalk Empire* also have revived style elements of vintage jewelry. *Mad Men* spawned an interest in 1960s culture that carried over from clothing to jewelry. Even multi-strand "granny" beads once considered common and undesirable were being worn by the young and fashionable set quite recently.

But when it comes right down to it, the timetable for defining vintage is based on a sliding scale that changes as we move from one decade to the next. It's loosely deemed newer than antique and older than collectible, and defined by many as Edwardian through the 1980s as of now. However, because Edwardian is more akin to Victorian in style than the Deco and "flapper" looks of the 1920s, that era is sometimes referenced as antique jewelry (and within a few short years it will, indeed, become antique without question). Some people even define jewelry from the early 1990s as vintage when there is great demand for it, as with costume pieces made by the House of Chanel and other couturiers that are still sought by both collectors and fashionistas, often prompted by what celebrities are wearing.

Collectible jewelry also has its fans and shouldn't be overlooked in terms of desirability and value. Even though it's not necessarily old – generally dating from the mid-1990s through today – it has a place in most jewelry collections, especially in the instance of "revival" pieces. These are inspired by older looks, and some of them even use old components but are newly made and offered for sale in boutiques and sometimes department stores or through individual reps.

For a vintage jewelry lover to take notice, newer pieces should be finely made of quality components and most often made in limited quantities, whether machine fabricated or artisan crafted. That rules out most mass imports and low quality discount store pieces in the costume jewelry realm, although who knows how many of those items will be considered collectible 20, 50 or 100 years from now? After all, no one would have ever suspected that cheap Bakelite figural brooches purchased at the local 5 & 10 in the 1930s would be so highly valued today, with celebrities Whoopi Goldberg and Lily Tomlin being rumored to collect them.

As long as we have art imitating life through pop culture, the response will be life imitating art. We may not know what the next trendsetting movie, television program or historical event will bestow on us, or what collecting whim will create a flux of demand. What we do know is that it will inevitably come, and collectors will respond – along with the general populace – by wearing and collecting jewelry.

STATE OF THE JEWELRY MARKET AND TODAY'S TRENDS

Today's collectible jewelry market is in somewhat of a flux, although that's always true to a certain extent. Trends in collecting aren't predictable, and at times they can be quite curious. A few collectors gathering items can cause a ripple of demand that impacts the antique and vintage marketplace on a larger scale as dealers compete to stock these items.

This happened in the vintage costume jewelry area with flowers made of cellulose acetate, a form of plastic, with rhinestone centers. Collectors also saw a rapid rise in demand for thermoset hinged clamper bangles studded

In the past several decades, there has been a surge in demand for Miriam Haskell pieces. Miriam Haskell pink glass grapes pin with glass leaves and pink glass beads, marked Miriam Haskell, 2 3/4" x 1 1/2". **200-$250**

with rhinestones in the not-too-distant past. Vintage Christmas jewelry and Bakelite have also had respective peaks in demand, and most shop owners specializing in antique and collectible goods remember the run on older brooches around 2005 after they appeared on modern designer runways. While still quite collectible, prices for all these items have cooled for now and dropped back to more reasonable levels than those seen during their respective rushes.

Designer costume jewelry demand ebbs and flows, and sometimes just as curiously since it's hard to pinpoint the reason for the flux. While always popular, jewelry marked "Miriam Haskell" has seen a number of surges in demand over the past several decades, and prices, especially for high quality, intricately crafted pearl pieces, remain strong for now. Demand for Juliana jewelry made by DeLizza & Elster, marked only with a paper hang tag when new so it's largely unmarked today, also remains strong for the most exquisite pieces, while more common designs can be purchased quite reasonably.

Some designer jewelry that was avidly sought a decade

Jewelry made by DeLizza & Elster is popular today. DeLizza & Elster coral gold stippled cabochon set in peach from the early 1960s, necklace, pin, bracelet and earrings; price depends on color.
$1,500-$2,500+ set

or two ago, like most anything made by Eisenberg, Hobé, Boucher, Trifari and others, has cooled considerably with only the rarest and most desirable designs bringing top dollar. That's not to say that the moderate pieces bearing these marks aren't just as nice as always, and most jewelry companies produced lines at a variety of price points and quality levels back in the day. But demand drives the market, and until desire for the mid-range pieces from these brands surges once again, it's largely a time for buyers in the low to moderate marketplace to reap the benefits.

In the fine jewelry sector, there's been an overwhelming trend to scrap jewelry during the recent past, due to the rise in the price of precious metals. Broken, battered and out-of-date jewelry made of karat gold and platinum brought a pretty penny for owners who had been holding these pieces. Most collectors have held onto their finest precious metal and gemstone treasures, but there's no doubt that some beautiful antique jewelry that should have never been con-

sidered for scrap was melted down, and to lovers of these old things, this is truly a tragedy.

In the long term, though, less antique fine jewelry available in the marketplace means higher prices for the items that survived. How much they will increase in value remains to be seen as the market for fine jewelry will likely remain soft until the economy does an uptick and purse strings are loosened for luxury purchases.

THE IMPORTANCE OF BEING AN EDUCATED COLLECTOR

The old adage that an educated consumer is the best customer couldn't be truer in the antique and vintage jewelry marketplace. Reputable dealers know educated buyers will recognize high-end pieces and be willing to pay the price to add rarities to their collections when they're fortunate enough to offer them for sale, and they appreciate that.

But as a vintage and antique jewelry collector, there are

Jewelry made by Trifari is among the designer jewelry that has cooled on the market, except for the most rarest pieces. Semi-circles and baguettes bracelet, 1950s, heavily gold-plated metal, articulated half moons or semicircle links, 20 central crystal baguettes, 58 smaller stones along perimeters, signed Trifari, 7 3/4". **$150-$250**

many varied reasons to work toward being an educated and confident consumer. This is especially true as shoppers become more discerning with their jewelry budgets. Everyone wants to get the most bang for their buck today, and education means knowing when you're getting a bargain and when you can find the same thing for less elsewhere with some patience and diligence.

Arming yourself with education goes beyond snagging a great find at a bargain price, although that's always fun for a collector. Answering questions about how old an item is, where it originated and who made it, what it's made of and how much it's worth will always lead jewelry owners to do a bit of research. They learn without looking too far that age doesn't necessarily make jewelry valuable, but good

design will always be fashionable and in demand. They also find that fine jewelry and costume jewelry styles can be very similar. Fine jewelry has inspired many fabulously fake designs, especially when it comes to pieces made from the 1940s back to the Victorian era.

Learning actually takes on a life of its own when collectors become obsessed with research. They go on to discover how greatly condition affects value, which repairs preserve value and which ones are detrimental, how to develop an all-important eye for quality, and even how to identify unsigned jewelry. While it might sound a bit daunting, for folks with a strong interest in any type of jewelry, it is effortless work that ends up feeling more like play. So where to begin?

Experienced collectors as well as those just getting their feet wet in the hobby often recommend *Warman's Jewelry Identification and Price Guide* for reliable information and a wide representation of what the antique and vintage jewelry market has to offer. Acquiring this book is a great first step in bolstering jewelry education. Other books on jewelry collecting are available as well, and the best will provide authoritative history to go along with the attractive photographs displayed on their pages.

It's important not to stop with books, however, because some are better than others when they are evaluated with frankness. One of the best ways to learn which books are top-notch, along with myriad other jewelry lessons, is by interacting with other collectors. Whether you do this on the Internet, in person at antique and collectible shows where jewelry is sold, taking classes related to jewelry history, or by participating in jewelry collecting clubs and organizations, don't ever underestimate the value of personal interaction.

One of the main benefits of interacting with others is the opportunity to hold vintage and antique jewelry and examine it closely, even if it's something you can only hope to own some day. Books will help you learn what to look for, but you'll never truly develop an eye for the preeminent and understand how to evaluate jewelry in terms of quality and condition until you hold the best of the best in your hand. This is where patronizing antique shows and attending events for collectors, such as conventions and workshops, will really pay off.

Of course, if it's impossible for you to attend these types of events, sharing information online is also very helpful once you've read everything you can find on a particular topic and learn which print-based information is reliable and what's not quite up to snuff. Through listserves, online groups, social media and other Internet-based resources, you can share photos, ask questions, and exchange information with other collectors and dealers that specialize in the items you're researching or contemplating adding to a collection.

Becoming part of an organization like Costume Jewelry Collectors International (CJCI) offers jewelry lovers, whether beginners or seasoned pros, an opportunity to not only glean information but to share it as well. Whether you participate through the organization's social networking site online, access its educational resources through its website, or attend the group's yearly conventions that include interacting with special guests and participating in jewelry workshops, you'll find a way to mingle with others you can learn from and/or mentor depending on your experience level. To find out more about all these facets of CJCI, visit its website at www.costumejewelrycollectors.com.

If you're interested in attending organized workshops that lean toward fine jewelry topics (costume jewelry is sometimes covered as well), consider a trip to the Antique Jewelry & Art Conference, also known as "Jewelry Camp," held each year in various locations around the country. You'll find more information on the next camp for adults interested in jewelry at www.jewelrycamp.org.

For a well-researched publication on jewelry of all kinds, along with regular email updates, consider joining the Association for the Study of Jewelry and the Related Arts (ASJRA). This organization focuses on jewelry ranging from fine to artisan to costume, publishes a quarterly journal titled *Adornment,* sponsors special events, and keeps members abreast of jewelry-related exhibits around the world. Learn more about the mission of ASJRA and the benefits of joining at www.asjra.net.

— *Pamela Y. Wiggins*

ABOUT PAMELA Y. WIGGINS

Pamela Y. Wiggins has avidly collected vintage costume jewelry for the past 25 years, and has sold antique and vintage jewelry for nearly as long, as the proprietor of Chic Antiques by Pamela Wiggins. She is the co-founder of Costume Jewelry Collectors International (CJCI) and is the Expert Guide to Antiques for About.com, where she often writes on jewelry and related topics. She has also written numerous features relating to adornment for national and regional publications as a freelance journalist specializing in antiques and collectibles, and has lectured on costume jewelry topics for numerous groups throughout her collecting career.

ORGANIZATION OF THE BOOK

Warman's Jewelry Identification and Price Guide is divided into three main sections: Late 18th and 19th Centuries, Turn of the Century, and 20th Century. A time line precedes and a glossary, references section, and index follow the main body of the book.

Time Line: One of the unique features of *Warman's Jewelry* is the "Time Line." Its purpose is to aid in circa-dating and put jewelry in context with other relevant historical events, discoveries, and inventions. It also summarizes some of the information included in the text of each section. The dates can be used to set the earliest and/or latest possible circa date for a piece. For example, the lowering of karatages of gold to 15, 12, and 9 karat was made legal in Great Britain in 1854. Therefore, gold jewelry with the British designation "9 ct" would date to after 1854. In 1932, the British law was changed, eliminating 15 and 12 karat in favor of 14 karat gold, which gives us the latest date for a piece marked "15 ct" or "12 ct."

Construction methods, materials, and findings, if unaltered, can also be helpful circa-dating clues. For example, commercially made safety catches for brooches were introduced around the turn of the 20th century (one version was patented in 1901, another in 1911). An original safety catch on a brooch, then, is a telltale sign of 20th century manufacture. Care must be taken, however, to ascertain that the finding is, in fact, original. Alterations on old pieces are common.

Patents are another useful circa-dating tool when used as a clue to a piece's age in addition to other factors, such as style and manufacturer's dates of operation. Prior to the 1930s, the patent's actual date of issue is more often stamped on a piece rather than the number. This is not necessarily the year in which the piece was made, as patents are valid for 17 years (design patents for a maximum of 14; some terms were shorter).

Clothing styles have often dictated or at least influenced types and styles of jewelry, so it is helpful to have some knowledge of fashion history when researching and dating a piece. Significant specific events related to fashion are listed in the Time Line, but space did not permit the inclusion of every stylistic change in clothing and jewelry fashion. Some of this information can be found in the text of each section, and, for further information, books on fashion history are included in the references.

The dates given in the Time Line are as accurate as could be ascertained. Research is never complete, however. New information continues to be discovered, which sometimes contradicts previously published "facts."

Different dates are often given in various sources for the same event. Sometimes there is a span of a number of years between date of first invention and dates of patenting, perfecting, publishing results, commercialization, and common use. One source may cite, for example, the date a new manufacturing process was patented, but another may give the date it was invented, perhaps five years earlier. Or it may have taken its inventor five years to perfect, and may not have been available to the public for another five. The difficult task for historians is to decide which date is the most accurate, significant, and helpful. Analysis of history is often a matter of subjective interpretation.

History: Jewelry does not exist in a vacuum. Fashion and history have a cause-and-effect relationship to jewelry designs. Events, discoveries, inventions, social trends, and fads play important roles in jewelry history. Each category of this book is prefaced by an encapsulated history so that readers will understand why a particular piece of jewelry was made and worn during a given period. Design elements that identify a particular style or period and well-known designers and manufacturers are also included.

It is not always possible to pinpoint the age of a piece of jewelry exactly. A dated publication can help to circa-date a piece, but relying on only one piece of evidence can also be misleading. Some models (manufacturers' name for designs) continued to be made for many years, even decades, as long as they were popular and sold well. There is a bell curve to every style or trend—an ascension, peak, and tapering off in popularity. Styles evolve, coexist, and overlap. This is better understood when history is viewed as a continuum of simultaneous events, rather than as a linear succession of events.

Improved methods of communication have hastened the rate of influence and change over the past two centuries; today, trends come and go at breakneck speed. Historians used to record changes in fashion by the decade; now changes occur annually.

References: For further information, the references that were consulted for the text for each section and category are listed in the appendix. This appendix also includes periodicals, collectors' clubs, Internet sites, and museums. Because of growing interest and the constant need for updated information, new titles and new editions appear every year. One good search engine that compiles the listings of several sites is www.bookfinder.com.

Marks: Categories with numerous makers' marks appear separately in an appendix, as do marks that span more than one category. Attribution of unsigned pieces must rely on provenance or documentation such as company catalogs or archives, sales receipts or owners' records, and fashion magazines or trade publications that picture the item in question along with its maker's name. Most old jewelry is unmarked and unattributable and must be evaluated solely on its own merits. Ideally, the same should be true of signed pieces, but the fact is that an important name on a piece scores points with collectors and adds value. Nevertheless, the name itself should not be the only or even the first thing taken into consideration when evaluating a signed piece. Marks and attributions are the frosting on the cake.

Photos and captions: The variety of jewelry is so great that it would be impossible to include examples of every kind. Unlike some other collectibles, with jewelry there is less likelihood of finding pieces identical to those shown. In certain categories, such as mass-produced costume jewelry of the mid-20th century, multiples of the same design can still be found. What you will find more often are comparable pieces—from the same period, of the same style, made from the same materials. The prices listed are for specific pieces of specific quality and condition.

Glossary: Jewelry has its own lexicon. Many jewelry terms are derived from the French, which became the language of choice when jewelry-making terminology was adopted internationally in the 18th century. This glossary lists terms used in *Warman's Jewelry* and is necessarily incomplete. The general references list jewelry dictionaries that the reader can use as supplements. Some jewelry-related websites have glossaries as well. Often there is more than one word that can be used to describe a piece of jewelry.

PRICE NOTES: BUYER'S GUIDE, NOT SELLER'S GUIDE

Most of the pieces pictured in this book were for sale or sold at auction within the past few years. Those that are from private collections were usually acquired at antiques shows, shops and malls, auctions, flea markets, and yard sales over the past several years, but are valued at current levels.

The marketplace where a piece of jewelry is sold affects price as much as other criteria, i.e., design, craftsmanship, condition, demand and scarcity, and intrinsic value of metals and stones in fine jewelry. Differences were often a result of the type of marketplace (e.g., an urban retail shop versus a rural flea market), rather than its region or locale.

LATE GEORGIAN PERIOD

Date	General History, Discoveries & Inventions	Date	Jewelry & Gemstone History, Discoveries & Inventions
		1730	Georges Frédéric Strass becomes famous for paste jewelry (c.)
1760	George III becomes king of Great Britain	1760	American goldsmith Paul Revere begins making jewelry (c.)
		1764	Josiah Wedgwood introduces fine ceramic known as jasperware in plaques with relief decoration resembling cameos, mounted in cut steel, manufactured by Matthew Boulton beginning in 1773
1774	Louis XVI becomes king of France	1769	Die-stamping machine patented by John Pickering, adapted for inexpensive jewelry in 1777
1775	American Revolution begins, Congress adopts the Declaration of Independence, 1776	1780	Burmese jadeite imported into China
1782	French scientist Antoine Laurent Lavoisier succeeds in melting platinum from its ore using pure oxygen	1785	Eye miniatures popularized by Prince George of England
1789	French Revolution begins, ends 1799	1786	Marc Étienne Janety, goldsmith to Louis XVI of France, crafts a sugar bowl out of platinum
	George Washington elected first President of the United States, dies 1799	1793	Seril Dodge of Providence, RI, advertises offering of jewelry items made to order, sells business to half-brother Nehemiah, 1796
		1795	Diamonds begin to be set à jour (c.)
1799-1815	Napoleonic Wars	1799	Amethysts discovered in the Ural Mountains of Russia
1800	Thomas Jefferson elected President of the U.S.	1800	À jour settings for colored stones begin to appear (c.)
	Alessandro Volta invents the first battery, the Volta Pile		Cannetille filigree developed by Parisian jewelers (c.)
	Metallurgist Wm. H. Wollaston, chemist Smithson Tennant begin collaboration, create commercial-grade platinum, discover platinum family of metals (palladium, rhodium, 1802; iridium, osmium, 1803)		
1801	Robert Hare of Philadelphia invents oxyhydrogen ("gas") blowpipe	1801	E. Hinsdale establishes first American factory for the manufacture of fine jewelry in Newark, NJ
1804	Napoleon crowns himself Emperor of France	1804	Royal Ironworks of Berlin opens, jewelry production begins 1806
1811	George III declared insane; Regency period begins in Britain		
1812-1815	War between U.S. and Great Britain		
1813-1815	Prussian War of Liberation against Napoleon	1813-1815	Berlin iron jewelry made in Germany as patriotic gesture during War of Liberation: "gold gab ich fur eisen" [I gave gold for iron]
1815	Kingdom of France (Bourbon dynasty) restored, Louis XVIII	1815	Fortunato Pio Castellani established in Rome, begins study of becomes king granulation in ancient goldwork, 1827
		1819	The Gas Blowpipe by E.D. Clarke is published
1820	George III of Great Britain dies, George IV becomes king	1820s	Ancient goldwork discovered in Etruscan excavations
	Platinum discovered in Russian Ural Mountains		
1824	Charles X becomes king of France	1824	Pinmaking machine for straight pins patented in England by Lemuel Wellman Wright, by John Howe in U.S. 1832
1829-1837	Andrew Jackson is President of U.S.	1829	Sir Walter Scott's Anne of Geierstein is published, describing the opal as "misfortune's stone"
			French square hallmark for doublé d'or (rolled gold) introduced by Paris Mint
1830	"India rubber" elastic first appears in women's clothing	1830	Claw/coronet settings of the Middle Ages revived
	Godey's Lady's Book first published		
	Louis-Philippe I becomes king of France		
	George IV of Great Britain dies, William IV becomes king		
1836	Edmund Davey discovers and identifies acetylene U.S. Patent Act passed. U.S. Patent Office issues Patent Number 1		

Time line images: George III courtesy of Wikipedia; George Washington courtesy of Wikipedia; Louis XVIII courtesy of Coutau-Begarie Auctions; Andrew Jackson public domain image courtesy of the U.S. Senate; filigree courtesy of Sotheby's.

Early Victorian (Romantic) Period

Date	General History, Discoveries & Inventions	Date	Jewelry & Gemstone History, Discoveries & Inventions
1837	Victoria becomes Queen of Great Britain	1837	Enameled garter armlet made for Queen Victoria; Order of the Garter strap and buckle motifs become popular
	Louis J. M. Daguerre perfects daguerreotype photographic process		Charles Lewis Tiffany founds company in New York City; becomes Tiffany & Co. 1853
	The telegraph is patented by Cooke and Wheatstone, improved by Samuel Morse, first message sent 1844		
1839	Charles Goodyear invents and patents (1844) vulcanized rubber; displays products at Crystal Palace (1851)		
1840	Victoria weds Prince Albert	1840	Electroplating commercialized, patented by Elkingtons of Birmingham. Large-scale jewelry manufacturing begins in U.S.
			Process for permanently foiled pastes (faceted glass) discovered
			Steam power first used for diamond cutting in Amsterdam
		c. 1840	Scottish motifs in "pebble" (agate) jewelry popularized, continuing through the rest of the century
			Repoussé and machine stamping replace cannetille (gold filigree)
			Algerian knot motif introduced in Paris
1842	Gutta percha introduced in Paris	1841	Duty on imported jewelry and mounted gemstones levied by U.S.
	Excavations of ancient Assyrian capital of Nineveh begin		
	British kite-shaped registry mark introduced	1846	Riker, Tay & Searing founded in Newark, NJ, become Riker Bros. 1892
		1847	Cartier founded in Paris
1848	Balmoral Castle in Scotland purchased by Queen Victoria	1848	Caldwell & Bennett becomes J.E. Caldwell & Co., Philadelphia
	Formation of the Pre-Raphaelite Brotherhood in England		Thomas H. Lowe of Birmingham introduces rolled gold plating process (a.k.a. gold filled) to Providence, RI, manufacturers
	Gold discovered in California		
1849	California Gold Rush	1849	Gold electroplating patented
	The safety pin invented and patented by Walter Hunt of New York (patent #6,281)		Opals first discovered in Australia, first with play of color, 1863
1850	High tariff placed on foreign goods imported into U.S.	1850	Tube-shaped ("trombone") safety catch patented by Charles Rowley of Birmingham England
			Brooches with swiveling compartments introduced (c.)
			Garnet-glass doublets introduced (c.)
1851	First international exhibition, the Great Exhibition of the Works of Industry of All Nations, held at The Crystal Palace in London	1851	Artificial aventurine ("goldstone") exhibited at Crystal Palace
	Gold and diamonds first discovered in Australia		
	Hard rubber (vulcanite) patented by Nelson Goodyear		
1852	Louis Napoleon becomes Napoleon III, beginning of French Second Empire	1852	Tiffany & Co. introduces the English sterling standard to the U.S.
			Machine for heat-pressing bog oak patented
1853	Commodore Matthew Perry sails American fleet into Japan, opens East-West trade relations	1853	Demantoid garnets discovered in Ural Mountains, identified as green andradite, 1864, named demantoid, 1878
	Crystal Palace Exhibition held in New York, modeled after London exhibition		Process for "bloomed gold" documented
1854	Results of first commercially successful aluminum reduction process	1854	Use of 15-, 12-, and 9-karat gold made legal in England published by Henri Ste. Claire Deville
1855	Paris Exposition Universelle	1855	Theodor Fahrner founds jewelry factory in Pforzheim, Germany
	Aluminum articles first exhibited		First aluminum jewelry made in France (c.)
	R.W. Bunsen begins using gas-air burner that is his namesake		Patents for Bois durci, Parkesine, and artificial coral issued
1856	Wm. Perkin accidentally discovers the first synthetic aniline (coal tar) dye, mauve		
1857	Financial "Panic of 1857" affects all U.S. industries	1857	Snake-chain making machine patented in U.S.
	Furnace to melt platinum and its alloys developed by Henri Ste. Claire Deville		
1858	First attempted laying of a transatlantic cable	1858	Boucheron founded in Paris
1859	Construction of the Suez Canal begins	1859	Jewels of Queen Ah-Hotep of Egypt discovered
	Comstock Lode (silver) discovered in Nevada		First attempt at organized jewelers' union in U.S., not successful until 1900 (International Jewelry Workers Union of America)
		1860	Henry D. Morse opens first American diamond-cutting factory in Boston, develops standards for American round brilliant cut, 1872-75
			English patent for machine to manufacture stamped settings (collets) for stones granted to Frenchmen Bouret and Ferré

Time line images: Queen Victoria and Price Albert wedding/public domain; comstock lode/public domain; gold stone image/GDK/Wikipedia.

MID VICTORIAN (GRAND) PERIOD

Date	General History, Discoveries & Inventions	Date	Jewelry & Gemstone History, Discoveries & Inventions
1861	U.S. Civil War begins [1861-1865]; Lincoln inaugurated	1861	Fortunato Pio Castellani turns business over to son Augusto
	Prince Consort Albert dies; Victoria enters prolonged period of mourning	1861-c.1880	Wearing of mourning (black) jewelry required at British court
1862	International Exhibition held in London	1862	Archeological Revival gold jewelry exhibited by Castellani of Rome at International Exhibition
			Reverse crystal intaglios by Charles Cook shown at Exhibition
1863	Edward, Prince of Wales, marries Alexandra of Denmark		Japanese decorative arts exhibited for the first time in the West
1865	Lincoln assassinated	1865	Sapphires found in Missouri River in Montana
1866	First successful transatlantic cable laid		
1867	Paris *Exposition Universelle*	1867	Egyptian Revival jewelry exhibited at Paris Exposition
			First authenticated diamond, the Eureka, discovered in South Africa
			Parisian firm Boucheron begins production of *plique à jour* enamels
1868	Celluloid, the first successful semi-synthetic thermoplastic, invented in U.S. by John Wesley Hyatt; commercial production begins in 1872; trade name registered, 1873	1868	Gorham Mfg. Co., Providence RI, adopts sterling standard of 925 parts per thousand
1869	First transcontinental railroad from Omaha to San Francisco	1869	Henry D. Morse cuts the Dewey diamond, largest found in America to date (23.75 cts, cut to 11.70 cts)
	Suez Canal opened		"Diamond rush" begins in South Africa with discovery of the "Star of Africa"
			American Horological Journal first published, merges with *The Jewelers' Circular* to become *The Jewelers' Circular and Horological Review*, 1873
1870	Fall of the French Empire	1870	*The Jewelers' Circular* founded, first issue published February 15
	British metallurgist George Matthey perfects lime furnace for platinum refining		Peter Carl Fabergé takes over father's business
			Diamonds discovered in Kimberley, South Africa
1870s	Recession in Europe	1870s	Influx of European craftsmen and designers into U.S.
			Japanese craftsmen introduce metal-working techniques and designs to the West
1872	International Exhibition held in London	1872	Black opals first discovered in Queensland, Australia
			Ferdinand J. Herpers of Newark, NJ, patents six-prong setting for diamonds, introduced as the "Tiffany setting" by Tiffany & Co., 1886
1873	Universal Exhibition held in Vienna	1873	Henry D. Morse and Charles M. Field obtain British and U.S. (1874, 1876) patents for steam-driven bruting (diamond cutting) machines
1874	Gold discovered in Black Hills of Dakota Territory		
1875	Arthur Lazenby Liberty founds Liberty & Co. of London	1875	The Celluloid Mfg. Co. begins jewelry production in Newark, NJ
1876	Centennial Exposition held in Philadelphia	1876	Alessandro Castellani presents and lectures on Etruscan Revival jewelry at Centennial Exposition
	Wearing of swords banned in Japan		
	Queen Victoria becomes Empress of India		
	Alexander Graham Bell patents the telephone		
1877	Advent of bottled oxygen (liquefied and compressed)	1877	Successful experiments with chemical manufacture of very small rubies and sapphires in Paris, published by Frémy
1878	Paris *Exposition Universelle*	1878	Tiffany & Co. awarded gold medal for encrusted metals technique in the "Japanesque" style at Paris Exposition
			Tiffany Diamond discovered in South Africa
			Unger Bros. of Newark, NJ, begins the manufacture of silver jewelry
			Earring covers for diamond earrings patented
			Patent for platinum-tipped prongs for setting diamonds (#202,402)
1879	T. A. Edison patents incandescent lightbulb	1879	Gem expert George F. Kunz joins Tiffany & Co.
			Hiddenite, green variety of spodumene, found in North Carolina

Time line images: Suez Canal and Paris Exposition Universelle/Wikipedia; sapphire/Heritage Auctions, Inc.; Etruscan Revival jewelry/Heritage Auctions, Inc.

LATE VICTORIAN (AESTHETIC) PERIOD

Date	General History, Discoveries & Inventions	Date	Jewelry & Gemstone History, Discoveries & Inventions
1880	Rational Dress Society founded in Britain	1880	Cecil Rhodes establishes the De Beers Mining Co. in South Africa (renamed De Beers Consolidated Mines in 1888)
1881	The first electrically-lit theatre, The Savoy, opens in London		Mass production of wrist watches begins in Switzerland, introduced in U.S. 1895, U.S. manufacture 1907 (c.)
1883	Metropolitan Opera House opens in New York City		
		1885	First appearance of the "Geneva" synthetic ruby
1886	Gold discovered in South Africa (Transvaal)	1886	Tiffany setting for diamond solitaires introduced
	Statue of Liberty dedicated		Richard W. Sears starts a mail-order company to sell watches (second company to sell jewelry and watches founded in 1889)
1887	Queen Victoria's Golden Jubilee	1887	Gold extraction by cyanide process invented by John Stewart Macarthur and the Forrest brothers
	Hall-Héroult process for refining aluminum developed; first commercial production in Switzerland, value drops		Tiffany & Co. purchases French crown jewels
	Celluloid photographic film invented by Hannibal W. Goodwin		Birmingham (England) Jewellers' and Silversmiths' Association formed by manufacturers
	Tiffany & Co. purchases French crown jewels		Black opals discovered in New South Wales, Australia; commercial mining at Lightening Ridge mine begins 1903
			The Belais brothers of New York begin experimenting with alloys for white gold (c.); David Belais introduces his formula to the trade in 1917 (referred to as "18k Belais")
1888	George Eastman introduces the first commercial box camera, the Kodak	1888	C.R. Ashbee's Guild of Handicraft founded in London, the first crafts guild to specialize in jewelry-making and metalwork
1889	Paris Exposition Universelle - Eiffel Tower constructed, first structure to serve as landmark for an exposition	1889	Tiffany & Co. exhibits enameled orchid jewels by Paulding Farnham at the Exposition Universelle
	Sapphires found in Dry Cottonwood Creek, Montana		
1890	Sarah Bernhardt plays Cleopatra on stage		
	Charles Dana Gibson's "Gibson Girl" first appears in the humor magazine Life (c.)		
1891	The marking of foreign imports with the name of the country of origin in English required by the enactment of the McKinley Tariff Act, October, 1890	1891	Power-driven bruting (girdling) machine for cutting diamonds patented in England
1892	Vogue Magazine founded in U.S.	1892	Marcus & Co., formerly Jaques & Marcus, established in New York
1893	World's Columbian Exposition in Chicago	1893	Cultured pearls first developed by K. Mikimoto in Japan; first spherical pearls grown 1905
			"Platingeld" introduced, used for simulated gold and platinum chains
1894	Thomas Edison's Kinetoscope Parlor ("peepshow") opens in New York City	1894	Screwback earring finding for unpierced ears patented (U.S.)
1895	Sigfried (aka Samuel) Bing opens his new Paris gallery of decorative art called "L'Art Nouveau"	1895	René Lalique exhibits jewelry at the Bing gallery and the Salon of the Societé des Artistes Français; begins work on a series of 145 pieces for Calouste Gulbenkian
	American Consuelo Vanderbilt marries the British Duke of Marlborough		Daniel Swarovski opens glass stone-cutting factory in Tyrol, Austria
	The wireless telegraph invented by Guglielmo Marconi (first transatlantic wireless signal in 1901)		Blue sapphires discovered in Yogo Gulch, Montana
	Bonanza Creek Gold Rush in Klondike (Yukon, Canada)		
1897	Queen Victoria's Diamond Jubilee	1897	Lacloche Frères established in Paris
	Casein plastics marketed in Germany		
	Boston and Chicago Arts and Crafts Societies founded		
1898	Alaska Gold Rush	1898	Commercial sapphire mining begins in Rock Creek, Montana
	Spanish-American War		
1899-1902	Boer War (South Africa)	1899-1902	Diamond supplies curtailed by Boer War; prices for De Beers' reserve stock rise

Time line images: Statue of Liberty/public domain; orchid jewels/LangAntiques.com; saphhire/public domain.

Edwardian Period (Belle Époque)

Date	General History, Discoveries & Inventions	Date	Jewelry & Gemstone History, Discoveries & Inventions
1900	Paris *Exposition Universelle*	1900	Synthetic rubies exhibited at Paris Exposition; Tiffany & Co. exhibits a life-size iris corsage ornament set with Montana blue sapphires
	U.S. officially adopts the gold standard with McKinley's signing of the Gold Standard Act (monometallism)		Boucheron, Fouquet, Lalique, Vever and other French jewelers display their Art Nouveau jewels at Paris Exposition
	Oxyacetylene torch invented by Edmund Fouché		The Kalo Shop founded by Clara Barck Welles in Chicago, begins jewelry-making 1905, closed 1970
			The diamond saw is invented by a Belgian working in the U.S. (c.)
1901	Queen Victoria dies. Edward VII becomes king	1901	Lever safety catch for brooches patented by Herpers Brothers of Newark
	McKinley assassinated. Theodore Roosevelt becomes President		
	Pan-American Exposition held in Buffalo, NY		Tiffany & Co. exhibits at Pan-American Exposition, special mark (beaver) used on exhibition pieces
	Gustav Stickley begins publishing his periodical, *The Craftsman*, (until 1916)		
1902	Vienna Secession Exhibition	1902	Flame-fusion process for synthesizing rubies presented in Paris by Verneuil, published and patented 1904
	Edward VII coronation		Joseph Asscher develops the Asscher cut for diamonds
			Cartier opens a London branch
			Pink variety of spodumene, kunzite, discovered in California, identified by and named for George F. Kunz
			Process for setting rhinestones or metal in celluloid patented
1903	Wiener Werkstätte founded in Vienna, Austria by Koloman Moser and Josef Hoffmann	1903	Fabergé opens London branch, selling mostly "gentlemen's things"
1904	Louisiana Purchase Exposition held in St. Louis	1904	Louis Comfort Tiffany exhibits his jewelry for the first time at the St. Louis Exposition
	New York City subway opens		Marshall Field & Co., Chicago, establishes a craft shop for jewelry and metalware (closed c. 1950)
	Construction begins on the Panama Canal		Georg Jensen opens his silversmithy in Copenhagen, Denmark
1905	Albert Einstein proposes his theory of relativity	1905	Forest Craft Guild founded by Forest Mann in Grand Rapids MI
	Henri Matisse and other fauvist artists exhibit at Salon d'Automne in Paris		The Kalo Shop begins jewelry-making in Chicago`
			Cullinan diamond (3,106 carats) discovered in Transvaal So. Africa, presented to Edward VII 1907
			First spherical cultured pearls grown in Japan by Mikimoto, patented 1908, U.S. patent, 1916
1906	San Francisco earthquake and fire	1906	National Stamping Act passed in U.S., requiring marking of gold and silver content
	Finland is first European country to grant women's suffrage		Van Cleef & Arpels founded in Paris
1907	First exhibition of cubist paintings held in Paris, including works by Pablo Picasso and Georges Braque	1907	Tiffany & Co. establishes Art Jewelry Dept. with Louis Comfort Tiffany as director
	Suffragettes demonstrate for the right to vote in London		Benitoite discovered in California, declared official state stone, 1985
1908	Henry Ford introduces the first mass-produced automobile, the Model T	1908	First spherical cultured pearls patented in Japan by Mikimoto (first grown in 1905, American patent granted in 1916)
	Couturier Paul Poiret opens "Boutique Chichi," introduces corsetless dresses and the vertical line in fashion (c.)		Synthetic spinel accidentally produced by flame fusion process
1909	Leo H. Baekeland patents first entirely synthesized plastic, Bakelite	1909	Cartier New York opens
	The Wright brothers begin large-scale manufacture of the airplane (first flight 1903, patented 1906)		
	Copyright symbol © introduced for printed works		
1910	The *Ballets Russes* production of *Schéhérazade* presented in Paris	1910	Eugene Morehouse invents the "bullet" safety catch for brooches, patented for B.A. Ballou & Co 1911
	Edward VII dies, George V becomes king of Great Britain	1910-1920	Suffragette jewelry in green, white, and violet (first initials for "give women votes") is popular in Britain and U.S.
	First major American women's suffrage parade held in New York City, demonstration in Washington DC, 1913		
	France classifies platinum as a precious metal, new hallmark (dog's head) issued 1912		
1911	George V coronation	1911	George V has Cullinan I and II set in Imperial State crown and scepter
			The Hope Diamond is purchased by Ned and Evalyn Walsh McLean
			Synthetic blue sapphires patented in U.S by Verneuil
1912	The Titanic sinks	1912	Oscar Heyman & Bros. founded in New York
			Cartier introduces the baguette cut for diamonds
1914	World War I begins	1914	Platinum declared a "strategic metal" during wartime, use in jewelry diminished
	First ship through Panama Canal (completed 1913)		
	The first U.S. fashion show is staged by Edna Woolman Chase, editor of *Vogue*		
1915	Panama-Pacific International Exposition held in San Francisco	1915	U.S. patent #1165448 granted to Karl Gustav Paul Richter of Pforzheim Germany, for a white gold alloy of gold, nickel and palladium
	Panama-California Exposition held in San Diego		
1917	Theda Bara plays Cleopatra in first (silent) film version	1917	David Belais of New York introduces his formula for 18k white gold to the trade, known as "18k Belais"
	The U.S. enters the war		
	Russian Revolution begins		Cartier designs the Tank wristwatch, first public sale 1919
1918	First regular airmail service, between Washington DC and New York City, begins, New York to San Francisco 1921		
	World War I ends		
	Bohemia, Moravia and Slovakia become the Republic of Czechoslovakia		

Time line images: Edward VII/public domain; Henri Matisse painting/public domain; suffragette jewelry/public domain.

EDWARDIAN PERIOD (BELLE ÉPOQUE)

Date	General History, Discoveries & Inventions	Date	Jewelry & Gemstone History, Discoveries & Inventions
1919	Bauhaus founded in Germany by Walter Gropius	1919	Marcel Tolkowsky publishes *Diamond Design*, detailing the cut and proportions of the modern brilliant ("American" or "ideal" cut), following scientific standards first discovered and developed by Henry D. Morse
	The Eighteenth Amendment to the U.S. Constitution is ratified (Prohibition)		
1920	The Nineteenth Amendment, giving women the right to vote, is ratified		
	First regular radio programs begin broadcasting in Pittsburgh		
1922	Howard Carter discovers King Tutankhamun's tomb in Egypt	1922	Raymond C. Yard, Inc. founded in New York City
1923	Cartoonist John Held Jr's "Betsy Co-ed" and "Joe College" first appear on the cover of humor magazine *Life*.	1923	Frederik Lunning comes to New York City, opens a shop for Georg Jensen, 1924
			Synthetic pearl essence for simulated pearls invented, called "H-scale"
		1924	Egyptologist Caroline R. Williams discovers the granulation technique used by ancient goldsmiths
1925	Exposition Internationale des Arts Decoratifs et Industriels Modernes held in Paris	1925	Synthetic spinel, inadvertently produced by flame fusion process 1908, in wide commercial use (c.)
	Josephine Baker appears in the Revue Nègre in Paris		Firm of Trifari, Krussman & Fishel established
1926	The first commercial injection molding machine patented by Eckert and Ziegler in Germany		
1927	Charles Lindbergh flies solo nonstop New York to Paris	1927	Cartier patents model with spring system for double clip brooch
	Motion pictures with sound first publicly shown (Al Jolson in *The Jazz Singer*)		
	Cellulose acetate, trade name Lumarith, introduced by Celluloid Corp.	1928	Schiaparelli establishes "Maison Schiaparelli" in Paris
			Paul Flato opens salon in New York
1929	The Great Depression begins with stock market crash	1929	Trabert & Hoeffer, Inc.-Mauboussin merger agreement
1930	Formation of the Union des Artistes Modernes in Paris		Black, Starr & Frost merger with Gorham Corp., until 1966
	Construction completed on Chrysler Building in New York		
1931	Empire State Building becomes New York's tallest	1931	The "Duette" pinback mechanism for double clip brooches patented by U.S. costume jewelry manufacturer Coro
			William Spratling opens the first silver workshop in Taxco, Mexico
1932	Franklin D. Roosevelt elected President	1932	14k gold replaces 12k and 15k in Britain, by decision of the Worshipful Company of Goldsmiths, London
	Radio City Music Hall opens		Harry Winston opens a retail jewelry business in New York City
1933	Construction begins on Golden Gate Bridge in San Francisco (completed 1937)	1933	The "invisible setting" (serti invisible) patented by Cartier and Van Cleef & Arpels (introduced in U.S. 1936)
	Prohibition repealed		Lost wax process, used in dentistry since c. 1910, reintroduced for mass production of jewelry castings with vulcanized rubber molds (c.)
	Gold taken out of circulation		
	"Century of Progress" World's Fair opens in Chicago		
1934	Cecil B. De Mille's *Cleopatra* starring Claudette Colbert in title role	1934	Ernest Oppenheimer creates the De Beers Consolidated Mines Ltd. diamond cartel
	Salvador Dalí exhibits surrealist paintings in New York City		Synthetic emeralds ("Igmerald") developed by IG-Farben, Germany, first seen by gemologists
			Van Cleef & Arpels introduces the "Ludo" flexible strap bracelet
			Patent for clipback earring finding for unpierced ears granted to Eugene Morehouse for B.A. Ballou
1935	French luxury cruise ship Normandie arrives in New York	1935	D. Lisner & Co. introduces "Bois Glacé" jewelry, their trade name for colorless phenolic plastic (Bakelite) laminated to wood
1936	George V dies. Edward VIII of Britain abdicates the throne to marry American-born divorcée Wallis Simpson, becomes Duke of Windsor, succeeded by George VI		*The Jewelers' Circular* merges with *The Keystone* to become *Jewelers' Circular-Keystone*
	Margaret Mitchell's novel, *Gone With the Wind*, is published		
	BBC inaugurates television service; general broadcasting begins in U.S. 1941		
	Life magazine founded by Henry Robinson Luce		
1937	Du Pont de Nemours & Co. introduces acrylic plastic, trade name "Lucite"; also patents nylon fiber	1937	Van Cleef & Arpels makes "marriage contract" bracelet for Wallis Simpson, the Duchess of Windsor
	The International Exhibition of Arts and Techniques in Modern Life held in Paris		Boucheron, Cartier, Mauboussin, Van Cleef & Arpels and others display figural jewels of colored gold and gemstones at Paris exhibition
	First feature-length animated film, Walt Disney's *Snow White and the Seven Dwarfs*		Paul Flato opens his Los Angeles establishment
			Double-pronged hinged (dress) clip introduced (c.)
1939	*Gone With The Wind* premiers	1939	First commercially successful synthetic emerald process marketed by Carroll Chatham of San Francisco, CA ("Chatham Created Emerald" term first used 1963)
	World War II begins in Europe		The House of Jewels at the New York World's Fair is sponsored by Tiffany & Co., Black, Starr & Frost-Gorham, Udall & Ballou, Marcus & Co., and Cartier New York
	First nylon stockings marketed		Van Cleef & Arpels opens an office in New York City
	The New York World's Fair, titled "The World of Tomorrow," opens		Verdura opens his own shop in New York
			Sam Kramer opens shop in Greenwich Village
1940	France falls under German occupation	1940	The Bank of France bans all gold trading

Time line images: Salvador Dali painting/public domain.

Edwardian Period (Belle Époque)

Date	General History, Discoveries & Inventions	Date	Jewelry & Gemstone History, Discoveries & Inventions
1941	The U.S. enters the war with the Japanese bombing of Pearl Harbor	1941	10% luxury tax on jewelry in U.S., raised to 20% 1944
	Craft Horizons, the first national magazine for crafts, is published by the Handcraft Cooperative League		Jean Schlumberger opens shop in New York, joins Tiffany & Co. 1956
	First U.S. television broadcasting begins		
1942	Rationing of consumer products (sugar, coffee, gasoline) begins in U.S.	1942	Use of platinum for jewelry prohibited in U.S.
	Polyethylene formulated by Earl S. Tupper and DuPont, Tupperware introduced 1946		White metal restricted by U.S. government, sterling silver used as substitute in costume jewelry
1943	Postal zones added to addresses of large cities in U.S.		
1945	Roosevelt dies. Harry Truman becomes President	1945	Suzanne Belperron forms partnership Herz-Belperron with Jean Herz in Paris
	World War II ends		Mexican government requires marking of sterling silver with "spread eagle" assay mark (c.)
	United Nations is formed, holds first session 1946	1946	Opal doublets first made in Australia, triplets c. 1960
			First national exhibit of American studio artists' jewelry held at Museum of Modern Art in New York City
			Jerry Fels founds "Renoir of Hollywood" in Los Angeles, CA
			David Webb opens office in New York, salon in 1963
1947	Couturier Christian Dior introduces "The New Look"	1947	Synthetic star rubies and sapphires ("Linde") first marketed
	Copyright laws re-enacted by U.S. Congress, expanded to include illustrations of merchandise and designs for art works		Costume jewelry manufacturers begin abandoning design patents in favor of copyrights, using © as part of maker's mark
			Synthetic rutile introduced as a diamond simulant
			Metalsmithing workshop series for war veterans begins, ends 1951
1948	Jewish State of Israel declared, admitted to U.N. 1949	1948	De Beers Diamond Corp. launches the slogan "a diamond is forever"
	Truman elected to full term as President		
1949	German Federal Republic (West Germany) proclaimed	1949	Harry Winston purchases Hope diamond. His "Court of Jewels" exhibit opens in New York, tours U.S. for the next four years
1951	Color television is introduced in U.S.	1951	The Metal Arts Guild organized in San Francisco
1952	George VI of Britain dies; succeeded by Elizabeth II	1952	Italian jewelers Buccellati establish a salon in New York City
	Dwight D. Eisenhower elected President		
1953	Marilyn Monroe sings "Diamonds Are a Girl's Best Friend" in *Gentlemen Prefer Blondes*	1953	Mamie Eisenhower wears Trifari faux pearls to inaugural ball
		1954	De Beers institutes the annual Diamonds International Awards for original designs in diamond-set jewelry
			First successful production of synthetic diamonds at General Electric, process patented 1960, large gem-quality crystals produced 1970
1955	Atomically generated power first used in the U.S.	1955	Swarovski Corp introduces the "aurora borealis" color effect for rhinestones and crystal in collaboration with Christian Dior
	Disneyland amusement park opens		Strontium titanate introduced to the public as a diamond simulant
1957	The U.S.S.R. launches the first "Sputnik" satellite on Oct. 4		
	Jack Kerouac's *On the Road* published, coins the term "Beat Generation"		
1958	Universal Exhibition opens in Brussels, Belgium		
1960	John F. Kennedy elected President of U.S.		
	Birth control pills introduced to the public		
1961	Audrey Hepburn stars in *Breakfast at Tiffany's*	1961	International Exhibition of Modern Jewelry (1890-1961) held in London
	Soviets, U.S., put first men in space		U.S. National Stamping Act amended, requiring a maker's trade mark
1963	Kennedy assassinated. Lyndon Johnson becomes President		
	U.S. Post Office introduces the ZIP code		
	Elizabeth Taylor stars in *Cleopatra*		
1964	The Beatles perform live for the first time in the U.S.		
	Vietnam War begins	1967	Tanzanite discovered in Tanzania
1969	U.S. moon landing		
	Woodstock music festival		
1972	Richard Nixon re-elected	1972	Cubic zirconia "skull melt" process patented, CZs commercially marketed, 1976
			Gilson produces synthetic opal and synthetic turquoise
1974	Nixon resigns as a result of Watergate (1973)	1974	Tsavorite garnet (green) discovered in Kenya, Africa
1976	U.S. bicentennial	1976	National Stamping Act amendment introduces the marking of "plumb" gold (e.g., "14 KP"), meaning exact (no tolerance)
	The microprocessor is introduced; Apple II personal computer, 1977	1979	Main pipe of the Argyle Diamond Mine in Australia discovered, mining company commissioned in 1985
			Sugilite, named for Professor Ken-ichi Sugi, begins appearing on the market (discovered 1944)

Time line images: United Nations emblem/public domain; Marilyn Monroe/20th Century Fox; Tanzanite and Tsavorite images/Heritage Auctions, Inc.

PART I

LATE 18TH AND 19TH CENTURY JEWELRY

Jewelry has always been worn for many purposes. In addition to social status, it can serve as a memento of loved ones living or dead. It also has a role as decorative and/or functional parts of clothing. A jewel can be worn as an expression of religious faith, and as a talisman or amulet to ward off evil and disease.

Souvenir jewelry and traditional jewelry symbolic of national or cultural origin or group membership are also common. In fact, more non-status antique jewelry, often made from non-precious materials, survives today in its original form than does gemstone and gold jewelry. Anything with components of value was more likely to be broken up for its gemstones and precious metal and reworked into pieces in keeping with current fashion.

Fine and expensive high-karat gold and gemstone pieces from the late 18th and early 19th centuries certainly do turn up at auctions and high-end antiques shows. However, most of the earliest accessible and affordable jewelry that exists today is memorial and sentimental jewelry.

The first section of this book is divided accordingly, covering what is known as the Late Georgian and Regency periods in Great Britain (the reigns of Georges III and IV), circa 1760-1837 (William IV reigned 1830-1837, but there is no "William period"). In the United States, these periods correspond roughly to the late Colonial and Federal periods.

Although it may seem arbitrary, the year 1837 is generally recognized by jewelry historians as the beginning of a new era, although some types and styles of jewelry carried over from the previous decade. The timespan of the period is lengthy, so it is usually divided into three sub-periods. While there is a difference of opinion as to the exact years when one sub-period ends and the next begins, there is general recognition of their names: They are called the Early or Romantic, the Middle or Grand, and the Late Victorian or Aesthetic Period.

Jewelry doesn't always fit neatly into one or another time-slot or category. Styles tend to overlap, and newer versions of old designs continued to be made in later periods. Many materials were worn throughout the late 18th and 19th centuries, e.g., coral, cut steel, and diamonds; many motifs recurred, such as snakes, flowers, and hands, and many types or forms of jewelry continued to be worn, like watch chains, bracelets, and cameos.

Precise dating can be difficult, unless there are clues like maker's marks, hallmarks with date letters, or engraved dated inscriptions. More often than not, late 18th and 19th century jewelry is unmarked. Identifying construction techniques and original findings can help to narrow the date range. Some findings, however, like the "C"-catch (a simple hook) and the "tube" hinge of brooch pin assemblies, were in use for the entire period, and often continued to be used in the 20th century. Furthermore, pieces with intrinsic value—precious metals and stones—do not always survive intact. Alterations are common.

Several thematic threads were woven into the fabric of society. Nature, history, symbolism, and above all, sentiment, were sometimes inextricably intertwined.

In Victorian times, naturalism was expressed in jewelry with exact depictions of flora and fauna in gold and gemstones or other materials. Distasteful as it may seem today, real insects and birds' heads were sometimes made into jewelry. Flowers were symbols of sentiment and nature.

Skinner, Inc.

Floral and flowers were among the popular motifs in jewelry from this period. Georgian topaz brooch, 18th century, designed as floral and foliate motifs and set throughout with faceted foil-back topaz, silver mount, 3 1/4" wide. **$3,851**

Every flower had a specific meaning, and their definitions were cataloged in several flower dictionaries. One book, published in 1866, was appropriately called *The Language and Sentiment of Flowers* (several versions are still available today).

The second half of the 19th century was the age of the international exhibition—what later came to be known as World's Fairs and Expos. Their historical importance should not be underestimated. In a period lacking mass communications media like television, exhibitions were the mass marketing tool of the era. They made it possible for manufacturers and merchants to display their wares over a period of six months or more to hundreds of thousands of potential customers.

The latest discoveries and developments, styles, and tastes were introduced to the general public at exhibitions. Instead of "as seen on TV," an item would be touted, for example, "as seen at the Paris Exposition." To have a booth at an exhibition conferred the highest status upon the goods and their maker. Jewelry was exhibited by such prestigious firms as Froment-Meurice of Paris and Phillips of London at London's Crystal Palace Exhibition in 1851; Castellani of Rome exhibited at the International Exhibition in London in 1862 and at the Philadelphia Centennial Exposition in 1876; and Tiffany & Co. of New York was also at the Philadelphia Centennial and the Paris Exposition in 1867, 1878, 1889, and 1900.

The designs of these and other exhibitors became fashionable by word of mouth and through reports in periodicals. They inspired many imitators.

The period 1837-1901 is called Victorian in the United States as well as Great Britain. In spite of our country's independence from hers, Victoria's tastes influenced Americans, as well as her own subjects. While the Western world looked to Paris for the latest styles and trends, English interpretations of French styles were acceptable to the more conservative American temperament. At times, these styles were modified even further by American artisans and manufacturers.

When the young queen ascended the throne of Great Britain in 1837, the United States was still a young country. Machine-made jewelry production had begun in New England and New Jersey, but a distinct American style had yet to emerge. Most of it was imitative of the English or French. Some jewelers, in fact, tried to "pass" their items as European. Other types of jewelry that were worn were usually imported from Britain and the Continent.

In the early years of this country's history, patriotism and lifestyles in general discouraged ostentatious displays of wealth. Aristocracy and all that symbolized it, like jewelry, was out. The Puritan work ethic was in. Many Americans wore little jewelry, except sentimental jewelry, until after the Civil War.

Wives of statesmen and presidents, the elite of Boston, New York, and Philadelphia, and other well-to-do Americans were the exception to this rule. Dolley Madison was known for her jeweled turbans, sent from Paris—the War of 1812 notwithstanding.

In the 1840s, President John Tyler's new wife, Julia, was the closest thing to royalty this country ever saw. She wore crowns and diamond tiaras.

REPRODUCTION ALERT

Manufacturers in Portugal, South America, Germany, Thailand, and the United States can and do reproduce late 18th and 19th century style pieces to any specification, using stones and findings identical to the originals. Unless you have one of their catalogs or are aware of the provenance of a piece, it is often extremely difficult to differentiate new from old.

LATE GEORGIAN JEWELRY, CIRCA 1760-1837

A quick look at the beginning of the "Time Line" in the front of this book will hint at the social and political upheaval that took place in Europe and America during this time period: The American and French Revolutions, England at war with France, France with the United States. George III was declared insane. Louis XVI was beheaded. Napoleon overran Europe and crowned himself emperor. Little wonder that changes in social customs, fashion, and attitudes about personal adornment occurred at the same time.

At the beginning of the period, royalty and nobility were the primary wearers of jewels of high intrinsic value. In 1762, Queen Charlotte, wife of George III, posed for her portrait wearing, among other jewels, a diamond stomacher that covered her entire V-shaped bodice. (Evidence that diamond-set jewels were made and worn in America in pre-Revolutionary times has been presented, but little of it survives or is documented.) Low necklines and upswept hair suggested long earrings and short necklaces. The girandole (French for chandelier) and pendeloque were popular shapes for earrings and pendants. The former usually consist of three pear-shaped diamond (or colored gemstone) drops suspended from a central element and small surmount. Pendeloques are single pear-shaped drops, sometimes suspended from a central bow and single-stone or cluster surmount. Short necklaces of graduated collet-set diamonds or other gemstones, known as rivières, were worn through the first two or three decades of the 19th century (this necklace style was revived in the 1880s). Diamonds began to be set à jour (open-backed) at this time, but colored gemstones such as garnets and topaz continued to be mounted in closed back settings lined with colored foil to enhance their natural color. Open settings for colored stones began appearing around the turn of the 19th century, but were not in the majority until the 1840s.

Large diamond-set bow brooches, known as sévigné, were fashionable when tight bodices were in style in the late 18th century, but when fashions changed, they

Jewelry courtesy the Steve Fishbach Collection; photo by Linda Lombardo

Queen Charlotte made stomachers, pieces of jewelry that covered bodices, fashionable. Georgian stomacher, circa 1820, chain added to convert to necklace in Victorian period; rose-cut diamonds, emeralds set in silver, with gold pinchbeck; 3 3/4", chain 30". **$8,500**

were no longer wearable. The bow motif itself remained, however. Floral spray and feather brooches were also set with diamonds. These tended to be stylized and flat until Early Victorian naturalism gave them dimension and a realistic look.

The 18th century is commonly called the Age of Diamonds, but it could also be called the "Age of Paste" (a high lead content glass invented by Georg Frédéric Strass in 1730). Those who could not afford to emulate the aristocracy still strove to imitate their style. Paste jewels were set in silver or gold closed-back mounts and foiled for added sparkle. A black spot was often painted on the culets of colorless brilliant-cut stones to further emphasize the look of diamonds of the period (now called "old mine cut," cushion-shaped with a small table and large culet, or bottom facet). The jewelry forms were identical to those set with diamonds and colored gemstones. Paste jewels were prized in their own right, not merely as a substitute or imitation, and were sold by many of the "best" jewelers of England, France, and in the Colonies before the American Revolution.

The American and French Revolutions, like most wars, were an impetus for change. Jewelry, a non-essential luxury, was one of the first things to go, sold or melted down for the war effort, or survival. In France, anything that smacked of aristocracy was frowned upon. Jewels were not part of the new republic's ideology. But by the end of the 18th century, a desire for personal adornment had returned, albeit in new forms.

Fashion changed drastically at the turn of the 19th century, when Napoleon's First Empire held sway. The late 18th century's full skirts, tight bodices, and three-quarter sleeves with deep lace ruffles, gathered draped collars (berthas), or ruffled lace necklines were discarded in favor of the Neoclassical look of filmy, high-waisted, and draped Grecian-style dresses with short puffed sleeves and deep décolletage. The style's simplicity and the fabrics' delicacy required changes in jewelry forms: Out went stomachers and large, heavy brooches. In came necklaces of plaques and draped chains, small buckles for sashes worn just under the bosom, smaller gem- or paste-set brooches, narrow link bracelets worn in multiples, aigrettes, and hair ornaments. Interest in Greek and Roman antiquities had been heightened by new archeological discoveries at Herculaneum and Pompeii in the mid-18th century, and was kept alive by Empress Josephine's preoccupation with classical motifs. Cameos and mosaics were worn as necklaces en esclavage, the plaques joined with two or three lengths of swagged chain encircling the base of the neck.

In the 1820s, fashions underwent another change. Sleeves were longer and grew larger toward the end of the decade. Waists remained high but skirts were fuller and heavier, embellished with ruffles and trimmings. By 1830, the waist had returned to its natural position, tightly sashed and buckled. Tight bodices returned. Sleeves were voluminous, necklines cut straight across. Jewelry forms included long draped chains, wide buckles and bracelets, long earrings (the "torpedo" shape was popular), and fancy combs in elaborately dressed hair. Cross pendants were also popular, especially Maltese crosses, which could be set with diamonds, colored gemstones, or pastes, carved from chalcedony or made entirely of gold. Gold was in short supply in the early 19th century, but the decorative technique known as cannetille, a type of scrolled filigree with tightly coiled spirals or rosettes, was used to make a small amount of gold go a long way. Substantial-looking chains were made of stamped thin gauge gold, and were lightweight. In the 1820s and 1830s, the romantic notion of the "language of stones," like that of flowers, gave rise to pieces with messages spelled out by the initial letter of the stone's name, known as "acrostic jewelry." "Regard," the most commonly expressed sentiment, was represented by ruby, emerald, garnet, amethyst, and diamond. "Dearest" was another favorite "acrostic."

As the Industrial Revolution gave rise to more mechanized methods of production in the first three decades of the 19th century, more jewelry was made for the middle classes, making way for the profusion and variety of the Victorian era.

CUT STEEL, BERLIN IRON, SILESIAN WIRE WORK

Jewelry made from riveted faceted beads or studs of polished steel dates at least as far back as the 16th century. Cut steel jewelry had its heyday in the late 18th century, when some of the most delicate and intricate ornaments were made to imitate the sparkle of diamonds. But it persisted as a craft and a fashion into the 20th century. Much of what survives today was made in France, especially in the form of buckles for shoes and waists.

Some sources say that circa dating can be determined by construction methods and the number of facets on the studs. Earlier pieces have numerous (up to 15) facets, while later ones have as few as five. Machine-stamped strips instead of individually riveted studs are an indication of later, lower-quality, manufacture. But, according to other sources, multi-faceted, individually studded examples of higher quality can also date as late as the 1900s. England was a primary source for cut steel in the 18th century, the most well-known manufacturer being Matthew Boulton of Soho, near Birmingham. But factories in France were still turning out cut steel trinkets as recently as the 1940s.

Although buckles are the form most often seen today (for which there is less demand), bracelets, brooches, earrings, chains, chatelaines, and necklaces can also be found. Considering the intricacies of their design and craftsmanship, and their relative scarcity, prices on these pieces remain quite reasonable.

Most of the black lacy cast iron jewelry known as Berlin iron was made in the early 19th century. Its manufacture began around 1806, but a quantity of it was made in Germany during the Prussian War of Liberation against

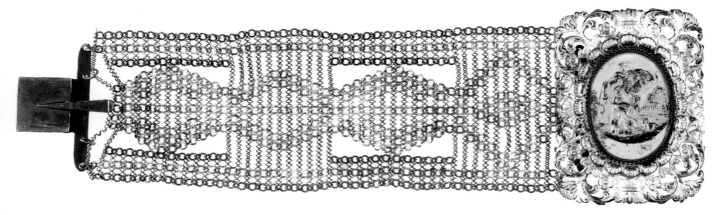

Private Collection

Silesian Ironworks bracelet, Georgian era, late 1700s, German, from Silesia, where iron mines were located; buckle portion is wider, features landscape scene on background of what is possibly mica; 7 1/4", 2" wide. **$500+**

Napoleon (1813-1815). Some pieces continued to be made in the 1850s and were exhibited by German manufacturers at the Crystal Palace in 1851. Berlin iron was sand-cast, then lacquered black. Earlier pieces tended toward the Neo-classical, with cast cameo-like profiles mounted on polished steel plaques, sometimes framed in gold. By the 1830s, Gothic Revival was the stylistic influence. Gothic arches and tracery were cast into lace-like necklaces, bracelets, earrings, cross pendants, and chains. Today, Berlin iron in any style is extremely scarce and expensive, but the Neo-Gothic forms are in the greatest demand.

Another unique type of iron and steel jewelry, associated with a part of Eastern Europe then known as Silesia (now mostly part of Poland, and parts of the Czech Republic and eastern Germany), is sometimes referred to as Silesian wire work. Wrapped and woven iron or steel wire mesh was fashioned into bracelets, necklaces, brooches, and earrings, sometimes decorated with cutout polished steel shapes known as "sequins" or paillettes. Little documentation or information is available about this work, including where it was made and by whom (the name "Silesian wirework" is itself of questionable origin, possibly a term coined by collectors). Although a number of examples are shown in Anne Clifford's *Cut Steel and Berlin Iron Jewellery,* cited in "References," the author can only conjecture about its origin. As yet, 31 years after that book's publication, no one has come up with any further information. Some theorize the work was done in England or France, but to date no documentation supports this theory.

The woven wire mesh was machine-made, which circa-dates the pieces to no earlier than the first quarter of the 19th century. Regardless of its origin, the intricacy of the workmanship is something to marvel at. Coupled with its rarity, Silesian wirework is certainly deserving of greater appreciation and respect than to be called "Brillo pad" jewelry, as once source would have it.

A more readily available type of iron jewelry dates to the latter part of the 19th century. It is inaccurately called "gun-metal," perhaps because its smooth burnished bluish-gray surface resembles the barrel of a gun. Chains and lockets are the predominant forms, but accessories and chatelaine appendages are also found on the market.

MEMORIAL, MOURNING, AND HAIR JEWELRY

One of the most popular expressions of sentimentality, on both sides of the Atlantic, was the making and wearing of jewelry containing human hair, a practice that originated in the 17th century. These pieces were worn as memento mori (mourning) and also as love tokens.

The earliest type of hair jewelry was made with glass or rock crystal-covered compartments to hold the hair of a loved one, living or deceased. These continued to be made and worn through the greater part of the 19th century, with some alterations in style. Eighteenth and early to mid-19th century mourning brooches might depict an entire funeral scene painted on ivory, complete with weeping willow, urn, and a despondent maiden standing forlornly by. The sepia tones of the paint were often derived from using macerated hair as a pigment. This was strictly for reasons of sentiment, not because the hair provided a superior form of paint. Sometimes the scene was made three-dimensional with snippets of hair forming, for example, the branches of the willow.

In some pieces, the hair is formed into curls, called "Prince of Wales plumes," or made into wheat sheaves, mounted on a white background. Another technique was to lay strands of hair flat on "goldbeater's skin," a type of adhesive backing, and cut out individual floral motifs that were then assembled as a three-dimensional "picture" under glass.

More commonly, locks of hair were simply braided or coiled, sometimes using more than one color (from different family members), and placed in compartments set into a frame and covered with glass.

On mourning pieces, the outer or inner frame could include a snake motif, symbolizing eternity. Seed pearls, symbolic of tears, were sometimes added, along with gold thread or wire tied around the lock of hair. In late Georgian and early Victorian pieces, the backs are gold or gold-filled, and slightly convex. They were often engraved with names or initials, and dates of birth and/or death. This personalization of a piece is desirable to collectors, and of course it takes the guesswork out of placing the piece in its time-frame.

Late Georgian mourning brooches or pins were often navette-shaped, oval, or oblong; circa 1820-1840, they were small rounded rectangles, ovals, or crescents, often worn pinned to black ribbon as a necklace or bracelet. They were bordered with pearls, garnets, coral, French jet (black glass), or black enamel around the glass-covered compartment (according to Shirley Bury [op. cit. "References"], these were sometimes called "handkerchief pins," later known as "lace pins."). Later brooches were larger, worn at the throat

Skinner, Inc.

Memorial ring, 14k gold and inkwork, late 18th century, depicting a mourning woman by an urn under the motto, "Not Lost But Gone Before," enamel shank reading: "John Dunbar OBt 23 Sep 1775 AEt 38," in an antique box (repair), size 8. **$652**

or in the center of the bodice. Black onyx plaques or black enameled borders inscribed "In Memory Of" around a central hair compartment became standardized forms for mourning pieces.

Double-sided rock crystal lockets with gem-set frames were popular in the mid-to-late 18th century. They could contain a lock of hair or other memento of a loved one.

Late Georgian mourning rings, like brooches, could also be navette-shaped or oblong, or wide bands with inscriptions encircling the outer surface. Others bore inscriptions around the outside of a narrow black-enameled shank surmounted by a hair compartment framed in garnets or pearls, or a gemstone. Some mourning rings have swiveling compartments, one side containing hair. Victorian mourning rings might be simple bands with woven hair channel-set around the outside, or an enameled inscription. Fancier rings had cutout or enameled names on compartments containing hair.

MINIATURES

Before the advent of photography, the miniature portrait

Unsigned miniature portrait on ivory of John Quincy Adams, image is as he might have appeared around the 1820s, housed in a mid-Victorian case that does not appear to be original, miniature is attached to what is probably original cloth backing, "John Quincy Adams 1825-29" written on mounting, painting itself is 1 7/8" x 2 3/8". **$478**

was the only way to capture a wearable likeness of a loved one. This was another popular form of sentiment in the 18th and early to mid-19th centuries.

Some miniatures were worn as memorials to a deceased spouse or parent, but others were simply a way of keeping a likeness as a reminder of the object of one's affections. Queen Victoria wore a portrait of Albert as a bracelet clasp from the beginning of their marriage, which she of course continued to wear after his death. Bracelets and pendants were the most common way of wearing a miniature, but brooches were also worn. Portrait miniatures in painted enamel often have a lock of the portrayed loved one's hair enclosed in a compartment on the reverse.

Portraits are relatively easy to circa-date, if one is familiar with fashion history, and notes the clothing, hair, and other details of the person depicted. These are usually rendered in the styles of the times.

Other types of miniatures have religious themes, and some simply depict a pretty scene. The Swiss were known for painted enamels (sometimes called Geneva or Swiss enamel), most often depicting people, usually women, in regional dress against a scenic background. These were at the height of fashion in the 1830s. Sylvan scenic Swiss landscapes were also rendered in enamels during this period.

One of the rarest and most desirable forms of miniature is the eye miniature, said to have originated with George IV in 1785, while he was Prince of Wales. He sent a minia-

ture of his eye in a letter to the widow Maria Fitzherbert, whom he later secretly married. The eye portrayed was difficult to identify, giving rise to the idea of a "secret lover" always watching. Eye miniatures were worn through the first half of the 19th century, although by the 1820s the fashion had waned considerably. They are not often seen on the market today (see "Reproduction Alert").

The masked ball was another context in which anonymity was sought as a form of amusement. These were a popular diversion among the wealthy of the late 19th century, who often dressed in pre-Revolutionary 18th century costume. Portraits of masked revelers were sometimes made in miniature.

By the second half of the 19th century, photographs began to supersede portrait miniatures, and were often inserted into one side of the swiveling compartment of a large gold or gilt metal brooch. The other side might contain a lock of the loved one's hair or a swatch of his or her clothing. Photographs were also contained in lockets, a tradition that continues to this day.

REPRODUCTION ALERT

Because they are scarce and sought-after, eye portraits have been faked, usually by taking the hair out of a brooch with a glazed compartment and replacing it with an eye. Some of the eyes aren't even actual paintings, rather they are printed. The small screened dots making up the picture are the giveaway.

Heritage Auctions, Inc.

Diamond and silver-topped gold pendant-brooch, European-, mine- and rose-cut diamonds weighing approximately 7.35 carats, set in silver-topped 14k gold, pendant wire, removable pinstem and catch on the reverse, 1 1/8" x 1 3/8". **$4,780**

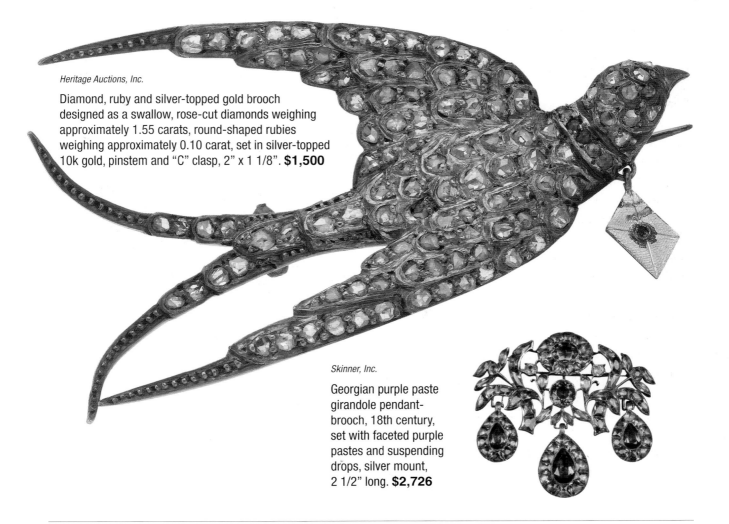

Heritage Auctions, Inc.

Diamond, ruby and silver-topped gold brooch designed as a swallow, rose-cut diamonds weighing approximately 1.55 carats, round-shaped rubies weighing approximately 0.10 carat, set in silver-topped 10k gold, pinstem and "C" clasp, 2" x 1 1/8". **$1,500**

Skinner, Inc.

Georgian purple paste girandole pendant-brooch, 18th century, set with faceted purple pastes and suspending drops, silver mount, 2 1/2" long. **$2,726**

Skinner, Inc.

Georgian rose-cut diamond and enamel star and moon brooch, the star set with a circular rose-cut diamond measuring approximately 8.50 mm, joined to a crescent moon with oval and circular rose-cut diamonds, blue enamel ground, silver mount with gold pinstem, 1 1/8" long. **$1,659**

Skinner, Inc.

Georgian diamond brooch set throughout with old pear and old mine-cut diamonds, approximate total weight 9 carats, silver-topped gold mount, 1 3/4" x 1 5/8". **$5,925**

Jewelry courtesy the Steve Fishbach Collection; photo by Linda Lombardo

French portrait miniature brooch, painting on ivory, 18k gallery, 1830s, 2 1/2". **$2,600**

Skinner, Inc.

Brooch, gold and hand-painted, mourning-type, a thin gold mount and frame enclosing a long oval hand-painted scene of a memorial obelisk centered by a covered urn above initials against a landscape of hairwork poplar trees and inked details, the back inscribed and dated 1782, England, 1 1/4" long. **$2,500**

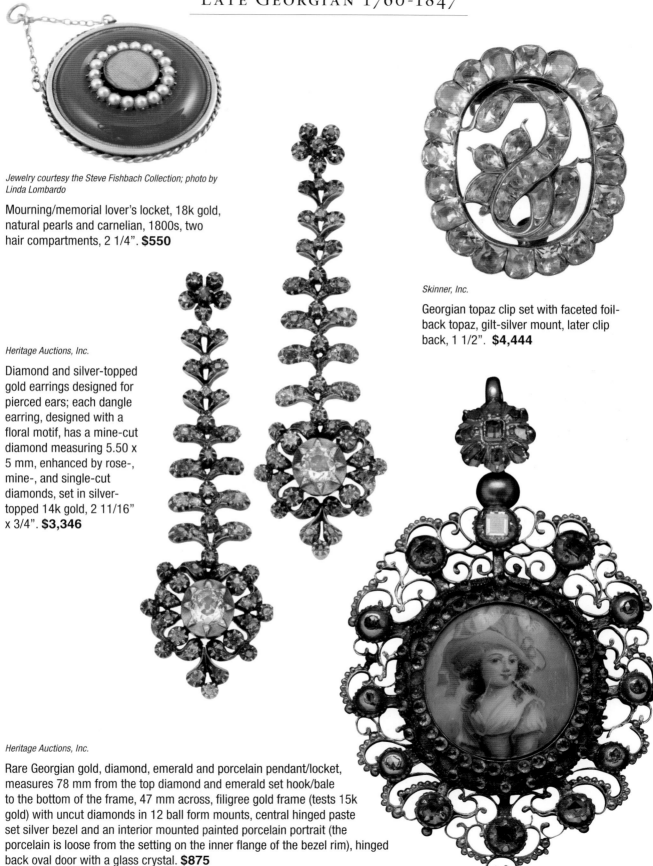

Jewelry courtesy the Steve Fishbach Collection; photo by Linda Lombardo

Mourning/memorial lover's locket, 18k gold, natural pearls and carnelian, 1800s, two hair compartments, 2 1/4". **$550**

Skinner, Inc.

Georgian topaz clip set with faceted foil-back topaz, gilt-silver mount, later clip back, 1 1/2". **$4,444**

Heritage Auctions, Inc.

Diamond and silver-topped gold earrings designed for pierced ears; each dangle earring, designed with a floral motif, has a mine-cut diamond measuring 5.50 x 5 mm, enhanced by rose-, mine-, and single-cut diamonds, set in silver-topped 14k gold, 2 11/16" x 3/4". **$3,346**

Heritage Auctions, Inc.

Rare Georgian gold, diamond, emerald and porcelain pendant/locket, measures 78 mm from the top diamond and emerald set hook/bale to the bottom of the frame, 47 mm across, filigree gold frame (tests 15k gold) with uncut diamonds in 12 ball form mounts, central hinged paste set silver bezel and an interior mounted painted porcelain portrait (the porcelain is loose from the setting on the inner flange of the bezel rim), hinged back oval door with a glass crystal. **$875**

Heritage Auctions, Inc.

Emerald, diamond, pearl and silver-topped gold necklace, French, rectangle-shaped emerald measuring 14.50 x 12 mm and weighing approximately 10 carats, emerald-shaped emeralds weighing approximately 10 carats, rose-cut diamonds weighing approximately 0.65 carat, and button-shaped pearls measuring 5.10 x 5.40 mm, set in silver-topped 18k gold, French hallmarks; total emerald weight is approximately 20 carats; necklace is accompanied by its original fitted box; 16" long. **$6,273**

Jewelry courtesy the Pearl Society; photo by Matthew Arden

Oriental pearl necklace sewn with white horsehair to mother-of-pearl plates, given to Miss Constance Wharton by her mother, late 19th century, with a note (in her hand) indicating it had been made circa 1820 for her great-grandmother. Accompanying fitted case originally held matching grand parure, likely dispersed to other members of the family. Note small neck size, under 13", 3/4" wide. Members of this family included writer Edith Wharton and founders of the Wharton School of Economics. **$2,150**

Skinner, Inc.

Late Georgian garnet fringe necklace designed as graduating collet-set foil-back garnets suspending pear-shape garnet fringe, gold mount, 15 7/8" long. **$3,437**

Skinner, Inc.

Late Georgian diamond ornament, circa 1840, designed as a feather and set throughout with 140 old mine-cut diamonds, approximate total weight 12 carats, silver-topped gold mount, 3 3/4" long. **$18,960**

Heritage Auctions, Inc.

Gold ring with topaz stone, 14k yellow gold (tested), late Georgian, circa 1830-1840, topaz set in a multi-rounded prong mount, topaz is an oval mixed cut, approximate measurement 15.5 x 12.2 x 7.9 mm for an approximate weight (measured in the mount by leverage gauge and calculated) of 11.10 carat. The ring was given by statesman and politician Sam Houston to his wife; inside shank is engraved in script "Sam Houston to Marga...L (?)..."; due to heavy wear it is not possible to determine the final lettering of the engraving, but Houston's wife's name was Margaret Moffette Lea. The shank measures 5 mm wide with an all-bright polish, size 5. **$49,500**

Skinner, Inc.

Late Georgian gold and garnet ring, circa 1810-1820, the cushion-cut garnet within a foil-back ribbed collet, flanked by fancy-cut diamonds set in silver, size 6. **$3,081**

Skinner, Inc.

Georgian ruby and diamond ring, circa 1820, collet-set with cushion-cut rubies and old mine-cut diamonds, floral and foliate shoulders, ribbed shank, silver and gold mount, size 8. **$533**

Heritage Auctions, Inc.

Two rare rose gold and hair bands: one size 7, 6 mm wide, rose gold with gold initialed rectangle frame and coin edges; one size 9 with pearls, 6.5 mm wide. **$167**

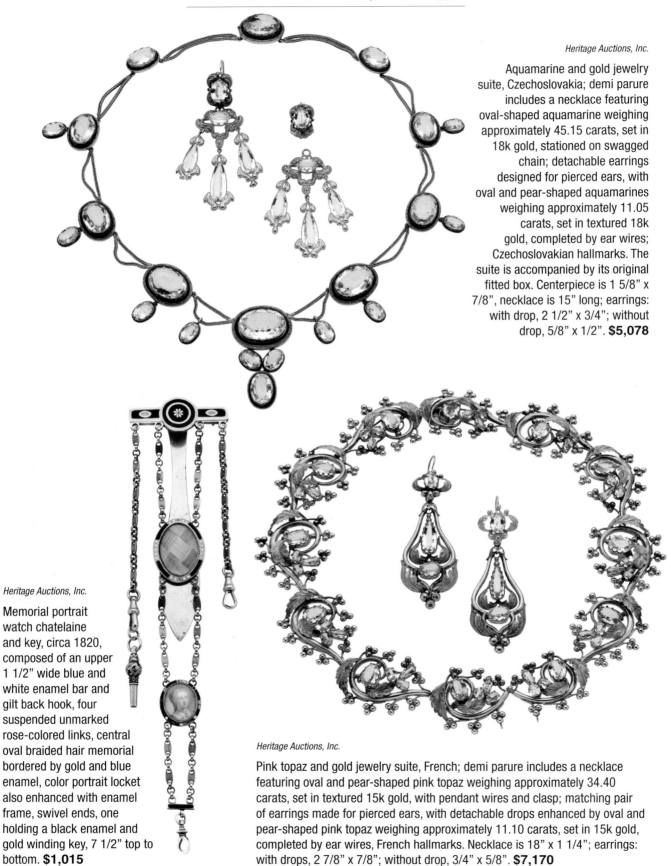

Aquamarine and gold jewelry suite, Czechoslovakia; demi parure includes a necklace featuring oval-shaped aquamarine weighing approximately 45.15 carats, set in 18k gold, stationed on swagged chain; detachable earrings designed for pierced ears, with oval and pear-shaped aquamarines weighing approximately 11.05 carats, set in textured 18k gold, completed by ear wires; Czechoslovakian hallmarks. The suite is accompanied by its original fitted box. Centerpiece is 1 5/8" x 7/8", necklace is 15" long; earrings: with drop, 2 1/2" x 3/4"; without drop, 5/8" x 1/2". **$5,078**

Memorial portrait watch chatelaine and key, circa 1820, composed of an upper 1 1/2" wide blue and white enamel bar and gilt back hook, four suspended unmarked rose-colored links, central oval braided hair memorial bordered by gold and blue enamel, color portrait locket also enhanced with enamel frame, swivel ends, one holding a black enamel and gold winding key, 7 1/2" top to bottom. **$1,015**

Pink topaz and gold jewelry suite, French; demi parure includes a necklace featuring oval and pear-shaped pink topaz weighing approximately 34.40 carats, set in textured 15k gold, with pendant wires and clasp; matching pair of earrings made for pierced ears, with detachable drops enhanced by oval and pear-shaped pink topaz weighing approximately 11.10 carats, set in 15k gold, completed by ear wires, French hallmarks. Necklace is 18" x 1 1/4"; earrings: with drops, 2 7/8" x 7/8"; without drop, 3/4" x 5/8". **$7,170**

EARLY VICTORIAN (ROMANTIC PERIOD), CIRCA 1837-1861

Queen Victoria set the tone for the era as the first female to rule Great Britain since Queen Anne (d. 1714). Like most women of her time, she was an incurable romantic—and she loved jewelry! The early years of her reign are aptly called The Romantic Period (also known as the Victoria and Albert period). In 1840, Victoria married Albert, who became Prince Consort in 1857 and died suddenly in 1861. The 21 years of their marriage were filled with love, devotion, and the births of nine children. Symbols of romance were predominant in the jewelry that Albert designed and had made for Victoria. Her betrothal ring was in the form of a snake with its tail in its mouth, symbol of everlasting love, a motif that recurs throughout the 19th century.

The snake also symbolized eternity, guardian spirit, and wisdom. Snake (or serpent) jewelry was especially popular in the 1840s. Gold snake necklaces, bracelets, and rings were set throughout with small turquoise cabochons or partly enameled and gem-set.

Flowers in jewelry were both symbolic of Victorian sentiment and a reflection of interest in nature. Flower motif brooches in diamonds and paste carried over from Georgian times, but became more three-dimensional and realistic. Flower heads were often set en tremblant. Gold and colored gemstone flowers were also realistically rendered.

The hand is another recurring romantic symbol in Victorian jewelry. It had a variety of meanings depending on how it was depicted. Hands holding flowers conveyed the flower's message. Yew wreaths symbolized mourning. Clasped hands symbolized friendship. Good luck and "evil eye" hand gesture amulets were carved in coral, ivory, jet, and mother-of-pearl. Hands were also used as clasps for bracelets and neck chains, especially in earlier period pieces.

Sentiment prevailed in the gifts of jewelry Victoria exchanged with others. She fostered the widespread practice of giving and wearing jewelry made with the hair of the giver as a memento or love token. And no one thought it at all strange that she had a bracelet made from her children's baby teeth.

The Great Exhibition of the Industry of All Nations, held in London in 1851, was perhaps the single most important event of the early Victorian period. It was dubbed "The Crystal Palace" after the gigantic all-glass structure that housed it. Never before had there been a multi-national exhibit of any kind, held anywhere. This monumental spectacle has been called "the focal point for the Victorian culture of the Western world." Its success spawned "Crystal Palace" off-spring in Cork in 1852, New York and Dublin in 1853, Munich in 1854, and Paris in 1855. In 1854, the Crystal Palace itself was re-created at Sydenham, outside London. The jewelers who took part in these exhibitions were the most highly esteemed trendsetters of jewelry fashion. If it had been seen at the Crystal Palace, it was "in."

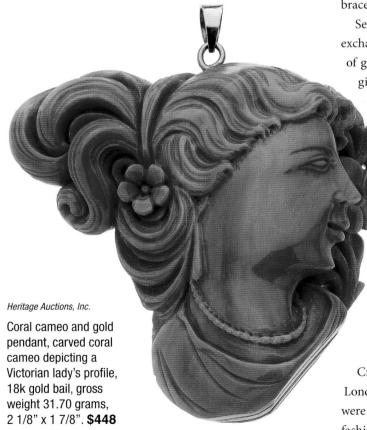

Heritage Auctions, Inc.

Coral cameo and gold pendant, carved coral cameo depicting a Victorian lady's profile, 18k gold bail, gross weight 31.70 grams, 2 1/8" x 1 7/8". **$448**

Heritage Auctions, Inc.

Necklaces with large pendant drops were worn on low-cut gowns during the Early Victorian period. Gilt metal necklace with enameled center piece under glass, alternating rose-gold links with pieced panel links, 55 mm x 34 mm shield pendant, raised glass crystal, colorful blue high relief bird motif, 57.1 grams, 16 1/2" long. **$310**

In 1851, naturalistic diamond flower brooches and hair ornaments, Celtic annular (ring) brooches, and Scottish "granite" bracelets, Berlin iron jewelry, and gemstone and enameled bracelets were among the jewels shown.

Early Victorian fashions determined the ways in which jewelry was or was not worn. The dresses of the period were full-skirted, worn with petticoats, and often had long sleeves. Lace collars with brooches pinned at the throat were common. Necklines on dresses worn by younger women were cut low and wide across the shoulders. Velvet or silk ribbons were sometimes worn around the neck, crossed in front and pinned with a small brooch. Large jeweled brooches with pendent drops, called bodice brooches, were worn on low-cut gowns in the evening. Unless otherwise altered, early Victorian brooches usually have an extended pinstem (meant to be pushed back through the clothing to keep the brooch in place), C-catch, and tube hinge.

In the late 1840s and early 1850s, bonnets were worn during the day, and for evening wear, center-parted hair covered the ears in loops or ringlets, trimmed in ribbons or flowers. Consequently, earrings were seldom worn.

Bracelets, worn in multiples on both wrists, were the most popular form of jewelry, especially snake-shaped coils or bangles. "Stretchy" expandable bracelets were introduced in the early 1840s, thanks to the invention of elastic, c. 1830. In spite of their prevalence, relatively few early Victorian bracelets survive today, having been subjected to considerably more wear and damage than brooches or necklaces might have been.

Romanticism inspired the beginning of a revival of medieval and Renaissance motifs and decorative elements that was to continue throughout the century. Gothic architecture was translated into jewels. Gold was still in relatively short supply at the onset of the Early Victorian period. In the 1830s, gold was mostly hand-wrought filigree (cannetille), but by the 1840s, filigree was out and hollow stamped or repoussé thin gauge metal was in, used as settings for gemstones, or as frames for portrait miniatures and enamels. While à jour settings for faceted gemstones were now common, foiled stones in closed-back mounts continued to be seen, especially "pinked" topaz (colorless topaz with pink foil backing).

Seed pearl jewelry was often made with little, if any, gold at all. Tiny pearls strung on horsehair and mounted on cut-to-shape mother-of-pearl backings were made into entire suites of delicate and fragile jewels, typically of floral and foliate design. It is unusual to find individual pieces intact, and even rarer to come across intact suites, many of which were made in England in the first half of the 19th century. The fashion for seed pearls persisted longer in the United States. It was traditionally worn as bridal jewelry, but seed pearl jewelry items were still being offered for sale for everyday wear in American trade catalogs of the 1910s.

CORAL

Coral was popular throughout the 19th century. Children wore coral necklaces to fend off disease and evil spirits because the Victorians held on to the ancient belief that coral had curative and protective powers. It also appealed to their interest in nature. Beads, carved cameos, floral motifs, good luck charms, and natural branches were made into jewelry of all types. Italy, particularly Naples, was the primary source for coral, and most carvers were Italian. Desirable, but rarer, colors were deep red and pale pink.

The most prevalent surviving forms are those in which the coral is protected by a metal mounting or frame, and beads. Intact examples of delicately carved all-coral pieces are more difficult to find.

HAIRWORK

Hairwork is a second type of hair jewelry, in which the entire piece is made of woven hair with the addition of gold or gold-filled fittings and decorative elements. These pieces were not necessarily meant for mourning. They were made by and for women and men out of their own or a loved one's hair and given as mementos or love tokens.

The technique involved the use of a type of worktable where individual strands of hair were weighted and woven together to form hollow tubes around a solid core of cording and/or wire. This core was sometimes removed, and the

Heritage Auctions, Inc.

Three mourning pins: two oval, one gold with turquoise has hair glass frame on the back, one gilt with braided hair; one smaller gold oval drop with hair and a back frame engraved with a heart, cross and anchor. **$75**

tubes were then tied or enclosed with gold rings at intervals to form spherical or elliptical hollow "beads."

After processing and weaving, the hairwork could then be made into necklaces, bracelets, earrings, or brooches. A commonly found form is a watch chain in which the tube or rope of hair is woven in a spiral pattern, with an added gold or gold-filled swivel hook, bar, and fob charms (sometimes also made of hair).

Hairwork jewelry dates back further than was previously thought. Documented examples survive going back to the

Scottish agate chain, composed of agate batons, with heart-shape agate padlock, silver mounts, 25 1/4" long. **$1,896**

late 18th century. But the height of hairwork's popularity was during the mid-19th century, when it was made commercially, as well as by "loving hands at home" from instructions found in women's magazines of the day, such as *Godey's Lady's Book* or *Peterson's Magazine*. Fittings for hair watch chains were advertised in Sears catalogs as late as 1911, but the practice of making and wearing hair jewelry had waned considerably by the 1880s.

While the thought of human-hair jewelry may be distasteful to some, collectors find both the idea and its execution fascinating. In recent years, there has been a growing appreciation for this lost art, as well as interest in reviving it.

The value of hair jewelry is in the workmanship: solid gold fittings enhance value only slightly over gold-filled. Watch chains are the form most usually found, while necklaces and earrings are scarce. Brown is the most common hair color; blond and white are scarce, and red is rare, not only because redheads are in the minority, but also because red hair was attributed to women of ill repute.

Damaged pieces are difficult to repair, so be sure to check condition carefully.

SCOTTISH JEWELRY

Gothic and Celtic Revivals were already well under way when Victoria ascended the throne. Her own romantic attachment to ancient and medieval history was certainly influential in furthering the public's preoccupation with the past. Britain's, particularly Scotland's, past was romanticized by historical novels, like those of Sir Walter Scott. And after Victoria purchased Balmoral, a castle in Scotland, in 1848, everyone became enamored of Scottish motifs. Circular Scottish plaid pins (sometimes called "target" brooches), heraldic crests, dirks and claymores (knives and swords), thistles and St. Andrew's crosses (Scottish national emblems), the Order of the Garter strap and buckle (symbol of the chivalric order headed by Victoria)—all were made into jewelry with varieties of agates, malachite, cairngorms (dark yellow-amber faceted quartz), and amethysts set in engraved silver or gold.

Unless a piece is hallmarked with a British date letter (and many pieces are not; in fact, "purist" collectors say that "real" Scottish agate jewelry is never hallmarked), precise dating of Scottish jewelry is difficult. Earlier pieces tend to be more faithful to traditional Scottish motifs. Mid- and late Victorian pieces incorporated anchors, hearts, serpents, arrows, and other non-Scottish forms. Subtle differences can be seen in later 19th century pieces, such as the cut of the stones and the absence of ornate engraving. Some traditional forms continued to be made, and C-catches and tube hinges continued to be used as brooch findings well into the 20th century. But rhodium plating and cast mountings are sure signs of more recent vintage and lesser quality. Brooches are the most common form; bracelets are scarcer, but they do turn up; necklaces, earrings, and buckles are rare. Scottish jewelry is very wearable with today's fashions and, consequently, demand is high, especially for larger, less-common pieces.

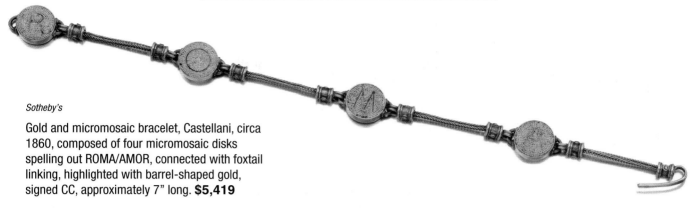

Sotheby's

Gold and micromosaic bracelet, Castellani, circa 1860, composed of four micromosaic disks spelling out ROMA/AMOR, connected with foxtail linking, highlighted with barrel-shaped gold, signed CC, approximately 7" long. **$5,419**

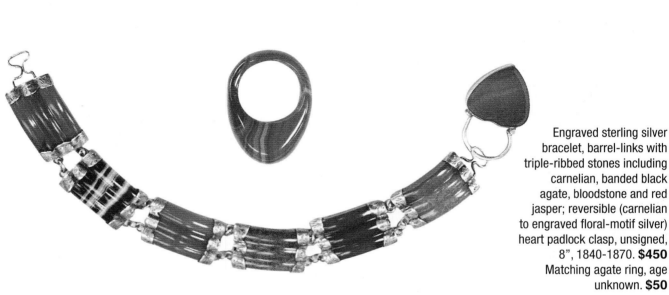

Engraved sterling silver bracelet, barrel-links with triple-ribbed stones including carnelian, banded black agate, bloodstone and red jasper; reversible (carnelian to engraved floral-motif silver) heart padlock clasp, unsigned, 8", 1840-1870. **$450** Matching agate ring, age unknown. **$50**

Sotheby's

Pair of micromosaic bracelets, Castellani, circa 1860, each designed as a series of square links set with eau de nil and silver colored tesserae with letters spelling AMOR/ROMA, within rope work borders, to foxtail chain connections, each signed with interlaced Cs, can be joined together and worn as a necklace, approximately 7" long. **$27,098**

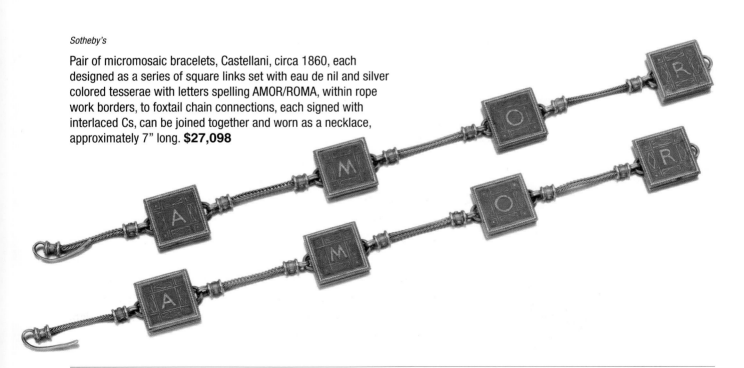

Diamond-shaped pendant/brooch with bezel-set pyramid-cut granite stones, colors of Aberdeen (gray) and Peterhead (pink), silver frame with slate back, also attributed to M. Rettie & Sons, circa 1850, 2 5/8". **$325**

Heritage Auctions, Inc.

Turquoise and pearl gold brooch, circa 1858, unmarked yellow gold tests 18k, 12.7 grams, 31 mm across, 14 mm high, accented with small pearls and turquoise, lightly engraved on the back, "June 28. 1858," dent on one side front and back, repair where the pin is attached on the back. **$275**

Heritage Auctions, Inc.

Gold and aquamarine brooch, upper section measures 57 mm across, fine repoussé gold work with faceted aquamarines, tests 15k, 14.1 grams, 3 3/4" top to bottom. **$657**

CameoHeaven.com

Cameo, Psyche and Eros, rare, Victorian shading, 15k gold setting (tested), c-clasp with a trombone closure pin, 1850, 2 1/2". **$1,595**

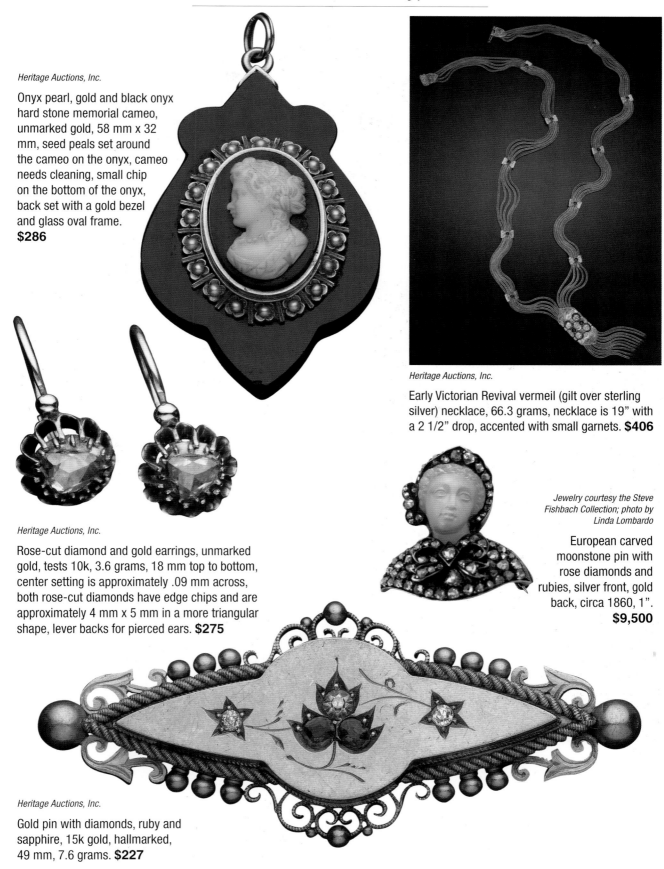

Heritage Auctions, Inc.

Onyx pearl, gold and black onyx hard stone memorial cameo, unmarked gold, 58 mm x 32 mm, seed peals set around the cameo on the onyx, cameo needs cleaning, small chip on the bottom of the onyx, back set with a gold bezel and glass oval frame. **$286**

Heritage Auctions, Inc.

Early Victorian Revival vermeil (gilt over sterling silver) necklace, 66.3 grams, necklace is 19" with a 2 1/2" drop, accented with small garnets. **$406**

Heritage Auctions, Inc.

Rose-cut diamond and gold earrings, unmarked gold, tests 10k, 3.6 grams, 18 mm top to bottom, center setting is approximately .09 mm across, both rose-cut diamonds have edge chips and are approximately 4 mm x 5 mm in a more triangular shape, lever backs for pierced ears. **$275**

Jewelry courtesy the Steve Fishbach Collection; photo by Linda Lombardo

European carved moonstone pin with rose diamonds and rubies, silver front, gold back, circa 1860, 1". **$9,500**

Heritage Auctions, Inc.

Gold pin with diamonds, ruby and sapphire, 15k gold, hallmarked, 49 mm, 7.6 grams. **$227**

Heritage Auctions, Inc.

Rose gold and diamond pin, mine cut diamonds, leaf motif, 54 mm, 7.4 grams. **$262**

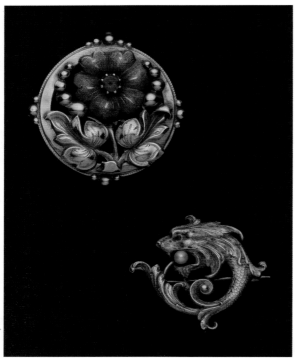

Heritage Auctions, Inc.

Portrait pin, unmarked gold, tests 14k, 7.1 grams, 30 mm x 34 mm, two chips on the top right sides on the edges, portrait has some wear. **$131**

Heritage Auctions, Inc.

Two gold pins, total weight is 8.3 grams, one 14k griffin pin, 29 mm with pearl and emerald eye, one unmarked early Victorian gold pin with amethyst (small side chip), 32 mm. **$286**

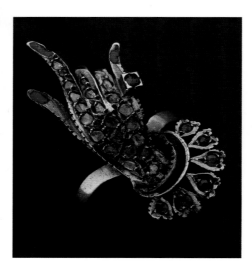

Heritage Auctions, Inc.

Diamond, ruby and enamel ring, set in unmarked rose gold, ring measures 35 mm end to end, mine cut diamonds, rubies, one emerald, blue and red enameled accents, 7.9 grams, size 6 3/4. **$203**

Heritage Auctions, Inc.

Vacheron & Constantin diamond, enamel and gold hunting case pocket watch with accompanying brooch, fob and key, circa 1850. A Victorian gold mourning brooch with applied black and white enamel accents supports the watch, key and fob. Case: 38 mm, hinged, circular 18k yellow gold with smooth edge and ornately decorated case front and back, black champleve enamel, accented by rose-cut diamonds; No. 83139 dial: white enamel with black Roman numerals, gilt "moon" hour and minute hands. Movement: 31 mm, gilt, 13 jewels, detached lever, keywind and set, No. 83139, signed Vacheron & Constantin on the center bridge, lateral bridge escapement; signed and numbered Vacheron & Constantin in Geneve. E. E. Rodgers on cuvette, triple signed Vacheron & Constantin on the dial, movement and dustcover. **$3,107**

Heritage Auctions, Inc.

Early coral and gold cameo, 14k gold, 8 grams, 38 mm top to bottom. **$118**

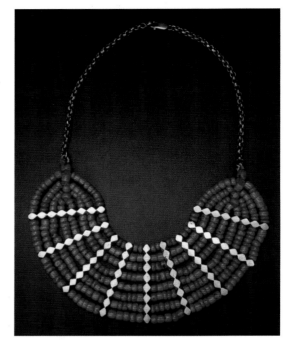

Heritage Auctions, Inc.

Coral and gold necklace, clasp and chain are 14k yellow gold, 156.3 grams, chain is 10", coral piece is 3" x 5 1/2". **$250**

Heritage Auctions, Inc.

Coral cameo gold pin/ pendant, 14k yellow gold, 7.6 grams, 32 mm x 27 mm, has a bale. **$300**

Heritage Auctions, Inc.

Two cameo pins, one 30 x 21 mm high relief coral cameo with gold frame, one 36 x 30 mm early Victorian hardstone cameo in a very fine unmarked rose gold fancy frame, 16.3 grams total. **$334**

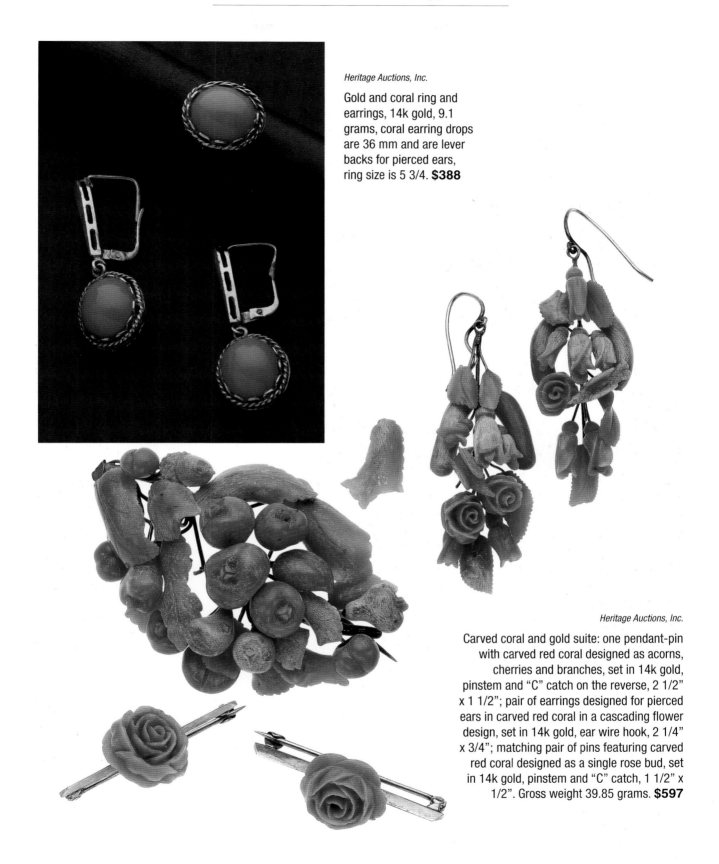

Heritage Auctions, Inc.

Gold and coral ring and earrings, 14k gold, 9.1 grams, coral earring drops are 36 mm and are lever backs for pierced ears, ring size is 5 3/4. **$388**

Heritage Auctions, Inc.

Carved coral and gold suite: one pendant-pin with carved red coral designed as acorns, cherries and branches, set in 14k gold, pinstem and "C" catch on the reverse, 2 1/2" x 1 1/2"; pair of earrings designed for pierced ears in carved red coral in a cascading flower design, set in 14k gold, ear wire hook, 2 1/4" x 3/4"; matching pair of pins featuring carved red coral designed as a single rose bud, set in 14k gold, pinstem and "C" catch, 1 1/2" x 1/2". Gross weight 39.85 grams. **$597**

Diamond, enamel and gold mourning hinged locket, European-cut diamonds weighing approximately 0.85 carat, black enameled star applied on 14k gold, locket opens to reveal a lock of hair and is personalized on the reverse, 1 1/4" x 7/8". **$875**

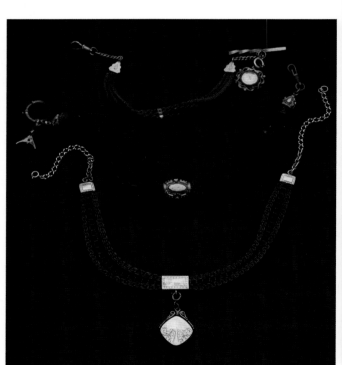

Three hair chains: 6" with gold-filled chain and fob and three small seed pearls; 10" chain with center gold-filled locket; 10 1/2" chain. **$100**

Five memorial hair pins: one with engraved oval bezel, back has four names and dates ranging from 1824 to 1846, missing the pin back; two in fancy unmarked gold oval frames, one missing the pin back; one small oval in rose gold with later metal pin back; one gilt tubular braided hair pin. **$174**

Linda Lombardo jewelry and photo, Worn to Perfection on Ruby Lane

Triple-strand woven hairwork watch chain, yellow gold-filled fittings with hearts, 1860s-1880s, 13". **$250**

Jewelry and image courtesy Linda Lombardo, Worn to Perfection on Ruby Lane

Graphite on vellum portrait miniature, circa 1830s, with two apertures containing hair and initials "L" and "O," 1 1/2". **$750**

Heritage Auctions, Inc.

Three pins, one rose gold with pearls and mine-cut diamond, one rose gold with hair cross, one gilt pin with pearls. **$310**

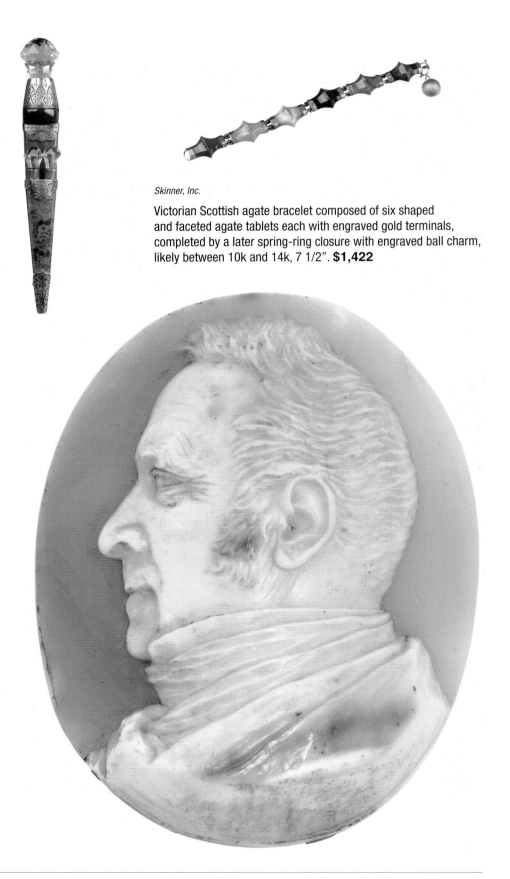

Skinner, Inc.

Victorian Scottish agate dirk brooch set with various agates and jasper, with shaped citrine highlights, engraved silver mount, 3 1/4" long. **$711**

Skinner, Inc.

Victorian Scottish agate bracelet composed of six shaped and faceted agate tablets each with engraved gold terminals, completed by a later spring-ring closure with engraved ball charm, likely between 10k and 14k, 7 1/2". **$1,422**

Heritage Auctions, Inc.

Unmounted Victorian Scottish shell portrait cameo depicting a gentleman's profile, 45 x 35 x 3.50 mm, bottom edge of the cameo is inscribed, "N. 185 King," reverse is inscribed, "N. 185, J. C. King, Boston, 28th May 1849." Attributed to John Crookshanks King (1806-1882), a Scottish-born machinist and sculptor, who immigrated to the United States in 1829. He was actively modeling busts and cameos of important public figures in New Orleans from 1837 to 1840, prior to continuing his craft in Boston. **$179**

Heritage Auctions, Inc.

Scottish opal and gold hardstone brooch, unmarked gold tests 14k, 12.3 grams, 27 mm x 24 mm, one stone has two scratches. **$325**

Skinner, Inc.

Antique silver and Scottish agate earpendants on wires, each drop set with agate bands, ribbed scroll tops, and engraved accents, 2" long. **$652**

Skinner, Inc.

Antique silver and Scottish agate earpendants on wires, each drop with flexible center and set with shaped agate tablets, engraved accents, 1 3/4" long. **$504**

Tiffany & Co. established itself as a reputable firm during this period. Renaissance Revival 18k gold figural locket, Tiffany & Co., with repoussé female herms among scrolling foliate and torch motifs, the sides with finely chased Muses in high relief, Terpsichore holding a lyre, Clio a trumpet, both wearing flowing garments leaving one breast exposed, lyre-form bail, and opening to reveal a compartment, inscribed signature to interior within repoussé, interior appears to be altered with one photo compartment, 1 1/2".
$5,925

MID-VICTORIAN (GRAND PERIOD), CIRCA 1861-1880

The Romantic Period ended abruptly with the death of Prince Albert in 1861, and the beginning of the Civil War in the United States—causes for deep mourning on both sides of the Atlantic. Wearing black was more than a correct form for mourning; it became fashionable.

Fashion, as always, played an important role in the changing look of jewelry. The voluminous skirt, supported by crinolines, or hoops, was introduced in the mid-1850s and became the look of the 1860s. This wider silhouette required larger jewelry. Brooches were massive, bracelets widened and were often worn in pairs, one on each wrist. Lower necklines prompted the wearing of necklaces and large lockets. Lockets and brooches often contained photographs, which gradually overtook portrait miniatures as a form of memorial jewelry. Hairstyles changed to once again reveal the ear, and earrings returned, growing to greater lengths towards the end of the period. Trains, bustles, ruffles, pleats, flounces, and fringe adorned the skirts of the 1870s. Tassels and fringe appeared in jewelry to complement the look.

For those who weren't in mourning, it was a colorful period. William Perkin discovered coal tar in 1856, which led to his accidental discovery of the first synthetic aniline dye. The first color he produced was purple, or mauve, which created such a sensation that it ushered in the era that followed, called the "Mauve Age." The fashion for bright colors continued through the 1870s. Colored gemstones and enamels complimented the look.

By the 1860s, Revivalism was in full swing. Women were piling on Etruscan-style amulets and other "classical" ornaments to the point of being satirized by the press. Revivalist Castellani's goldwork was displayed at the International Exhibition in London in 1862. Egyptian-style jewels were seen at the Exposition Universelle in Paris in 1867. Enameled Renaissance Revival jewels were seen in fashionably colorful social circles as well.

International exhibitions whetted appetites for exotic jewels from exotic places, like India. Mogul jewelry, Jaipur enamel, and gold-mounted tiger's claws from Calcutta became the rage in the 1870s, especially after Queen Victoria was proclaimed Empress of India in 1876. These pieces also inspired the work of English, European, and American jewelers.

After the Civil War, it became acceptable for American women to wear jewelry in greater quantities. Prosperity was growing, and with it the desire to display signs of wealth. What better way for a man to proclaim his status than to bedeck his wife in jewels? For the upper classes, at least, The Grand Period was indeed grand.

Working-class women were also decking themselves in baubles, bangles, and beads, although they were of the mass-produced "imitation" variety. Frankly fake costume jewelry was still an unheard of idea. Even if it wasn't "real," women wanted it to look like it was. Manufacturers were now capable of turning out machine-made goods in quantity to satisfy their demand. Electroplated trinkets set with glass "stones" were made to look like gold and diamond jewels.

Men continued to drape their vests with the requisite watch chains and fobs. Cuff links, also known as sleeve buttons, tie pins (also called scarfpins, stickpins, stockpins, cravat pins), signet rings, collar buttons, and shirt studs were additional forms of male adornment. Most of these were gold or gold-filled. Gemstones were added on occasion, particularly to stickpins.

By the 1860s, Tiffany & Co. had established itself as America's most prestigious and reputable firm, first by importing the best of European goods, then by manufacturing their own wares of the highest quality. From 1867 until the end of the century, Tiffany exhibited and won medals at international expositions in Paris and the United States. They promoted an appreciation of American craftsmanship and resources by exhibiting pieces with American themes, and newly discovered American gemstones, like Montana blue sapphires and Maine tourmalines. They also displayed newly discovered diamonds from South Africa and opals from Australia.

The Centennial Exposition in Philadelphia was a landmark event in American jewelry history. It gave Tiffany and other American jewelers the opportunity to "strut their stuff" in a grand manner and capture the world's attention. It furthered the recognition of the United States as an industrial nation with a talent for invention and production.

BLACK JEWELRY

Sentiment was the glue that held Victorian lives together. It was also the preservative that has saved many pieces of jewelry from being discarded or sold for scrap. Surely one prevailing sentiment was that of bereavement. Victoria had an unswerving sense of propriety and issued rules and regulations governing strict codes of behavior for herself,

Heritage Auctions, Inc.

Jet cameo pendant-brooch, Bacchanalian theme depicting the god of wine with rams and grapes, dangling flowers, carved in jet, pendant bail, pinstem and "C" catch on the reverse, gross weight 23.80 grams, 1 3/4" x 1 7/8". **$298**

her family, her court, and her subjects. These rules of etiquette included dress codes for all occasions, particularly for mourning, including the proper jewelry to be worn.

After Prince Albert died, Victoria went into a period of mourning that lasted for the rest of her life, a full 40 years. For much of this time, all members of the royal court were required to wear black. This funereal atmosphere spread throughout the populace, creating a demand for black jewelry, the only color permitted during periods of full mourning. Jet was the material of choice. An entire industry grew up around the mining and carving of jet, a fossilized coal found near the town of Whitby in England. The area became famous for its artisans, and tourists went to Whitby to watch them work. They brought home jet souvenirs, sometimes personalized with the names of loved ones, not necessarily departed.

Brooches, bead necklaces, and bracelets were the most commonly worn types of jet jewelry. Bracelets were often of the stretchy type, strung on elastic and usually worn in pairs (as were many types of bracelets). Pendent earrings were worn, but are not found as often today as are brooches and bracelets.

Jet jewelry became so popular that it spawned a number

Heritage Auctions, Inc.

Black onyx, seed pearl and gold suite: pendant with rectangular and drop-shaped black onyx, set in 14k gold, pinstem and "C" catch on the reverse, 1 3/4" x 1 3/4"; matching pair of earrings designed for pierced ears, set in 14k gold, completed by a shepherd's hook, 2 1/2" x 3/4"; pendant featuring oval-shaped black onyx measuring 36 x 45 mm, seed pearls ranging in size from 3.50 to 1.50 mm, set in 14k gold, pinstem and catch on the reverse, 1 1/2" x 1 3/4"; gross weight 41.05 grams. **$597**

of imitations. Two of the most common were black glass, misleadingly called "French jet" (also known as "Vauxhall glass") and vulcanite, a hardened (vulcanized) rubber that is sometimes mistakenly called gutta-percha. Gutta-percha is a natural substance from the Malayan palaquium tree. It was occasionally used for jewelry but it is not stable in air, so little survives. Other materials are also erroneously labeled gutta-percha, including shellac-based compositions molded into daguerreotype ("union") cases, hand mirrors and brushes, buckles, and other jewelry, and pressed horn (processed and dyed black), often seen in mourning jewelry. Bog oak, from the peat bogs of Ireland, is sometimes included in this group of jet imitations, but although it is black to dark brown and carved (usually with Irish motifs) or heat press-molded, it was never meant as a substitute for jet.

True jet tends to command higher prices than do comparable pieces made from its imitations. Many dealers do not know how to tell the difference. The word "jet" has become synonymous with "black," so any black shiny jewelry material may be misidentified as jet.

Black onyx is another material used in mourning jewelry, and about which there is some confusion. Gemologically, the correct name is dyed black chalcedony. Onyx by definition is a banded, or layered, stone, most often seen carved into cameos. The black color is almost always a result of soaking in sugar solution and heating in sulfuric acid, a process that was known to the Romans.

Black enamel was often the material of choice for mourning jewelry, usually applied to gold brooches and rings. The surface might be smooth or engraved, sometimes with the words "In Memory Of" in old English lettering on the enameled ground.

At times it can be difficult to determine where mourning left off and fashion began in black jewelry. Massive necklaces, diamond-enhanced brooches, and elaborately carved bracelets might lead one to question the depth of the wearer's mourning. But considering that some women wore black for most of their adult lives, it is not surprising that they would want to enliven their "toilet" with a bit of fashionable elegance. Because it was fashionable, black jewelry was also worn by women who were not in mourning.

TORTOISESHELL AND PIQUÉ

Tortoiseshell was another popular 19th century jewelry material. It was also considered suitable for half-mourning. Lockets, hair combs, and bracelets were made from this natural plastic taken from the shell of the hawksbill turtle, now an endangered species.

A technique known as piqué, originally used in ornamental objects in the 17th century, was applied to jewelry and popularized in the mid-to-late 19th century. After softening it with heat, the tortoiseshell was inlaid with gold and/or silver in floral or geometric patterns. The technique using inlaid strips of metal cut into ornate designs is called piqué posé. Piqué point refers to dots or other small geometric shapes inlaid in an overall pattern.

Animal rights were not a big issue in Victorian times. Animals or parts of animals were used with impunity. It is now illegal to buy or sell tortoiseshell in this country. Antique pieces are exempt, but there are restrictions regarding import and export to and from other countries. Not all mottled brown lightweight material is tortoiseshell, however. Toward the end of the century, many hair combs and other jewelry and objects were made of celluloid in imitation of tortoiseshell (see "Early Celluloid" in "Late Victorian" section).

REVIVALIST JEWELRY

Victorians were fascinated with ancient history. For them, history meant revivals. Archeological discoveries and published accounts of ancient historical events and epics prompted revivals of jewelry styles from ancient and medieval cultures: Assyrian, Celtic, Egyptian, Etruscan, Gothic, Hellenistic and Roman, Mogul (India), Moorish, and Renaissance. Exact copies were favored over interpretations. With some exceptions, originality and creativity were not notable characteristics of Revivalist style, although exquisite workmanship and attention to details often were.

A number of noted jewelers of the mid- to late-19th century worked in the Revivalist mode, copying ancient forms. Among these, the most famous were the Castellani family of Rome, and Carlo Giuliano (c. 1831-1895) and sons Carlo and Arthur of London.

Heritage Auctions, Inc.

Two Etruscan Revival gold brooches: one is a carved scarab with a 18k gold lotus blossom frame, signed Blanchard, Cairo, 1 3/4" x 1 7/8"; the other one is a real dung beetle resting within a 22k gold winged frame, 2" x 1/2". **$956**

Skinner, Inc.

Renaissance Revival Limoges enamel brooch depicting a helmeted figure with flowing hair against a fantastic landscape with trees and castle, gold mount with split pearl accents, 1 1/8" diameter. **$474**

ETRUSCAN

Revivalism reached its height during the 1860s and 1870s. A mania for all things Italian promoted the popularity in particular of Etruscan Revival jewels, most closely associated with what is generically called the "archaeological style," which also includes copies of Roman cameos and intaglios, mosaics, and "Hellenistic" (of Greek history, language and culture, 4th to 1st century BC) gold jewelry. The discovery of gold treasures from antiquity in Tuscany, in west-central Italy, near Rome, instigated the attempt to copy the ancient technique of granulation. Minute beads of gold were applied side-by-side to a gold surface to create a design. The difficulty lay in soldering the beads to the surface without melting them. Fortunato Pio Castellani (1794-1865), while unable to duplicate the technique exactly, came closest to perfecting it. Twisted, or "corded," wirework was also applied to gold jewels in the Etruscan style. Others made the attempt at granulation and wirework, but were not always as successful.

The ancient jewels themselves were copied by the Castellani family, as well as the techniques. The bulla, a two-sided round pendant worn by the Etruscans as an amulet, and the fibula, a safety-pin type of brooch used to fasten garments, were among the favorite forms.

The popularity of the Castellani family's work was of course a motive for their imitators—copyists of copyists, as it were. Skill in craftsmanship, or the lack of it, is what separates the wheat from the chaff. Some craftsmen were very skilled indeed, but the range of quality in Etruscan-style jewels is wide. Although quality workmanship is of primary consideration, a signature can add a great deal of value. The Castellani marks, back-to-back overlapping Cs, are important ones to know. It is also important to note that their marks, as well as their techniques, were copied, but some unsigned pieces can be attributed to the Castellani.

Large numbers of pieces in the archaeological style were produced by anonymous manufacturers throughout the last half of the 19th century. Many unsigned examples of varying quality can be found today of Etruscan decoration on gold and gold-filled pieces.

RENAISSANCE

The Giulianos were Revivalists of another sort. They specialized in jewels in the Renaissance style, and were famous for their enameling. One trademark was an enameled white background with black dots, or black with white dots. Carlo Giuliano's work reached its peak in the 1870s. Although he, too, employed granulation as well as other ancient techniques, unlike most Revivalists, he was an interpreter of the style. He improved upon techniques and forms with original ideas rather than exact copies. He signed his pieces C.G. in an applied or impressed oval plaque.

Sons Carlo and Arthur (mark: C. & A.G.) carried on after their father's death in 1895, but changing styles affected their business. Early 20th century pieces were not as successful. The business closed in 1914, the year of Arthur's death. Both Giuliano marks have been counterfeited.

Other noted archaeological and Renaissance revivalist jewelers were John Brogden of London, Ernesto Pierret (1824-1870) of Rome, and Eugène Fontenay (1823-1887), Froment-Meurice (1802-1855), Jules Wièse (1818-1890) and son Louis of Paris.

Enamel, colored gemstones, and pearls are characteristic materials for Renaissance Revival jewels. Austrian and Hungarian Renaissance Revival jewelry was produced in quantity in the late 19th and early 20th centuries (see "Beaux-Arts and Neo-Renaissance Jewelry" in Part II). It is cruder in execution and materials—usually silver gilt, enamel, low-quality gemstones (sometimes glass) and freshwater pearls. Nevertheless, these pieces have a certain appeal and are of growing interest, particularly among collectors of costume jewelry. Accordingly, prices have risen. Most pieces are unmarked, but sometimes a piece will have an Austro-Hungarian silver quality hallmark, usually a dog's head in a coffin-shaped lozenge (see "Marks on Metals" appendix; for other less commonly seen Austrian hallmarks, see Tardy, *International Hallmarks on Silver*, English translation, Paris, 1985.)

EGYPTIAN

The discovery of the tomb and treasures of Queen Ah-Hotep and the start of construction of the Suez Canal in 1859 (completed 10 years later), inspired the return of the Egyptian style, which had been revived once before in the late 18th and early 19th centuries. Familiar Egyptian symbols—scarabs, pharaohs, lotus blossoms, falcons, and vultures—found their way into jewels by Castellani, Giuliano, Brogden, Robert Phillips, and several famous French jewel houses, including Froment-Meurice and Boucheron. These pieces were worked in gold, enamel, gemstones, and mosaics in much the same manner as other Revivalist jewelry.

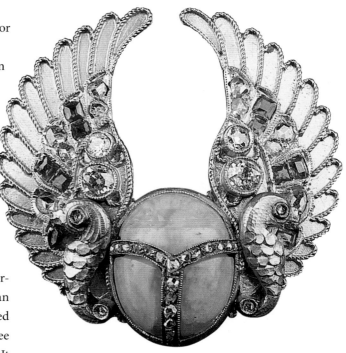

Egyptian Revival scarab brooch, gem-set 14k gold, designed as winged scarab, oval amazonite cabochon forms body enclosed by thin diamond-set bands, flanked by small S-scroll snakes, tall curved feathered gold wings bezel-set with old European-cut diamonds, step-cut rubies, European assay marks, possibly Austrian. **$4,230**

Revivalism caught on in the United States, too, although somewhat later. When Alessandro Castellani exhibited his family's work at the 1862 International Exposition in London, America was in the throes of the Civil War. But in 1876, at the Centennial Exposition in Philadelphia, Castellani presented his ideas and his jewelry to the receptive American public.

Soon after, classical motifs and "Etruscan" worked gold began making their appearance in American-made jewelry, most of it mass-produced.

Today it is not unusual to find American pieces, both signed and unsigned, that reflect the widespread appeal of the past during the mid- to late-Victorian era.

REPRODUCTION ALERT

Faked signatures and reproductions are common. Signed pieces should be authenticated by an expert.

CAMEOS AND INTAGLIOS

The cameo has come to be known as a classic form of jewelry, the epitome of the "old-fashioned" look. But its widespread popularity began in the 19th century as a tourist souvenir. Hardstone cameos date to ancient Rome; shell cameos to the Renaissance. Late 18th century Neoclassicists revived the art, inspired by Napoleon's preoccupation with Roman Imperialism. But it was the Victorians who popularized (some say vulgarized) the cameo made from a variety of materials—shell, lava, coral, ivory, jet, as well as gemstones—as a part of a Greco-Roman Revival that remained in vogue from mid-century onward.

Travelers touring Europe (on guided excursions organized and conducted by the West's first travel agent, Thomas Cook) helped promote cameo-carving to the point of mass production. Italy was a favorite destination, especially, due to the Victorian preoccupation with ancient history, the ruins of Pompeii at Mount Vesuvius. "Lava" cameos were purchased as souvenirs. The material, actually a form of limestone mixed with volcanic particles called pyroclastics (real lava is molten rock), was found in the region, and associated with the volcano that was Pompeii's downfall. Nearby, in the seaside town of Torre del Greco, Italian

Heritage Auctions, Inc.

Shell cameo and gold brooch, rectangular-shaped, depicting a bouquet of flowers, measuring 39 x 46 mm, set in 14k gold, pinstem and "C" catch on the reverse, gross weight 11.30 grams, 1 1/2" x 1 7/8". **$187**

cameo carvers made shell and coral cameos for the tourists, as they continue to do today.

A true cameo is a miniature sculpture in relief, carved from a single piece of material. When the material is layered, as are agate (onyx) and shell, the carver uses the light and dark layers as contrasting background and foreground. When a design is carved into only the thin white layer of onyx with a thick black layer underneath, the background of the design appears translucent bluish-white. This is called "nicolo." The subject matter of cameos can range from classic mythological and Biblical scenes, floral bouquets and landscapes, to the more commonly seen heads or busts of women or men. Male cameos predominate the Neo-classical period.

A woman's profile is the motif most closely associated with cameos by their wearers today. These can date anywhere from 1840 to the present. Their look is usually in keeping with the style of the times.

One favorite technique for circa-dating is to look at the nose of the woman in profile. Aquiline, or Romanesque, noses are found on the classic beauties of the mid-19th century. Pert, turned-up noses are found on 20th century interpretations of female attractiveness. It's important to remember that carvers could only carve what they knew; hairstyles and attire can also help in circa-dating.

The most common material for cameos is shell, which is soft and easy to carve. Portrait cameos were sometimes made with the depicted woman wearing a necklace or other jewelry set with a small diamond. These are called cameos habillés (French for "dressed up"), and are still being made. Hardstone "blackamoor" cameos habillés of the mid-19th century, depicting the profiles of African women, are much less commonly seen and highly desirable collector's items.

Nineteenth century lava and coral cameos are also found today, although not as abundantly. While most shell cameos are carved in bas-relief, due to the relative shallowness of the material's layers, lava and coral, being monochromatic, can be and often are carved in high relief. The protruding noses on these cameos are most susceptible to damage.

Some of the best and most highly prized cameos are made from hardstone. These cameos are more difficult

Heritage Auctions, Inc.

Coral and gold cameo brooch, oval-shaped, measuring 28 x 20 mm, depicting a lady's profile, resting in a decorative 14k yellow gold frame, pinstem and catch mechanism, gross weight 11.60 grams, 1 7/16" x 1 1/8". **$537**

and time-consuming to fashion, and require a great deal of skill with lathe-held tools. Cameo experts point out that the word "carved" is technically incorrect when applied to stone cameos and intaglios. The correct word is "engraved." The art of engraving gemstones is called "glyptics" or "the glyptic arts." Hardstone cameos are occasionally engraved within a concave depression in the stone, where the edge of the stone is level with the highest part of the cameo itself. Chevet or chevée, cuvette, or curvette are the terms, used interchangeably, for this type of cameo. The British term is dished.

The quality of a cameo's carving can range from breathtaking to abysmal. Values also range widely, depending on the skill of the carver, depicted subject, size, and the materials used for the cameo and the mounting or frame. Quickly made mass-produced shell cameos—most of which come from Idar-Oberstein, Germany, not Italy—are of little value. Ultrasonic machine-made stone cameos have been produced for the past 30 years. These have a faintly textured surface referred to as the "fresh-fallen snow" syndrome by author Anna Miller. Their quality and value are low. Pseudo or assembled cameos are molded from natural or synthetic materials and laminated to a backing or set in a metal frame.

Brooches are the usual form, but cameos can also be found set into necklaces, bracelets, earrings, rings, and stickpins.

Intaglios, which actually preceded cameos in ancient times, are the opposite of cameos, in that the design is recessed, engraved into the stone, below the surface. The most common association is with fob seals or signet rings, in which the intaglio is used to create an impression in relief when pressed into sealing wax. These fobs and rings are also worn for ornamental purposes, but the design is less perceptible than that of a cameo. Intaglios are engraved in hardstone, never shell or other soft material. Molded glass imitation intaglios are found in inexpensive jewelry.

Reverse-painted rock crystal intaglios were popular from the time of their invention circa 1862 well into the 20th century, especially in sporting jewelry featuring animal motifs (see "Edwardian Jewelry" in Part II). Dogs, horses, or other animals were engraved into the backs of rock crystal quartz cabochons. The intaglios were then painted in real-istic colors and backed with mother-of-pearl before setting. From the front, the animals appear three-dimensional. These were imitated with molded and painted glass in the 20th century.

MOSAICS IN JEWELRY

The rise and fall of mosaics developed along parallel lines to that of cameos. Also based on ancient Roman techniques and revived by Neo-classicists, mosaics of the late 18th and early 19th centuries were miniature works of art in glass or stone, resembling paintings.

Like cameos, mosaics reached their height of popularity in the mid-19th century, during the Revivalist rage for all things Italian. And like cameos, too, it was the tourist trade that brought them to that height and was their downfall in terms of quality.

There are two types of Italian mosaics: Roman, or micromosaics, in which tiny bits of colored glass called tesserae are pieced together to form a picture, held in place with cement in a glass or stone background; and Florentine, or pietra dura (literally, "hard stone," plural: pietre dure), in which thin slices of colored stones are cut in shapes and fitted together like a jigsaw puzzle to produce a picture, usually using a bed of black marble as the foundation.

Jewelry courtesy the Steve Fishbach Collection; photo by Linda Lombardo

Italian micromosaic bracelet in silver gilt setting, circa 1890, 7".
$700

The subject matter for mosaics is also of two distinct types. Roman mosaics, catering to the tourist trade, often depict Roman ruins and landscapes or are copies of ancient mosaics, like the Capitoline doves, often called "Pliny's doves."

King Charles spaniels were another favorite motif. Mythological and religious figures are also seen in Roman mosaics. Florentine mosaics most commonly have floral motifs, but other figurative motifs, such as butterflies and birds, are found as well.

Value depends on quality of workmanship and condition. Mosaics are easily cracked or otherwise damaged. In Roman mosaics, the size of the tesserae helps determine age and quality. Micromosaics that look less like pieces of glass and more like a painting to the naked eye are usually earlier and better.

Entire parures, or suites, of jewelry were made from both types of mosaics. Demi-parures of pendant or brooch and earrings are also found.

The brooch is the most common single form of mosaic jewelry. Mosaics continue to be made in Italy today, still for tourists, but with much larger tesserae and much less workmanship.

MANUFACTURED GOLD, GOLD-FILLED, GOLD-PLATED

The Revivalists inspired an interest in goldwork. All-gold jewelry was a novelty in the mid-19th century. Before discoveries in California and Australia in 1849 and 1851 made larger quantities of gold more accessible, gemstones were the focal point of most jewelry. Gold was used sparingly in very thin filigree (cannetille) or repoussé work in the early part of the century (see "Late Georgian" and "Early Victorian" sections). Later, heating, rolling and pressing, and electroplating made a little gold go a long way, and gave machine-made articles the look of gold without the expense.

By the 1830s, the Industrial Revolution had come to jewelry manufacture. Birmingham became a major center for machine-made goods in England. The invention of electroplating in 1840 helped launch what was to

Heritage Auctions, Inc.

Gold bracelet, unmarked gold tests 10k, 66.4 grams, with seed pearls and black enamel, bracelet is a circular link weave pattern at 25 mm wide, buckle is 32 mm wide, accented by tassels, the double slide clasp opens to 7 1/2" and slides to make the bracelet smaller to any size under 7 1/2". **$1,673**

become a huge costume jewelry industry in England and the United States, although the term "costume" jewelry wasn't coined until the early 20th century.

The rolled gold-plating process was brought to the United States from Great Britain in 1848 and was a big hit with New England jewelry manufacturers. Unlike electroplating, which was applied to a finished base metal article, rolled gold was a mechanical process for sheet and wire that was then used to manufacture a finished piece. The technique was derived from Sheffield plate, developed in 1743, which was copper clad with silver and rolled to the desired thickness. Rolled gold is copper or brass clad with gold, known as gold-filled in the United States, and called doublé d'or by the French, who began using the technique as early as the 1820s. The metal "sandwich" was treated exactly the same as karat gold: stamped, engraved, and fashioned into pieces that were identical to their solid gold counterparts.

In the United States, manufacturing centers grew along the Eastern seaboard: in Philadelphia, New York, Boston, and especially in Providence, Rhode Island, and the neighboring towns of Attleboro and North Attleboro, Massachusetts, and in Newark, New Jersey. Some of these manufacturers are still in business today.

It is worth noting that during the height of mid-Victorian Revivalism, several Newark firms produced quality pieces in Revivalist styles, comparable to those made in Europe. These jewels met with acceptance, however, only when they were sold as French or English-made (makers' marks were often absent at this time). America's well-to-do believed their own country's product was inferior to that of Europe. Perhaps this was because Americans excelled in the mass production of inexpensive gold and gold-filled or plated items. Many of the factories that made these items were in Providence and the Attleboros, but Newark produced a sizable portion of them as well. Although the pieces were mass-produced, there still some craftsmanship involved. The forms may have been die-stamped by machine (the preferred method at the time), but engraving, enameling, and finishing were done by hand.

Stamped jewelry backed with a flat plate is sometimes called "hollow work," and resembles hand-raised repoussé metalwork, in which the metal is worked from the back to create a design in relief. Engraving or chasing may be added to the front of the piece. This is the type of work that many people today consider typically Victorian, probably because it was produced in such quantities that a great deal of it has survived. Often, particularly in American pieces, the engraved depressions were partly filled with black enamel to enhance the design, called taille d'épargne, or "black enamel tracery."

The addition of gold fringe or bead-tipped foxtail chain tassels was common in pieces of the 1870s, a time when women's dresses were trimmed with abundant quantities of fringe. Long pendent earrings were in vogue and were especially well-suited to tassels and fringing.

Garter bracelets, or jarretières, of gold or gold-plated brass mesh with fringed and tasseled ends, were worn in pairs. The bracelets were secured with an ornamental slide, often engraved and enameled or set with a small cameo. They are sometimes referred to as slide bracelets, which can be confusing. Another type of bracelet is also called a slide bracelet, because it is made up of a collection of slides from longchains—a practice that began earlier in this century, after longchains went out of fashion. These slide bracelets became, and still are, popular enough to have been reproduced. The reproductions are fairly easy to detect. They don't have the hodgepodge look of a piece made up of old parts, as the originals are. Sometimes each slide is hallmarked in exactly the same way—a dead giveaway.

Hinged hollow bangles, both gold and gold-filled, are another kind of bracelet that remained popular throughout the Victorian period. They have become a classic form and are still made today. Widths and decorative elements vary from wide and ornately engraved or decorated to narrow and plain. The "bypass" or "crossover" design, in which decorated ends of a narrow tubular bangle cross parallel to one another at the top, gained favor in the later part of the century.

With the discovery of diamonds in South Africa in 1867 leading to a greater supply—and demand—a clever American invention was patented in 1878 that was designed to protect diamond drop earrings from being lost or

Heritage Auctions, Inc.

Gold suite: mesh choker necklace in 14k gold and a matching 14k gold mesh pin, black enamel, pinstem and catch on the reverse, gross weight 74.40 grams; necklace is 13" x 1"; pin is 3" x 7/8". **$2,629**

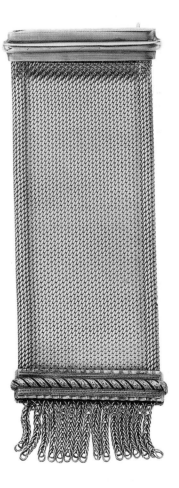

stolen: a spherical hinged hollow cover that snapped on over the diamond and concealed it from view. These were usually made of plain yellow gold, sometimes enameled or repoussé.

Another unique mid-to-late Victorian ornament involved the recycling of an outdated component of 18th century pocket watches, the escapement cover, or "watchcock." These gilt brass inner parts were actually rather decorative, each one engraved with a variety of floral and foliate motifs and other embellishments, including faces. In the 1880s, they were linked together to form necklaces or bracelets, or joined for brooches. Today these are quite scarce and collectible.

One variety of necklace of typically Victorian manufacture is called a "bookchain" necklace. Stamped, flat, folded-over rectangles, resembling the shape of a book, form the links of a double-sided chain, usually engraved or decorated on both sides. The chain is held together in front by an ornate clasp or slide, often with a small cameo set in it, the ends extending like tassels. The design may have evolved from the practice of wearing a ribbon around the neck, pinned with the ends crossed in front. Another variety of bookchain has a front spring ring clasp with an extension and a second spring ring for suspending a locket or pendant.

Lockets, another classic jewelry form, were popular in the 19th century, varying in size and shape. Large oval gold and gold-filled lockets on wide or thick chains were in keeping with style proportions of the Grand Period, 1860-1880. Round and somewhat smaller lockets appeared toward the end of the century.

Gold and gold-filled longchains and slides were practical as well as popular. A watch, lorgnette, or other useful (or decorative) item could be attached by means of a swivel hook and suspended from the chain. The ornamental slide was drawn up and the pendent piece pinned or tucked into a pocket or belt, causing the chain to drape attractively.

Gold-filled and electroplated jewelry was affordable to nearly everyone.

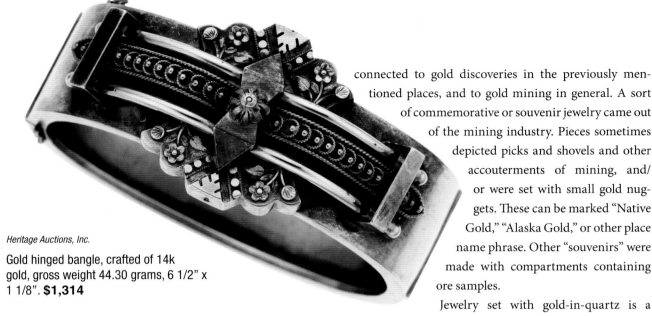

Heritage Auctions, Inc.

Gold hinged bangle, crafted of 14k
gold, gross weight 44.30 grams, 6 1/2" x
1 1/8". **$1,314**

Since it was manufactured in the same forms and styles as
solid gold jewelry, unless there is enough wear on a piece to
reveal base metal (usually brass), jewelry should be tested to
determine if it is gold or gold-filled, as it is seldom marked.
Gold-filled pieces sell for a little more than half the price of
their all-gold counterparts.

Occasionally, one hears the term "pinchbeck" used to
refer to gold-filled or gold-plated brass jewelry (more commonly heard in Britain). This is a word that has taken on
mystic proportions. In reality, pinchbeck is an alloy of
copper and zinc formulated in the early 18th century by
Christopher Pinchbeck as an inexpensive imitation gold.
It fell out of favor as a substitute for gold when electroplating was invented (c. 1840), and truly met its demise
when 9 karat gold was made legal in Britain in 1854. Most
pinchbeck jewelry was made in England. It was imported
by American jewelers, although some work was done here.
Pre-Victorian pieces made from pinchbeck are rarely seen
today, despite some dealers' claims. If they are of the period,
they are highly collectible and expensive. The problem for
collectors is one of circa-dating. There is no readily available
test for pinchbeck, as it is really one of several alloys of brass,
all of which differ only in percentages of copper to zinc.

The California Gold Rush of 1849 was followed by gold
discoveries in Australia in 1851, the Black Hills of the Dakota
territory in 1874, South Africa in 1886, and Alaska in 1898,
thus ensuring a more plentiful supply of gold for the rest of
the century. Two unique types of gold jewelry are directly

connected to gold discoveries in the previously mentioned places, and to gold mining in general. A sort
of commemorative or souvenir jewelry came out
of the mining industry. Pieces sometimes
depicted picks and shovels and other
accouterments of mining, and/
or were set with small gold nuggets. These can be marked "Native
Gold," "Alaska Gold," or other place
name phrase. Other "souvenirs" were
made with compartments containing
ore samples.

Jewelry set with gold-in-quartz is a
second type of mining-related jewelry, most
closely associated with California. Quartz is the usual
host mineral for gold, but it was more expensive to extract
gold from the hard-rock mines than from placer mining,
where natural forces had already separated the metal from
its matrix. Gold-in-quartz was therefore called "rich man's
gold." Jewelry set with polished pieces of it was considered
status-symbol jewelry, now highly collectible, especially in
California.

Nineteenth century gold jewelry is often unmarked.
If hallmarks are present, however, they can help determine age and country of origin. The United States had no
legal standards until 1906, but 14 and 10 karats were the
most common alloys for mass-manufactured gold of the
Victorian period. A few prestigious firms, such as Tiffany
& Co., used 18k exclusively; others used it occasionally.
The British used 9, 12, and 15 karat gold after 1854, when
standards were lowered from 18 karat. According to some
experts, unassayed (unmarked) gold before 1854 can be
lower than 18k. Britons spell karat with a c; the abbrevia-
tion is "c" or "ct." If a British piece is hallmarked, the date of
assay is indicated by a letter.

Assayed French gold is never lower than 18k; the hallmark is an eagle's head. Makers' marks are in a lozenge.
Other European countries use three-digit numbers that are
karat equivalents in thousandths, e.g., 750 equals 18k, 585
is 14k, etc. (see appendices, "Marks on Metals" and "Basic
Hallmark Identification").

Heritage Auctions, Inc.

Gold and black enamel memorial locket, unmarked gold tests 14k, 11.4 grams, 27 mm x 21 mm, memorial inscription on the inside of the locket with dates of "June 17, 1856, April 18, 1879 & November 28, 1879" with names for each date, both sides of the locket contain memorial hair, light surface scratches on both sides of the locket. **$375**

Stag head brooch, mid-Victorian era, cast-silver, garnet eyes, 1" faceted cairngorm bezel-mounted between antlers, unsigned, 2 7/8". **$450**

Jewelry and image courtesy Linda Lombardo, Worn to Perfection on Ruby Lane

Low-karat gold mourning pin with hair aperture and lock of hair, 1870s, 1 1/4". **$150**

Jewelry courtesy the Steve Fishbach Collection; photo by Linda Lombardo

English Mizpah photo locket in original jewelry case, Bright and Sons, Scarborough, England, dated, with inscription, "from Mama, October 26, 1873" and "May the Lord watch between you and me when we are absent one from the other," 14k gold, 2 1/4". **$7,500**

Heritage Auctions, Inc.

Diamond, hair and gold mourning locket-pendant, rose-cut diamonds set in 18k gold, opens to reveal a lock of hair, engraved "Augusta John May 24th, 1871," 2" x 1 1/8". **$507**

Skinner, Inc.

Victorian smoky quartz pendant, designed as a fly resting on a faceted oval berry capped by carved leaves, white metal mounts, 2 1/4" long. **$563**

Bonhams

Antique turquoise and diamond locket pendant, circa 1880, gross weight approximately 34.4 grams, mounted in 18 karat gold, 2 1/4" long. **$1,500**

Sotheby's

Archaeological-Revival gold and carnelian scarab bracelet, circa 1860, the articulated bracelet set with seven carved carnelian scarabs, the reverse of each engraved in a globolo style featuring figures and scenes from ancient Greek and Etruscan mythology, each scarab held within wirework and filigree bezels, spaced by batons accented by gold wire, 7" long. **$25,000**

Sotheby's

Archaeological-Revival gold and carnelian scarab necklace, circa 1860, suspending 21 carved carnelian scarabs, the reverses of each are engraved in a globolo style featuring figures and scenes from ancient Greek and Etruscan mythology, each scarab framed within wire and beadwork surrounds, spaced by twisted wire rondelles, completed by a carved carnelian intaglio clasp and supported on a gold loop-on-loop chain, 15" long. **$47,500**

Jewelry courtesy the Steve Fishbach Collection; photo by Linda Lombardo

Victorian Etruscan two-color gold earrings on wires, circa 1880s, 1 3/4". **$1,800**

Skinner, Inc.

Renaissance Revival silver and enamel pendant depicting a pelican feeding its young, suspending pearl drops, hallmarks, in a fitted box, 2 1/2" long. **$1,838**

Skinner, Inc.

Renaissance Revival gold, enamel, and diamond architectural-style pendant depicting an enamel swan wrapping its neck around a rose-cut diamond cross, the blue enamel ground with rose-cut diamond sun, all within a tabernacle-form mount bordered by twisted columns with rose-cut diamond and pearl swags and suspending pearl drops, engraved foliate accents, with indeterminate signature, 3" long. **$5,925**

Heritage Auctions, Inc.

Etruscan Revival gold jewelry suite: one pair of earrings designed for pierced ears, with a matching convertible pendant-brooch, with two locket compartments on the reverse, all in 14k yellow gold, gross weight 45 grams. Earrings are 2" x 1 3/4", pendant-brooch is 2 13/16" x 1 15/16". **$2,390**

Skinner, Inc.

Renaissance Revival silver brooch and earpendants, the brooch Austro-Hungarian, set with green beryls and pastes, reverse with engraved accents, hallmarks, the earpendants set with rose-cut diamonds spaced by pearls, brooch is 1 1/4", earrings 1 1/8". **$474**

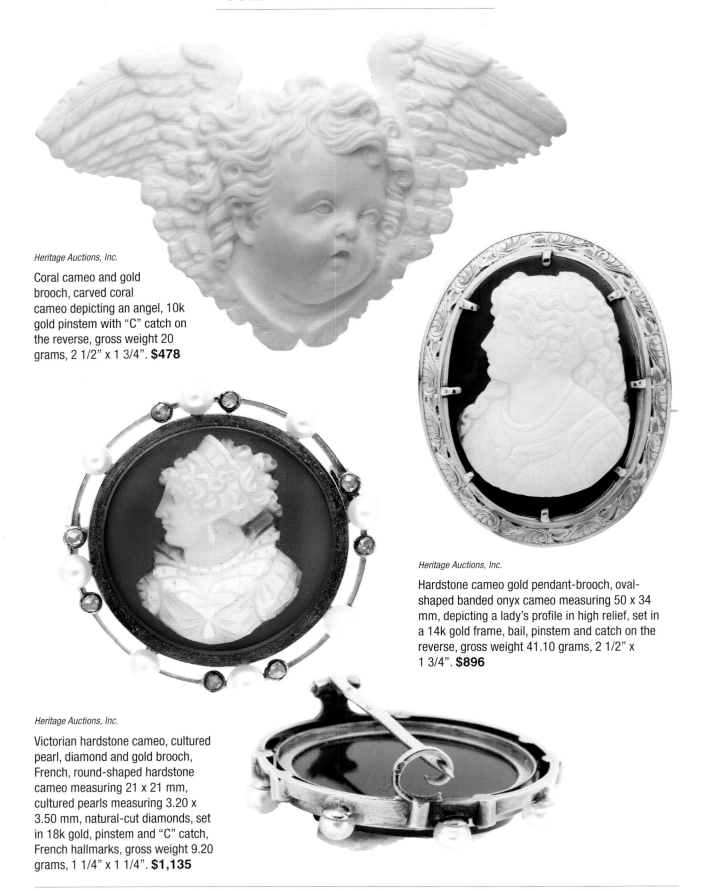

Heritage Auctions, Inc.

Coral cameo and gold brooch, carved coral cameo depicting an angel, 10k gold pinstem with "C" catch on the reverse, gross weight 20 grams, 2 1/2" x 1 3/4". **$478**

Heritage Auctions, Inc.

Hardstone cameo gold pendant-brooch, oval-shaped banded onyx cameo measuring 50 x 34 mm, depicting a lady's profile in high relief, set in a 14k gold frame, bail, pinstem and catch on the reverse, gross weight 41.10 grams, 2 1/2" x 1 3/4". **$896**

Heritage Auctions, Inc.

Victorian hardstone cameo, cultured pearl, diamond and gold brooch, French, round-shaped hardstone cameo measuring 21 x 21 mm, cultured pearls measuring 3.20 x 3.50 mm, natural-cut diamonds, set in 18k gold, pinstem and "C" catch, French hallmarks, gross weight 9.20 grams, 1 1/4" x 1 1/4". **$1,135**

Camelot Cameos and Antiques jewelry; Kerry Davidson photo

Historical cameo, Italian, circa 1861-1862, carved from lava in high relief to depict Cupid holding up a picture of Garibaldi, 2", gold brooch mount; representing the high esteem and affection of the Italian people for Giuseppe Garibaldi, military hero of the Italian Risorgimento (rebirth) that resulted in the unification of Italy. **$1,450**

Heritage Auctions, Inc.

Hardstone cameo, cultured pearl, gold pendant-brooch, oval-shaped banded onyx cameo measuring 34 x 25 mm, depicting a lady's profile in high relief, cultured half-pearls, set in 10k rose gold, retractable bail and pinstem and "C" catch on the reverse, gross weight 19.40 grams, 2 1/4" x 1 3/4". **$717**

Heritage Auctions, Inc.

Hardstone cameo, seed pearl and gold pendant-brooch, carved banded onyx cameo measuring approximately 26 mm x 26 mm, depicting a woman's profile, encircled by seed pearls, set in an openwork 14k yellow gold frame, retractable pendant bail, pinstem and catch on the reverse, gross weight 8.80 grams, 1 3/8" x 1 3/8". **$59**

Heritage Auctions, Inc.

Lava cameo and silver brooch, oval-shaped lava cameo measuring 30 x 26 mm, depicting a gentleman's profile, set in silver, pinstem and "C" catch, gross weight 12.10 grams, 1 1/2" x 1 3/4". **$418**

Heritage Auctions, Inc.

Shell cameo and gold brooch, oval-shaped shell cameo measuring 47 x 40 mm depicting mother Mary and a praying child, set in an openwork design frame of 18k gold, pinstem and catch on the reverse, gross weight 22.10 grams, 2 1/8" x 2 1/2". **$717**

Heritage Auctions, Inc.

Onyx cameo, half-pearl, pearl and gold pendant-brooch, oval-shaped and banded, depicting a lady's profile, resting within an 18k yellow gold frame, freshwater pearls with half-pearl accents, bail hook, pinstem and hinged "C" clasp on the reverse, gross weight 29.30 grams, 2 7/8" x 1 3/4". **$1,852**

Skinner, Inc.

Seed pearl cameo brooch, 14k gold, molded glass, enamel, diamond, seed pearls, depicting an Elizabethan lady within blue enamel foliate frame set with diamond melee and pearls, 2". **$415**

Heritage Auctions, Inc.

Shell cameo gold pendant-brooch, shell cameo measuring 54 x 41 mm, depicting a lady's profile, set in textured 14k gold frame, bail, pinstem and "C" catch on the reverse, gross weight 25.45 grams, 2 5/8" x 2". **$896**

Heritage Auctions, Inc.

Shell cameo and gold brooch, oval-shaped shell cameo depicting a mythological scene, resting within a 9k yellow gold frame, safety chain, gross weight 15.90 grams, 1 3/4" x 1 1/2". **$298**

Heritage Auctions, Inc.

Cameo and gold pendant-brooch, oversized ivory cameo measuring 63 x 48 x 8.75 mm, depicting Tatiana, Queen of Fairies, from William Shakespeare's "A Midsummer Night's Dream," resting within a 14k yellow gold frame; the cameo, carved in high relief, is inscribed on the backside, "HB 1669"; collapsible pendant bail, pinstem and catch on reverse, gross weight 42.30 grams, 2 1/2" x 2". **$956**

Camelot Cameos and Antiques jewelry;
Kerry Davidson photo

Carved high relief hardstone cameo of the Madonna set in a fine 18k gold, circa 1880, pearl and black enamel brooch mount, Italian, 2". **$3,750**

Camelot Cameos and Antiques jewelry; Kerry Davidson photo

Coral cameo habille of Athena Parthenos, set in gold pendant mount, Italian, late 19th century, carved after a work by the Greek sculptor Phidias; Athena's helmet is adorned with a sphinx and horse and is inset with a diamond; she wears her aegis (breastplate) complete with head of Medusa, 2 1/8". **$2,500**

Camelot Cameos and Antiques jewelry

Eos (also called Aurora), with the genius of light on her back, ushering in the new morning; Italian, circa 1870, 18k fancy etched gold brooch mount, carved in high relief, 2 3/4". **$2,250**

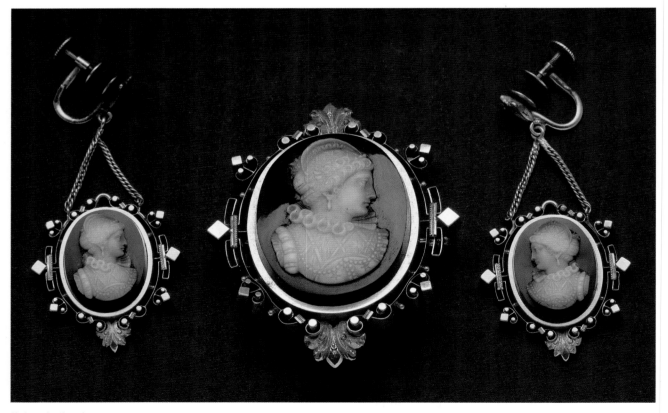

Heritage Auctions, Inc.

Cameo hardstone on black onyx pin and earrings, heavy gold frames, 36.8 total grams, cameo pin has a bale and is 50 mm x 40 mm, earrings are screwbacks and 29 mm x 25 mm, with a 20-mm chain drop. **$750**

Heritage Auctions, Inc.

Lady's gold slide chain with shell cameo, circa 1875, 10k rose gold slide, black enamel designs and small multicolor gold leaf accent, 14k yellow gold chain, double circular link design, swivel end, 60" long. **$956**

Heritage Auctions, Inc.

Three cameo rings: one hardstone with pearls in rose gold, size 7 1/4; one in a 14k white filigree mount with pearl border, size 6; one 26 mm round shell in a rose mount, size 4, gross weight is 23.5 grams. **$657**

Jewelry and image courtesy Linda Lombardo, Worn to Perfection on Ruby Lane

Gutta percha link chain with later Bakelite and Lucite cameo attached, 1870s, 18". **$195**

Skinner, Inc.

Victorian 14k bicolor gold bangle, the ornate cuff with braided ropetwists and leaf accents, centering a seed pearl, 6 1/4" interior circumference. **$1,185**

Sotheby's

Gold and micromosaic brooch, circa 1870, circular mosaic depicting a seated woman in peasant costume holding a basket of grapes, elaborate frame of gold wire and beadwork with mosaics of doves, floral sprigs and leaves, the reverse with glazed compartment, some tesserae missing. **$3,600**

Heritage Auctions, Inc.

Victorian 14k gold bangle with a scarab and double ram's head design, weight 9.20 grams, 5 3/4". **$516**

Heritage Auctions, Inc.

Micromosaic and gold hinged bangle depicting a Greek scene with cherubs, set in 22k gold, gross weight 20.60 grams, 6 1/2" x 7/8". **$1,375**

Skinner, Inc.

Pair of Victorian 14k gold bracelets, each hinged bangle with black tracery enamel and engraved ornament, 6 1/4" interior circumference. **$948**

Heritage Auctions, Inc.

Gold brooch crafted of 18k gold, pinstem and "C" catch on reverse, gross weight 23.27 grams, 2 1/8" x 1 3/4". **$1,075**

Skinner, Inc.

Victorian 14k gold and enamel bracelet, the woven bracelet with slide and terminal in black tracery enamel, foxtail fringe, adjustable length. **$652**

Skinner, Inc.

Victorian 14k gold demi-parure, comprising brooch and earpendants with applied bead and wirework motifs, brooch is 1 5/8" and earrings are 1 1/4". **$593**

Heritage Auctions, Inc.

Rare Victorian gold and enamel sword pin, unmarked, 18k gold, finely detailed with white enamel, eagle motifs, 13.4 grams, 5 3/4" long. **$750**

LATE VICTORIAN (AESTHETIC PERIOD), CIRCA 1880-1901

By the 1880s, Victorian society was beginning to change. In celebration of 50 years on the throne in 1887, Queen Victoria was willing to relax her strict rules of mourning a little, much to the relief of her subjects. Fashions had changed, too. Victoria was no longer as influential as her beautiful daughter-in-law, Princess Alexandra, who was already a trend-setting fashion plate.

In keeping with a new "aestheticism," lines were simpler, fabrics lighter. Flounces and trains were abandoned in favor of smooth curves. Delicate lace replaced heavy fringe. After a short period of protruding emphasis, the bustle became a vestige of its former self as fullness transferred to "leg-o'-mutton" and "balloon" sleeves. Collars grew higher and tighter. The tailored look was in vogue. Women were becoming more active, in the work force and at leisure, and required proper attire. Their only remaining extravagance was their headgear. Hats were large and decorated profusely with bows, ribbons, lace, flowers, plumes, and feathers—sometimes entire birds. Ornamental hatpins grew to great lengths to keep them in place.

Attitudes about jewelry were also affected. Elaborate ostentation gave way to refined simplicity. Heavy, dark, somber, massive, and ornate jewelry was losing favor. Lighthearted, light-colored, and delicate pieces took its place. Silver replaced gold for daytime wear. Many female aesthetes—early feminists rebelling against constricting fashions and protesting the notion of woman as decorative object—no longer wore any jewelry at all during the day. Diamonds continued to be the evening jewels of choice amongst most ladies of wealth and status, however.

Jewelry in general was reduced in dimension even when worn in quantity. Brooches were smaller, often worn in multiples. Crescents and stars were popular motifs. Some had utilitarian purposes as veil, lace, hat, bodice, skirt, or cuff pins. These were also called "handy pins" or "beauty pins." Earrings shrank to diminutive proportions. Sometimes they were nothing more than a single small stone, pearl, or stud. Until the 1890s, earrings were made for pierced ears. By the end of the century, however, women were beginning to look upon ear-piercing as a barbaric practice. The screwback finding was invented as a solution. The earliest "attachment for holding ear-jewels" for unpierced ears was patented in 1894. Its use gradually superseded the earwire and stud post; by the 1920s, screwbacks were predominant.

Necklaces were fringes or festoons of linked gemstone drops and chains. Princess Alexandra was the instigator of the dog-collar necklace, a high, wide choker, usually of diamonds and/or pearls, which became an Edwardian trademark when she became Queen. In the United States, the American "royal," Consuelo Vanderbilt, who became the Duchess of Marlborough in 1895, popularized the look with her dog collar of 19 rows of pearls and diamond clasps. Both ladies had the requisite long slender necks for wearing such a jewel. Bracelets continued to be worn in multiples, growing narrower toward the end of the period. Bangles were tubular or open knife-edge wires joined by an ornamental device in front. Curb-link bracelets in gold or silver were also fashionable, often joined with a heart-shaped padlock clasp. Small waists were a fashion focal point; wide belts and ornamental buckles were commonly worn.

Chatelaines, derivatives of a chain worn by medieval keepers of keys, were once again in fashion, having returned in a slightly altered state from those of the early 19th century. Perhaps this was because of the focus on the waist, but it was also because Alexandra favored them. Late 19th century chatelaines performed a number of different specialized utilitarian and decorative functions. Various implements were suspended by chains from a decorative clasp that hooked over a belt or waist sash. They were a sort of housewife's tool kit. Scissors, needle cases and other sewing tools, notepads and pencils, match safes, coin purses, spectacles cases, and other assorted useful items could be hung from swivel hooks on a chatelaine. Most of these were decorated with repoussage, stamping or engraving. Those made of silver appealed to aesthetic tastes, especially after the trend-setting Princess Alexandra was seen wearing one.

Sporting jewelry grew in popularity as women became

more involved in outdoor activities. Horseshoes and animal motifs—fox and hounds, horses, game birds, etc.— were worn with tailored clothing. Both women and men wore reverse-painted crystal intaglios, an often-used decoration for stickpins, cuff links, and small brooches.

Animal and bird motifs showed up in gem-set novelty brooches and stickpins. The ubiquitous snake was joined by lizards and salamanders, bats, frogs, mice, butterflies and other insects, and swallows.

Japanese motifs and designs gained approval after new trade relations were opened with Japan in the 1850s, and Japanese decorative arts and crafts were introduced to the West at international exhibitions in the 1860s and 1870s. Interest in things Japanese coincided with the growth of the Aesthetic Movement in Britain, France, and the United States. The tenets of the movement embraced the Oriental approach to design: simplicity of form and inspiration from nature. Japanese fans, bamboo, scenes, and other ornamental devices, collectively referred to as japonaiserie (also called "Japanesque" and "japonisme"), began to crop up in jewelry, particularly in silver and mixed-metals, imitating metalworking techniques used in Japanese sword-making. Tiffany & Co. won the Grand Prix for its "Japanesque" mixed-metals designs in silverware at the Paris Exposition of 1878. They applied the same techniques to jewelry.

International expositions continued to play an important role in the dissemination and marketing of new ideas and trends in fashion and jewelry. Two more Expositions Universelles were held in Paris in 1889 and 1900. The World's Columbian Exposition in Chicago in 1893 was another exhibition that brought international prestige and recognition to the United States. Tiffany and Gorham each had their own pavilion, and numerous other American and European manufacturers were well represented with displays of jewelry.

EARLY CELLULOID

The first uses for the first commercially successful semi-synthetic plastic, invented in 1868 and dubbed "celluloid" by its inventor, John Wesley Hyatt, were utilitarian. The initial motive for its invention was as a substitute for ivory billiard balls.

Skinner, Inc.

Chatelaines came back into fashion in the Late Victorian period. American Victorian sterling chatelaine, late 19th century, Rococo Revival brooch-form body suspending five oval link chains holding sterling Renaissance Revival notepad with celluloid pages, a retractable pencil, heart-shaped monogrammed locket, round mirror, and rectangular etui; sold together with a silver plated mesh purse. **$459**

Although that use proved impractical, celluloid was in fact an acceptable material for other uses, such as for detachable collars and cuffs, piano keys, and hair combs. Manufacturers of the latter took advantage of celluloid's ability to imitate tortoiseshell, a natural plastic.

Makers of inexpensive jewelry found a use for celluloid, too, as imitation coral and ivory. The earliest jewelry was made by the Celluloid Manufacturing Co. in 1875.

It wasn't until the 1920s that "frankly fake" celluloid jewelry was made (see "Plastics and Novelty" section).

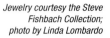

English silver locket with inlaid multicolor gold, circa 1880s, 18".
$2,800

SILVER AND MIXED METALS

Silver as a metal for jewelry has fluctuated in popularity and application. In the 18th and 19th centuries, it was customarily used for setting diamonds and colorless paste, or, disguised with gilding, for making imitation jewels look real. It wasn't until the latter part of the 19th century that silver came into its own as a material to be used for its aesthetic and sculptural qualities alone. Changing fashions, historical events and discoveries, and the Aesthetic Movement itself contributed to the metal's appreciation.

In 1876, Japan banned the wearing of swords and ended the feudal system, thus sounding the death knell for the samurai warrior. But the masterful metalwork of Japanese sword makers lived on in jewelry. Sometimes the sword fittings themselves became jewelry, and were exported to the West. The Japanese also made jewelry to suit Western tastes. It is important to clarify the meanings of the Japanese words "shakudo" and "shibuichi": these are words for Japanese metal alloys (not the decorative metalwork technique itself), similar to the English word "sterling" for an alloy of silver and copper. Japanese metalworking techniques have a number of different names, but what Westerners erroneously refer to as "shakudo" is usually a raised design with gold and silver inlaid into (or overlaid onto) a background

metal (shakudo or shibuichi). The inlay technique is known as "damascene work" in Western culture. The general Japanese term for this type of work is "zogan," but each variation of the technique has a different name. Japanese inlay is often imitated with die-stamped designs in shakudo or shibuichi overlaid with thin gold and silver foil accents.

The discovery of the Comstock Lode in Nevada in 1859 made silver readily available to manufacturers in the United States and Britain. Its relatively low cost meant that silver jewelry was now affordable to almost everyone. The japonaiserie craze of the 1870s and early 1880s led British and American manufacturers to produce stamped silver "trinkets" engraved with Japanese motifs. In the United States, it was permissible to include copper in a fashion similar to the way in which Japanese alloys of copper and silver (shibuichi) and copper and gold (shakudo) were used, but assay laws prohibited British manufacturers from doing so. Touches of rose and yellow gold were added to silver for a "mixed-metals" effect.

The locket and the hinged bangle were favorite forms in silver. They were stamped, engraved, and embellished with beaded edges and applied motifs such as buckles, flowers and leaves, crosses, and anchors. Pastes continued to be set in silver brooches and buckles.

After a decline in the wearing of daytime jewelry in the mid-1880s, silver jewelry regained favor in the waning years of the century. Message and "love brooches" were all the rage amongst the working class. These were stamped and engraved with the names of loved ones or other endearing terms. A Biblical reference, "Mizpah," sent the message: "The Lord watch between me and thee when we are absent one from another." The language of flowers was also used to send sentimental signals to loved ones—forget-me-nots (remembrance), ivy (friendship), and a different meaning for every variety of rose. Other popular symbols were the anchor of hope, cross of faith, heart of charity, good-luck horseshoe, and lovebirds. Silver coins were also used for love tokens, engraved with ciphers or names of family members or loved ones and made into bracelets or brooches. Jubilee jewelry was another sentimental working-class favorite, commemorating Queen Victoria's Diamond Jubilee, the

60th anniversary of her reign. Brooches would usually bear Victoria's cipher (VR or VRI) and the years 1837 and 1897 along with other engraved decoration. Touches of gold might be added. Those who could afford it wore gem-set versions.

Silver belts, buckles, clasps, and chatelaines were frequently worn during the Aesthetic period, emphasizing the tiny corseted waist that women suffered so much to achieve.

Only a few American makers are associated with silver jewelry of this period. Those that are made jewelry as an adjunct to their other silver wares, notably Tiffany, Gorham, and George W. Shiebler. Tiffany's and Gorham's pieces were generally in keeping with the style of the times, mostly buckles and bracelets in the aesthetic taste.

Shiebler's work followed a different bent, which proved successful enough to be imitated by others. Most well known is Shiebler's "curio medallion" series, depicting profiles of Greek and Roman deities, which can be found on brooches, bracelets, cuff links, and also on the handles of flatware. Greek lettering was sometimes added. It seems Revivalism was still alive and well in the 1880s and 1890s, but in a new form, with hand-crafted overtones. The company also produced quirky designs from nature, such as insects and spiders on leaves, seashells and sea creatures, and other flora and fauna. Shiebler pieces are usually marked "sterling" with a winged S and are numbered.

A technique known as "niello" was applied to silver ornaments in the late 19th century. Based on a medieval Russian technique, niello is a grayish-black mixture of silver, lead, copper, and sulfur that is applied to engraved designs on the silver's surface, then fired and polished smooth. Allover geometric or floral patterns yielded the best effect. An alloy of 800 silver (parts per thousand) was usually used because it withstands firing temperatures better than higher grades of silver.

Like gold, 19th century silver jewelry is not always hallmarked. When marks are found, however, they can be helpful clues. The American standard for silver was 900 parts per thousand until 1906. Pieces marked "standard" or "coin" are 900 silver of American origin. Some manufacturers, such as Tiffany, Gorham, and Shiebler, used the British sterling standard of 925 considerably earlier and marked pieces "sterling." The British mark for sterling is a "lion passant," or walking lion. The place of assay and date letter hallmarks correspond to those used on gold. European countries used alloys ranging from 750 to 950 with various devices as indications of silver content for hallmarks (see "Marks on Metals").

DIAMONDS AND COLORED GEMSTONES

The diamond has been the stone of choice among nobility and the wealthy for centuries. Although the 18th century has been called The Age of Diamonds, improved cutting and setting techniques to enhance the diamond's brilliance were developed in the 19th and 20th centuries.

Until the use of platinum found favor as a metal for setting diamonds at the end of the 19th century, silver was used to complement the stone's whiteness, almost always laminated to a yellow gold backing, sometimes called silver-topped yellow gold.

Closed-back and foiled settings were still in use at the beginning of the century. Open-backed (à jour) mounts gradually replaced them. It was discovered that brilliance was increased when light was reflected from the back as well as the front of the stone. The shape and cut of the diamond also evolved. Flat-backed rose cuts and cushion-shaped "old mine" cuts were eventually outnumbered (but not entirely replaced) by the circular "old European" brilliant cut toward the end of the century.

Credit for the development of the modern brilliant cut usually goes to Marcel Tolkowsky, who published his treatise Diamond Design in 1919. But the work of a little-known American diamond cutter, Henry D. Morse (1826-1888), preceded Tolkowsky's by more than 40 years. It was Morse who first discovered the scientific principles and precise cutting angles of what has come to be known as the "American" or "ideal" cut. And it was Morse's foreman, Charles M. Field, who developed and patented with Morse the first steam-driven diamond-cutting machines in 1874 and 1876, which preceded the European bruting (girdling) machine by 16 years. Unfortunately, to date no known pieces of 19th century jewelry set with Morse's brilliants have been identified.

The discovery of diamonds in South Africa in 1867 increased the stone's availability. Subsequent discoveries led to greater supplies and lower prices in the early 1880s. In spite of a worldwide depressed economy, diamond-encrusted jewels were well represented at the 1889 Paris Exposition and found favor among the wealthy. By the 1890s, the De Beers Co. had begun to control prices and dominate the South African diamond market.

Diamonds have always been considered formal jewels for important occasions, usually reserved for nighttime wear. The Victorians had strict rules of etiquette concerning when diamonds should be worn and who should wear them. They were considered inappropriate for unmarried young women; most married matrons reserved them for balls and court appearances. However, toward the end of the century, when both diamonds and wealth were in greater supply in the United States, most rules were forgotten.

When electric lighting was introduced in the 1880s, sparkling diamond-set jewelry became even more desirable. Fashion would never be the same after electric lights began brightening up homes and public places, like the Savoy Theatre in London, opened in 1881, and the Metropolitan Opera House in New York in 1883, where the privileged class went to see and be seen, decked in diamonds. The first tier of the Met was christened "The Diamond Horseshoe" in reference to its bejeweled patrons. At the turn of the century, the fashion for pale fabrics and colorless platinum-set jewels further heightened the demand for diamonds.

Diamonds found their way into every conceivable form

Heritage Auctions, Inc.

Diamond and platinum-topped gold brooch, European-cut diamonds weighing approximately 4.35 carats set in platinum-topped 14k gold, hook, pinstem and catch on the reverse, gross weight 17 grams; 2" x 1 7/8". **$2,250**

of jewelry, from tiaras to rings. The diamond brooch lent itself to a variety of motifs that reflected the Victorian preoccupation with nature.

Flower bouquets and sprays were worn throughout the 19th century, sometimes with parts mounted en tremblant, on springs or wires that trembled when the wearer moved. Animal and insect motifs were popular in the 1880s and 1890s, as were crescents and stars. These were often worn scattered about the neckline or as veil or lace pins. Figural motifs remained in vogue through the turn of the century.

In 1886, Tiffany & Co. introduced the "Tiffany setting"

for diamond solitaires. The high-pronged mount elevated the stone to show off its brilliance to the best advantage. It became the standard setting for engagement rings. This type of setting was originally patented by Ferdinand J. Herpers of Newark, New Jersey, in 1872. It is perhaps not coincidental that the 14-year interval between Herpers' patent and Tiffany's setting is the length of time for which a design patent was granted.

However, if it weren't for the prestigious firm's promotions, not only of solitaires, but of all diamond jewelry (including its purchase of a major portion of the French crown jewels in 1887), Americans might have worn far fewer diamond-set jewels.

Other gemstones were in and out of style according to the vagaries of fashion.

Pavé-set small turquoise cabochons were used extensively in jewelry of the 1840s, particularly in snake motifs. Turquoise made a return appearance in the latter part of the century. Seed pearl jewelry, a tradition since the early 19th century, continued to be worn.

Besides their familiar use in Scottish jewelry, agates, variegated varieties of quartz, are found in other types of Victorian jewelry. Factories in Idar-Oberstein, Germany— the actual suppliers of many a "Scottish" pebble—have been the primary centers for the cutting and polishing of agates for three centuries. The soaking and heating processes for staining the stones has been done there as well. During the mid- to late 19th century, color-enhanced banded agates were formed into beads and figural or geometric shapes. Although agate's value as a gemstone is low, Victorian agate jewelry is valued for its design, craftsmanship, and collectiblity.

Both faceted and cabochon garnets had their day at various times. There are several varieties and colors of garnets. Among them, the types most closely associated with the Victorian period are the reddish-brown pyrope and the reddish-purple almandite.

In the early 19th century, memorial brooches and "handkerchief pins" were often set with flat-cut pyrope or almandite garnets around a compartment containing hair. Large almandite cabochons, called carbuncles, are most often seen in mid-Victorian Revivalist pieces.

In the later part of the century, small faceted rose-cut and single-cut pyropes (also called Bohemian garnets) were set in low-karat gold and gilt base metal or silver. This type of jewelry was mass-produced in Bohemia.

Green demantoid garnets were discovered in the Ural

Jewelry courtesy the Steve Fishbach Collection; photo by Linda Lombardo

Bracelets, Bohemian rose-cut garnets, circa 1880s, 3/4" wide. **$1,500 each**

Mountains of Russia in 1853 but were not identified as a variety of andradite until 1864, and not named "demantoid" (diamond-like, referring to the stone's luster) until 1878. Demantoids are found in late 19th and early 20th century pieces. The green color was especially favored for the salamander and lizard brooches that were in vogue at the time. The Russian Revolution of 1917 curtailed mining there, and by the 1920s, supply had dwindled. Demantoids are rarer, more desirable, and more costly than most other varieties of garnet.

Pyropes and almandites are the least expensive, but the quality and style of a piece set with these garnets may outweigh the stones' intrinsic value.

Opals were also popular in the late Victorian era, their wearers having overcome the superstition that the stone brought misfortune.

In keeping with the pale look of the period's fashions, moonstones were worn, sometimes carved as cameos. The "man in the moon" was a favorite motif.

Pearls, another pale gem, were worn as necklaces alone or in combination with diamonds, setting the tone for what would become the classic Edwardian style of the early 20th century (see "Edwardian" section in Part II).

REPRODUCTION ALERT

Late Victorian-style garnet jewelry is mass-reproduced. Wholesalers advertise in antiques publications and on the Internet; some participate in jewelry trade shows. Most of them have catalogs with photographs. Other gemstone-set reproductions/repros are imported from Portugal, South America, Germany, and Thailand. Some pieces are good enough to fool the experts.

Heritage Auctions, Inc.

Diamond, sapphire, ruby, enamel and gold hinged bangle, European-cut diamond measuring 7.70 x 7.50 x 4 mm and weighing approximately 1.50 carats, oval-shaped sapphire measuring 9.20 x 7.60 x 4.60 mm and weighing approximately 2.70 carats, cushion-shaped ruby measuring 7 x 6.50 x 3.50 mm and weighing approximately 1.45 carats, round-shaped sapphire weighing approximately 0.65 carat, European-cut diamond weighing approximately 0.45 carat, European-cut diamonds weighing approximately 3.90 carats, set in 18k white gold, blue enamel applied on 18k yellow gold; total diamond weight is approximately 5.85 carats, gross weight 46.70 grams, 6 3/4" x 1 1/2". **$10,755**

Heritage Auctions, Inc.

Enamel, ruby, diamond and gold bracelet, round-shaped rubies weighing approximately 3.50 carats, rose-cut diamonds weighing approximately 0.50 carat, green enamel applied on 18k gold, articulated gold tongue, gross weight 83.37 grams, 6 1/2" x 3/4". **$7,187**

Heritage Auctions, Inc.

Diamond, enamel and gold mourning bracelet, hinged, mine-cut diamonds weighing approximately 0.60 carat, rose-cut diamonds, black enamel applied on 14k gold, gross weight 44.87 grams, inside diameter 6 1/2". **$3,883**

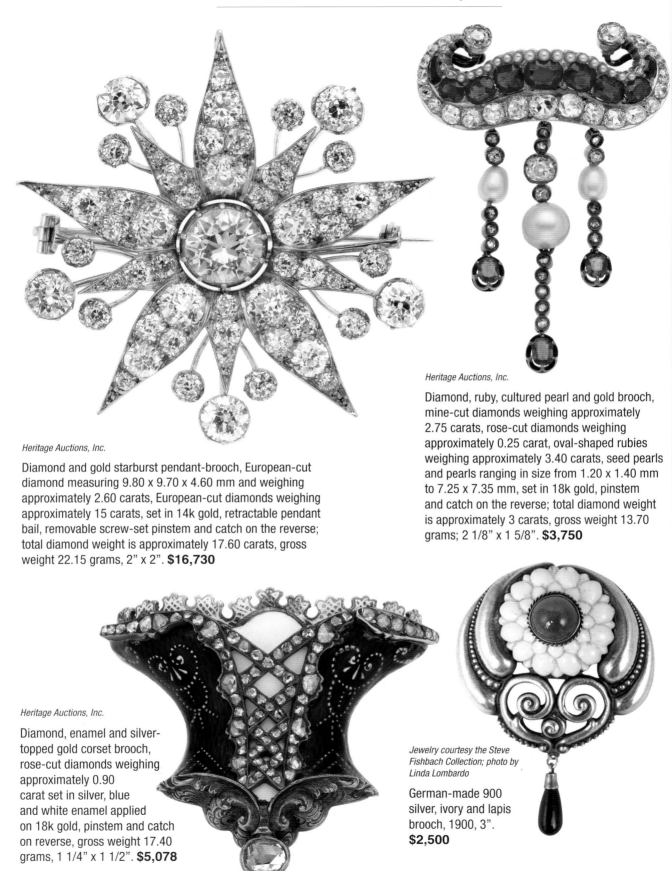

Heritage Auctions, Inc.

Diamond and gold starburst pendant-brooch, European-cut diamond measuring 9.80 x 9.70 x 4.60 mm and weighing approximately 2.60 carats, European-cut diamonds weighing approximately 15 carats, set in 14k gold, retractable pendant bail, removable screw-set pinstem and catch on the reverse; total diamond weight is approximately 17.60 carats, gross weight 22.15 grams, 2" x 2". **$16,730**

Heritage Auctions, Inc.

Diamond, ruby, cultured pearl and gold brooch, mine-cut diamonds weighing approximately 2.75 carats, rose-cut diamonds weighing approximately 0.25 carat, oval-shaped rubies weighing approximately 3.40 carats, seed pearls and pearls ranging in size from 1.20 x 1.40 mm to 7.25 x 7.35 mm, set in 18k gold, pinstem and catch on the reverse; total diamond weight is approximately 3 carats, gross weight 13.70 grams; 2 1/8" x 1 5/8". **$3,750**

Heritage Auctions, Inc.

Diamond, enamel and silver-topped gold corset brooch, rose-cut diamonds weighing approximately 0.90 carat set in silver, blue and white enamel applied on 18k gold, pinstem and catch on reverse, gross weight 17.40 grams, 1 1/4" x 1 1/2". **$5,078**

Jewelry courtesy the Steve Fishbach Collection; photo by Linda Lombardo

German-made 900 silver, ivory and lapis brooch, 1900, 3". **$2,500**

Heritage Auctions, Inc.

Diamond, emerald, ruby, cultured pearl and gold pierced brooch, one mine-cut diamond measuring 7.15 x 5.30 mm and weighing approximately 0.75 carat, one pear-shaped diamond measuring 6.20 x 4 mm and weighing approximately 0.45 carat, European-, mine- and rose-cut diamonds weighing approximately 7.55 carats, pear- and oval-shaped emeralds weighing approximately 4.40 carats, cushion- and rectangular-shaped rubies weighing approximately 2.10 carats, pearls measuring 4.70 x 5 mm, set in 18k gold, pinstem and "C" catch, gross weight 31.40 grams, 2" x 2 5/8". **$4,780**

Jewelry and image courtesy Linda Lombardo, Worn to Perfection on Ruby Lane

Sash pin with large red faceted glass, circa 1900, unmarked, 3". **$120**

Jewelry and image courtesy Linda Lombardo, Worn to Perfection on Ruby Lane

Sash pin with large amethyst colored glass, circa 1900, 2 1/2". **$95**

Heritage Auctions, Inc.

Victorian diamond, multi-stone, seed pearl, gold and silver brooch, circa 1880, designed as a butterfly, round-cut rubies, sapphires, emeralds and an opal set in 14k yellow gold, seed pearls and rose-cut diamonds set in silver, 1 3/4" x 1". **$597**

Jewelry courtesy the Steve Fishbach Collection; photo by Linda Lombardo

European miniature portrait painting on enamel pin, circa 1880s, 18k gallery with diamonds, 1 5/8". **$2,500**

Three late-Victorian figural sterling dirk pins used to secure kilts or as lapel decorations, 1911, each with cairngorm mounted on its handle; larger two 3 5/8" and 2", unsigned, various inlaid agates; smallest 1 1/4" with inlaid gray granite, signed by Joseph Cook & Sons, Birmingham. **$275, $50, and $75, respectively**

Jewelry and image courtesy Linda Lombardo, Worn to Perfection on Ruby Lane

Sash pin with large amber-colored glass, circa 1900, unmarked, 2 1/2". **$125**

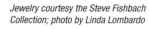

Jewelry courtesy the Steve Fishbach Collection; photo by Linda Lombardo

Enameled portrait pin, circa 1880s, 18k gold, 1". **$950**

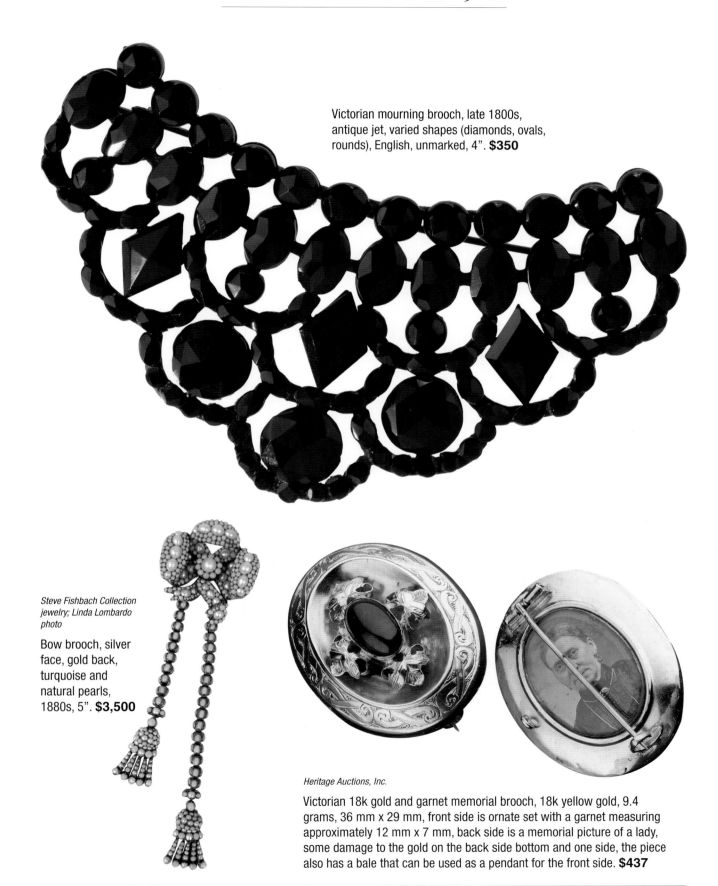

Victorian mourning brooch, late 1800s, antique jet, varied shapes (diamonds, ovals, rounds), English, unmarked, 4". **$350**

Steve Fishbach Collection jewelry; Linda Lombardo photo

Bow brooch, silver face, gold back, turquoise and natural pearls, 1880s, 5". **$3,500**

Heritage Auctions, Inc.

Victorian 18k gold and garnet memorial brooch, 18k yellow gold, 9.4 grams, 36 mm x 29 mm, front side is ornate set with a garnet measuring approximately 12 mm x 7 mm, back side is a memorial picture of a lady, some damage to the gold on the back side bottom and one side, the piece also has a bale that can be used as a pendant for the front side. **$437**

Heritage Auctions, Inc.

Diamond, enamel and gold earrings, French, designed for pierced ears, mine- and rose-cut diamonds weighing approximately 4.90 carats, black enamel applied on 18k gold, French hallmarks, gross weight 16.80 grams, 2" x 1". **$4,481**

www.Topazery.com

Victorian Danish crucifix, circa 1900, 14k rose gold, the base has a punched surface for a textured effect, rounded off into a fleur de lis at the four points, the cross culminates at the center with a starburst flower, a collection of 16 spherical and half spherical pearls are threaded down the middle, hallmark of the Netherlands. **$650**

Victorian earrings, 1900, jet, polished faceted balls dangle from decorative pearl and enamel panel, later converted to screwbacks, 1 1/4". **$100**

Heritage Auctions, Inc.

Sapphire, diamond and silver-topped gold earrings designed for pierced ears, oval-shaped sapphires weighing approximately 10.70 carats, European-cut diamonds weighing approximately 3.70 carats, set in silver-topped gold, leverbacks, gross weight 11.63 grams, 1 5/8" x 3/4". **$3,883**

Victorian malachite and gold necklace features octagonal-shaped malachite tablets ranging in size from 19 x 19 mm to 12 x 12 mm, wrapped in 18k yellow gold, 17" long. The necklace is accompanied by a fitted box. **$2,629**

Steve Fishbach Collection jewelry; Linda Lombardo photo

European 18k gold, amethyst, rose diamond and purple enamel necklace, circa 1890s, 24" with chain. **$6,500**

Jewelry courtesy the Steve Fishbach Collection; photo by Linda Lombardo

Gold locket with mine-cut diamonds, rubies and emeralds, 15k gold on 14k gold slide chain, circa 1880s, 2 1/8" on 26" chain. **$12,000**

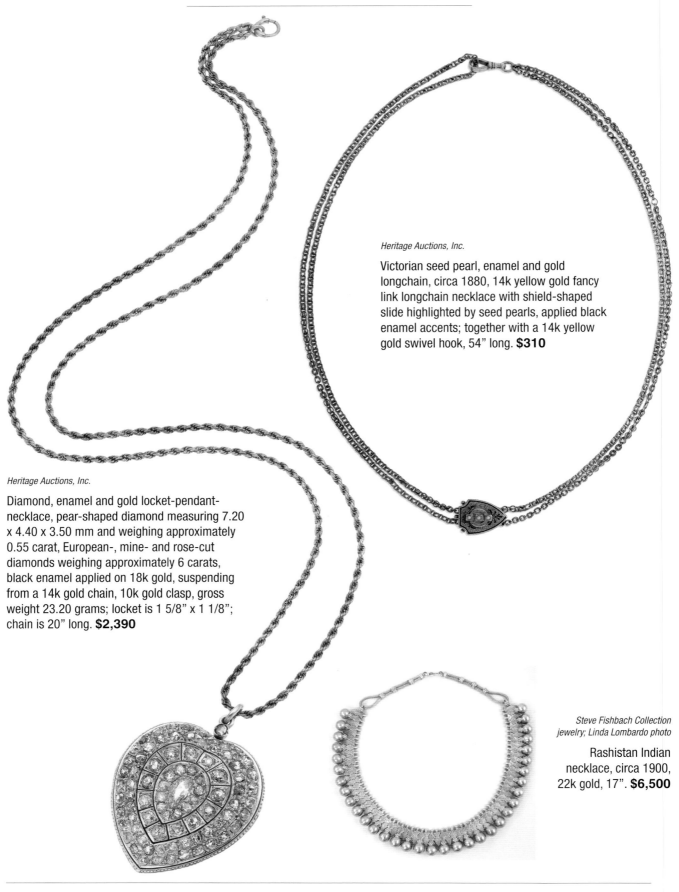

Heritage Auctions, Inc.

Victorian seed pearl, enamel and gold longchain, circa 1880, 14k yellow gold fancy link longchain necklace with shield-shaped slide highlighted by seed pearls, applied black enamel accents; together with a 14k yellow gold swivel hook, 54" long. **$310**

Heritage Auctions, Inc.

Diamond, enamel and gold locket-pendant-necklace, pear-shaped diamond measuring 7.20 x 4.40 x 3.50 mm and weighing approximately 0.55 carat, European-, mine- and rose-cut diamonds weighing approximately 6 carats, black enamel applied on 18k gold, suspending from a 14k gold chain, 10k gold clasp, gross weight 23.20 grams; locket is 1 5/8" x 1 1/8"; chain is 20" long. **$2,390**

Steve Fishbach Collection jewelry; Linda Lombardo photo

Rashistan Indian necklace, circa 1900, 22k gold, 17". **$6,500**

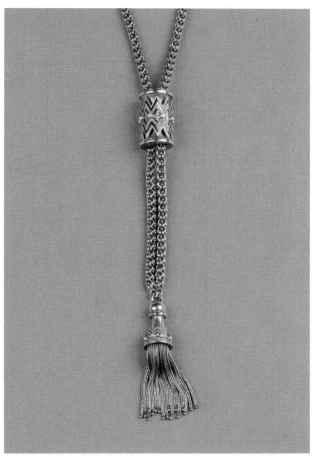

Skinner, Inc.

Victorian 14k gold slide necklace, barrel slide with black tracery enamel and split pearls, suspending a tassel with conforming cap, 38.9 dwt, 32 1/2" long. **$2,640**

Skinner, Inc.

Victorian 14k gold tassel necklace, longchain of fine circular links with engraved slide set with split pearls and black tracery enamel, foxtail fringe, and ending in a tassel, 27 dwt, 43 1/2" long. **$1,680**

Heritage Auctions, Inc.

Amethyst, diamond and silver-topped gold necklace, Netherlands, oval and cushion-shaped amethysts weighing approximately 89.35 carats, European-cut diamonds weighing approximately 17.25 carats set in silver-topped 14k gold, gross weight 84.30 grams, 15" long, centerpiece is 3 1/2" x 2". **$27,485**

Heritage Auctions, Inc.

Diamond silver-topped gold necklace, French, mine-, European- and rose-cut diamonds weighing approximately 5.90 carats set in silver-topped 18k gold, stationed on a sterling silver chain, French hallmarks, gross weight 50 grams, 2 1/8" x 4"; 22" long. **$5,975**

Heritage Auctions, Inc.

Seed pearl, enamel and gold mourning pendant/locket, hinged, seed pearls, black enamel applied on 14k gold, suspending from a black cord, gold spacers with black and white enamel, locket opens to reveal two photo panes, gross weight 25 grams, locket is 2" x 1", cord is 22" long. **$537**

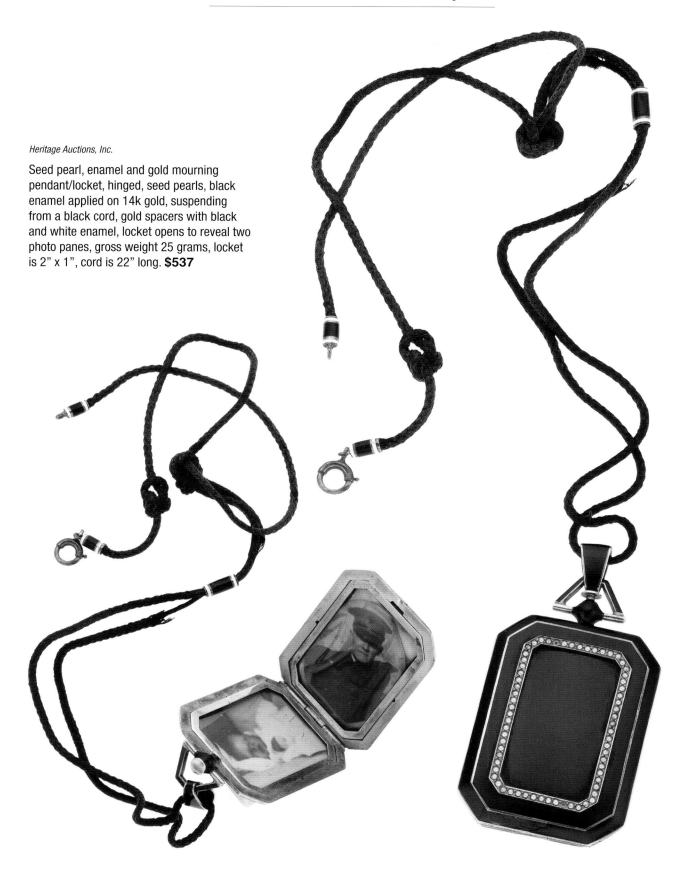

Heritage Auctions, Inc.

Sapphire, diamond and platinum-topped gold ring, cushion-cut sapphire measuring 9 x 9 x 4.15 mm and weighing approximately 2.65 carats, European-cut diamonds weighing approximately 1.65 carats set in platinum-topped 14k gold, Austrian hallmarks, gross weight 4 grams, size 6 1/2 (sizeable). **$2,151**

Jewelry courtesy the Steve Fishbach Collection; photo by Linda Lombardo

Bohemian garnet necklace and brooch in low-karat gold setting, 1880s, 14 1/2" with 3 1/2" drop. **$3,500**

Heritage Auctions, Inc.

Diamond and gold heart-shaped pendant, pear-shaped rose-cut diamond measuring 12 x 8.90 mm and weighing approximately 1.10 carats, rose-cut diamonds weighing approximately 3.95 carats set in textured 14k gold, total diamond weight is approximately 5.05 carats, gross weight 13.20 grams, 1 1/2" x 1 1/8". **$2,600**

Heritage Auctions, Inc.

Diamond and silver-topped gold articulated pendant, combination of mine- and rose-cut diamonds weighing approximately 7.15 carats set in silver-topped 14k gold, gross weight 20.40 grams, 2 1/2" x 1 5/8". **$2,375**

Heritage Auctions, Inc.

Diamond and silver-topped gold ring, rose-cut diamond measuring 6.50 x 6 mm, rose-cut diamonds set in silver-topped 14k gold, gross weight 3.90 grams, size 6 3/4 (sizeable). **$1,912**

PART II

TURN-OF-THE-CENTURY JEWELRY

The year 1900 did not signal the beginning of a new era so much as the continuation of the old and the continuing evolution of the new. The Victorian age did not end with Queen Victoria's death in 1901; Victorianism held sway until World War I. But while a large proportion of the populace continued to cling to late Victorian fashions, three more stylistic trends emerged to establish themselves among various segments of society by the turn of the century.

This did not happen overnight. What is usually referred to as the Edwardian style had already begun to make its mark on fashionable society long before Edward became king. Aesthetic influences that led to the Arts and Crafts Movement and the beginning of modernism had made their presence felt as early as the mid-19th century. And the "New Art" had made its debut in Paris in the 1890s. So, in fact, at the turn of the century, there were four concurrent jewelry styles: Victorian, Arts and Crafts, Art Nouveau, and Edwardian, plus a fifth "revivalist" style that was yet to be named.

This section is divided into four styles. As with 19th century jewelry, it can be difficult to clearly identify turn-of-the-century pieces as one particular style or another. At times, two or more styles are commingled in a single piece of jewelry. Historians, collectors, and dealers seem to have a need to pigeonhole and label everything. It may be hard to accept that this is not always possible. A label for a style always crops up after the style has come and gone. It is artificial by nature. While an attempt has been made to categorize the pieces in the following sections, individual interpretations vary. Up until recently, historians usually grouped all turn-of-the-century "art" jewelry under

Art Nouveau. Now, most make a distinction between Art Nouveau and Arts and Crafts. Even more recently, a new label has come into use: Beaux-arts, which is now treated as a separate style in this edition. But one person's Arts and Crafts is another's Art Nouveau. Edwardian pieces sometimes include Art Nouveau elements, and confusion still exists over that which is neither, hence the new style designation, Beaux-arts. Some stylistic details clearly belong in one or the other camp. These will be described in the sections that follow. What is important is to understand the part that each style played in jewelry history, to recognize its characteristic components, to see how the styles influenced one another, and how designs evolved over time.

As always, events and fashion trends played an important part in the evolution of fin de siècle jewelry design. The pace of change was quickened by new developments. The advent of the automobile and the airplane revolutionized transportation and increased mobility. "Motoring" became a fashionable pastime. The wireless telegraph and the telephone improved communication. The motion picture industry made its humble debut as the "peepshow" at Thomas Edison's Kinetoscope Parlor in New York City. By 1910, thousands of movie theaters were showing films whose stars were already influencing fashion. Jewelers advertised wares in the new trend-setting fashion magazine, *Vogue*.

The 1900 Paris Exposition Universelle heralded the pinnacle of Art Nouveau. Sarah Bernhardt's stage jewels by René Lalique and Georges Fouquet inspired many designers. The 1904 St. Louis Exposition showcased the remarkable jewels of Louis Comfort Tiffany for the first time, as well as Jugendstil designs from Austria.

Skinner, Inc.

Cuff links were worn by both men and women during this time period. Art Nouveau 14k gold cuff links, each double link depicting buds, maker's mark for Sloan & Co. **$563**

In 1890, artist Charles Dana Gibson introduced the public to what was to become the epitome of turn-of-the-century American womanhood, the Gibson Girl. Her hair, figure, and attire were considered the height of fashion in a trend that continued through the early 1900s.

The head and neck were emphasized with large hats, upswept bouffant hairdos, and high collars for day, décolleté for evening. Hatpins, hair combs, tiaras, "dog collar" chokers, and delicate lace pins and watchpins complemented the look. Festoon necklaces, pendants and their diminutive form, the lavalier, also focused attention on the neck. The lorgnette, usually worn suspended from a chain, became a symbol of period sophistication. Corsage, or bodice, ornaments decorated "pouter pigeon" bosoms. The waist was a focal point of the hourglass silhouette, and anything that adorned it was fashionable. One- and two-piece buckles, sewn onto fabric or leather belts, were often-worn accessories, as were belts of swagged chains linking small plaques. Large brooches known as sash ornaments or pins were also worn at the waist. Many have open centers; some include a simulated hasp. The pinstem is invisible when the brooch is pinned to a ribbon or belt, and the brooch imitates the look of a buckle. Cuff links and scarf pins continued to be worn by both sexes. Mainstream and avant-garde designs alike were rendered in these forms, made from both precious and non-precious materials.

ARTS AND CRAFTS, CIRCA 1890-1920

Arts and Crafts was more than a style. It was called a Movement, which encompassed a philosophy, an attitude, and a way of living. The practitioners of the Movement were revivalists of a sort, but unlike the Etruscan and Greco-Roman Revivalists, they were not copyists; they were interpreters of the past. They revived the ideas of handicraft, of medieval guilds and individual craftsmanship. Their philosophical point of view influenced their creative impulses, which found expression in a number of different forms and incorporated a variety of stylistic elements. So Arts and Crafts is not one style, but many.

Historians usually classify the various interpretations of Arts and Crafts by country of origin. While it may be that an identifiable characteristic approach to design is shared by artisans of the same nationality, it is dangerous to generalize. Without documentation or identifying marks—and many Arts and Crafts pieces are unmarked—attribution to country or maker is a guessing game at best. In terms of history, however, it can be useful to trace the movement as it developed from it origins in Great Britain and spread to Europe and the United States.

GREAT BRITAIN

As early as the 1870s, when Victorian Classical Revivalists were in the majority, the seeds of dissent were germinating. The dissidents were counter-revolutionaries to the Industrial Revolution. They rebelled against increased mechanization and mass-production and the consequent loss of the human touch in the making of decorative and utilitarian objects. They also rebelled against the excesses of Victorian ornament, setting the stage for the advent of modernism at the beginning of this century. The rebellion had its roots in Great Britain, then the greatest of industrial nations. The Crystal Palace Exhibition of 1851 had shown the world the achievements of the British in the use of the machine. For some, it was the beginning of the end of craftsmanship. John Ruskin and William Morris, generally recognized as the instigators of the insurrection, went on to formulate a rather utopian philosophy that would gather steam and become the Arts and Crafts Movement. The earliest application of the philosophy was in architecture, interior design, and furnishings. Jewelry-making wasn't included until C.R. Ashbee founded his Guild of Handicraft in London in 1888.

The Aesthetic Movement of the 1870s may have given impetus to Arts and Crafts and Art Nouveau. The influence of Japanese art began with the aesthetes and also found expression in the later styles. The adherents of the Aesthetic movement were a splinter group of intellectuals that included the Pre-Raphaelites of the art world and the advocates of dress reform, such as members of The Rational Dress Society in Britain and The Free Dress League in the United States. While mainstream fashion kept women tightly corseted, boned, and laced into hourglass figures, clothing reformists attempted to liberate fashion from the confines of the corset. Reform dress for Arts and Crafts proponents was loose and high-waisted in the medieval or Renaissance style. This was part of their preoccupation with the past—recalling simpler, idealistic times in hopes of liberating themselves from the dehumanizing mechanized world. Types of jewelry made to complement the clothing were primarily necklaces and pendants, buckles, sash ornaments, and brooches. Hatpins, hair ornaments, and tiaras, an important part of period fashion, were also interpreted by Arts and Crafts designers. Rings and bracelets were less commonly made, earrings rarely.

The prime directive of the Arts and Crafts Movement purists was for one artisan to make everything entirely by hand from start to finish. No matter how varied the style, the one thing they all had in common was the desire for their handcraftsmanship to be apparent. Hammer marks and irregularities were left intact as evidence of human handiwork. Simplification of line and form and the use of stylized organic motifs were also common threads.

Staunch social idealists, the leaders of the movement hoped to bring art to the people "in an acceptable form at realistic prices." In jewelry, the intrinsic value of the materials was of secondary importance to design and workmanship. Most Arts and Crafts artisans preferred silver to gold and inexpensive cabochon gemstones, like turquoise and moonstone, to faceted diamonds and rubies. Enameling was a favorite technique of many. Some worked in brass, copper, and glass.

Although the materials were inexpensive, the time and workmanship involved in producing entirely handmade pieces made them too labor intensive to be affordable for any but the well-to-do. The rejection of the use of all machinery made production in multiples difficult and expensive. The guild artisans were unable to produce sufficient quantities of jewelry to supply the masses. The irony of the situation was that the very manufacturers whose techniques they rejected were successful where the purists failed. British firms such as Liberty & Co., W. H. Haseler, Murrle, Bennett & Co., and Charles Horner commercialized the style, but in so doing made it affordable.

Liberty & Co.

Liberty & Co.
Cymric Ltd.
(1903 only)

Murrle, Bennett
& Co.

Foremost among the success stories was Liberty & Co., founded by Arthur Lazenby Liberty in 1875 as an importer of Near and Far Eastern goods, just as the japonaiserie craze was in full swing. The company's own popular "Cymric" (pronounced "kim′-rik," from the word for the Celts of Wales) line of metalware and jewelry was first exhibited in 1899. Liberty employed a number of designers to create what were then called "modern" designs. The "Liberty Style," which really was the people's style, was mass-produced interpretations of one-of-a-kind handmade pieces, and much more accessible and affordable to the middle and working classes. The prototypes for these pieces were designed by talented artists whose names were kept from the public at the time, but who are well-known today. Liberty's principal designer, whose work is most sought-after, was Archibald Knox (1864-1933).

Knox's work is characterized by Celtic knot motifs (also called entrelac) and whiplash curves in silver and enamel. In

Skinner, Inc.

Liberty was a top company and the work of its top designer, Archibald Knox, was highly sought after. Arts and Crafts sapphire and diamond pendant, Archibald Knox, Liberty & Co., British, set with a cushion-cut sapphire measuring approximately 10 x 8.80 x 5.35 mm, weighing approximately 4.25 carats, and rose-cut diamonds, and suspending a cushion-cut sapphire drop, platinum-topped gold mount, suspended from delicate platinum chain, in original Liberty & Co. fitted box, pendant is 1 1/2" long, chain is 15 1/2" long. **$6,000**

his pieces, he popularized the use of intermingled "floating" blue and green enamels pooled in central depressions. He occasionally worked in gold. Some other known designer-jewelers and craftspeople who worked for Liberty were Jessie M. King of Glasgow, Scotland, Oliver Baker, Arthur and Georgie Gaskin of Birmingham, and Charles Fleetwood Varley (a scenic enamellist). These same designers also worked independently, creating entirely handmade pieces. When Liberty appropriated their designs, the pieces were made by machine, but with hand-finished details. They

retained the look of the hand-wrought designs, and, except by purists' standards, are still considered Arts and Crafts. Unfortunately, the pieces were only marked with one of several Liberty hallmarks ("L & Co.," "Ly & Co.," "LC&C Ld"). Attribution is based on characteristic motifs and techniques, and at times, archival documentation in the form of drawings and company records.

W. H. Haseler and Murrle, Bennett & Co. also produced designs for Liberty's retail establishment. In 1901, W. H. Haseler, a Birmingham manufacturer, formed a partnership with Liberty to produce their Cymric line. Pieces can be marked for Liberty or "W.H.H." for Haseler. Murrle, Bennett was founded in 1884 as wholesale distributors. It was based in England, but also had manufacturing connections in Pforzheim, Germany, where it imported pieces for Liberty and also worked with Theodor Fahrner. Its mark is a conjoined "MB" inside a large C, followed by a small o, which is often used together with British hallmarks or Fahrner's marks. Some pieces are marked "M.B. & Co." World War I brought association with Fahrner to a halt, and Murrle Bennett ceased to be known as such in 1916. The company was renamed White, Redgrove and Whyte.

Charles Horner was a mass-marketed manufacturer in Halifax, which produced silver and enamel jewelry that was entirely made by machine, but maintained the appearance of Liberty-style Arts and Crafts. It was known for small brooches, pendants and chains, and hatpins. The winged scarab, Celtic knot, and thistle were favorite motifs. Pieces are marked "C.H.," usually with Chester assay marks and date letters. For more on these four firms, see "Liberty and His Rivals" in Becker's *Antique and 20th Century Jewellery*.

GERMANY AND AUSTRIA

By the late 1890s, the Arts and Crafts Movement had found its way across the English Channel to Europe, where it was interpreted and renamed by German, Austrian, and Scandinavian artisans. In Germany and Austria, it was called *Jugendstil* ("young style"). Scandinavians (particularly the Danes) called it *skønvirke*. The Italians mostly stuck with classic revivalism, but its few practitioners called the new style *Stile Liberty*.

Theodor
Fahrner
(Germany)

German *Jugendstil* has been classified both as Arts and Crafts and as Art Nouveau, but it can also be viewed as the genesis of modernism. It seems best to analyze each piece individually rather than make a judgment call on the entire body of work. Certain pieces exhibit English Arts and Crafts influence while others take inspiration from French Art Nouveau. If it is possible to generalize at all, the *Jugendstil* "look," whether abstract or figural, is characterized by strong lines and bold designs. A number of individual artists worked independently or anonymously. Several manufacturers also produced *Jugendstil* jewelry. The most well-known of these was Theodor Fahrner of Pforzheim, which brought the work of many individual designers to the attention of the general public.

Theodor Fahrner could be called the Liberty of Germany, in terms of *modus operandi*, although Fahrner manufactured jewelry exclusively, while Liberty traded in a variety of goods. What the two had in common was employing skilled freelance designers to produce "modern" designs for a commercial market. The designs themselves were sometimes the same, thanks to the connection with Murrle, Bennett & Co. Unlike Liberty, however, many of Fahrner's pieces produced between 1900-1919 were also signed by the designers. Most of these designers came from the Darmstadt Colony, an artists' community founded on the same philosophical ideals as the British guilds. It is during this period that Fahrner's *Jugendstil* jewelry was produced. Today it is highly sought-after, especially if it is artist-signed. Some important designers were Patriz Huber, Max Gradl, Franz Boeres, and Georg Kleemann.

Founded in 1855 in Pforzheim, the company's distinctive mark, a conjoined "TF" in a circle, was not introduced until 1901. The death of Theodor Fahrner (Jr.), son of the company's founder, in 1919 brought changes to the factory. Keeping up with new styles under new ownership, the company went on to become known as a producer of Art

Deco fashion jewelry in marcasite, enamel, and gemstones set in silver (see "Costume Jewelry, c. 1920-1935"). The firm closed in 1979. A great deal of information, painstakingly compiled by its authors, can be found in the book on Fahrner cited in the "References."

Heinrich
Levinger
(Germany)

Heinrich Levinger was another Pforzheim manufacturer, which is not as well-known as Fahrner, but the pieces the company made are equally desirable to collectors. They were noted for stylized organic forms in *plique-à-jour* enamel and silver. They made designs attributed to Viennese designer Otto Prutscher (1880-1949), but unlike Fahrner, no designer's mark was ever put on the pieces. In fact, sometimes the maker's mark is absent. Both Fahrner and Levinger pieces dating before 1915 can be marked with the French word "déposé," which means the design is registered (similar to a design patent). This mark was used for exports to both French and English-speaking countries. After World War I, the German phrase *ges. geschützt* (protected by law) replaced the French.

In Austria, Vienna was the center of *Jugendstil* activity. Among its practitioners, the best-known is a guild of multimedia craftspeople who were part of the Vienna Secession, the Wiener Werkstätte (Viennese Workshop). Founded in 1903 by Josef Hoffmann (1870-1956) and Koloman Moser (1868-1918), it was patterned after C.R. Ashbee's Guild of Handicraft. The style that evolved there is geometric and simplified, a harbinger of modernism. Jewelry by any of the Wiener Werkstätte designers, especially the work of Hoffman and Moser, is now highly collectible. The most often seen of the shop's marks is a superimposed "WW." An extensive history and examples of both German and Austrian *Jugendstil* can be found in Becker's *Art Nouveau Jewelry*, listed in the "References" section in the back of the book.

Wiener
Werkstätte
(Austria)

Some of Moser's designs were executed by the Viennese firm Georg Anton Scheid before the founding of the Wiener Werkstätte. The mark is G.A.S. with Austrian hallmarks. The Scheid pieces tended to be non-representational Art Nouveau in style.

UNITED STATES

British and European Arts and Crafts jewelry has been well documented in several books. American Arts and Crafts jewelry, however, has been given relatively little attention. Aside from brief chapters in two books, the only other sources of information are articles in periodicals, exhibition catalogs, and the semiannual sales catalogs published by Aram Berberian of ARK Antiques. There are a great many more extant, accessible examples of American Arts and Crafts jewelry than some historians would lead one to believe. Some examples are by makers about whom very little published information exists, but whose work is available on the market today.

The handicraft aesthetic caught on a bit later in the United States but lasted longer. Some say it never ended, but that is a matter of personal interpretation. It began with guilds of craftspeople inspired by and patterned after British models. The most well known are the Roycrofters and Gustav Stickley's Craftsman group. Perhaps the fact that these guilds were not known for jewelry-making explains why some collectors are unaware that American Arts and Crafts jewelry was made by many others. The movement's jewelry makers were concentrated in the Northeast (Boston, New York), the Midwest (especially Chicago), and California. Arts and Crafts societies were founded in several major cities and promoted the work of their members.

In Boston, the Society of Arts and Crafts was the guiding light of the movement. Founded in 1897, the Society began conferring the award and title of Medallist to its most highly skilled members in 1913. Four of these Medallists were jewelers whose oeuvre is recognized today as the best

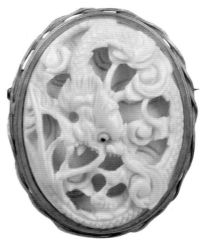

Skinner, Inc.

The Society of Arts and Crafts in Boston was the guiding light of the Arts and Crafts jewelry made in the United States. Carved ivory brooch depicting an exotic dragon amongst scrolling foliage, braided gold frame, with a pouch from The Society of Arts and Crafts, 32 Newbury St., Boston; 1 5/8" long. **$237**

of American Arts and Crafts. This Boston group seems to have been directly inspired by the British in terms of design and execution, if not use of materials. Its pieces incorporate organic motifs, wire and beadwork in open, delicate, and refined designs. Unlike its British counterparts, however, the society worked primarily in gold and used faceted stones of high intrinsic value, as well as cabochon gemstones and pearls. It relied on stones and metal for color, rather than enamel. But like the British, the group's pieces are not always signed. Documentation in the form of drawings or photographs in the Society's archives have aided attribution.

Among the earliest recipients of the Medallist award was Josephine Hartwell Shaw (1865-1941), to whom it was given in 1914. Examples of her work are rare and sought-after today. Margaret Rogers (? - c. 1945) became a Medallist in 1915. She exhibited in Boston and at the annual exhibitions sponsored by the Art Institute of Chicago. Frank Gardner Hale (1876-1945) studied at C.R. Ashbee's Guild of Handicraft in England and in Europe. His work reflects the influence of his studies. He, too, won the Medallist award in 1915. Edward Everett Oakes (1891-1960) studied under both Shaw and Hale.

The youngest and most prolific of the four, Oakes was awarded the Society's medal in 1923. Even though he was a latecomer, his pieces retained the motifs and the aesthetic

Skinner, Inc.

The work of prolific jewelry designer Edward Oakes was influential with other designers. Arts and Crafts moonstone ring, Edward Oakes, circa 1930s-1940s, set with a high-domed cabochon moonstone, with foliate shoulders and scrolling tendrils, full-cut diamond and circular-cut sapphire accents, gold and platinum mount, unmarked, size 4 1/2. **$2,489**

of Arts and Crafts. He developed distinctive repoussé leaf and flower forms that were combined with wire tendrils and beadwork in layers around gemstones. He used his own alloys of colored gold, particularly green gold, and also worked in combinations of gold and silver. His mark is his last name within an oak leaf, but, like the others, he did not always sign his work. Gilbert Oakes (1919-1987), his son, followed in his father's footsteps stylistically, and when his work is signed, it is an oak leaf with an acorn.

Laurence Foss (b. 1920) was a close friend of Gilbert Oakes who also learned jewelry-making from Edward Oakes. He was a machinist by trade, but he started making jewelry "for fun" from his own dies. He made pieces for Georg Jensen U.S.A. from the mid-1940s through the early 1950s, which he marked with his initials L/F in a shield. Shreve, Crump and Low in Boston also carried his work, which is not always signed.

Stavre Gregor Panis (1889-1974) became a Craftsman member (the first of three levels of membership) of the Boston Society of Arts & Crafts in 1925. He was another latecomer whose work resembles that of the Chicago metalsmiths (especially c. 1930s Kalo) more than that of his Boston colleagues. His trademark style was hand-hammered cutout sterling plaques and figural shapes with simple engraved

lines. His mark is his initials in a convex-sided triangle.

Mary Gage (1898-1993) was a woman who, like Oakes, worked in a mode that wasn't in keeping with the period in which she lived. She was behind, not ahead of, her time. Her style is much more akin to Arts and Crafts, but the period in which she worked corresponds with that of modernist studio artist-jewelers. She began silversmithing in the mid-1920s in New York City, then later moved to New England, ending up in Portland, Maine. She continued to make jewelry until her death at the age of 94 in 1993. Because her style varied little over the years, it's difficult to pinpoint circa-dates for her pieces exactly. Large flower and lily pad motifs were her specialty.

In New York, the eccentric artistic genius Louis Comfort Tiffany (1848-1933), son of the founder of Tiffany & Co., turned his attention from interior design to jewelry after his father's death in 1902. His pieces were first exhibited at the St. Louis Louisiana Purchase Exposition in 1904. Until 1907, his jewelry was made by his own firm, Tiffany Furnaces. After 1907 and until 1933, all L.C.T. pieces were made by and marked Tiffany & Co. There is ongoing controversy over the identification of L.C. Tiffany jewelry made after 1907, particularly when a Tiffany & Co. piece of the period comes up for sale at auction. An authentic, identifiable piece of Louis Tiffany jewelry sold at auction today may bring tens of thousands of dollars.

Perhaps because of his association with the most prestigious jewelry firm in the country, some may find it difficult to reconcile Tiffany's jewelry with the Arts and Crafts Movement's tenets. Many classify it as Art Nouveau, along with his glass, lamps, and other decorative art objects. Jewelry historian and L.C. Tiffany biographer Janet Zapata points out that his sources and influences were many, including Oriental, Islamic, Egyptian, and Byzantine motifs, and, especially, the colors and forms found in nature. Tiffany was such an individual artist that the diverse body of his work defies classification. However, Zapata considers his jewels to be very much in keeping with Arts and Crafts philosophy: "Louis's conception of jewelry was at odds with the pieces being made at Tiffany & Co. To him, color was paramount; gemstones were to be selected for their poly-

Heritage Auctions, Inc.

Brooch, Tiffany & Co., circa 1907, moonstone, Montana sapphire, plique-à-jour enamel and platinum, faceted cushion-shaped moonstone measuring 9.36 x 8.08 4.61 mm and weighing approximately 2 carats, round-shaped Montana sapphires weighing approximately 0.20 carat, opalescent plique-à-jour enamel, set in platinum, marked Tiffany & Co. and likely designed by or under the direction of L.C. Tiffany, 1 13/16" x 1/2". **$3,750**

chromatic effects, not for their monetary value." (p. 40, op. cit.). She further states that "each piece was hand-crafted... nothing was stamped out or cast. This craftsmanship ideal was followed at the time by Arts and Crafts designers in England and Boston…" (ibid., p. 100).

Marcus & Co. was a New York firm whose output included both British-influenced Arts and Crafts and French-influenced Art Nouveau. They are noted for their enameled gold, gemstone and pearl jewels. They occasionally made sterling pieces.

Another latecomer who worked in the Arts and Crafts idiom was Peer Smed (1878-1943) of Brooklyn, New York. Smed came to the United States from Denmark around 1904, having apprenticed with the well-known Danish firm A. Michelsen. Little information has been recorded about him or his work. He is known to have designed for Tiffany & Co. from his own studio in the 1930s. He made sterling flatware and hollowware as well as jewelry. He followed the Arts and Crafts philosophy in producing individual pieces made by hand from start to finish by one person—he employed a few Scandinavian silversmiths in his shop. He marked his pieces with his name and the words "handwrought" or "hand chased." According to Charles L. Venable of the Dallas Museum of Art, Peer Smed had a son named Dan, also a silversmith. He made jewelry in Los Angeles beginning in the late 1930s or very early 1940s, and died in 1951. He used his full name as his mark, "Dan Smed."

In upstate New York, Heintz Art Metal Shop of Buffalo made jewelry and decorative objects of patinated bronze with sterling overlay in cutout patterns. They were in business from 1906 to 1929. Their style is so distinctive that although their mark was not used on jewelry, it is readily identifiable.

The crafts community known as the Elverhöj Colony was founded in upstate New York in 1913 (the name Elverhöj comes from a Danish fairy tale). The members of the Colony followed the Arts and Crafts credo of making everything completely by hand. One of their primary products was jewelry. James Scott was a member of the colony who made gold and silver jewelry set with gemstones; unfortunately, he did not sign his work. According to catalog #00-1 from ARK Antiques, Scott's work was among 27 items of jewelry exhibited by the Elverhöj Colony at the 13th annual exhibit of Arts and Crafts held at the Art Institute of Chicago in 1914.

The Chicago Arts and Crafts Society was founded in 1897, the same year as Boston's. Chicago fostered a number of Arts and Crafts silversmiths and jewelers, many of whom were both. Collectors were made aware of their work as a result of an exhibition and catalog titled, *The Chicago Metalsmiths*, sponsored by the Chicago Historical Society in 1977. The catalog is still the best source of information on this group of artisans and shops. The largest and best known of them is The Kalo Shop, in operation from 1900 to 1970. The shop's early jewelry designs are the essence of simplicity in line and form. Most are sterling, although it made some 14k gold pieces, often set with blister or baroque pearls, mother of pearl or abalone shell, coral, moonstones, or other inexpensive gemstones. Pendants are suspended from handmade "paper clip" chains, so called because of the elongated oval shape of the links. This is a typical type of chain used by turn-of-the-century Arts and Crafts designers. In the 1920s and 1930s, the Kalo look changed to cutout and pierced repoussé floral and foliate motifs with

Arts and Crafts 18k gold and diamond bangle, bezel-set overall with old European- and old mine-cut diamonds, approximate total weight 3.10 carats, with foliate motifs and scrolling tendrils, interior circumference 7 1/2".
$7,703

Carence Crafters   George W. Frost

engraved details. Later Kalo designs reflect the modern trend of the times. The word "kalo" in block letters is found as part of the mark on all of its pieces. Some are numbered with order or design numbers.

The Art
Silver Shop

Some other noted Chicago shops and silversmiths who also made jewelry were the Art Silver Shop (Art Metal Studios after 1934), the T.C. Shop, James H. Winn, Madeline Yale Wynne, Frances Glessner, and Matthias W. Hanck. Lebolt & Co., a retail jewelry establishment founded in 1899, installed a workshop around 1912 to produce its own line of hand-wrought silver and jewelry. Marshall Field & Co., a Chicago department store, catered to the demand for handcrafted metalware and jewelry by opening its own Craft Shop around 1904. It made jewelry in silver and brass using acid-etching and patination, techniques that were apparently unique to American Arts and Crafts jewelry, particularly in the Midwest. These two processes were usually combined to create a design on a shaped plaque of hammered raised metal. The effect was an "antique," aged look, more crude and rough in appearance than the polished, refined pieces of the Boston jewelers. The craft shop closed in the 1950s.

Other Midwestern shops made brass, copper, and nickel silver ("German silver") jewelry of the same genre: Carence Crafters of Chicago (who also made sterling and gemstone pieces), George W. Frost of Dayton, Ohio, and the Forest Craft Guild in Grand Rapids, Michigan, founded by Forest Mann around 1905. Most, but not all, pieces are marked.

The Billiken is a whimsical character that became an early 20th century fad. He was designed and patented in 1908 by Florence Pretz, an art student from Kansas City, Missouri. She called him the "God-Of-Things-As-They-Ought-To-Be." The rights for the original design were purchased from her by the Craftsman's Guild of Chicago, which produced many different kinds of articles in the Billiken image, including buckles and sash pins of patinated and acid-etched brass with an Arts and Crafts look. The exclusive right to manufacture Billikens in silver and gold was held by Paye & Baker silversmiths of North Attleboro, Massachusetts. Today the Billiken has a devoted following.

There were a number of other lesser-known American guilds or shops based outside of Boston and Chicago. Several of them were in other parts of the northern Midwest, particularly Ohio: In Cleveland, Potter Studios, founded by Horace Potter, and the Rokesley Shop, founded around 1907. The latter produced pleasing designs in silver, enamel, pearls, and gemstones. It was one of the few American shops to use enamel in the English manner.

Pasadena, California, silversmith Clemens Friedell (1872-1963) worked for Gorham Co. in Providence, Rhode Island, before coming to California in 1910. His style has the Art Nouveau overtones of that company's "Martelé" line. His earlier work was mostly commissioned silverware. He opened a retail shop in 1929 that carried jewelry as well as a large array of decorative silver objects and hollowware.

As with any other type of jewelry, one should always evaluate an Arts and Crafts piece on its own merits, regardless of where, when, or by whom it was made. Because so much Arts and Crafts jewelry is unmarked and often unattributable, this may not be just the first, but the only, handcrafted jewelry in the Arts and Crafts mode. Some of it is well done; some is not.

Moonstone and 14k gold Arts and Crafts brooch, the oblong gold mount decorated with leaves and delicate scrolls, centered by an oval moonstone flanked by round cabochon moonstones, unsigned work of Edward Oakes, 1 1/2". **$5,875**

Jewelry courtesy Didier Antiques London; image by Adam Wide

Nelson and Edith Dawson Arts and Crafts dragonfly brooch, gold, circa 1900 1", British. **$4,50**

Jewelry courtesy Didier Antiques London; image by Adam Wide

Newlyn School pansy brooch, enamel and gold, 1900, British, 1 1/8". **$2,740**

Skinner, Inc.

Arts and Crafts 18k gold, moss agate, and carnelian bracelet, Margaret Rogers, Boston, the bezel-set moss agate tablets spaced by carnelian disks with foliate accents, signed MR, 6 5/8". **$4,740**

Arts and Crafts open cuff bracelet, American, silver (tested), abstract floral pattern, 1939, signed by artist Mabel S. Nicoll with date (April 1939). **$150+**

Heritage Auctions, Inc.

Arts and Crafts black opal and gold brooch, oval-shaped black opal cabochon measuring 20.88 x 11.32 x 3.28 mm and weighing approximately 3.80 carats, set in 14k gold, pinstem and catch, 1 1/4" x 7/8". **$2,000**

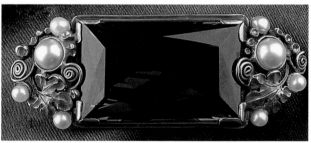

Green tourmaline, seed pearl and 14k gold Arts and Crafts brooch, centered by a long rectangular fancy-cut green tourmaline flanked by scroll and floret gold ends accented with seed pearls, unsigned piece by Edward Oakes, early 20th century, 5/8 x 1 1/2". **$5,600**

Doyle New York

Arts and Crafts gold and amethyst brooch, circa 1900, 14k one cushion-shaped amethyst, approximately 40 carats, amethyst is deep purple with deep lavender hues, several minor scratches and nicks not visible to eye, 1 1/16" x 1 5/8". **$875**

Gem-set 18k gold Arts and Crafts brooch, early 20th century, openwork lacy gold mount in a winged design, set in the center top with a ring of circular-cut amethysts enclosing a large oval-cut amethyst, surrounded by various bands of gems including blue, purple and yellow sapphires, peridots, amethysts, rubies, green tourmalines, aquamarines and seed pearls, three gem-set pendant drops at the bottom, designed and signed by Frank Gardiner Hale, 2" x 2 1/2". **$10,575**

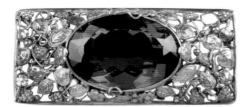

Skinner, Inc.

Arts and Crafts 14k gold and amethyst brooch set with cushion-cut amethyst measuring approximately 29 x 20 x 13.10 mm, in a plaque of grapevine motifs, 2 3/8" long. **$1,200**

Jewelry courtesy GreatVintageJewelry.com; photo by Veronica McCullough

Arts and Crafts porcelain enamel pin, Eastern Turret Fleur-de-Lys motif in primary enamel colors, handmade silver filigree flower frame and bezel, old c-clasp. Purchased in Russia, brought to United States in 1940s. Probably dates from the 1880-1900 era. Unsigned, 1 1/2". **$125-$150**

Skinner, Inc.

Arts and Crafts ivory brooch, carved to depict a bouquet of flowers, gold frame with scroll and foliate devices, with a box from The Society of Arts and Crafts, 9 Park St., Boston; 1 3/4" long. **$296**

Skinner, Inc.

Arts and Crafts silver and blister pearl pin, Josephine Hartwell and Frederick Shaw, set with two blister pearls and a cabochon sapphire, signed J&F Shaw, 7/8". **$1,541**

Arts and Crafts bar pin, garnet, amethyst and 14k gold, early 20th century, long oblong form centered by a cabochon amethyst flanked by rose-cut garnets bezel-set among leaves and berries, signed. **$650**

Skinner, Inc.

Arts and Crafts 18k gold cuff links, Tiffany & Co., each double link of cushion form with scroll and bead borders, 13.4 dwt, letter date M for 1907-1947, directorship of John C. Moore II, signed Tiffany & Co., Makers. **$2,760**

Skinner, Inc.

Arts and Crafts gold nugget and hardstone cuff links, each oval cabochon framed by gold nuggets, reverse marked "Native Gold Nuggets." **$948**

Skinner, Inc.

Arts and Crafts 14k gold and Favrile glass dress set, Potter Mellen, comprising a pair of cuff links and three shirt studs each set with molded glass, maker's mark. **$1,080**

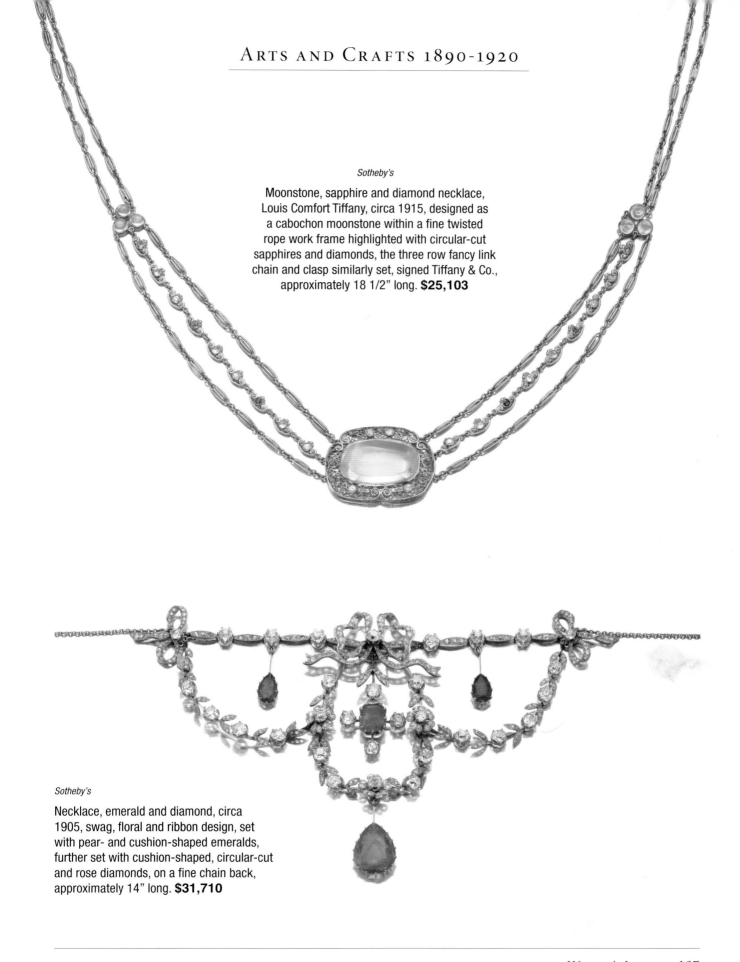

Sotheby's

Moonstone, sapphire and diamond necklace, Louis Comfort Tiffany, circa 1915, designed as a cabochon moonstone within a fine twisted rope work frame highlighted with circular-cut sapphires and diamonds, the three row fancy link chain and clasp similarly set, signed Tiffany & Co., approximately 18 1/2" long. **$25,103**

Sotheby's

Necklace, emerald and diamond, circa 1905, swag, floral and ribbon design, set with pear- and cushion-shaped emeralds, further set with cushion-shaped, circular-cut and rose diamonds, on a fine chain back, approximately 14" long. **$31,710**

Skinner, Inc.

Arts and Crafts 18k gold, sapphire and freshwater pearl necklace, Margaret Rogers, Boston, designed as a circular pendant bezel-set with a sapphire measuring approximately 10 x 8.90 mm, framed by circular-cut sapphires, shaped pearls and wire scrolls, suspended from a chain of navette-form links each set with bezel-set sapphires and pearls, signed MR, pendant is 1 5/8" diameter, chain is 16 1/4" long. **$10,665**

Skinner, Inc.

Arts and Crafts moonstone and split pearl necklace, Tiffany & Co., circa 1915-1920, the large oval cabochon moonstone measuring approximately 30 x 16.10 x 10.50 mm, within a platinum bezel with foliate engraving, suspended from a chain of 18k gold and split pearl lyre-form links spaced by cabochon moonstones in platinum bezels, signed Tiffany & Co. on drop and on clasp, chain is 18 5/8" long. **$21,600**

Skinner, Inc.

Arts and Crafts moonstone and amethyst necklace, pendant set with oval and circular moonstone cabochons with amethyst center among scrolling floral and foliate devices, suspended from a conforming chain, pendant is 1 3/4" long, necklace is 17" long. **$1,353**

Skinner, Inc.

Arts and Crafts 14k gold and faience scarab necklace, F.G. Hale, designed as a bezel-set faience scarab among lotus blossom motifs, suspended from baton- and ball-link chain, signed, pendant is 1 3/4" and chain is 16 1/4" long. **$5,036**

Jewelry courtesy Didier Antiques London; image by Adam Wide

Omar Ramsden Arts and Crafts garnet and silver pendant, numerous small garnets in circular pattern, circa 1910, English, 1 3/4." **$1,120**

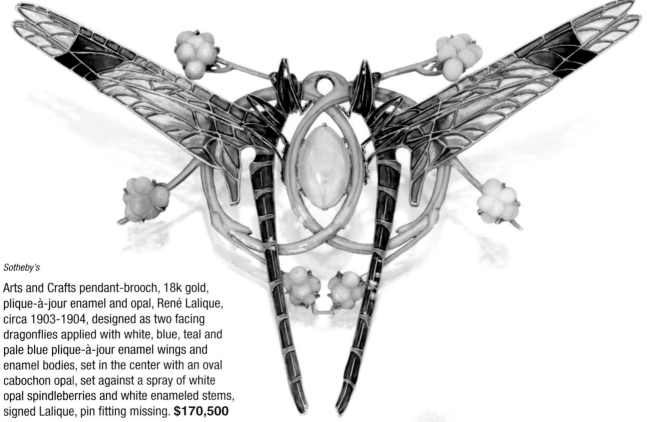

Sotheby's

Arts and Crafts pendant-brooch, 18k gold, plique-à-jour enamel and opal, René Lalique, circa 1903-1904, designed as two facing dragonflies applied with white, blue, teal and pale blue plique-à-jour enamel wings and enamel bodies, set in the center with an oval cabochon opal, set against a spray of white opal spindleberries and white enameled stems, signed Lalique, pin fitting missing. **$170,500**

Skinner, Inc.

Arts and Crafts gold, opal, and pearl cross and chain, Edward Oakes, circa 1930, set on one side with opals and circular-cut sapphires and on the other with half pearls and onyx tablets, all among foliate motifs and scroll and gold bead accents, suspended from trace link chain with open cylinder and bead links, unmarked, cross is 2 1/8", chain is 23 1/2". **$20,145**

Skinner, Inc.

Arts and Crafts 18k gold and diamond necklace, Edward Oakes, the central triangular element with bezel-set old mine-cut diamonds and elaborate foliate motifs, suspended from conforming old mine-cut diamond and floret links, ending in delicate chain, unsigned, 17" long. **$8,591**

Black opal, diamond and 14k gold Arts and Crafts pendant-necklace, delicate fancy link gold chain fitted with an oblong gold slide decorated with tiny pine cones and leaves, and enclosing an oblong black opal, suspending an ornate long gold-frame pendant with open leafy scrolls with tiny pine cones flanking a large almond-shaped black opal above an openwork spear-point frame set with five old European-cut diamonds suspending a black opal teardrop, mark of William Bramley, Montreal and "14B," 15". **$17,625**

Skinner, Inc.

Arts and Crafts 14k gold, sapphire and diamond ring, centering an old European-cut cognac diamond, further set with four old European-cut diamonds, and sapphire melee, foliate mount, indistinct maker's mark, size 5 1/4. **$2,133**

Skinner, Inc.

Arts and Crafts 18k gold and purple sapphire ring, bezel-set with a sapphire measuring approximately 11.50 x 8.50 x 6.50 mm, framed by foliate devices and seed pearls, size 8 1/2. **$2,370**

Skinner, Inc.

Arts and Crafts 14k gold, citrine and diamond ring, attributed to Edward Oakes, set with an emerald-cut citrine measuring approximately 16.45 x 12.40 x 7.40 mm, the shoulders with bezel-set old European-cut diamonds and floral and foliate motifs, size 6, unsigned. **$2,607**

Skinner, Inc.

Arts and Crafts 14k gold, sapphire and diamond ring, attributed to Edward Oakes, bezel-set with a circular-cut sapphire measuring approximately 6.20 x 3.65 mm, old European-cut diamond weighing approximately 0.60 carat, and another circular-cut sapphire, among floral and foliate motifs, conforming shoulders with old mine-cut diamond accents, unsigned size 5 3/4. **$5,629**

Skinner, Inc.

Arts and Crafts chrysoprase ring, attributed to Edward Oakes, set with a cabochon chrysoprase with gold leaf form shoulders, old mine-cut diamond accents, silver mount, unsigned, size 5 1/2. **$948**

Skinner, Inc.

Arts and Crafts zircon and cultured pearl suite, attributed to Edward Oakes, the brooch designed as a branch of leaves with clusters of bezel-set zircons and cultured pearls, earrings en suite, unsigned, brooch is 2 1/2" and earrings are 1". **$2,370**

Skinner, Inc.

Arts and Crafts 14k gold and serpentine necklace and earrings set with shaped and oval cabochons, with cabochon sapphire accent, quatrefoil motifs centering blue stones, and joined by seed pearls, earstuds en suite, 13 3/4" long, 2 7/8" drop. **$4,622**

ART NOUVEAU, CIRCA 1895-1910

In 1895, Sigfried (aka Samuel) Bing (1838-1905) converted his Oriental art gallery in Paris into a gallery for a new style, which gave the style its name, *L'Art Nouveau*. The Art Nouveau style caught fire and burned with a passion for a short while at the turn of the century before it flamed out and died. Its rise and fall spanned less than 20 years, but Art Nouveau had quite an impact on jewelry history. The quintessence of Art Nouveau was distilled by the French, but the ingredients for its heady mix of line and form came from the British Arts and Crafts Movement. It was the British insistence upon artistic integrity and individual expression that inspired the French to break away from constricting, traditional, imitative realism. This may explain the difficulty in determining which elements constitute which style.

The two have much in common: the use of inexpensive gemstones and other materials, enameling, the "whiplash" curve, motifs taken from nature, Japanese influence. But something changes in the translation from English to French. French pieces are figural, more three-dimensional and asymmetrical. The female face and body, naked and clothed, are predominant subjects for Art Nouveau interpretation, nearly absent in Arts and Crafts. Other Art Nouveau favorites include dragonflies and butterflies—some with female bodies—writhing snakes, and mythical creatures (chimera). The peacock and peacock feathers have been interpreted by both the British and the French in different ways. Irises, poppies, winged sycamore and maple seeds,

Doyle New York

Art Nouveau gold, plique-à-jour enamel and freshwater pearl brooch, circa 1900, centering three flared leaves applied with green plique-à-jour enamel, gold veins, outlined in gold, the stem continuing to an open modified oval, supporting drooping flowers fashioned with freshwater pearls, gold caps and curved stems, missing one small enamel section at tip of one leaf, center pearl possibly replaced, 3 1/8" x 2". **$3,000**

water lilies and trailing vines are part of the botanical repertoire of Art Nouveau.

Arts and Crafts floral and foliate motifs are stylized, the designs more abstract and controlled. Art Nouveau motifs have an element of fantasy, with exaggerated lines and sensual overtones. It might be oversimplifying to say categorically that if it's British, it's Arts and Crafts; if it's French, it's Art Nouveau. It would be fair to say, however, that the British retained too much of their Victorian sensibility to embrace Art Nouveau wholeheartedly. The French, on the other hand, were more than willing to take off in Art Nouveau's exuberant and, some say, decadent direction. Other countries followed: Belgium, Spain, and to a lesser extent, Russia. In Germany, Austria, and the United States, both British and French influences were felt.

Although there were many practitioners of the style in France, the work of one man has come to represent everything that Art Nouveau jewelry is about: René Lalique (1860-1945). His life has been well-documented and his work well-preserved (see "References" in the back of the book). A student of jewelry history should be familiar with his work because to understand Lalique is to understand Art Nouveau at its finest.

Other important French Art Nouveau designers and houses include Maison Louis Aucoc, under whom Lalique apprenticed, Georges Fouquet, Lucien Gaillard, Lucien Gautrait, and Maison Vever.

Frédéric Charles Victor de Vernon (1858-1912) was a medallist and engraver whose work was sold in Paris by Cartier, and made by Maison Duval and Lacloche Frères. He exhibited every year at the Paris Salons and was awarded a first-class medal in 1895. He specialized in Art Nouveau medal-jewels with religious themes, often enhanced with *plique-à-jour* enamel.

Enameling is one the most important decorative elements in Art Nouveau jewelry. One of the techniques that Lalique was noted for, and which became closely associated with Art Nouveau, is enameling. The usual explanation is that it looks like a stained glass window; a piece has no metal backing and the enamel colors are translucent. *Plique-à-jour* is particularly effective when used to depict insect wings (butterflies, dragonflies) and landscapes with sky and water. It is a difficult technique, and the results are fragile. Intact pieces are scarce.

When an enameled piece does have a backing, or groundplate, there are several other possible techniques, all of which were used in Art Nouveau as well as other styles of jewelry: *basse-taille, champlevé, cloisonné,* and Limoges, or painted enamel are the ones most commonly seen. An explanation of these techniques can be found in the "Glossary."

Basse-taille and *champlevé* enameled flowers on sterling or brass plaques, resembling miniature paintings, are often found in American Art Nouveau brooches and sash ornaments/pins, particularly by New England makers.

The style itself was a departure from what had gone before, but jewelry forms followed fashion's dictates. Hatpins, hair combs, necklaces and pendants, ornamental *plaques de cou* for dog collars, brooches, sash ornaments/pins, and buckles, and to a lesser extent, bracelets, cuff links, rings, and stickpins, were all interpreted by Art Nouveau designers. Another commonly seen form is sometimes referred to as "medal" jewelry. This was a French idea (called *bijou médaille* in France) that was also popular in the United States. It replaced the classic cameo with a medallion in gold or silver of the profile, full face, or torso of a woman or man in repoussé, stamped or cast relief. Borders and backgrounds were appropriately decorated with undulating vines, leaves, and flowers in the Art Nouveau style. The medallion could be a pendant, locket, brooch, or scarf pin. Less expensive versions were made in gilt base metals.

In the United States, Americans were torn between English pragmatism and French chic. In New York City, Tiffany & Co. and Marcus & Co. produced beautiful enameled and gemstone-set Art Nouveau jewels that rivaled most French pieces. And, although Arts and Crafts jewelry was gaining popularity in Boston, Chicago, and other cities, Newark, New Jersey, jewelry makers were turning out pieces influenced by Art Nouveau.

In the spirit of American entrepreneurship, the style was commercialized with great, if short-lived, success, particularly by two Newark silver manufacturers, Wm. B. Kerr and

Choker, gem-set 14k yellow gold, Art Nouveau, late 19th/early 20th century, composed of openwork looped and serpentine links highlighted with seed pearls, diamonds, rubies, sapphires or turquoise, joined by trace link chains, American hallmark, 13" long. **$3,800**

Unger Bros. Both firms were noted for their die-stamped relief designs that imitated repoussé handwork. They are easily recognized and circa-dated.

The pieces are backed with flat soldered-on sterling plates that bear the companies' marks. Kerr used a fasces, a bundle of rods bound around a battle-ax; Unger Bros.' mark is its interlaced initials, UB. Typical motifs were women's faces with flowing hair, and flowers, particularly poppies, waterlilies, and irises. Kerr was purchased by Gorham in 1906, retaining its name, but not its style, for some time afterward. Unger Bros. stopped making Art Nouveau designs in 1910. Brooches and buckles by either firm sell in the low to high three-figure range.

Other manufacturers, some based in Providence, Rhode Island, and Attleboro, Massachusetts, produced similar die-stamped jewelry in sterling and silver-plated brass. The quality varies. Inexpensive pieces are usually made from a single thin sheet of unbacked metal.

The genre of American hand-painted porcelain brooches is difficult to classify. The craft itself, begun around 1876, has been practiced as a hobby by women for many decades, but was especially popular around the turn of the 20th century. Floral motifs were a perennial favorite. An informative and thorough book on the sub-ject by Dorothy Kamm is cited in "References."

Several notable Newark manufacturers specialized in gold jewelry in the Art Nouveau style, often enameled and/or set with gemstones: Alling & Co., Bippart, Griscom & Osborn, Carter, Howe (later Gough) & Co., Krementz & Co., Riker Bros, and Whiteside & Blank, to name a few. Many Newark makers' marks can be found in Dorothy Rainwater's *American Jewelry Manufacturers*. Details on the companies' histories, compiled by Janet Zapata, are in *The Glitter & the Gold*, cited in "References."

The commercialization of Art Nouveau also brought about its demise. Perhaps its stylistic excesses, like a rich dessert, became cloying and difficult to digest in large quantities. After 1910, relatively little Nouveau jewelry was produced. By 1915, it was completely out of fashion.

REPRODUCTION ALERT

Since the 1960s' revival of Art Nouveau, many cast knockoffs of die-stamped period pieces have been made, especially in sterling. The reproduction pieces are solid instead of hollow, and the details are not as sharp. Reproductions of gold and gemstone Nouveau jewels can be cast or stamped, but also lack detail and signs of wear. Enameling is not as skillfully done.

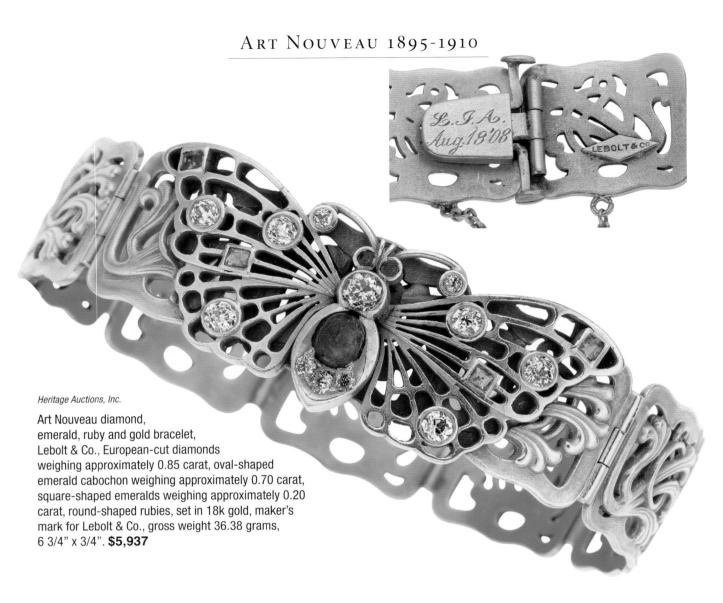

Heritage Auctions, Inc.

Art Nouveau diamond,
emerald, ruby and gold bracelet,
Lebolt & Co., European-cut diamonds
weighing approximately 0.85 carat, oval-shaped
emerald cabochon weighing approximately 0.70 carat,
square-shaped emeralds weighing approximately 0.20
carat, round-shaped rubies, set in 18k gold, maker's
mark for Lebolt & Co., gross weight 36.38 grams,
6 3/4" x 3/4". **$5,937**

Heritage Auctions, Inc.

Art Nouveau diamond and gold bracelet, full-cut diamonds weighing approximately 0.40 carat,
set in 18k gold, French hallmarks, gross weight 36.83 grams, 7 7/8" x 1/2". **$3,000**

Heritage Auctions, Inc.

Art Nouveau gold bracelet, 14k, weighs 29.19 grams, 6 1/4" x 9/16". **$1,187**

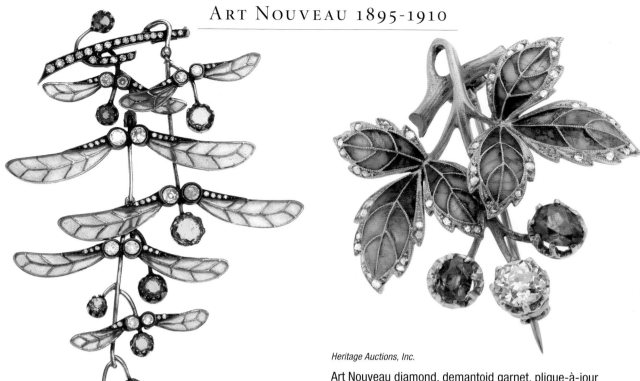

Heritage Auctions, Inc.

Art Nouveau brooch, demantoid garnet, diamond, plique-à-jour enamel, and silver-topped gold, round-shaped demantoid garnets weighing approximately 2.30 carats, European- and single-cut diamonds weighing approximately 0.90 carat, green plique-à-jour enamel, set in silver-topped gold, pinstem and catch, gross weight 13.55 grams, 3" x 2 1/8". **$4,687**

Heritage Auctions, Inc.

Art Nouveau diamond, demantoid garnet, plique-à-jour enamel, platinum-topped gold brooch features a European-cut diamond measuring 6.30 x 6.20 x 3.80 mm and weighing approximately 0.95 carat, oval-shaped demantoid garnets weighing approximately 1.65 carats, plique-à-jour enamel in shades of green and lavender, native-cut diamonds set in platinum-topped 14k gold, pinstem and "C" catch on the reverse. Marked AH for August Wilhelm Holström, Fabergé workmaster, Russian hallmarks, gross weight 12.70 grams, 1 3/4" x 1 1/2". **$5,975**

Sotheby's

Art Nouveau gold, diamond, enamel and glass brooch, Lalique, circa 1900, stylized insect decorated with a scarab beetle of pale blue opalescent glass above a calf's-head-cut diamond measuring approximately 15.3 by 18.3 by 5.1 mm, within a modified navette-shaped frame with fin terminals applied with opalescent enamel in shades of blue, signed Lalique. **$217,000**

Didier Antiques London jewelry; Adam Wide photo

Dorrie Nossiter comet brooch, pink tourmalines and pearl, 1920s, British, 2 1/3". **$2,735**

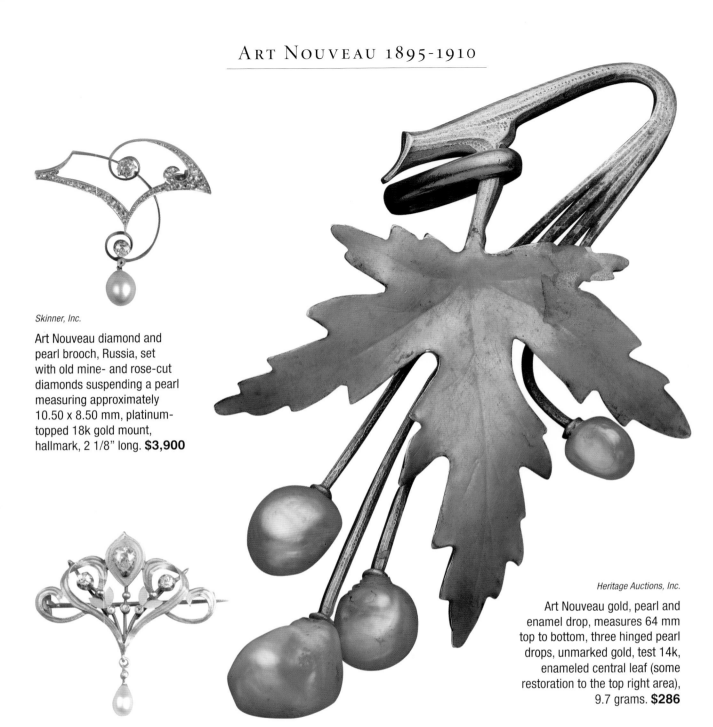

Skinner, Inc.

Art Nouveau diamond and pearl brooch, Russia, set with old mine- and rose-cut diamonds suspending a pearl measuring approximately 10.50 x 8.50 mm, platinum-topped 18k gold mount, hallmark, 2 1/8" long. **$3,900**

Heritage Auctions, Inc.

Art Nouveau gold, pearl and enamel drop, measures 64 mm top to bottom, three hinged pearl drops, unmarked gold, test 14k, enameled central leaf (some restoration to the top right area), 9.7 grams. **$286**

Skinner, Inc.

Art Nouveau diamond pendant/brooch, France, set with a pear and old mine-cut diamonds, rose-cut diamond accents, maker's mark and guarantee stamp, 1 1/2" long. **$563**

Skinner, Inc.

Art Nouveau Mesoamerican-style 14k gold, opal, and diamond brooch designed as a figure with outstretched arms, centering a cabochon opal, old European-cut diamond melee accents, reverse inscribed "Julie from Spencer 3-28-1900," 1 1/4". **$711**

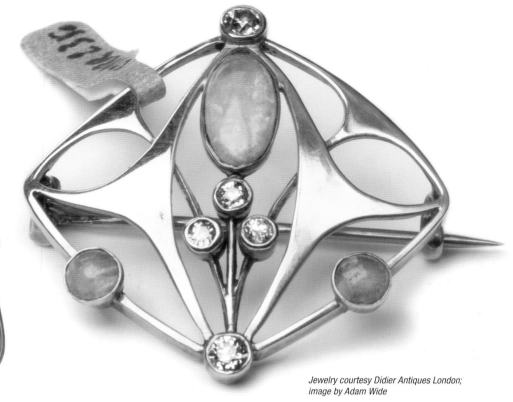

Jewelry courtesy Didier Antiques London; image by Adam Wide

Skinner, Inc.

Art Nouveau 18k gold locket-brooch depicting elegant lady with high collar and wearing elaborate floral hat, rose-cut diamond accents, opening to a compartment, signed Holy Frs, 1 1/4" long. **$652**

Murrle Bennett and Co. opal diamond brooch, 15k gold, circa 1900, Germany, 2". **$3,900**

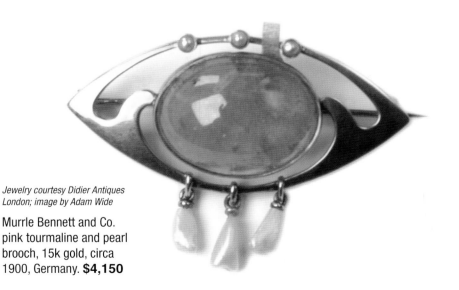

Jewelry courtesy Didier Antiques London; image by Adam Wide

Murrle Bennett and Co. pink tourmaline and pearl brooch, 15k gold, circa 1900, Germany. **$4,150**

Skinner, Inc.

Art Nouveau 18k gold brooch, Wiese, designed as finely pierced gold scrollwork, 7/8" diameter, replaced pinstem, no French marks, only signed WIESE. **$889**

Diamond, enamel and 18k gold Art Nouveau pin, designed as a pair of large scrolled leaves enameled in bluish green and framed by looping leaves and arching blossoms and buds bead-set with single-cut diamond, suspending a freshwater pearl drop, early 20th century. **$2,250**

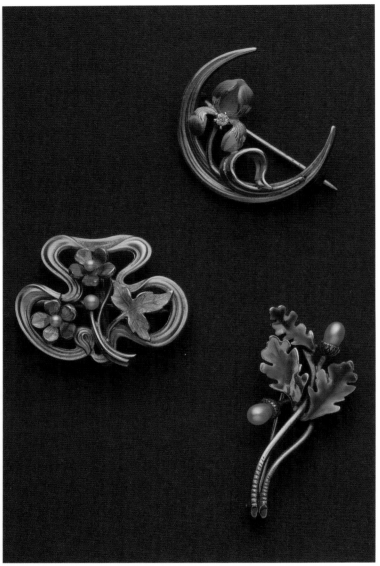

Heritage Auctions, Inc.

Three gold and enamel Art Nouveau pins, one a cloverleaf motif with watch loop on back, one acorn motif with pearls, one crescent (later added pin back). **$244**

Enameled 14k gold Art Nouveau pin designed as a three-petal blossom enameled in peach and yellow and attached to a green-enameled bud stem and a gold curled stem with two green-enameled leaves, small freshwater pearl accents, small enamel chip, late 19th/early 20th century. **$775**

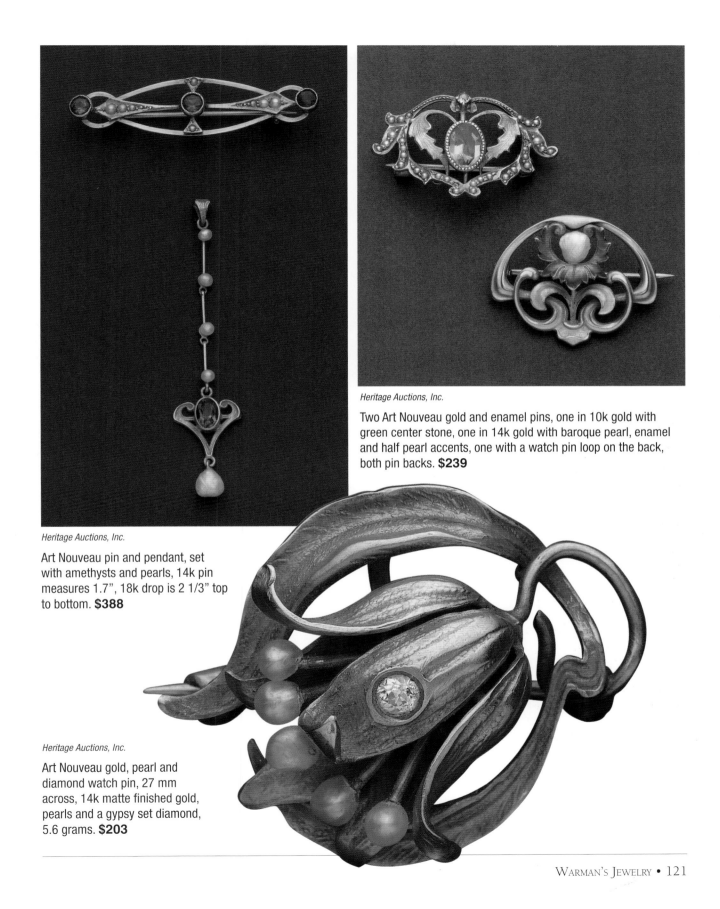

Heritage Auctions, Inc.

Two Art Nouveau gold and enamel pins, one in 10k gold with green center stone, one in 14k gold with baroque pearl, enamel and half pearl accents, one with a watch pin loop on the back, both pin backs. **$239**

Heritage Auctions, Inc.

Art Nouveau pin and pendant, set with amethysts and pearls, 14k pin measures 1.7", 18k drop is 2 1/3" top to bottom. **$388**

Heritage Auctions, Inc.

Art Nouveau gold, pearl and diamond watch pin, 27 mm across, 14k matte finished gold, pearls and a gypsy set diamond, 5.6 grams. **$203**

Sotheby's

Rare and important corsage ornament, enamel, gold, emerald and diamond, Fédor Anatolevitch Lorie, circa 1900, designed as a hybrid dragonfly, helmeted female head set with two cabochon sapphires to a winged torso, the lilac plique-à-jour enamel wings highlighted with circular-cut diamonds and cabochon emeralds to a similarly set tapering articulated body, suspended by the arms from a pair of pink enamel and gem-set stag beetles, mounted in 14k yellow gold. **$234,579**

Skinner, Inc.

Art Nouveau 14k gold and enamel stickpin, depicting a maiden in profile with diamond and gem-set bandeau, seed pearl border, 5/8" diameter. **$385**

Skinner, Inc.

Art Nouveau fire opal owl stickpin, rose-cut diamond eyes, perched on a gold branch, 3/4" long. **$1,067**

Skinner, Inc.

Art Nouveau 14k gold and demantoid garnet cuff links, each lion's head with demantoid garnet eyes, 5/8". **$1,440**

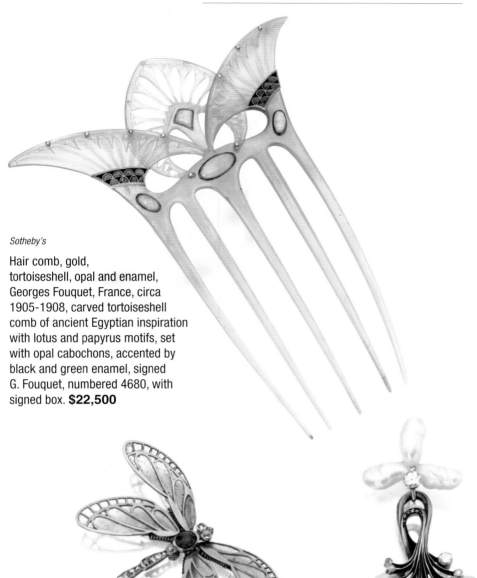

Sotheby's

Hair comb, gold, tortoiseshell, opal and enamel, Georges Fouquet, France, circa 1905-1908, carved tortoiseshell comb of ancient Egyptian inspiration with lotus and papyrus motifs, set with opal cabochons, accented by black and green enamel, signed G. Fouquet, numbered 4680, with signed box. **$22,500**

Skinner, Inc.

Earrings, pearl and 18k gold, Art Nouveau, pendant-type, late 19th/early 20th century, the top designed as an open flower and leaves centered by a small European-cut diamond and suspending a foliate designed gold framework enclosing a rounded blister pearl, European hallmarks, each 2 5/8" long. **$4,994**

Sotheby's

Art Nouveau dragonfly brooch and pair of pearl and enamel pendant-earrings, circa 1900, dragonfly mounted en tremblant, wings of green plique-à-jour enamel, body set with an oval sapphire and rose-cut diamonds, mounted in gold, Russian assay marks for St. Petersburg; earring pendants designed as whiplash scrolls applied with shaded green translucent enamel, set with four baroque pearls and old European-cut and rose-cut diamonds, mounted in 18k gold, maker's mark and French assay marks, supported on freshwater pearl and diamond tops, tops not original and later added. **$12,500**

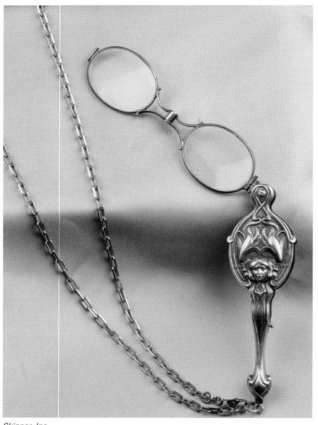

Skinner, Inc.

Art Nouveau sterling silver lorgnette, Krementz & Co., mask and tiger lily motifs, maker's mark, suspended from a later chain, 7" long. **$356**

Skinner, Inc.

Art Nouveau 14k gold lorgnette, Krementz & Co., with flower and scroll border, suspended from trace link chain, 32.3 dwt, 4 1/8" long. **$1,440**

Skinner, Inc.

Art Nouveau 14k gold and diamond locket, Pierrot figure set with old mine-cut diamond melee, reverse monogrammed, 1" diameter. **$563**

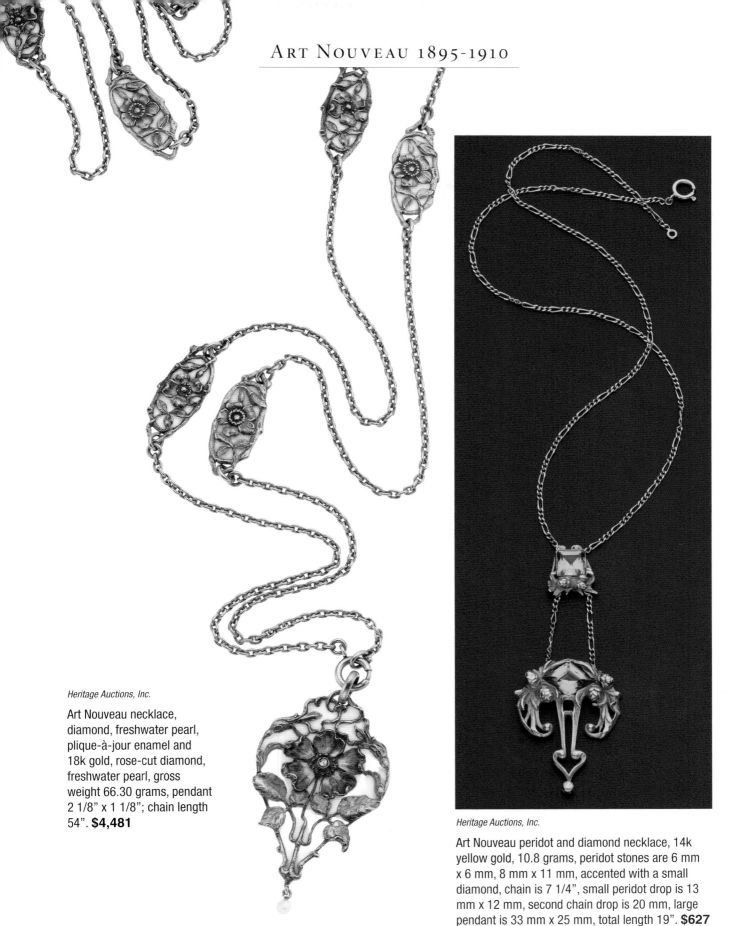

Heritage Auctions, Inc.

Art Nouveau necklace, diamond, freshwater pearl, plique-à-jour enamel and 18k gold, rose-cut diamond, freshwater pearl, gross weight 66.30 grams, pendant 2 1/8" x 1 1/8"; chain length 54". **$4,481**

Heritage Auctions, Inc.

Art Nouveau peridot and diamond necklace, 14k yellow gold, 10.8 grams, peridot stones are 6 mm x 6 mm, 8 mm x 11 mm, accented with a small diamond, chain is 7 1/4", small peridot drop is 13 mm x 12 mm, second chain drop is 20 mm, large pendant is 33 mm x 25 mm, total length 19". **$627**

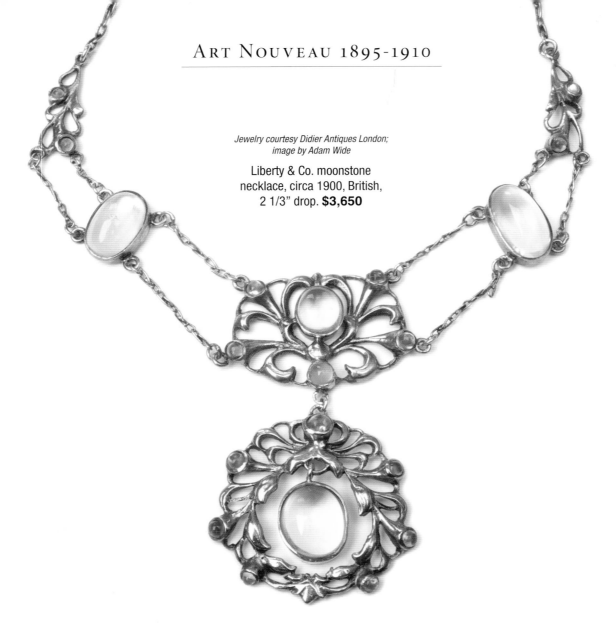

*Jewelry courtesy Didier Antiques London;
image by Adam Wide*

Liberty & Co. moonstone
necklace, circa 1900, British,
2 1/3" drop. **$3,650**

Heritage Auctions, Inc.

Art Nouveau enamel and gold pearl necklace, gold
14k enameled leaf and pearl pendant, 14k 15" chain,
measures 30 mm across the top frame. **$448**

Heritage Auctions, Inc.

Art Nouveau pearl and amethyst necklace,
10k gold, 22 mm across the main frame,
14" chain. **$262**

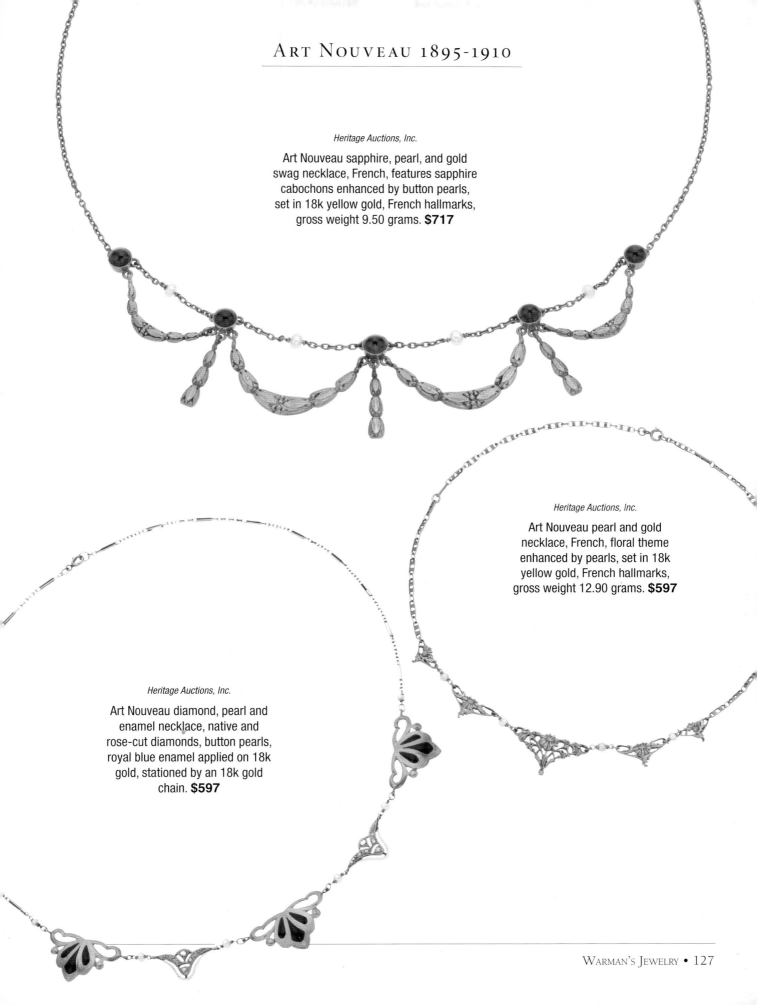

Heritage Auctions, Inc.

Art Nouveau sapphire, pearl, and gold swag necklace, French, features sapphire cabochons enhanced by button pearls, set in 18k yellow gold, French hallmarks, gross weight 9.50 grams. **$717**

Heritage Auctions, Inc.

Art Nouveau pearl and gold necklace, French, floral theme enhanced by pearls, set in 18k yellow gold, French hallmarks, gross weight 12.90 grams. **$597**

Heritage Auctions, Inc.

Art Nouveau diamond, pearl and enamel necklace, native and rose-cut diamonds, button pearls, royal blue enamel applied on 18k gold, stationed by an 18k gold chain. **$597**

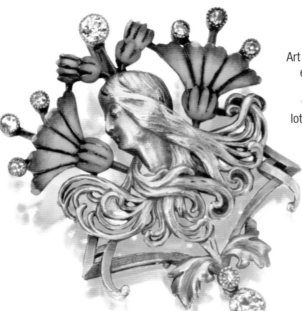

Sotheby's

Art Nouveau gold, diamond and enamel pendant, circa 1900, designed as a female figure with long flowing hair within lotus flowers applied with pink and green ombré enamel, accented by old European-cut diamonds weighing approximately .40 carat. **$6,875**

Skinner, Inc.

Art Nouveau plique-à-jour enamel, ruby and diamond necklace, shaped plique-à-jour enamel plaques set with cabochon and circular-cut rubies, old European- and rose-cut diamonds, platinum-topped 18k gold mount, 14k white gold filigree chain, Continental hallmark, 20 3/8" long. **$8,888**

Sotheby's

Art Nouveau pendant, gold, platinum, opal, diamond and plique-à-jour enamel, Paul Robin, France, circa 1900, large pendant applied with plique-à-jour enamel depicting pink trees, mountains and clouds framed by gold branches, pine cones and needles, the top set with old mine- and old European-cut diamonds weighing approximately 1.75 carats, set with a modified cushion-shaped opal measuring approximately 4.5 by 4 cm, the pendant set with a drop-shaped opal measuring approximately 4.5 by 2.3 cm, maker's mark, French assay mark. **$92,500**

Skinner, Inc.

Art Nouveau 18k gold and seed pearl necklace, designed as a shield-shape fringe with seed pearls and urn motifs, completed by filigree links, 15 3/4" long. **$1,422**

Sotheby's

Art Nouveau gold, diamond and enamel landscape pendant and chain, René Lalique, circa 1898-1900, pendant designed as a partially clad woman in diaphanous drapery strolling through a forested landscape against a sky of diamonds, leafy flourishes above and below, variously applied with blue and pale green enamel accents and small rose-cut diamonds, back of pendant finished in pale bluish-green enamel, signed Lalique, completed by an oval gold link chain, three diamonds missing, 18 1/2" long. **$326,500**

Skinner, Inc.

Heritage Auctions, Inc.

Art Nouveau pearl and enamel gold pendant and neck chain, 14k gold drop measures 46 mm top to bottom, enamel, seed pearls and large Baroque pearls, chain is 14k gold and 18". **$418**

Skinner, Inc.

Art Nouveau 18k gold and plique-à-jour enamel gem-set pendant, L. Gautrait, France, designed as a maiden with plique-à-jour enamel tresses wearing a diamond and rose-cut diamond diadem, opal accents, diamond and pearl drop, suspended from fancy link chain, pendant signed L. Gautrait, chain with partial maker's mark for Leon Gariod, guarantee stamps, 2" x 2 1/2"; chain 20" long. **$21,600**

Sotheby's

Art Nouveau gold, diamond, enamel and pearl pendant-necklace, attributed to Louis Aucoc, France, circa 1900, depicting the Birth of Venus with her bust supported on a diamond-set starfish, white diamond star an allusion to Venus as the white star in the night sky, framed by an openwork floral motif accented by peach and yellowish-green enamel, supporting a pearl drop measuring approximately 7.9 by 6.8 mm, gold link chain with small plaques of similar design to the pendant, set throughout with old European-cut, single-cut and rose-cut diamonds weighing approximately 1.50 carats, unsigned, French assay mark, 22" long. Accompanied by a fitted box signed Tiffany & Cie. **$37,500**

Art Nouveau pendant, snakes headdress, gold, enamel, rubies; original, "Sylvia," circa 1900 Paris, out of Maison Vever. Value unknown.

Didier Antiques London jewelry; Adam Wide photo

W.S. Hadaway enamel on silver ship pendant, circa 1900, English, 2" drop. **$7,465**

Skinner, Inc.

Art Nouveau plique-à-jour enamel pendant, France, set with a white resin Madonna within a plique-à-jour enamel frame, rose-cut diamond accents, maker's mark and guarantee stamp, 1 1/2". **$444**

Pendant, moonstone and 14k gold, Art Nouveau, late 19th/early 20th century, a long oval openwork gold mount with scrolling cattails suspending a long narrow oval cabochon moonstone, mark of Gorham Mfg. Co., Providence, R.I. **$600**

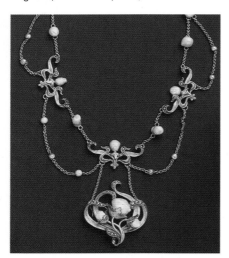

Pendant-necklace, enamel, pearl and 14k yellow gold, Art Nouveau, late 19th/early 20th century, the bottom pendant in the form of stylized freshwater pearl blossoms on scrolling leafy stems enameled in shaded orange and pale green and trimmed with seed pearls, suspended on trace-link chains below a necklace composed of three leafy scroll enamel and pearl blossoms along double trace-link chains accented with seed pearls, Bippart Griscom & Osborn, 15 1/2" long. **$4,400**

Pendant La Bretonne, Art Nouveau enamel and multi-gem piece, circa 1900, sculpted gold female bust in profile, calibré-cut opal costume, bonnet extending to form scrolling frame, enhanced with single old European rose-cut diamond trim, carved amethyst sleeve against openwork green and yellow enamel floral background suspending drop-shaped amethyst cabochon from detachable rose-cut diamond foliate hoop, mounted in gold, showing a traditional motif (young French Breton woman) in the new style; signed Vever for Henri Vever, Paris. **$400,000-$600,000**

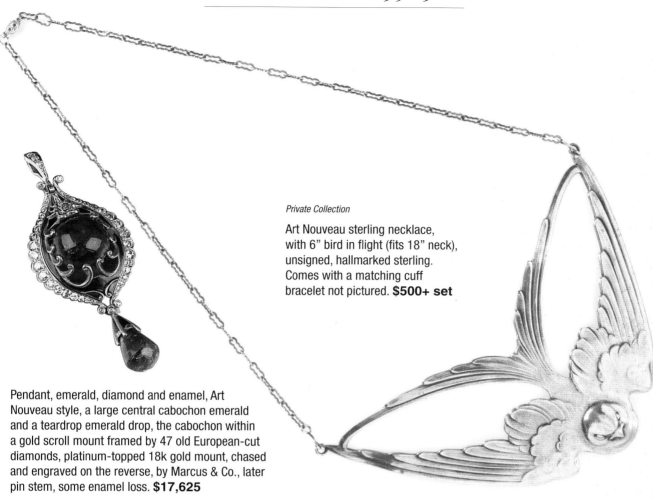

Private Collection

Art Nouveau sterling necklace, with 6" bird in flight (fits 18" neck), unsigned, hallmarked sterling. Comes with a matching cuff bracelet not pictured. **$500+ set**

Pendant, emerald, diamond and enamel, Art Nouveau style, a large central cabochon emerald and a teardrop emerald drop, the cabochon within a gold scroll mount framed by 47 old European-cut diamonds, platinum-topped 18k gold mount, chased and engraved on the reverse, by Marcus & Co., later pin stem, some enamel loss. **$17,625**

Pendant-brooch, enameled 14k gold, diamond and seed pearl, Art Nouveau style, designed as an enameled dark purple and white pansy blossom centered by a diamond and edged with a thin band of seed pearls. **$1,550**

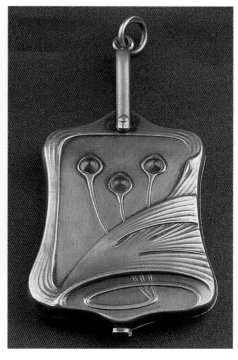

Art Nouveau slide locket, silver, early 20th century, flattened waisted rectangular shape, top embossed with sinuous vine and abstract leaf designs highlighted by green cabochons, gilt interior, European assay marks, 1 3/8 x 2". **$550**

Sotheby's

Art Nouveau pendant-brooch, gold, pearl, diamond and enamel, France, circa 1900, designed as a bare-breasted maiden with flowing hair and diaphanous drapery with arms outstretched in the form of American dancer Loïe Fuller, applied with peach, cream and pale green enamel, star at the top set with an old European-cut diamond, set at bottom with two old mine-cut diamonds, supporting a pearl drop measuring approximately 8.4 by 7.6 mm, indistinct maker's mark, French assay mark. **$18,750**

Pendant-necklace, plique-à-jour enamel, 18k gold and diamond, Art Nouveau style, designed as the gold dancing figure of a maiden wearing a swirled long gown enameled in turquoise and gold, the figure flanked by heavy gold vines curling up to suspend a pair of three-petal blossoms with blue and lavender plique-à-jour enamel and accented with old-European- and rose-cut diamonds, the base suspending a long freshwater pearl drop, the whole suspended by a pair of trace links joined to another three-petal blossom suspending a diamond drop, later trace-link chain, overall 18" long. **$8,000**

Jewelry courtesy Didier Antiques London; image by Adam Wide

Newlyn School large garnet pendant, silver, circa 1900, 3 1/2" drop, British. **$2,740**

Jewelry courtesy Didier Antiques London; image by Adam Wide

Murrle Bennett and Co. natural chrysophase and 15k pendant, circa 1900, 1 1/8" drop, Germany. **$6,640** (Company founded by Ernst Murrle and J.B. Bennett, specialized in reasonably priced quality jewelry in Art Nouveau [Jugendstil] style. Based in London with production in Pforzheim, Germany.)

Jewelry courtesy Didier Antiques, London; image by Adam Wide

Art Nouveau bat ring, 14k gold, circa 1900, J.F. Chatellier, New York. **$9,200**

Skinner, Inc.

Art Nouveau 18k gold and diamond ring, designed as a lion's head with an old European-cut diamond in its mouth, size 7 1/4. **$1,778**

Heritage Auctions, Inc.

Gold and pearl Art Nouveau ring, 31 mm end to end, set in unmarked gold, two baroque pearls, one round (later with nacre loss), size 3 3/4. **$79**

Skinner, Inc.

Art Nouveau 18k gold and enamel ring, Wiese, France, depicting a winged Nike with elaborate scroll motifs, maker's mark and guarantee stamps, signed, size 9 1/2. **$6,518**

Doyle New York

Group of antique and Art Nouveau gold, enamel, pearl and gem-set jewelry, 14k, clockwise from top left: amethyst, enamel, pearl and diamond pendant-brooch, green enamel and pearl leaf pin, locket with one old mine-cut diamond, gold and diamond heart locket, miniature portrait enamel pendant-brooch. **$1,375**

Doyle New York

Group of antique and Art Nouveau 14k gold, gem-set, enamel and pearl jewelry, top row from left: gold, peridot and split pearl pin; gold, amethyst and seed pearl pin; middle: gold and cabochon amethyst chain, 48 3/8" long; bottom: gold, peridot, freshwater pearl and enamel lavaliere, 16 1/2" long. **$1,500**

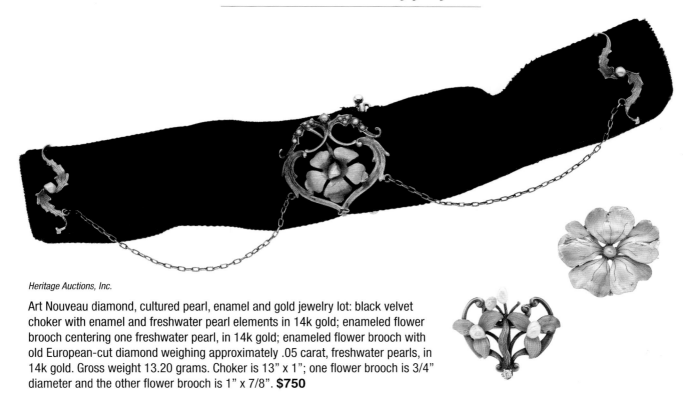

Heritage Auctions, Inc.

Art Nouveau diamond, cultured pearl, enamel and gold jewelry lot: black velvet choker with enamel and freshwater pearl elements in 14k gold; enameled flower brooch centering one freshwater pearl, in 14k gold; enameled flower brooch with old European-cut diamond weighing approximately .05 carat, freshwater pearls, in 14k gold. Gross weight 13.20 grams. Choker is 13" x 1"; one flower brooch is 3/4" diameter and the other flower brooch is 1" x 7/8". **$750**

Skinner, Inc.

Art Nouveau 14k gold, enamel, and seed pearl suite, Krementz & Co., comprising a pin and earrings, maker's mark, pin is 2" and earrings are 1". **$1,225**

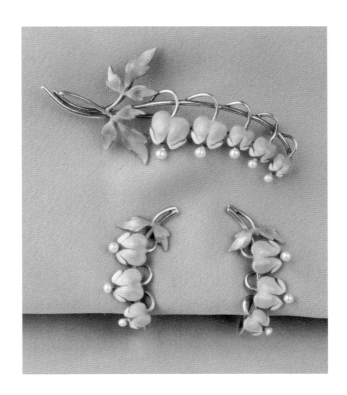

BEAUX-ARTS AND "NEO-RENAISSANCE," CIRCA 1890-1920

All turn-of-the-century jewelry made in Newark, N.J. was not made in the Art Nouveau style. A new term has entered the jewelry historian's vocabulary, taken from architecture: Beaux-arts. This is a term for a turn-of-the-century style that cannot be called Art Nouveau, Arts and Crafts, or Edwardian. It is clearly derived from the Revivalist

Heritage Auctions, Inc.

Edwardian jewelry emphasizes diamonds, pearls and platinum and has a lacy and delicate appearance. Diamond and platinum articulated brooch, European-cut diamonds weighing approximately 1.70 carats, rose-cut diamonds weighing approximately 0.70 carat, set in platinum, attached to a white metal frame, pinstem and catch, total diamond weight is approximately 2.40 carats, gross weight 12.34 grams, 2 1/4" x 1 5/8". **$3,750**

styles of the previous few decades, particularly those that came from a Viennese design source book called *Die Perle*, published in 1879 in German, English, and French. Finely detailed griffins, cherubs, and foliate scroll motifs often show up in circa 1890-1920 pieces by Wm. B. Kerr, Riker Bros., Krementz, Alling & Co., and others, which up until now have been called Art Nouveau, even though the name didn't fit. "Beaux-arts" seems to fill the need for a label for this style, and sufficient numbers of examples are on the market today to warrant giving it recognition and a separate classification.

Although they were making 90 percent of the country's karat gold jewelry at the turn of the century, Newark makers were not alone in producing the Beaux-arts style in the United States. Gorham Manufacturing in Providence, for example, also made sterling jewelry with similar motifs and decoration.

Considering the country of origin of one of the primary sources of these motifs (Austria), it seems logical to find similar ones cropping up in Austro-Hungarian jewelry during the same period. This is really a continuation of the Renaissance Revival style of the 1870s, hence the name "neo-Renaissance" to distinguish it from the earlier period. The turn-of-the-century pieces tend to be heavier in style and execution than earlier examples, but still feature enamel on silver-gilt, low-quality gemstones, and freshwater pearls, materials that are not usually seen in American Beaux-arts jewelry.

EDWARDIAN, CIRCA 1890-1920

Historically, the Edwardian period lasted for only the nine years that King Edward VII was on the throne, 1901-1910. The style most often referred to as Edwardian, however, began to evolve more than 10 years earlier and continued to be seen for more than 10 years after Edward's death. By the time Edward and Alexandra became king and queen, they were past middle age, and the style they influenced was firmly entrenched.

The period was a time of social reform, but it also saw the rise of an incredibly wealthy upper class, even within the so-called "classless" democracy of the United States. Unlike Victoria, who was the people's queen, Edward and Alexandra set the tone for an international high society separated from the lower classes by a social whirl of balls, sporting events, yachting, and all the other accoutrements of the well-to-do. Elegance and delicacy were the watchwords of the day. Jewels, of course, were an important part of the trappings.

Edwardian jewelry contrasts markedly with other concurrent styles. While Arts and Crafts and Art Nouveau were part of the aesthetic avant-garde, Edwardian jewelry clung to tradition. The former attracted the intellectual elite; the latter, the social elite. Arts and Crafts and Art Nouveau emphasized design and workmanship over intrinsically valuable materials. Edwardian emphasized diamonds, pearls, and platinum, in skillfully worked designs. Arts and Crafts and Art Nouveau jewelers used enamels and gemstones in a palette of colors. Edwardian jewels were monochromatic, mostly white or colorless.

Arts and Crafts was inspired by the medieval and Renaissance periods; Edwardian looked back to the Neoclassical and Rococo of the 18th century and the French courts of Louis XV and particularly Louis XVI. Not so much the jewelry of that time, but rather the ornamental motifs found on furniture, architecture, and decorative objects: bows, tassels, lace, and the foliate wreaths and swags that gave the style a name: "the garland style."

One of the most distinctive aspects of Edwardian jewels is their lacy, delicate appearance, made possible by the use of platinum, an extremely strong and ductile metal. Although platinum had been used earlier (contrary to popular belief, decorative and utilitarian platinum objects were being made as early as the late 18th century), demand for it—and consequently its value—was not as high, nor was it worked in the same way as it was at the turn of the century.

For a while, jewelers continued to treat platinum as they had silver, laminating it to gold. This was unnecessary because platinum does not tarnish and is strong enough to be used alone. The speculation is that jewelers were striving to maintain the tradition of 19th century diamond jewels set in silver-topped gold. Later, in the teens and 1920s, when platinum's value exceeded that of gold, platinum was once again layered with yellow gold in the manufacture of less expensive jewelry items, such as stamped filigree bar pins and flexible bracelets.

Platinum was not considered a precious metal until its advantageous qualities for setting diamonds were more widely recognized. Platinum wasn't officially recognized by the French government as a precious metal until 1910—years after platinum had become the metal of choice for setting diamonds. The French hallmark for platinum, a dog's head, wasn't introduced until 1912.

The Edwardian look is characterized by "knife-edge" platinum wires joining millegrained collet-set diamonds in openwork designs and saw-pierced platinum plaques set throughout with diamonds. The colorless all-diamond and pearl-and-diamond jewels complemented the all-white and pale pastel feminine fashions of the period, which were made of lightweight fabrics and lace.

While we are accustomed to referring to this style as Edwardian, as noted by Penny Proddow and Marion Fasel in their book, *Diamonds, a Century of Spectacular Jewels* (see "References"), "Edwardian" is not an entirely accurate appellation. For one thing, the style has French derivations, and the French would never name a style after an English king! And while it's true that King Edward VII was a well-known patron of the delineator of the style, Cartier, whom he dubbed "the king of jewelers and the jeweler of kings," he himself would not have called the style Edwardian. As Proddow and Fasel note, other names, while French, are also found lacking: *belle époque* (beautiful era) covers a much longer period, and includes Art Nouveau. *Fin de siècle*, turn of the century, must also include other styles. "The garland style," *style guirlande* in French, is perhaps the most appropriate or evocative name, but there is certainly no consensus on its use.

We usually think of what to call a style after some distancing of elapsed time has occurred. It should come as no surprise then, according to Judy Rudoe in the exhibition catalog, *Cartier 1900-1939*, that it was Hans Nadelhoffer, author in 1984 of the comprehensive book, *Cartier, Jewelers Extraordinary*, who first christened diamond and platinum Louis XVI-inspired jewelry "the garland style." Cartier was at the forefront in developing the style, introducing it in 1899.

The style's emphasis on diamonds coincided with improvements in diamond-cutting technology, which gave rise to new cuts, such as the marquise or navette, the emerald cut, and the baguette. The term "calibré cut" was used to refer to any stone cut to a special shape to fit a setting. The briolette cut, a three-dimensional teardrop shape, was often used for stones meant to be suspended, e.g., in earrings or lavaliers. All of these cuts were also used for other transparent gemstones. Colored stones were often combined with diamonds and pearls in Edwardian jewelry, particularly amethysts, peridot (Alexandra's and Edward's favorites, respectively), blue sapphires, demantoid (green) garnets, alexandrites, rubies, opals, and turquoise.

The motifs of the garland style combined floral and foliate swags with bows, tassels, and lace motifs to produce the jewelry forms of the day: dog collars, fringe and festoon necklaces, brooches, corsage ornaments and larger bodice ornaments (also called "stomachers," as they were in the 18th century), tiaras, lavaliers, pendants, and earrings.

The *négligée* pendant and the *sautoir* were uniquely Edwardian jewels of the period. A variation on the lavalier, the defining feature of the *négligée* is a pair of pendent drops suspended from unequal lengths of fine chain, usually joined to a small gem-set plaque. The drops are often pear-shaped pearls or gemstones. The *sautoir* is a long necklace terminating in a tassel or pendant. The necklace can be a rope or woven band of seed pearls, or a platinum chain interspersed with diamonds; the tassels are usually of pearls with diamond-set caps, the pendants pierced diamond-set plaques.

The probable originator of the garland style was Louis Cartier (1875-1942), who designed for an international clientele of the rich, royal, and famous. American bankers and industrialists, as well as French aristocrats and English nobility, commissioned jewels from Cartier's *atelier* in Paris. The firm was so successful with its new line of garland-style diamond and platinum jewelry that it soon expanded, opening branches in London in 1902 and New York in 1909.

Other famous French houses working in the same mode were Lacloche Frères, Boucheron, Chaumet, and Mellerio. Georges Fouquet and Lucien Gautrait, also known for their

Skinner, Inc.

Edwardian seed pearl sautoir, the finely woven strap suspending a tassel with platinum and rose-cut diamond cap, 42" long, the tassel 2 3/4". **$6,000**

Art Nouveau designs, made garland-style jewels as well.

Peter Carl Fabergé (1846-1920), the celebrated jeweler of the Russian Imperial court, was noted for his objects of vertu. Most of his jewels could be classified as Edwardian, but others have definite Art Nouveau lines and motifs. He was a master of enameling and a technical perfectionist, capable of great versatility. His clientele, however, tended certain restraint. Because the Fabergé name on a piece brings high prices, there are many fakes and forgeries to beware of.

Although the style was predominantly white, pastel colors were also in fashion. Enameling played an important part in lending color to Edwardian jewels. Fabergé was the firm with which this type of enameling was most closely associated, called *guilloché* enamel, which was a transparent-colored enamel over a machine-engraved repeating pattern. Cartier was also a proponent of enameling in the Russian taste, which was still very much in keeping with Louis XVI themes.

In the United States, by the first decade of this century, Tiffany & Co., Marcus & Co., Black, Starr & Frost, Udall & Ballou, and Dreicer & Co. all had retail establishments on Fifth Avenue in New York, where their garland-style jewels found favor with the wealthy denizens of that prestigious neighborhood.

For those unable to afford the opulence of Cartier et al, more modest adornments were available. Even if she owned no other piece of fine jewelry, a woman might have a diamond and platinum or white gold ring in the elongated oblong or navette shape and pierced scrollwork of the Edwardian style (some of these date to the 1920s and early 1930s). Bar brooches were very much in vogue; stars and crescents, sporting, and novelty jewelry continued to be popular, particularly reverse-carved and painted rock crystal intaglios, as were slim bangles, narrow flexible and link bracelets with pierced or filigree plaques; inexpensive gold lavaliers were prevalent. Most of these pieces were set with small diamonds and seed pearls. Moonstones, opals, peridots, demantoid garnets, pink tourmalines, and amethysts were also used. Synthetic rubies were introduced in 1902, and synthetic sapphires made their appearance after 1911. White gold came into common usage during World War I when platinum was appropriated for the war effort and banned for use in jewelry, and necessity prompted a search for a workable substitute. Karl Gustav Richter was granted a patent for his ternary (three-part) formula for white gold in 1915. The Belais Brothers of New York came out with their formula for white gold in 1917, dubbed "18k Belais," which can sometimes be found marked on white gold jewelry of the late teens and 1920s.

Less expensive still was "imitation" (the word "costume" had yet to be coined) jewelry in colorless rhinestones ("paste"), glass and silver made in exactly the same styles as "real" jewelry. It has been overlooked by many of today's costume jewelry collectors because of its small size and delicacy. Non-precious jewelry in the Edwardian or garland style has not survived in quantity. Whether little was made to begin with, or it was discarded, is unclear.

The latter part of the period, c. 1910-1920, interrupted by war, saw both gradual and abrupt stylistic changes. It has been called a transitional period, from Edwardian to Art Deco, in both fine and costume jewelry. The transitional style continued through the 1920s, becoming more geometric but retaining the open, lacy filigree and white or pale palette of high Edwardian, moving toward Art Deco's stronger contrasts in black and white, and red and white.

Aiding this change was what is considered a landmark event: the presentation in Paris of the Ballets Russes *Schéhérazade* in 1910. The ballet's Oriental-inspired costumes by Léon Bakst, stage design, and vibrant colors influenced trendsetters such as Paul Poiret, the progressive couturier, whose designs changed the fashion silhouette from curvilinear to vertical. Tassels and turbans were favorite Poiret accessories, and tasseled pendants and long pendent earrings were complementary jewelry forms. The *sautoir* evolved into long diamond-set geometric chain links and pendants, eventually reaching the masses as tasseled "flapper beads" in faceted glass.

At the same time that Paris was being swept away by the Ballets Russes, women in England and the United States were battling it out on the political front for women's suffrage. The colors for the movement in England, used by the Women's Social and Political Union (WSPU), were purple, white and green. But purple amethysts, white pearls, and green peridots (and other green stones) were all popular period gemstones. Many Edwardian and Art Nouveau-style jewels were made with these stones.

In the United States, the colors purple, white and green were adopted by some suffragist organizations, but others used gold instead of green. Yellow was used alone by the National American Woman's Suffrage Association (NAWSA).

Even today, it is difficult to say if a particular brooch or lavalier was meant for wear as a suffragist "badge" or is just a typical period piece.

REPRODUCTION ALERT

The open, lacy look of Edwardian jewels has been reproduced in recent renditions of the style in diamonds and white gold, which tend to be heavier and not as finely articulated as diamond and platinum pieces of the period. While the cut of the diamonds might be antique, the use of white gold is the tip-off that the piece is new.

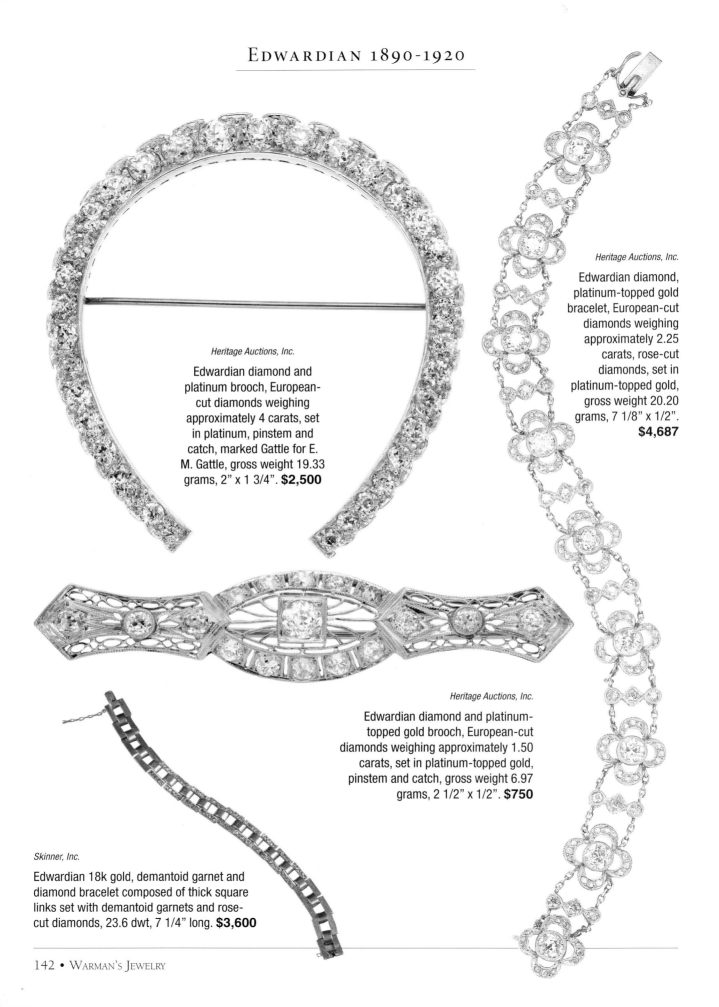

Heritage Auctions, Inc.

Edwardian diamond and platinum brooch, European-cut diamonds weighing approximately 4 carats, set in platinum, pinstem and catch, marked Gattle for E. M. Gattle, gross weight 19.33 grams, 2" x 1 3/4". **$2,500**

Heritage Auctions, Inc.

Edwardian diamond, platinum-topped gold bracelet, European-cut diamonds weighing approximately 2.25 carats, rose-cut diamonds, set in platinum-topped gold, gross weight 20.20 grams, 7 1/8" x 1/2". **$4,687**

Heritage Auctions, Inc.

Edwardian diamond and platinum-topped gold brooch, European-cut diamonds weighing approximately 1.50 carats, set in platinum-topped gold, pinstem and catch, gross weight 6.97 grams, 2 1/2" x 1/2". **$750**

Skinner, Inc.

Edwardian 18k gold, demantoid garnet and diamond bracelet composed of thick square links set with demantoid garnets and rose-cut diamonds, 23.6 dwt, 7 1/4" long. **$3,600**

Heritage Auctions, Inc.

Edwardian diamond, platinum and gold brooch, European-cut diamond measuring 6.92 x 6.85 x 4.71 mm and weighing approximately 1.35 carats, enhanced by European-cut diamonds weighing approximately 1.30 carats, set in platinum, 14k gold pinstem and catch, total diamond weight 2.65 carats, gross weight 8.50 grams, 2 5/8" x 1/2". **$4,062**

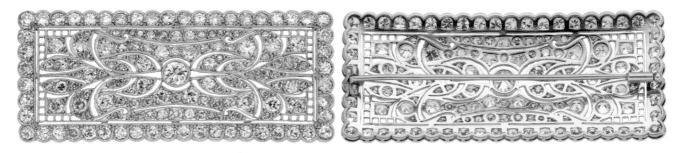

Heritage Auctions, Inc.

Edwardian diamond and platinum-topped gold brooch, centering a European-cut diamond measuring 5.20 x 5.40 x 2.90 mm and weighing approximately 0.50 carat, with European-cut diamonds weighing approximately 9.20 carats, single-cut diamonds weighing approximately 0.80 carat, set in platinum-topped 18k gold, pinstem and catch, total diamond weight is approximately 10.50 carats, gross weight 24.80 grams, 2 5/8" x 1 1/8". **$5,312**

Heritage Auctions, Inc.

Edwardian diamond and platinum brooch, European-cut diamonds weighing approximately 2.25 carats, set in platinum, gross weight 7 grams, 3/4" x 2". **$1,375**

Edwardian diamond and platinum brooch, European-cut diamonds weighing approximately 2.70 carats, set in openwork platinum, pendant bail, pinstem and catch on the reverse, gross weight 7.90 grams, 1 3/8" x 1 1/4". **$2,151**

Edwardian diamond, sapphire and platinum brooch, European- and single-cut diamonds weighing approximately 3.60 carats, pear and square-shaped sapphires weighing approximately 1.65 carats, set in platinum, pinstem and catch on the reverse, gross weight 11.65 grams, 1" x 2 1/4". **$2,390**

Edwardian bar brooch, diamond, cultured pearl and platinum-topped gold, cultured pearl measuring 4.80 x 5 mm, enhanced by European-cut diamonds weighing approximately 0.85 carat, set in platinum-topped 18k gold, pinstem and "C" catch on reverse, gross weight 7 grams, 2 1/4" x 3/8". **$625**

Edwardian brooch, diamond, seed pearl and platinum-topped gold, European-cut diamonds weighing approximately 0.40 carat, native-cut diamonds and seed pearls, set in platinum-topped 18k gold, pinstem and catch on reverse, gross weight 4.10 grams, 1 3/8" x 3/4". **$500**

Doyle New York

Edwardian platinum, diamond and plique-à-jour enamel swallow brooch, circa 1915, pierced plaque centering a soaring diamond-set swallow, atop a plique-à-jour enamel ocean scene with blue sky, the clouds outlined in platinum, framed by pierced florets set with diamonds, edged by black onyx, approximately 13.8 dwt. **$18,750**

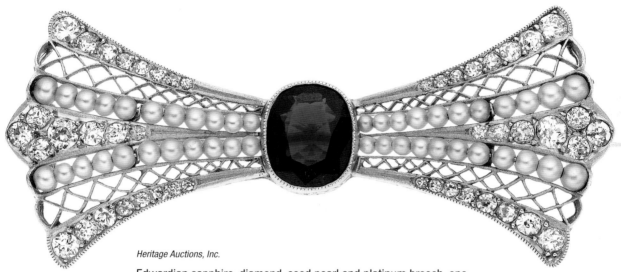

Heritage Auctions, Inc.

Edwardian sapphire, diamond, seed pearl and platinum brooch, one oval-shaped sapphire measuring 8.50 x 6.50 x 2.90 mm and weighing approximately 1.30 carats, European, Swiss and single-cut diamonds weighing approximately 0.85 carat, accented by seed pearls measuring 2-2.50 mm, set in platinum, gross weight 7.50 grams, 2" x 7/8". **$2,151**

Doyle New York

Edwardian pierced and fancy-shaped brooch, circa 1910, platinum, diamond and sapphire, centering one old European-cut diamond weighing approximately 1.45 carats, flanked by bows, with ribbons of French-cut sapphires, tipped by four old European-cut diamonds weighing approximately 1.20 carats, set throughout with small old European- and single-cut diamonds, approximately 8.8 dwt. **$8,125**

Doyle New York

Edwardian platinum, diamond and sapphire filigree brooch, circa 1915, four old European-cut diamonds weighing approximately 1.20 carats, 66 old European-cut diamonds weighing approximately 2.25 carats, gross weight approximately 18.66 grams. **$3,438**

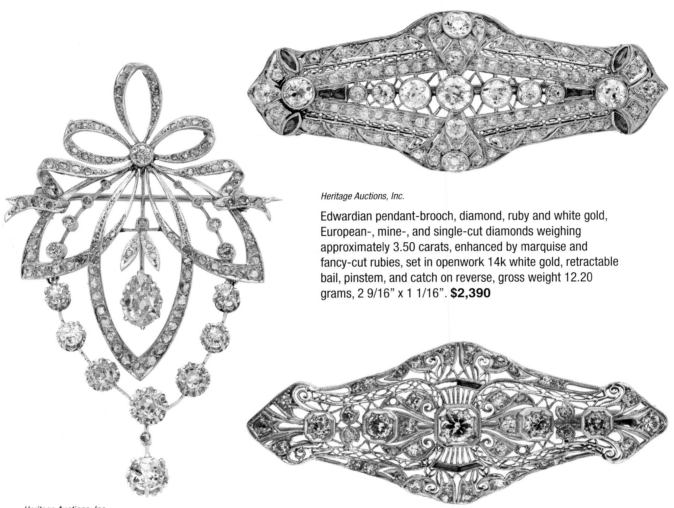

Heritage Auctions, Inc.

Edwardian pendant-brooch, diamond, ruby and white gold, European-, mine-, and single-cut diamonds weighing approximately 3.50 carats, enhanced by marquise and fancy-cut rubies, set in openwork 14k white gold, retractable bail, pinstem, and catch on reverse, gross weight 12.20 grams, 2 9/16" x 1 1/16". **$2,390**

Heritage Auctions, Inc.

Edwardian diamond and gold pendant-brooch, French, pear-shaped diamond weighing approximately 0.90 carat, mine- and rose-cut diamonds, set in 18k white gold, 18k yellow gold pinstem and "C" catch on the reverse, French hallmarks, total diamond weight is approximately 3.50 carats, gross weight 17.20 grams, 2 11/16" x 1 5/8". **$2,629**

Heritage Auctions, Inc.

Edwardian diamond and platinum brooch, European, Swiss and single-cut diamonds weighing approximately 3.25 carats, accented by blue stones, set in platinum, pinstem and catch on the reverse, gross weight 12.91 grams, 3" x 1 1/4". **$1,971**

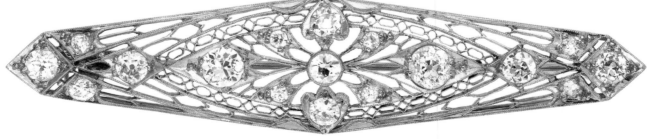

Heritage Auctions, Inc.

Edwardian diamond and platinum bar brooch, European-cut diamonds weighing approximately 3 carats, set in platinum, pinstem and catch on reverse, gross weight 7.75 grams, 2 3/4" x 5/8". **$1,135**

Doyle New York

Edwardian platinum and diamond brooch, circa 1915, features one old European-cut diamond weighing approximately .90 carat, 86 old European-cut diamonds weighing approximately 3.35 carats, gross weight approximately 14.6 grams. **$4,688**

Doyle New York

Edwardian platinum and diamond brooch, circa 1915, stylized flower with filigree decoration set with five old European-cut diamonds weighing approximately 4.50 carats, and 56 old European-cut diamonds weighing approximately 4.85 carats, weight approximately 30.3 grams. **$11,875**

Heritage Auctions, Inc.

Edwardian diamond and white gold pendant-brooch, European-, mine-, and single-cut diamonds weighing approximately 2.50 carats, set in openwork 14k white gold, retractable bail, pinstem, and catch on reverse, gross weight 11.20 grams, 2 1/4" x 1 1/8". **$836**

Heritage Auctions, Inc.

Edwardian brooch, circa 1910, diamond and platinum-topped gold, European-cut diamonds weighing approximately 2 carats, rose-cut diamonds, set in pierced platinum-topped 18k yellow gold, total diamond weight is approximately 3 carats, gross weight 8.80 grams, 2" x 7/8". **$2,629**

Skinner, Inc.

Edwardian demantoid garnet and diamond snake brooch set with circular-cut demantoid garnets framed by old mine-cut diamonds, cushion-cut ruby head, platinum-topped 18k gold mount, 2 1/4" long. **$8,100**

Skinner, Inc.

Edwardian 18k gold, enamel, and diamond brooch designed as a silver and rose-cut diamond trophy on blue guilloche enamel ground, French import stamps, 1" diameter. **$480**

Skinner, Inc.

Edwardian moonstone and diamond crown brooch set with five cabochon moonstones and old mine-cut diamonds, approximate total diamond weight 3 carats, platinum-topped 14k gold mount, 2 1/8" long. **$1,020**

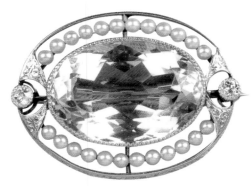

Skinner, Inc.

Edwardian freshwater pearl and diamond brooch-pendant set with pear-, old mine-, and rose-cut diamonds suspending a freshwater pearl, platinum-topped 18k gold mount, 3" long. **$1,920**

Skinner, Inc.

Edwardian platinum, aquamarine, seed pearl and diamond brooch, bezel-set with a cushion-cut aquamarine measuring approximately 19.50 x 13.90 x 8.95 mm, framed by seed pearls and old European-cut diamonds, engraved gallery, 1 1/8" long. **$1,680**

Doyle New York

Edwardian platinum, emerald and diamond bar pin and white gold and diamond filigree pin: diamond pin has one old European-cut diamond weighing approximately .40 carat and 44 old European-cut diamonds weighing approximately 2.20 carats; bar pin, circa 1915, is approximately 13.9 grams. **$2,375**

Skinner, Inc.

Edwardian opal and diamond brooch, bezel-set with three cabochon opals, further set with old mine-cut diamonds, approximate total diamond weight 1.20 carats, platinum-topped gold mount, millegrain accents, 1 7/8" long. **$1,440**

Skinner, Inc.

Edwardian amethyst, pearl and diamond brooch, navette form, set with a fancy-cut amethyst measuring approximately 30 x 19.30 x 11.20 mm, and old European- and old single-cut diamonds, framed by seed pearls, platinum and 18k gold mount, 1 3/4" long. **$2,040**

Skinner, Inc.

Edwardian platinum and diamond brooch, bezel-set with an old European-cut diamond weighing approximately 0.90 carat, and further set with old European-cut diamonds on knife-edge bars, millegrain accents, 1 1/2". **$3,198**

Heritage Auctions, Inc.

Edwardian stickpin, diamond and platinum-topped gold, mine-cut diamonds weighing approximately 0.50 carat, set in openwork platinum-topped 14k yellow gold, gross weight 3.40 grams, 2 5/8" x 7/16". **$262**

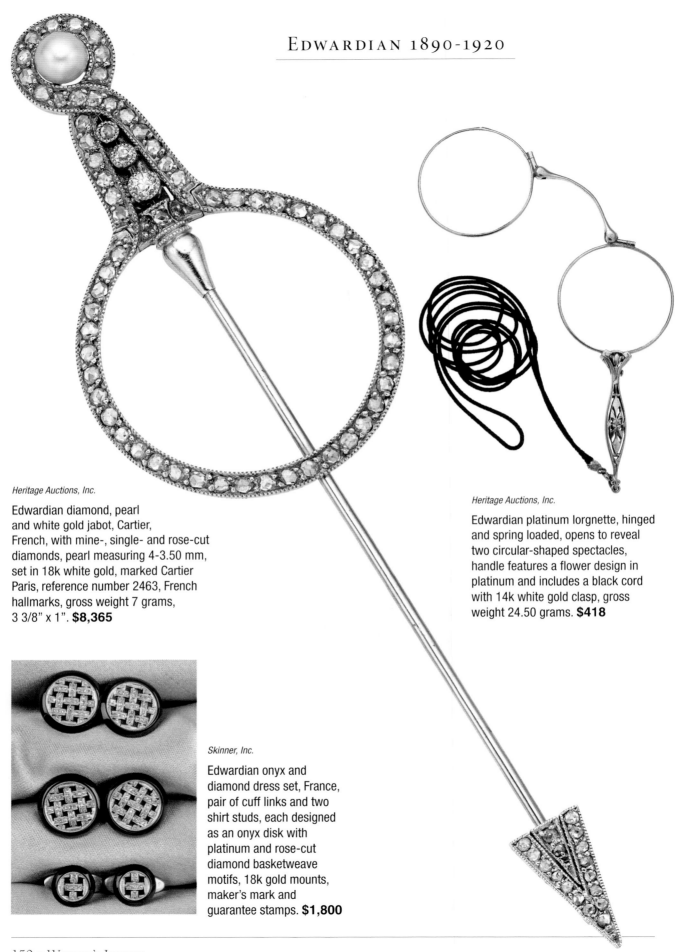

Heritage Auctions, Inc.

Edwardian diamond, pearl and white gold jabot, Cartier, French, with mine-, single- and rose-cut diamonds, pearl measuring 4-3.50 mm, set in 18k white gold, marked Cartier Paris, reference number 2463, French hallmarks, gross weight 7 grams, 3 3/8" x 1". **$8,365**

Heritage Auctions, Inc.

Edwardian platinum lorgnette, hinged and spring loaded, opens to reveal two circular-shaped spectacles, handle features a flower design in platinum and includes a black cord with 14k white gold clasp, gross weight 24.50 grams. **$418**

Skinner, Inc.

Edwardian onyx and diamond dress set, France, pair of cuff links and two shirt studs, each designed as an onyx disk with platinum and rose-cut diamond basketweave motifs, 18k gold mounts, maker's mark and guarantee stamps. **$1,800**

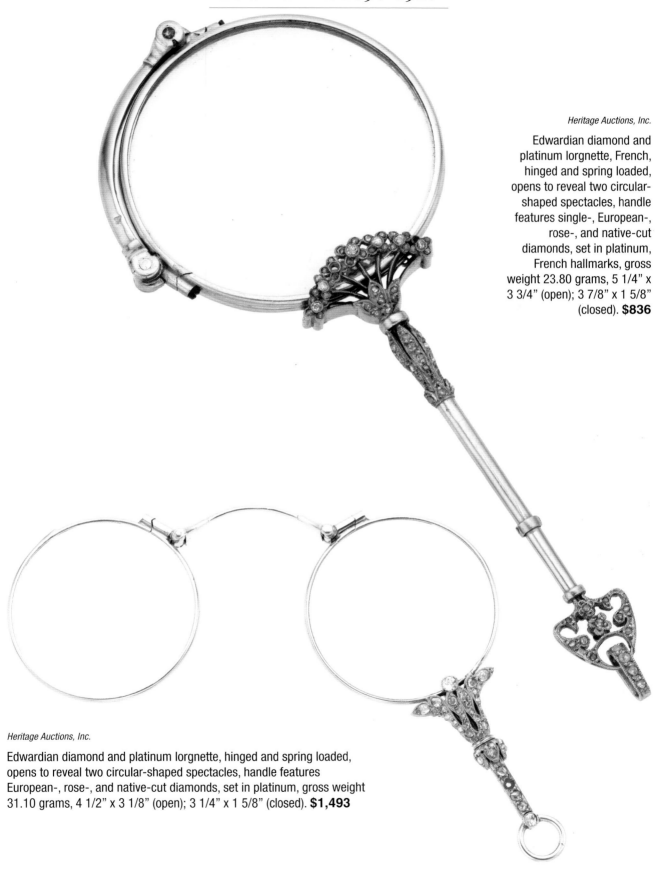

Heritage Auctions, Inc.

Edwardian diamond and platinum lorgnette, French, hinged and spring loaded, opens to reveal two circular-shaped spectacles, handle features single-, European-, rose-, and native-cut diamonds, set in platinum, French hallmarks, gross weight 23.80 grams, 5 1/4" x 3 3/4" (open); 3 7/8" x 1 5/8" (closed). **$836**

Heritage Auctions, Inc.

Edwardian diamond and platinum lorgnette, hinged and spring loaded, opens to reveal two circular-shaped spectacles, handle features European-, rose-, and native-cut diamonds, set in platinum, gross weight 31.10 grams, 4 1/2" x 3 1/8" (open); 3 1/4" x 1 5/8" (closed). **$1,493**

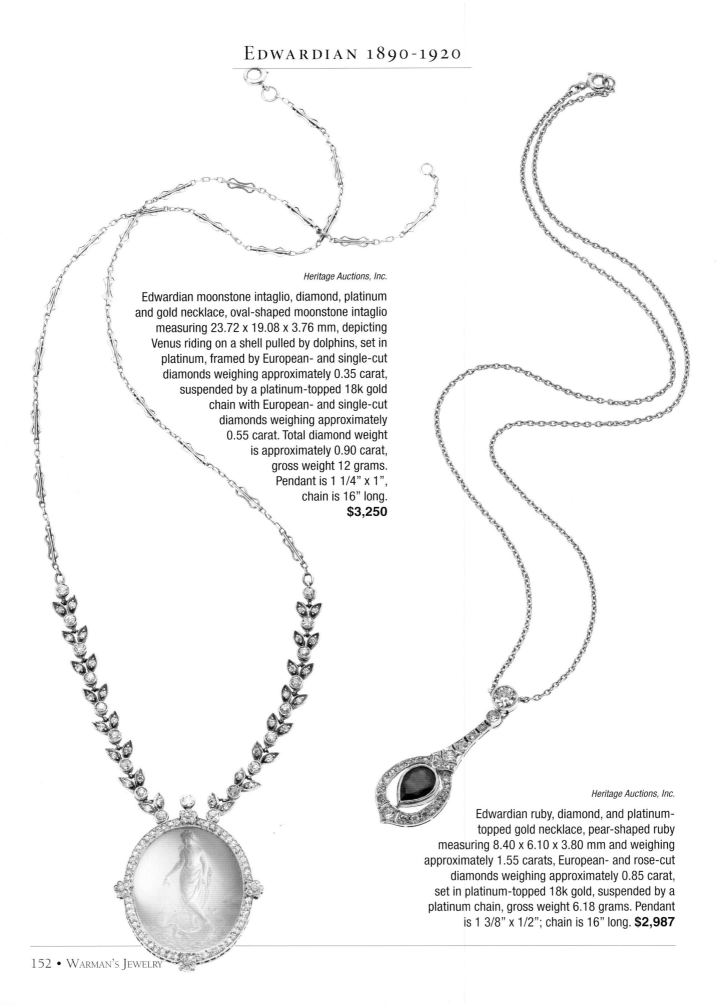

Heritage Auctions, Inc.

Edwardian moonstone intaglio, diamond, platinum and gold necklace, oval-shaped moonstone intaglio measuring 23.72 x 19.08 x 3.76 mm, depicting Venus riding on a shell pulled by dolphins, set in platinum, framed by European- and single-cut diamonds weighing approximately 0.35 carat, suspended by a platinum-topped 18k gold chain with European- and single-cut diamonds weighing approximately 0.55 carat. Total diamond weight is approximately 0.90 carat, gross weight 12 grams. Pendant is 1 1/4" x 1", chain is 16" long. **$3,250**

Heritage Auctions, Inc.

Edwardian ruby, diamond, and platinum-topped gold necklace, pear-shaped ruby measuring 8.40 x 6.10 x 3.80 mm and weighing approximately 1.55 carats, European- and rose-cut diamonds weighing approximately 0.85 carat, set in platinum-topped 18k gold, suspended by a platinum chain, gross weight 6.18 grams. Pendant is 1 3/8" x 1/2"; chain is 16" long. **$2,987**

Heritage Auctions, Inc.

Edwardian necklace, pearl, diamond, green stone, platinum and gold, strand of pearls has a clasp with European-cut diamonds weighing approximately 0.45 carat, surrounded by green stones, set in platinum-topped 14k gold, gross weight 8.70 grams, 20". **$750**

Jewelry and image courtesy Linda Lombardo, Worn to Perfection on Ruby Lane

Edwardian gold-color dog collar necklace with open back blue glass stones, 14". **$275**

Heritage Auctions, Inc.

Edwardian sautoir, diamond, seed pearl, enamel, platinum and gold, French, the woven seed pearl necklace has openwork platinum sections, with European- and rose-cut diamonds, suspending a detachable pendant, with European- and rose-cut diamonds, seed pearl tassel with a rose-cut diamond and enameled platinum cap, French hallmarks, total diamond weight is approximately 4.20 carats, gross weight is 62.50 grams, necklace is 27" long, pendant is 4" x 1 1/2", combined dimensions: 31" x 1 1/2". Clasp is shown in the photo below. **$15,000**

Heritage Auctions, Inc.

Edwardian sapphire, diamond, gold and platinum necklace, cushion-shaped sapphire measuring 16.78 x 11.24 x 3.01 mm and weighing 7.34 carats, four European-cut diamonds measuring 6 x 6 x 3.30 mm, 7 x 7 x 4.10 mm, 5.10 x 5.40 x 3.10 mm and 5 x 5.40 x 3.10 mm and weighing approximately 0.75, 1.25, 0.50 and 0.50 carats, respectively, European- and single-cut diamonds weighing approximately 2.85 carats, set in platinum, 14k white gold pinstem and catch on the reverse; together with a detachable platinum chain with rose-cut diamond accents. Total diamond weight is approximately 5.85 carats, gross weight 23.10 grams. Pendant-brooch is 2" x 1 1/2"; chain is 16" long. **$9,560**

Heritage Auctions, Inc.

Edwardian diamond, seed pearl and platinum sautoir, European- and single-cut diamonds set within an open wire work and pierced quatrefoil motif platinum shield, framed by wired seed pearls measuring 2.50-3 mm, supported by a finely wrought platinum fancy link chain, surmounted by an open wire work crown, set with European- and single-cut diamonds, total diamond weight is approximately 1.20 carats, gross weight 9.80 grams, 22" long. **$3,883**

Steve Fishbach Collection jewelry; Linda Lombardo photo

Late Edwardian pierced metal cameo necklace, 18". **$185**

Jewelry and image courtesy Linda Lombardo, Worn to Perfection on Ruby Lane

Late Edwardian/early Art Deco pierced segmented rhodium plated necklace, 17 1/2". **$195**

Steve Fishbach Collection jewelry; Linda Lombardo photo

Edwardian 14k white gold pendant, blue and white enamel, diamonds, from one of the Newark, New Jersey jewelers, circa 1910, 19" chain with 1 1/2" drop. **$3,500**

Doyle New York

Edwardian platinum, diamond and pearl pendant, circa 1915, four old mine-cut diamonds weighing approximately 1.10 carats, nine diamonds weighing approximately .70 carat, one pearl measuring approximately 5 mm, approximately 6.6 grams. **$3,200**

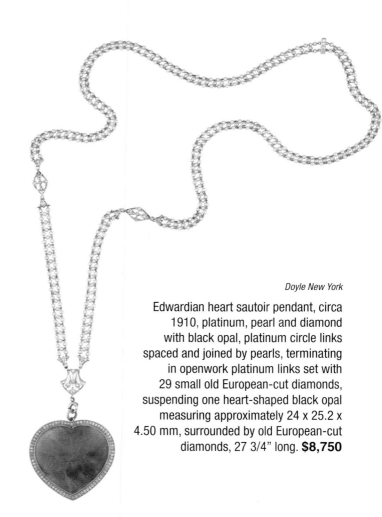

Doyle New York

Edwardian heart sautoir pendant, circa 1910, platinum, pearl and diamond with black opal, platinum circle links spaced and joined by pearls, terminating in openwork platinum links set with 29 small old European-cut diamonds, suspending one heart-shaped black opal measuring approximately 24 x 25.2 x 4.50 mm, surrounded by old European-cut diamonds, 27 3/4" long. **$8,750**

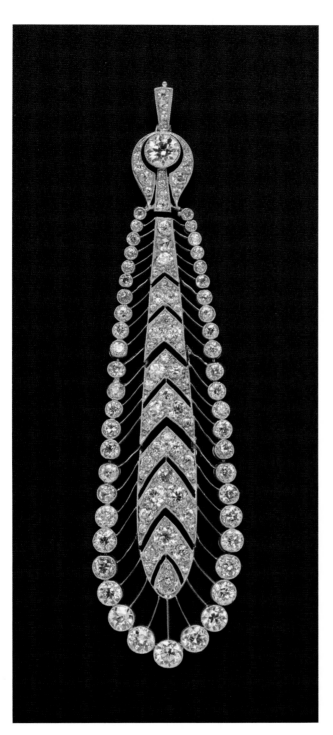

Skinner, Inc.

Edwardian platinum and diamond pendant, old mine-cut diamond drop weighing approximately 1.75 carats, suspended from a garland of old mine-cut diamonds with diamond swags, approximate total weight 7.09 carats, 2 1/8" long. **$10,200**

Skinner, Inc.

Edwardian platinum and diamond pendant, Tiffany & Co., set throughout with old European-cut diamonds on knife-edge bars, approximate total weight 7.75 carats, millegrain accents, signed, 3 3/4" long. **$18,000**

Skinner, Inc.

Edwardian enamel and diamond pendant, L. Gautrait, France, the guilloche enamel panel set with marquise- and rose-cut diamonds, foliate frame, and rose-cut diamond bail, platinum and 18k gold mount, maker's mark and guarantee stamps, signed, 1 1/2" diameter. **$8,040**

Heritage Auctions, Inc.

Edwardian diamond, cultured pearl and platinum ring, two European-cut diamonds weighing approximately 1.50 carats, cultured pearl measuring 5.95 x 6.20, European-cut diamonds weighing approximately 0.50 carat, set in platinum, total diamond weight approximately 2 carats, gross weight 7.92 grams, size 7 1/4 (sizeable). **$2,750**

Doyle New York

Diamond ring, circa 1915, platinum and vertically set European-cut diamonds, weighing approximately 4.25 carats, elongated pierced openwork mount set throughout with numerous single-cut diamonds, approximately 4 dwt, 1 3/16" long. **$12,000**

Heritage Auctions, Inc.

Edwardian diamond and platinum ring, mine-cut diamonds weighing approximately 3.55 carats, single-cut diamonds, set in platinum, total diamond weight is approximately 3.60 carats, gross weight 4.50 grams, size 6 1/4 (sizeable). **$2,750**

Sotheby's

Platinum and fancy blue diamond ring, Tiffany & Co., circa 1900, modified marquise-shaped diamond of fancy blue color weighing 3.54 carats, within a delicate mounting set with old European-cut and single-cut diamonds weighing approximately .35 carat, bearing partial signature "T" for Tiffany & Co., two diamonds missing, size 3 1/2. With fitted box signed Tiffany & Co. **$2,434,500**

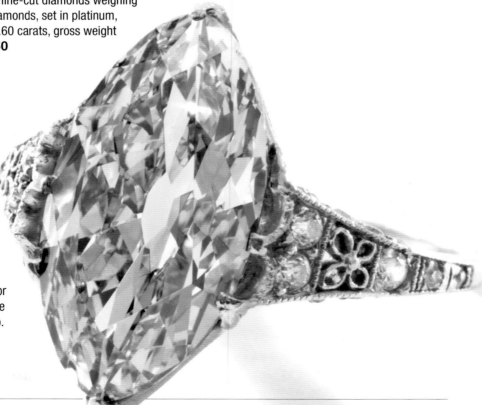

Skinner, Inc.

Edwardian fire opal and diamond ring set with a cushion-cut opal measuring approximately 14 x 11.70 x 5.10 mm, framed by rose-cut diamonds, rose-cut diamond shoulders, platinum-topped 18k gold mount, approximate size 5 1/2 (sizeable). **$5,100**

Doyle New York

Edwardian platinum, sapphire and diamond ring, circa 1915, pierced platinum mount centering one cushion-shaped sapphire weighing approximately 2 carats, flanked by two old European-cut diamonds weighing approximately 2 carats, with numerous small single-cut diamonds, hinged shank, size 8 1/4. **$21,250**

Skinner, Inc.

Edwardian ruby and diamond bypass ring, Tiffany & Co., set with an old European-cut diamond weighing approximately 0.95 carat, further set with a circular-cut ruby measuring approximately 6.40 x 4 mm and weighing approximately 1 carat, old European-cut diamond accents, platinum-topped 18k gold mount, signed, size 5 1/2. **$6,000**

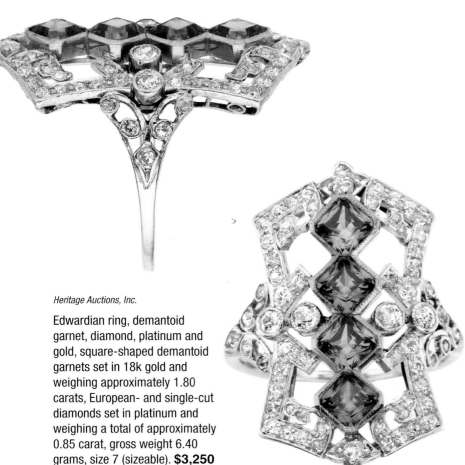

Heritage Auctions, Inc.

Edwardian ring, demantoid garnet, diamond, platinum and gold, square-shaped demantoid garnets set in 18k gold and weighing approximately 1.80 carats, European- and single-cut diamonds set in platinum and weighing a total of approximately 0.85 carat, gross weight 6.40 grams, size 7 (sizeable). **$3,250**

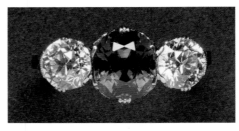

Heritage Auctions, Inc.

Edwardian diamond and platinum ring, navette form, mine-cut diamond measuring 6.50 x 6.40 x 4.80 mm and weighing approximately 1.25 carats, enhanced by mine- and single-cut diamonds, set in platinum, total diamond weight approximately 3.75 carats, gross weight 7.50 grams, size 6 3/4 (sizeable). **$3,585**

Skinner, Inc.

Edwardian platinum, sapphire and diamond ring set with an oval-cut sapphire measuring approximately 7.92 x 6.92 x 5.64 mm, weighing approximately 2.48 carats, flanked by old European-cut diamonds weighing approximately 0.78 and 0.75 carat, old European-cut diamond accents, approximate total diamond weight 2.10 carats, millegrain details, size 8 1/2. **$48,000**

Heritage Auctions, Inc.

Edwardian diamond and platinum ring, mine- and rose-cut diamonds weighing approximately 2.30 carats, set in platinum, gross weight 6.40 grams, size 6 3/4 (sizeable). **$2,750**

Heritage Auctions, Inc.

Edwardian diamond and white gold ring, European-cut diamond measuring 6.50-6.45 x 4.10 mm and weighing approximately 1 carat, European- and single-cut diamonds weighing approximately 0.50 carat, set in 14k white gold, total diamond weight is approximately 1.50 carats, gross weight 4.50 grams, size 3 (sizeable). **$2,031**

Sotheby's

Set of necklace, bracelet and pair of
earrings, Tiffany & Co., designed by
Louis Comfort Tiffany, circa 1910,
formed of sculpted gold links of foliate
and scroll design, set with a variety of
colored stones, including sapphires in
multiple hues, blue and purple spinel,
pink tourmaline, amethyst and zircon,
in round, cushion and various fancy
shapes, necklace is 18 1/2" long
and bracelet is 6 7/8", earrings with
later-added backs, signed Tiffany & Co.
$121,000

20TH CENTURY JEWELRY

The 20th century truly began with World War I, a cataclysmic event that transformed society. Women would never be the same after "the war to end all wars."

When the smoke cleared, the Gibson Girl had become Thoroughly Modern Millie. Her fashions, her attitude, her way of life, were marked departures from all that had gone before. The war and–at last–the right to vote gave American women a stronger voice in the affairs of the country and a greater awareness of the affairs of the world. This worldly sophistication was aided by the advent of radio, the growth of fashion magazines and popular culture periodicals, and perhaps most importantly, the motion picture industry. Changes in fashion occurred at an ever-accelerating pace.

Although Paris continued to be regarded as a fashion mecca through mid-century, British and European royalty were no longer as influential as America's Hollywood elite. Movie stars were the new queens. What they wore was closely monitored, reported, and emulated. Purveyors to these new "royals" achieved instant fame and success by association. Names of designers attained new importance, and "name-dropping" became a pastime of a new social class.

Indeed, "new" and "novelty" were watchwords of the day. The latest was considered the best. In jewelry, new designs and materials were incorporated into manufacturers' repertoires. Except for a hiatus during World War I, diamonds and platinum still ruled, but the avant-garde opted for chrome, rock crystal, glass, and that most novel of materials, plastic. Costume jewelry was given its stamp of approval by Coco Chanel and other haute couturiers. It was no longer looked down upon as a mere imitation of the real thing, although there were surely many rhinestone and rhodium-plated knockoffs masquerading as diamonds and platinum. Frankly fake jewels, however, were now being worn to complement one's outfit, or costume.

A method for producing dental castings, introduced in 1907, led to a new application of the ancient art of lost-wax casting in the 1930s: the mass-production of both fine and costume jewelry. Multiple copies of one design were made possible with the aid of vulcanized rubber molds, using the vulcanization process invented by Charles Goodyear in 1839, along with the development of an improved casting investment plaster in 1932.

Stylistic trends evolved more rapidly in the 20th century. Whereas a 19th century style could span several decades, after World War I, each decade was characterized by a different look. And while the general term "modernism" can be applied to the entire era, we tend to group the changing styles within it by 10-year periods, i.e., the 1920s, '30s, '40s, '50s, etc. This is not necessarily an accurate classification, nor are the appellations Art Deco, Streamline Moderne, or Retro Modern correctly applied to each decade. These are styles, not periods, which, as always, tend to overlap and coexist along with revivals and traditions. It can be said, for example, that Art Deco was a popular style in the '20s, but certainly not the only style. Consequently, rather than label each of the following subdivisions of 20th century jewelry with a style name, they are divided by period, with a prefacing explanation of the predominant styles in each.

In this section, it is also necessary to introduce a separate classification based on certain materials from which some jewelry was made. "Costume jewelry" is too all-encompassing and unwieldy a term for the several types of non-precious jewelry that proliferated from the 1920s onward. Therefore, there is a special category for plastic and novelty jewelry, the whimsical and "fun" costume jewelry that does not fall clearly into any other stylistic category. Because of its growth as a collectible, the classification of "designer signed" costume jewelry is divided into two sub-sections, with the chronological dividing line drawn at 1950.

Sotheby's

The jabot pin was a new form introduced in the 1920s. Platinum, gold, jade, ruby, sapphire, and diamond jabot pin, Mauboussin, circa 1920, the carved jade wreath adorned with cabochon rubies, cabochon sapphires and rose-cut diamonds, topped and surmounted by round, baguette, and single-cut diamonds, the bar pin accented by carved ruby and emerald terminals, signed Mauboussin, France, with French assay and workshop marks. **$31,250**

FINE JEWELRY

CIRCA 1920-1935

After a period of wartime austerity, the 1920s woman burst forth with a frenetic exuberance. She cut off her hair, her sleeves and her hems, bound her chest and dropped her waistline to become *la garçonne*, the female boy. She celebrated her new post-war prosperity and freedom by piling on the jewels.

Bare arms and waistless dresses changed fashion's focus from the wide waist-cinching belts, sash and corsage ornaments of the *belle époque* to multiple bracelets and small plaque brooches or jeweled ornaments worn at the hips and shoulders. There were endless variations of the diamond and platinum bracelet variously referred to as the plaque, flexible link or box, strap, band, or straightline. Some were accented with natural or synthetic sapphires or rubies, or emeralds, or a combination of these. Short hairstyles gave rise to long pendent drop earrings. The screwback finding (called the "French back" by some in the trade) was now the norm, as most women no longer pierced their ears. Large hats, hatpins, tiaras and haircombs disappeared, to be replaced by bandeaux and cloche hats embellished with small hat ornaments.

The *sautoir* remained, but in modified "modernized" form, becoming more geometric. It was often made entirely of diamonds and platinum, terminating in a diamond-set drop instead of a tassel, and it was convertible, forming bracelets, choker, and pendant. Lorgnettes continued to be fashionably suspended from long chains or cords; in the 1930s, they adapted for wear as clips. Tasseled ropes of gemstone beads were also worn.

Pearls remained popular, worn as *sautoirs* or long ropes, or twisted about the wrist. The recently marketed cultured pearl was affordable to the middle classes, although it caused a furor among natural (Asian) pearl merchants. Dog collars narrowed to become short delicate necklaces, often worn in addition to a *sautoir*. The bar pin and plaque brooch continued to be worn as transitional jewels in addition to two new forms introduced by Cartier: the circle or ring brooch (Cartier called it *broche de ceinture*, "belt brooch") and jabot pin, or *cliquet*. Both could be worn as hat ornaments. Pierced platinum or white gold and diamond rings retained the elongated outline of the past two decades, but became increasingly geometric in design. New ring shapes were hexagonal or octagonal, with colored gemstones and diamonds set in domed or stepped mounts.

The excesses of the 1920s were sharply curtailed by the 1929 stock market crash and the onset of the Great Depression. But even though it was out of reach for most pocketbooks, and production diminished, precious jewelry continued to be made. The elite of Hollywood and New York could still afford it; women of wealth everywhere continued to wear their status symbols. Indeed, jewelry grew larger and more three-dimensional as fashions became less severe. During the early 1930s, the waistline returned, sleeves grew longer and/or fuller, and a woman's curves were emphasized by bias-cut gowns in soft and satiny fabrics.

The dress clip became the most important jeweled accessory of the 1930s. Usually worn in pairs at the neckline, they were held in place by means of a flat-backed hinged mechanism that snapped shut over the fabric's edge. The story goes that Louis Cartier came up with the idea for the clip while watching a woman use clothespins to hang laundry out to dry. These versatile ornaments could also be worn on jacket lapels, hats, purses, belts, and, with the attachment of an additional pinback mechanism, a pair could be joined for wear as a brooch.

The all-white look of diamonds and platinum that began with the Edwardians at the turn of the century persisted well into the 1930s, with the additional use of colorless rock crystal. Over the years, geometric forms insinuated upon, then replaced the garland style. By the early 1920s, diamond cutting had advanced to such a degree that unusual shapes, such as the half-moon, the obus or bullet (a narrow pentagon), the epaulet (a wide pentagon), the trapeze, and the triangle, could be produced for added geometric interest in all-white jewels. At the same time, color was injected into some jewelry designs in the form of rubies, emeralds, sapphires, jade, coral, lapis, onyx, and enamels, as the style which later came to be known as Art Deco exerted its influence.

Art Deco itself was influenced by a number of design sources: Asian, Persian/Islamic, East Indian, ancient Egyptian and pre-Hispanic Mexican, African, American Indian, and, most directly, by turn-of-the-century Austrian and German Secessionist and *Jugendstil* designs.

While the commonly held view is that the Art Deco style arose as a result of the 1925 Paris exposition from which it derives its name, *L'Exposition Internationale des Arts Décoratifs et Industriels Modernes*, in fact that date is more correctly a culmination of developments that occurred throughout the previous two decades. It should be noted that the outbreak of war forced the exposition's postponement. It was originally planned for 1916, the idea having been discussed since 1907, according to Sylvie Raulet in her book *Art Deco Jewelry*. So we see the seeds of modernism being planted at the turn of the century and reaching full flower after World War I. Still, the popularization of the style was not widely felt in the United States until after the exposition–an event in which the United States did not participate. (Herbert Hoover, Secretary of Commerce at the time, was noted as saying this country did not have any "modern" decorative arts, and thus could not meet the entry requirements of newness and originality.)

The name Art Deco was not applied to what was then called "modernistic" or "moderne" until 1968, when it appeared in the title of a book by Bevis Hillier, *Art Deco of the '20s and '30s*. This probably explains why there are several different interpretations of what the style really is, and why there is debate over the period in which it flourished. For some, it is an all-encompassing label that includes what others separate into Art Deco, Zig-Zag Moderne, Streamline Moderne, and the International Style. Some say the style ended in 1925; others claim it spanned the entire period between the world wars. Mr. Hillier takes the inclusive, evolutionary point of view that although "there was a difference in character between the 'twenties and the 'thirties... Art Deco was a developing style...There was a strong continuity." (From the introduction to *The World of Art Deco*, catalog of an exhibition at the Minneapolis Institute of Arts, 1971).

The credo of the modernists was "form follows function," and all excess ornamentation was to be avoided, on a parallel with the tenets of the Arts and Crafts Movement. Unlike the purists of that movement, however, the modern-

The double-clip brooch was patented by Cartier in 1927. Diamond and platinum double-clip brooch, circa 1950, full-cut diamonds weighing approximately 1.40 carats, single-cut diamonds weighing approximately 5.90 carats, baguette-cut diamonds weighing approximately 2.35 carats, set in platinum, clip mechanisms on reverse; clips are joined by a box catch with hinged locks. Total diamond weight for the assembled double-clip brooch is approximately 9.65 carats. Combined dimensions 2" x 2". **$5,000**

ists espoused and embraced the use of the machine. The style is characterized by the simplification and stylization of motifs from nature and the introduction of abstract, non-representational, structural and geometric forms. Futuristic and speed-associated motifs were also part of the repertoire. Suffice it to say that whatever the label, there is general agreement that the design developments of the period between the wars were as much a departure from Victorianism as the chemise was from the hoop skirt.

In jewelry, too, one often hears the term Art Deco applied to everything from slight variations on Edwardian pierced platinum-and-diamond plaque brooches to starkly simple abstract metal and enamel pendants or bangles. The tendency is to call any piece from the '20s or '30s Art Deco–a matter of subjective interpretation. In fact, the evolution of the style in jewelry can be traced through several different lineages, from the traditional French haute *joailliers* to the avant-garde artist-designers, continuing to popular adaptations and modifications by American jewelers inspired by French designs.

Cartier is the most famous of the former for its version of Art Deco, which tended toward the figurative and exotic Eastern-influenced designs. Notable were Cartier's use of carved gemstones in circular "belt brooches," jabot pins (called *cliquet* pins by Cartier), multicolored "fruit salad" arrangements of leaves and berries in flexible band bracelets, flower vase brooches, and double clip brooches (patented by Cartier in 1927). It celebrated its 150th anniversary in 1997 with a major exhibition in New York and London.

Van Cleef and Arpels also contributed a great deal to the genre. They were particularly known for their Egyptian Revival motifs executed in calibré-cut colored gemstones and pavé diamonds on strap bracelets, inspired by the discovery of Tutankhamen's tomb in 1922 (an event that launched a general mania for Egyptian motifs). The firm also excelled at creating convertible diamond and platinum jewels in the prevailing geometric forms, e.g., a *sautoir* necklace that separated into bracelets and a pendant.

Other famous French houses whose pieces come up for sale at important jewelry auctions include Boucheron, Mauboussin, Chaumet, and Lacloche. Less often seen is the work of the French avant-garde designers: Jean Desprès (1889-1980), Jean Dunand (1877-1942), Georges Fouquet (1862-1957) and son Jean Fouquet (b. 1899), Gérard Sandoz

(b. 1902), and Raymond Templier (1891-1968). When a significant piece by any of these houses or designers is offered, it can realize five or six figures.

Several American firms made and sold noteworthy Art Deco jewels inspired by the French, especially after the 1925 exposition: the manufacturing jewelers William Scheer, Inc. and Oscar Heyman & Bros., retailers J.E. Caldwell & Co., Black, Starr & Frost, Tiffany & Co., Marcus & Co., C.D. Peacock, and the New York branches of Cartier and Van Cleef & Arpels. The French manufacturing firm Rubel Frères, established in the United States in 1939 as John Rubel Co., was affiliated with VC & A until 1943.

Raymond C. Yard opened his own salon on Fifth Avenue in New York in 1922. He was known for catering to an elite clientele. In the late 1920s and early '30s, he designed a series of whimsical anthropomorphic animals engaged in human activities. His rabbit figures were especially charming.

Many anonymous French and unsigned American-made pieces of the period are sold at auction. Price is often determined by the number, size, quantity, and quality of the gemstones used as much as, if not more than, the design, which can be repetitious and unoriginal. Less-than-important commercial pieces signed by the famous houses are also auctioned regularly. Their names are often cause for an escalation in price, but astute buyers always evaluate a piece on its own merits before taking its marks into consideration.

REPRODUCTION ALERT

The Deco revival that began in the early 1980s has generated a plethora of knockoffs and "Deco style" pieces that never existed during the 1920s and 1930s. Many of these come from Thailand and Hong Kong, where the workmanship is rarely as good as the originals, but European and American manufacturers are producing quality reproductions, some of which defy detection. Among them: Branca de Brito of Portugal, Hermes of Munich, Germany, and Authentic Jewelry in New York City. Ask questions, read auction catalog warranties, conditions, and descriptions carefully—if a piece is described as "Art Deco style," it is not of the period—and examine pieces thoroughly. Be aware that descriptions are the opinions of the auction houses.

CIRCA 1935-1945

The stylistic developments of the '30s started taking a markedly different path about half-way through the decade. By the mid-'30s, the all-white look of diamonds and platinum that had been a mainstay of fine jewelry fashion since the turn of the century began to fade. Colored gold and gemstones gradually became more prominent, encouraged by changes in clothing styles and later, by wartime shortages and restrictions. The repeal of Prohibition and the abandonment of the gold standard in 1933 may have precipitated the change.

Although the Depression had the nation and Europe in its grip for the duration of the decade, these two events could have sparked hope for better days ahead. Nightclubs were once again in business and gold jewelry was once again in fashion, as publicized by Hollywood and its stars, the epitome of glamour. Jewelry was still desirable to own in hard times, not only as personal adornment, but also as portable wealth, a concept that remained viable throughout the war years. In the "make-do" spirit of the period, however, fewer and less expensive gemstones were used, including synthetic rubies and sapphires, and less expensive gold took the place of platinum, which became totally unavailable for jewelry during the war.

A resurgence of romanticism in the mid- to late '30s generated a desire for femininity in fashion and a return to Victorian sentimentality. There was even a reprise of British royal influence, which nearly upstaged all of Hollywood. The abdication of King Edward VIII in 1936, and his subsequent marriage to Wallis Simpson, was "the most famous love story of modern times." Jewelry played a well-publicized, prominent and sentimental role in that story. (Not to be outdone, Margaret Mitchell and Hollywood gave us "Gone With the Wind," the most famous love story of Victorian times.) The Duke and Duchess of Windsor, as they became known, were the equal of Victoria in their influence on the jewelry-buying public. The most famous of the Duchess' jewels were made by Cartier and Van Cleef & Arpels, but designs by Suzanne Belperron, Harry Winston, Verdura, David Webb, and Seaman Schepps were also part of her collection. (All of these were sold by Sotheby's in

Geneva at its renowned record-breaking auction in April 1987.)

Retro Modern is the somewhat controversial name coined for the fluid 1940s jewelry style that began to emerge around 1935. It is an appropriately contradictory term, carrying the suggestion of looking backward and forward at the same time. The style's characteristics were truly an infusion of past and futuristic themes. The Machine Age, streamlined look of the late 1920s and early 1930s continued to evolve, becoming larger and more three-dimensional. But geometric severity was tempered by curvilinear softness, asymmetry, and a return to naturalistic motifs, usually interpreted on a larger scale and in more stylized forms than their Victorian counterparts.

In the gradual move away from abstraction, flowers, animals, and birds became increasingly popular. Buckles, bows, ribbons, and fabric-like folds were often executed in combined contrasting colors of gold alloys in overtones of pink (rose) and green as well as yellow (called bicolor and tricolor gold). Pieces were massive-looking, but hollow and, especially during wartime, the gold was of a thin gauge. In German-occupied France, the customer supplied the gold and gemstones, and the government took a percentage of the gold's value. While the United States was under no such restriction on gold, patriotism dictated restraint. Patriotism itself was a prevalent theme in wartime jewelry, both in colors (rubies and sapphires, often synthetic, accented with small diamonds) and motifs (flags, eagles, and military insignia).

Elements of the Machine Age style were reinterpreted in yellow and rose gold, including large geometric link and wide strap bracelets in "tank track" and other repeating patterns. In 1934, Van Cleef & Arpels designed a flexible strap of honeycomb or brickwork patterned segments with a large ornamental buckle-shaped clasp. They christened it the "Ludo" bracelet, after Louis "Ludovic" Arpels, but it appears to have been inspired by Victorian gold mesh *jarretières*, or "garter" bracelets. The design was copied by many others and remained popular throughout the '40s. Bangles were wide and three-dimensional, often with a single large rectangular-cut gemstone (aquamarine and citrine were

Doyle New York

Birds became an increasingly popular motif during this time. "Bird on a Rock" brooch, platinum, 18k gold, pavé-set with 70 round diamonds of 2.75 carats, polished gold beak, feathers and legs, ruby eye, perched atop cushion-cut citrine measuring 29 mm, signed Schlumberger, Tiffany, approximately 18.3 dwt.; 2 1/2". Doyle catalog note: In the late 1950s, Jean Schlumberger was invited to design for Tiffany & Co., creating whimsical and surrealist pieces incorporating natural and organic forms in his work. This iconic design was originally created in the 1960s for the Tiffany yellow cushion-cut diamond of 128.50 carats. **$25,000**

favored) in the center of a scroll or bow of gold with small colored stone accents. Sentiment was expressed in charms of personal significance, some suspended from the traditional link bracelet, others mounted on wide hinged bangles or cuffs. Charms were also fine jewelry's form of whimsy. Disney cartoon characters became popular, especially after the appearance of the first feature length animated film, "Snow White and the Seven Dwarfs," in 1937.

Dress clips, the ornamental mainstay of the early '30s, became even more versatile as the central removable decoration of bangle bracelets, and as the *passe-partout*—another Van Cleef & Arpels invention (introduced in

Skinner, Inc.

Earclips came into vogue with the introduction of the clipback finding. Gold and cultured pearl "fireworks" earclips, 18k, Tiffany & Co., signed, 1 1/8". **$1,020**

1938)—an enhancer for a snake chain necklace. The ubiquitous double clip brooch also continued to be worn through the '40s. Early '30s pairs of clips were flat, geometric, symmetrical twins; later they became more three-dimensional and asymmetrical mirror images or figurals. The double-pronged hinged clip finding took the place of the flat-backed clip by the end of the '30s. This type of fastening continued to be used on fine jewelry, often with the addition of a safety catch for one or both prongs.

During the war years, clothing fashions grew more severe and masculine, but jewelry, especially brooches, became more feminine. Large floral sprays were prevalent, worn high on a square-shouldered jacket, like a corsage of real flowers. Bicolor gold ribbon bows were another favorite, as were gem-set birds and butterflies. Necklaces became a focal point, shortened to collarbone or choker length. The flexible, slinky flattened gold tube, known variously as snake chain, gas pipe, or mouse tail, first exhibited in 1934, remained popular throughout the '40s. Earrings became earclips with the introduction of the clipback finding, patented in 1934. The emphasis was on the lobe rather than below it. Multi-petaled flower heads, scrolls and cornucopia were popular motifs. Pendant earrings continued to be worn at night, but were usually wider at the top, narrower at the bottom. Rings were massive, generally set with a large central colored gemstone flanked by scrolls of gold

or small gemstones of contrasting color. Suites and demi-parures returned to favor after a hiatus of several decades, in matched brooches and earrings, clips and earrings, and necklaces, bracelets and earrings.

French jewelers continued to be innovative and influential designers until 1940, when France fell under German occupation. Suzanne Belperron (1900-1983) was a celebrated French artist-jeweler whose distinctive style must be studied to be recognized because she seldom signed her work. She favored inexpensive gemstones like citrine and rock crystal, often sculpturally carved or set in clusters. She worked briefly for Cartier and also ran her own shop; her longest association was with Jean Herz, with whom she formed the partnership Herz-Belperron in 1945.

Van Cleef & Arpels was one famous firm whose designs came to prominence during the prewar period. In addition to the aforementioned creations, they are credited with the invention of the "invisible setting" of calibré-cut gemstones, used primarily for sapphires and rubies. Another of their well-known designs was the ballerina clip or brooch. This design actually originated in the United States, executed in the early '40s by John Rubel Co. for Van Cleef & Arpels, New York. It inspired a host of female figurals that remained popular through the '50s.

Cartier, long renowned for its impeccably crafted original designs, continued to produce distinctive, mostly figural pieces before the war. They even managed to create some new designs during wartime. Their famous "Bird in a Cage" and "Liberated Bird" brooches, executed in 1942 and 1944, respectively, symbolized the occupation and the liberation of Paris.

After 1940, most European jewelry production was curtailed, although the large French houses managed to stay afloat with a limited output of mostly prewar designs. By contrast, having been cut off from Europe during World War II and with no Paris fashions to emulate, American jewelers and their designs came to the fore. Some of these jewelers were transplanted Europeans, others were home-grown. One house, which became particularly well-known for their Retro Modern designs, was a merger of American and French firms: Trabert & Hoeffer-Mauboussin. Joining forces just after the stock market crash in 1929, the company became famous for their line of Retro-styled jewels named "Reflection" in 1938. Their slogan was "Reflection–your personality in a jewel." The unique feature of this line was a standardized array of elements that the customer could arrange and combine to suit her fancy. Trabert & Hoeffer-Mauboussin were among the first to take advantage of the recently developed method of mass-production using lost-wax casting with vulcanized rubber molds, which facilitated the making of interchangeable components for the Reflection line. While the firm of Trabert & Hoeffer, Inc. continues today, the association with Mauboussin was terminated in the 1950s.

Texas-born Paul Flato (b. 1900) opened his first salon in New York in the late '20s. His fame and fortune seemed assured when he opened a second establishment in Los Angeles in 1937, catering to Hollywood's elite. He was known for a wide variety of original, whimsical, naturalistic, and surrealistic designs. Fame and fortune were fleeting, however. His business closed in the early 1940s. He was later "rediscovered" in Texas, consequently, more information about him and his work is available.

One of Flato's designers, a European émigré who had already made a name for himself working for Chanel in Paris, was Fulco Santostefano della Cerda, duc di Verdura (1898-1978), known simply as Verdura. After leaving Flato in 1939, he opened his own shop in New York. He was known for his bold and imaginative designs and figural conceits. He emphasized design rather than large gemstones, the importance of which he dismissed, reputedly saying that "mineralogy is not jewelry." He occasionally incorporated shells and pebbles in his work.

Seaman Schepps (1881-1972), a native American, opened his first shops in California, but he moved to New York in 1921, where his establishment remained, except for a five-year hiatus from 1929 to 1934. His work reflects influences by Belperron, Flato, and Verdura in his sculptural and figural pieces. His most-often seen design is for clip earrings, a pair of gem-set turbo (snail-shaped) shells, inspired by Verdura.

Less well-publicized perhaps than their prestigious New York competitors, manufacturers in Newark, New Jersey, continued to produce well-made and affordable gold jewelry in the prevailing style of the period. Geared to conservative tastes, the pieces were more restrained examples of the "tailored" look that was popularly worn with suits at the time.

CIRCA 1945-1960

History records wars as lines of demarcation. What happens after them is usually a radical departure from what was happening before and during wartime. World War II was no exception.

Post-war prosperity unleashed an indulgence in luxury long frustrated by deprivation. All aspects of popular culture changed, including a marked change in fashion. Christian Dior introduced his "New Look" in 1947: long, full skirts, nipped-in waists, unpadded, sloping shoulders, tight bodices, and décolleté necklines. Femininity was back in style. To complement the look, jewelry had to change, too.

In fact, jewelry design took off in two divergent directions, that of the "traditionalists" of fine jewelry, including the large houses and those who designed for them, and that of the new modernist designs of avant-garde studio artists. Among the former group, there was a return to an extravagant display of all kinds of gemstones, but especially, diamonds were a girl's best friend once again. In 1948, De Beers Corp. set the tone for the era with its now-famous slogan, "A diamond is forever." A nearly imperceptible flexible platinum wire setting (said to have been inspired by a holly wreath), pioneered by diamond magnate Harry Winston around 1946, allowed clusters of stones to dominate a jewel. Fancy cuts, such as marquise and pear, were particularly favored in diamond jewelry.

The motifs and forms of traditional jewelry in the '50s and early '60s were not a radical departure from those of the '40s, but their execution was decidedly different. Where '40s pieces had a heavy, solid, and smooth polished look (even though they may have been hollow and light in terms of actual weight), '50s pieces were open and airy with textured surfaces such as Florentine (brushed metal), ropetwisted or braided wire, mesh, reeding, fluting, and piercing. Yellow gold was predominant except for all-diamond jewels, for

Whereas 1940s pieces had a heavy, solid look, pieces in the '50s and '60s were open and airy with textured surfaces such as Florentine. Ruby, diamond and gold bracelet, circa 1960, full-cut diamonds weighing approximately 1.75 carats, alternating with round-cut rubies weighing approximately 2 carats, framed by Florentine finished 14k yellow gold chevron-shaped links, 7" x 3/4". **$836**

which the preferred metal was once again platinum.

Following the trend for matching accessories, the suite returned in force as a full *parure* of necklace, bracelet, earrings, and brooch. Floral motifs were still in vogue, as well as a variety of leaf shapes, with increasing emphasis on gemstones and texture. Necklaces remained short as chokers, collars, or bibs. These could be draped, swirled, or fringed in gold or entirely gem-set. Diamond necklaces typically featured a row or fringe of baguette and/or marquise diamonds flanked by scrolled or draped side elements. Bracelets were primarily of the flexible sort, often gemstone-encrusted. Charm bracelets also maintained their popularity. Earrings were usually circular, floral, or foliate yellow gold clips for day, long fringes of gemstones, usually diamonds, for evening wear. Upswept styles that enveloped the ear were also common. Brooches in the forms of animals and people continued to amuse, more often as cartoon-like caricatures than realistic portrayals. Stylized foliate sprays entirely set with numerous baguette, marquise, and pear-shaped stones were another often-seen form. Modernism exerted its influence in the form of starburst and "atomic" shapes. Rings were domed clusters of gemstones or one large stone surrounded by smaller stones, usually marquise or other fancy-cut diamonds.

The famous *haute joaillerie* houses—Cartier, Van Cleef & Arpels, et al—continued to produce opulent jewels in new designs as well as reprising pre-war classics that were finding a wider audience among the newly prosperous. One French house that began making its mark in the early 1950s was Sterlé, founded by Pierre Sterlé (1905-1978) in 1934. Most famous among his designs is a fantastic "Bird of Paradise" brooch–a bird, not a plant, with a carved amethyst head, textured yellow gold body, fringes of foxtail chain (called *fil d'ange*) for tail and wings, set with turquoise, with diamond-set edges and beak. The company was purchased by Chaumet in 1976.

American jewelry firms began achieving greater recognition in the 1950s. Harry Winston (1896-1978), a retailer, broker and manufacturer since the 1930s, made an even bigger name for himself with his touring "Court of Jewels" exhibit, which opened in 1949, the same year he purchased the Hope Diamond. (He donated it to the Smithsonian Institution in 1958.) For obvious reasons, Winston became known as the "King of Diamonds."

Julius Cohen (d. 1995) began working for Harry Winston in 1942, after leaving his uncle's firm, Oscar Heyman & Bros. He opened his own salon in New York in 1955. Perhaps because of his association with Winston, he continued to incorporate large diamonds in his original designs. The "Fantasy of the Phoenix" brooch is an example of a collaboration between jewelry Cohen and client Robert Tobin.

Hammerman Bros., founded in New York in 1946, was a manufacturing jewelry firm known for fine quality mainstream jewelry. Their mark is a conjoined HB, which is sometimes confused with a similar mark used by Oscar Heyman & Bros., another prestigious New York jewelry manufacturer, founded in 1906.

Although it comes up for sale at auction from time to time, no written documentation has yet been discovered for a distinctive type of oxidized steel jewelry made for an Asian art and antiques store, G.T. Marsh & Co., in Monterey, California.

San Francisco antique jewelry dealer Lynne Arkin provided the following information: "Founded by George Turner Marsh in 1876 in San Francisco, it became familiarly known as Marsh's. It is recognized as the oldest retail business in the U.S. dealing in Japanese and Chinese art. In 1927, the Marsh family built the architectural landmark in Monterey, California, that was their shop until February 2001. The senior Mr. Marsh had a jeweler-craftsman who worked for him, and created the unique black matte finish steel jewelry set with pearls, diamonds, gold…etc. in the 1940s, '50s, and '60s."

Marsh pieces are not always signed, but the style and materials are characteristic enough to safely attribute them.

CIRCA 1960-1975

Beginning in 1955 under Walter Hoving's directorship, Tiffany & Co. gained new distinction with designs by Jean Schlumberger (1907-1987), a former associate of Elsa Schiaparelli. Known for his use of colored gemstones, enamels, and animals and other motifs inspired by nature, Schlumberger became the first Tiffany designer whose jewels bore his signature. American-born Donald Claflin (d. 1979), noted for his whimsical animal designs, joined Tiffany's in 1965. Claflin had previously worked for David Webb.

After opening an office in New York in 1946 and a salon in 1963, David Webb (1925-1975) came to prominence in the mid-1960s when both clothing and jewelry styles were undergoing a significant change. He fostered, if not initiated, a trend for wearing quantities of large-scale, flamboyant jewels of Renaissance and fantasy-inspired design. Webb's animal motifs were influenced by Jeanne Toussaint of Cartier, creator of the famous panther jewels for the Duchess of Windsor and other wealthy clients. Webb's "make a statement" jewels are readily identifiable.

Designers Verdura, Seaman Schepps, and Suzanne Belperron remained active through the 1960s.

In the late 1950s and '60s, the fashion world turned its eyes to Italy, where clothing designers like Emilio Pucci were garnering attention. Italian jewelers were also creating a stir. The fashion for yellow gold created a new demand for Italian goldsmiths' talents. Foremost among Italian jewelers are the two family-run houses of Bulgari and Buccellati. The former house is famous for its Renaissance-inspired colored gemstone pieces and classical designs incorporating ancient coins with heavy gold chains. Buccellati is known for its patterned textured engraving using a bulino graver, a technique also inspired by Renaissance goldwork, particularly that of Benvenuto Cellini. Both firms expanded to international branches, including the United States in 1952 (Buccellati) and 1970 (Bulgari).

The 1960s were indeed a time of extreme changes, in fashion and in society at large. "Flower power" and the sexual revolution were watchwords of the day. There was a rejection of "the establishment" in favor of radical ideas and behavior. The mid-1960s also signaled the beginning of a renaissance of international style and multi-cultural consciousness, incorporating American, French, English, Italian, Islamic, and East Indian motifs, materials, and artistry. Ethnic looks became fashionable. New trends in art also inspired fashion and jewelry design: the black-and-white geometry of Op Art and the colorful irreverence of Pop Art found expression in jewelry and fabrics.

New practitioners of a new jewelry style emerged in the mid-1960s as well. Although conventional precious materials continued to be used, the designs themselves were decidedly unconventional and large in scale. Abstract, textured, jagged-edged, and amorphous organic forms took shape in yellow gold, sometimes accented with diamonds and/or pearls. Other more unusual stones were also used, including clusters of rough crystals, nodules and irregularly

Sotheby's

Platinum, 18k gold, rock crystal, diamond, ruby, enamel and cultured pearl bracelet, David Webb, circa 1973, composed of 29 strands of cultured pearls, ranging in size from approximately 3.4 to 3.1 mm, the carved rock crystal clasp depicting a panther head set with numerous round and marquise-shaped diamonds weighing approximately 3.95 carats, with two pear-shaped ruby eyes weighing 1.30 carats, applied with black enamel, signed David Webb, with signed box, 8" long. **$46,875**

polished colored stones, and organic materials. In England, the master of this style was Andrew Grima (b. 1921), who opened his own business in 1965. Arthur King (1921-1986), based in New York, also worked in a similar vein, as did Gilbert Albert in Switzerland. Like the Modernists of the 1950s, these and other designers of the period all followed a similar path, but each had his own individual mode of expression.

Wendy Ramshaw's (b. 1939) mode of expression was a decided departure from other jewelry designers of the late 20th century. The London jeweler's work straddled the line between the artistic and the commercial. Her "Picasso's Ladies" series is perhaps the most well-known of her signature styles, particularly the stacks of multiple gold and gemstone rings mounted on lathe-turned Perspex (acrylic) stands that become part of the design.

The firm of Kutchinsky was founded in London by Polish immigrant jewelers in 1893, but although it was successful from the beginning, it wasn't until after World War II that its international reputation was established. Kutchinsky jewels of the 1960s reflect a cosmopolitan approach to design.

More traditionally designed jewels of the late 1960s and early 1970s also display a unique period twist: the setting of diamonds in yellow gold rather than a white metal (platinum, white gold, or silver). Diamonds were often combined with colored gemstones, especially turquoise and rubies, or emeralds and rubies, typically framed in textured yellow gold or corded yellow gold wire. These stone combinations were also worked into Mogul-inspired pendants, necklaces, and suites.

William Ruser (1908-1994?) was a mainstream jeweler whose Beverly Hills salon catered to Hollywood stars, including Joan Crawford and Loretta Young. He was noted for incorporating freshwater pearls into his whimsical poodle and cherub designs, some of which were actually created by the husband and wife team of Cy and Vera Wood (known as "Cyvra") of Topanga, California. One of the most popular series they designed was the "child of the week," based on the well-known nursery rhyme ("Monday's child is fair of face, Tuesday's child is full of grace," etc.).

A few auction houses have recognized the 1950s as a "period," including circa dates in their descriptions; others do not. Most 1960s and 1970s jewelry is still described as contemporary or simply not dated. Auction house catalogs of "important" or "magnificent" (i.e., very high end) jewelry usually include biographical information on designers and manufacturers, which can be helpful. Now that the 20st century is here, historians will undoubtedly acquire a clearer perspective on later 20th century styles, and perhaps someone will even come up with names for them, and more reference material will continue to be published.

Sotheby's

Fine diamond bracelet, Boucheron, circa 1925, flexible wide band composed of four rows of square links set with circular-cut diamonds, embellished with pairs of stylized roses each centering on a circular-cut stone, mounted in platinum, signed Boucheron Paris, French maker's and assay marks, approximately 7" long. **$625,980**

Sotheby's

Silver, gold and diamond bracelet, Mario Buccellati, circa 1925, articulated strap of openwork design, the rectangular panels set with numerous rose-cut diamonds weighing approximately 4 carats, signed M. Buccellati, with signed box, 7" long. **$32,500**

Jewelry courtesy the Steve Fishbach Collection; photo by Linda Lombardo

Amethyst cabochon and rose diamond bracelet set in 14k gold, circa 1900s, 7 1/4". **$3,500**

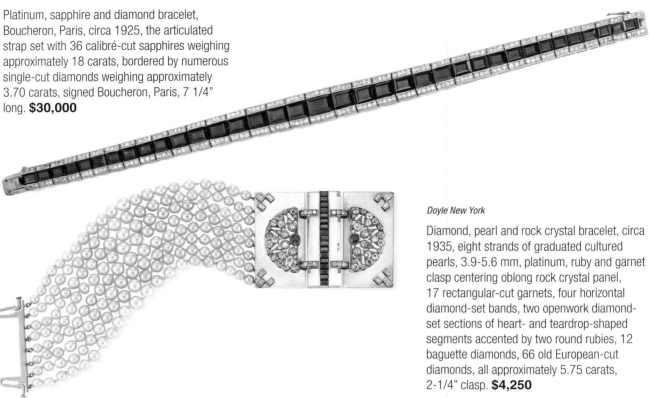

Sotheby's

Platinum, sapphire and diamond bracelet, Boucheron, Paris, circa 1925, the articulated strap set with 36 calibré-cut sapphires weighing approximately 18 carats, bordered by numerous single-cut diamonds weighing approximately 3.70 carats, signed Boucheron, Paris, 7 1/4" long. **$30,000**

Doyle New York

Diamond, pearl and rock crystal bracelet, circa 1935, eight strands of graduated cultured pearls, 3.9-5.6 mm, platinum, ruby and garnet clasp centering oblong rock crystal panel, 17 rectangular-cut garnets, four horizontal diamond-set bands, two openwork diamond-set sections of heart- and teardrop-shaped segments accented by two round rubies, 12 baguette diamonds, 66 old European-cut diamonds, all approximately 5.75 carats, 2-1/4" clasp. **$4,250**

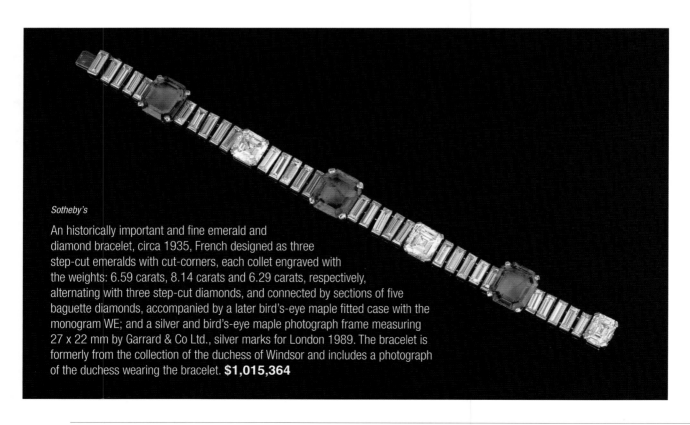

Sotheby's

An historically important and fine emerald and diamond bracelet, circa 1935, French designed as three step-cut emeralds with cut-corners, each collet engraved with the weights: 6.59 carats, 8.14 carats and 6.29 carats, respectively, alternating with three step-cut diamonds, and connected by sections of five baguette diamonds, accompanied by a later bird's-eye maple fitted case with the monogram WE; and a silver and bird's-eye maple photograph frame measuring 27 x 22 mm by Garrard & Co Ltd., silver marks for London 1989. The bracelet is formerly from the collection of the duchess of Windsor and includes a photograph of the duchess wearing the bracelet. **$1,015,364**

Kenneth Jay Lane jewelry

Double dragons simulated carved jadeite spring-hinged cuff bracelet, 1960s, faux coral cabochons, emeralds and diamonds, fancy cast 22k gold-plated metal, signed © KJL, 3 1/2" wide. **$240**

Sotheby's

Platinum, 18k white gold and diamond bangle-bracelet/brooch combination, circa 1935, Raymond Templier, France, hinged sculptural bangle supporting a detachable diamond-set clip of oval shape with two arms affixed at the opening set with old European-cut, round and single-cut diamonds weighing approximately 6.25 carats, internal circumference 5 7/8", signed Raymond Templier, French assay marks. **$128,500**

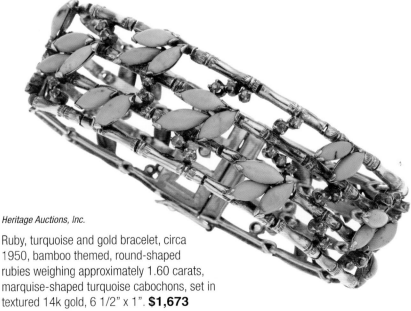

Heritage Auctions, Inc.

Ruby, turquoise and gold bracelet, circa 1950, bamboo themed, round-shaped rubies weighing approximately 1.60 carats, marquise-shaped turquoise cabochons, set in textured 14k gold, 6 1/2" x 1". **$1,673**

Skinner, Inc.

Diamond bracelet, France, circa 1940s, set with three old European-cut diamonds weighing approximately 1, 0.90, and 0.85 carats, further set with old European- and single-cut diamonds, approximate total weight 17 carats, rhodium-plated silver mount, French maker's mark and guarantee stamp, 7 1/4" long. **$9,600**

Clip and bangle bracelet combination, 18k gold, Cartier, Paris, circa 1940, centered by three flowers accented by gold ropetwists, set with round diamonds weighing approximately 3.25 carats, bangle-bracelet and two flower clips signed Cartier Paris, all components numbered 09003, with French workshop and assay marks, internal circumference approximately 6". **$43,750**

Turquoise, sapphire and gold bracelet, circa 1950, turquoise cabochons and round-cut sapphires set in 18k yellow gold, tongue-in-groove clasp with two figure-eight safeties, 7 1/4" x 1/2". **$4,780**

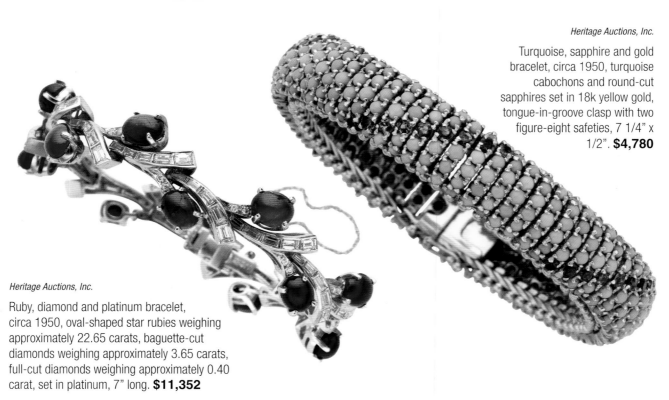

Ruby, diamond and platinum bracelet, circa 1950, oval-shaped star rubies weighing approximately 22.65 carats, baguette-cut diamonds weighing approximately 3.65 carats, full-cut diamonds weighing approximately 0.40 carat, set in platinum, 7" long. **$11,352**

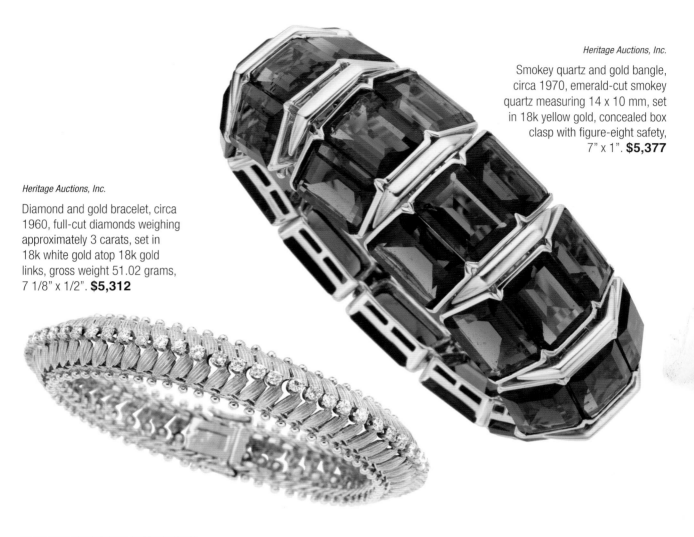

Heritage Auctions, Inc.

Smokey quartz and gold bangle, circa 1970, emerald-cut smokey quartz measuring 14 x 10 mm, set in 18k yellow gold, concealed box clasp with figure-eight safety, 7" x 1". **$5,377**

Heritage Auctions, Inc.

Diamond and gold bracelet, circa 1960, full-cut diamonds weighing approximately 3 carats, set in 18k white gold atop 18k gold links, gross weight 51.02 grams, 7 1/8" x 1/2". **$5,312**

Heritage Auctions, Inc.

Diamond and gold hinged bangle bracelet, Van Gogh, circa 1960, full-cut diamonds weighing approximately 0.70 carat, set in 14k white gold, applied on heavily textured 14k yellow gold, marked Van Gogh, 6 1/4" x 5/8". **$2,390**

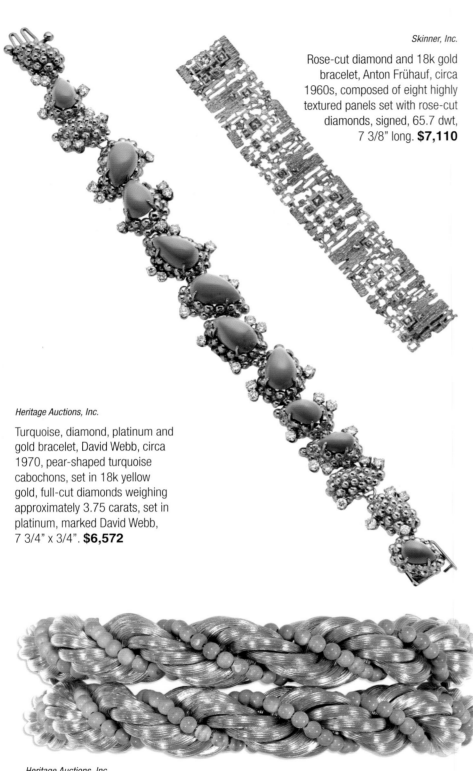

Skinner, Inc.

Rose-cut diamond and 18k gold bracelet, Anton Frühauf, circa 1960s, composed of eight highly textured panels set with rose-cut diamonds, signed, 65.7 dwt, 7 3/8" long. **$7,110**

Heritage Auctions, Inc.

Turquoise, diamond, platinum and gold bracelet, David Webb, circa 1970, pear-shaped turquoise cabochons, set in 18k yellow gold, full-cut diamonds weighing approximately 3.75 carats, set in platinum, marked David Webb, 7 3/4" x 3/4". **$6,572**

Heritage Auctions, Inc.

Turquoise and gold bracelets, circa 1960, fashioned with a rope motif featuring turquoise beads measuring 3 mm, wire wrapped around textured 18k yellow gold links, forming soft bangles, box clasps with safeties, 7" x 1/2". **$2,151**

Heritage Auctions, Inc.

Diamond, blue enamel and gold bangle bracelet, Tiffany & Co., circa 1960, single-cut diamonds weighing approximately 1 carat, set in 18k white gold, blue enamel applied on 18k yellow gold, 6 1/2" long. **$2,270**

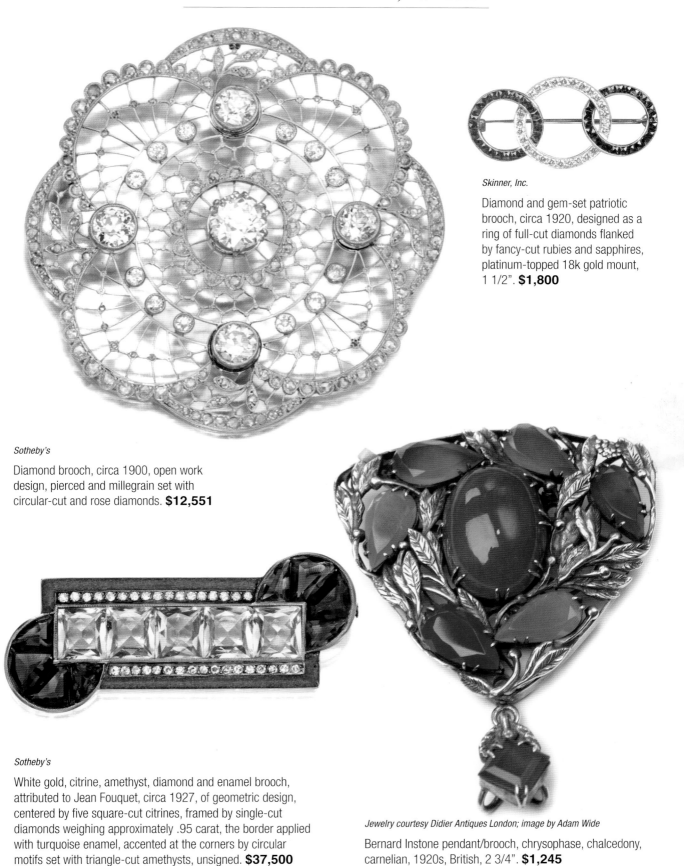

Skinner, Inc.

Diamond and gem-set patriotic brooch, circa 1920, designed as a ring of full-cut diamonds flanked by fancy-cut rubies and sapphires, platinum-topped 18k gold mount, 1 1/2". **$1,800**

Sotheby's

Diamond brooch, circa 1900, open work design, pierced and millegrain set with circular-cut and rose diamonds. **$12,551**

Sotheby's

White gold, citrine, amethyst, diamond and enamel brooch, attributed to Jean Fouquet, circa 1927, of geometric design, centered by five square-cut citrines, framed by single-cut diamonds weighing approximately .95 carat, the border applied with turquoise enamel, accented at the corners by circular motifs set with triangle-cut amethysts, unsigned. **$37,500**

Jewelry courtesy Didier Antiques London; image by Adam Wide

Bernard Instone pendant/brooch, chrysophase, chalcedony, carnelian, 1920s, British, 2 3/4". **$1,245**

Skinner, Inc.

Cartier Pendulette, circa 1949, jadeite, diamond, coral and MOP dial carved with bird and leaf motif, faceted coral beads and green jadeite ring, engraved with no. 200, signed, including Cartier box. **$13,000**

Sotheby's

Moonstone, ruby and diamond brooch, Raymond Yard, circa 1950, circular brooch set with 20 oval cabochon moonstones, 15 round rubies and five round diamonds, mounted in platinum, signed Yard. **$9,375**

Heritage Auctions, Inc.

Retro ruby, diamond and two-tone gold brooch, circa 1940, flower design, round-cut rubies, single-cut diamond, set in 14k pink and yellow gold, pinstem and catch on reverse, 2 3/16" x 2 3/16". **$478**

Heritage Auctions, Inc.

Diamond and platinum clip-brooch, circa 1950, pear-shaped diamonds weighing approximately 2.30 carats, marquise-shaped diamonds weighing approximately 2.10 carats, full-cut diamonds weighing approximately 1.35 carats, baguette-cut diamonds weighing approximately 1.90 carats, set in platinum, clip mechanism and catch on reverse, total diamond weight is approximately 7.65 carats, 1 3/4" x 1 1/4". **$4,182**

Heritage Auctions, Inc.

Diamond and platinum pendant-brooch, circa 1950, full-cut diamonds weighing approximately 4 carats, baguette-cut diamonds weighing approximately 0.60 carat, set in platinum, retractable bail, pinstem and catch on reverse, total diamond weight is approximately 4.60 carats, 1 3/4" x 1 1/2". **$2,125**

Heritage Auctions, Inc.

Diamond and platinum brooch, Linz, circa 1950, marquise-cut diamond measuring 12 x 6.10 x 4 mm and weighing approximately 1.65 carats, European- and full-cut diamonds weighing approximately 5.35 carats, set in platinum, pinstem and catch, marked Linz, total diamond weight is approximately 7 carats, 2 1/4" x 7/8". **$5,078**

Heritage Auctions, Inc.

Diamond and platinum pendant-brooch, circa 1950, suspends pear-shaped diamonds weighing approximately 0.70 carat, framed by full-cut diamonds weighing approximately 2.65 carats, baguette-cut diamonds weighing approximately 2.30 carats, set in platinum, pendant hanger, pinstem and catch on reverse, total diamond weight is approximately 5.65 carats, 1 5/8" x 1 3/8". **$3,250**

Skinner, Inc.

Gem-set and 18k gold flower brooch, Cartier, circa 1950s, set with a carved ivory rose blossom with cabochon turquoise center, ribbed leaves set with full-cut diamond melee accents, signed, 2 3/4". **$23,700**

Heritage Auctions, Inc.

Diamond and platinum pendant-brooch, circa 1950, pear and marquise-shaped diamonds weighing approximately 2.30 carats, full-cut diamonds weighing approximately 4.40 carats, baguette, tapered baguette and triangle-cut diamonds weighing approximately 5.05 carats, set in platinum, bail, pinstem and catch on reverse, 2 3/8" x 1 3/4". **$6,572**

Heritage Auctions, Inc.

Diamond, turquoise, cultured pearl and gold brooch, circa 1950, round and oval-shaped turquoise cabochons ranging in size from 11.10 x 8.15 mm to 7 x 6.90 mm, cultured pearls ranging in size from 6.50-6 mm to 5.50-5 mm, full- and single-cut diamonds weighing approximately 0.20 carat, set in 18k white and yellow gold, pinstem and catch on reverse, 3 1/2" x 1 3/4". **$1,015**

Heritage Auctions, Inc.

Turquoise, diamond, ruby, cultured pearl and gold brooch, circa 1950, kingfisher features round-shaped turquoise cabochons weighing approximately 0.50 carat, single-cut diamonds weighing approximately 0.03 carat, round-shaped ruby cabochon weighing approximately 0.05 carat, cultured pearl measuring 3.50 mm, set in textured 18k gold, pinstem and catch on reverse, 1 5/8" x 1 5/8". **$2,151**

Heritage Auctions, Inc.

Cultured pearl, diamond and platinum clip-brooch, circa 1950, cultured pearls ranging in size from 4.20 x 4.40 mm to 6.60 x 6.70 mm, full- and single-cut diamonds weighing approximately 2.35 carats, baguette-cut diamonds weighing approximately 0.40 carat, set in platinum, double pinstem and catch mechanism on reverse, 1 5/8" x 1 3/8". **$1,792**

Heritage Auctions, Inc.

Turquoise, diamond, lapis lazuli and gold domed clip-brooch, circa 1960, oval-shaped turquoise cabochon measuring 19 x 13.50 mm, full-cut diamonds weighing approximately 1.60 carats, surrounded by pear-shaped turquoise and lapis lazuli cabochons, set in textured 18k yellow gold, double pinstem and catch mechanism on reverse, 1 7/8" x 1 5/8". **$3,824**

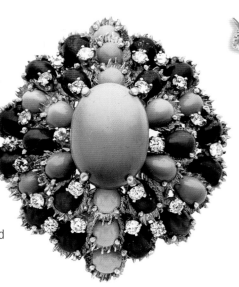

Heritage Auctions, Inc.

Diamond and gold brooch, circa 1960, full-cut diamonds weighing approximately 1.10 carats, set in 18k gold, clip mechanism on reverse, 2 1/2" x 1 1/2". **$687**

Heritage Auctions, Inc.

Turquoise, diamond, platinum and gold clip brooch, circa 1950, Boucheron, designed as a floral display resting within a Grecian urn-style vase, round and fancy-shaped turquoise cabochons set in 18k yellow gold, full-cut diamonds weighing approximately 3 carats, set in platinum, clip mechanism on reverse, marked Boucheron, Paris, reference #45443, French hallmarks, 2 1/2" x 1 1/4". **$7,767**

Skinner, Inc.

Palm tree brooch, 18k gold, coral and diamond, Cartier, France, circa 1960, with full-cut diamond and heart-shape coral accents, numbered, export stamps, signed Cartier Inc., made in France, 2 1/4" long. **$5,500**

Heritage Auctions, Inc.

Ruby, diamond, and platinum pendant-brooch, circa 1950, designed as a butterfly, round-cut rubies ranging in size from 4 mm to 5 mm, full-, baguette- and marquise-cut diamonds weighing approximately 3.70 carats, set in platinum, pendant bail, pinstem and catch on reverse, 1 1/4" x 1 1/2". **$1,792**

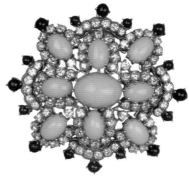

Jewelry courtesy Lee Shau Kwan, Esther Woo Jan; image by John F. Pipia

Peacock brooch, jadeite cabochons, rubies, diamonds, 1968-'72, 2 1/4". Betty Ma notes, "Chinese artists are partial to peacocks, from paintings, embroideries and carvings. The jadeite stones are vibrant, translucent, colors well matched. Use of rubies and sapphires is well integrated. This peacock represents what I would like Chinese-Americans, Americans and all jewelry lovers to think of jadeite: a piece of art in its natural, untreated form, and modern when done tastefully. This piece has it all. The person who created it was well trained and knew when to stop with the materials on hand." **$5,000-$7,000**

Skinner, Inc.

Coral, 18k gold, lapis, and diamond pendant-brooch, Italy, circa 1960s, set with oval coral and round lapis cabochons and full-cut diamonds, approximate total diamond weight 5 carats, two "maker's mark" panels, one a spiral, another an M, 2 1/4". **$4,740**

Skinner, Inc.

Carved coral, 18k gold and diamond pendant-brooch, circa 1960s, depicting a Buddha head with full-cut diamond melee collar and headdress, within a textured surround, 2 1/2". **$1,422**

Heritage Auctions, Inc.

Turquoise, diamond and gold flower clip-brooch, circa 1960, one oval-shaped turquoise cabochon measuring 17 x 12 mm, encircled by full-cut diamonds, framed by round turquoise cabochons measuring 8.50 x 9 mm, single-cut diamonds, set in heavily textured 18k yellow gold, French hallmarks, 2 3/4" x 1 3/4". **$5,377**

Heritage Auctions, Inc.

Diamond, emerald, ruby, lapis and turquoise pendant-brooch, J.G. Jlry (Jack Gutschneider, NYC), circa 1960s, 60 mm across, 18k gold, centered by a 12 x 10 mm lapis lazuli cabochon, round diamonds and emeralds, four ruby cabochons, four large Persian turquoise cabochons, pin back and a bale, 27.4 grams, signed on the back center bar. **$2,270**

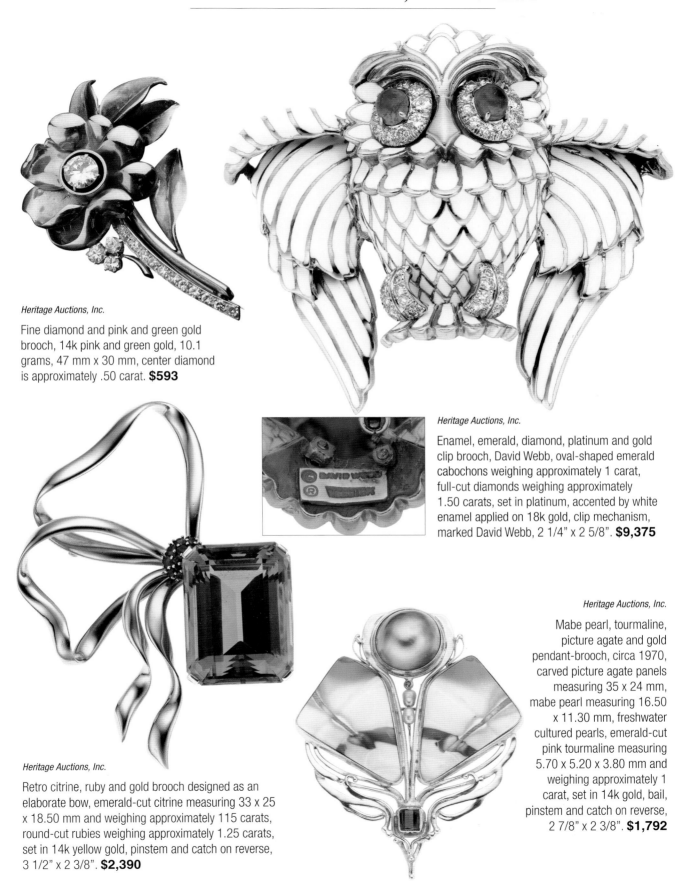

Heritage Auctions, Inc.

Fine diamond and pink and green gold brooch, 14k pink and green gold, 10.1 grams, 47 mm x 30 mm, center diamond is approximately .50 carat. **$593**

Heritage Auctions, Inc.

Enamel, emerald, diamond, platinum and gold clip brooch, David Webb, oval-shaped emerald cabochons weighing approximately 1 carat, full-cut diamonds weighing approximately 1.50 carats, set in platinum, accented by white enamel applied on 18k gold, clip mechanism, marked David Webb, 2 1/4" x 2 5/8". **$9,375**

Heritage Auctions, Inc.

Mabe pearl, tourmaline, picture agate and gold pendant-brooch, circa 1970, carved picture agate panels measuring 35 x 24 mm, mabe pearl measuring 16.50 x 11.30 mm, freshwater cultured pearls, emerald-cut pink tourmaline measuring 5.70 x 5.20 x 3.80 mm and weighing approximately 1 carat, set in 14k gold, bail, pinstem and catch on reverse, 2 7/8" x 2 3/8". **$1,792**

Heritage Auctions, Inc.

Retro citrine, ruby and gold brooch designed as an elaborate bow, emerald-cut citrine measuring 33 x 25 x 18.50 mm and weighing approximately 115 carats, round-cut rubies weighing approximately 1.25 carats, set in 14k yellow gold, pinstem and catch on reverse, 3 1/2" x 2 3/8". **$2,390**

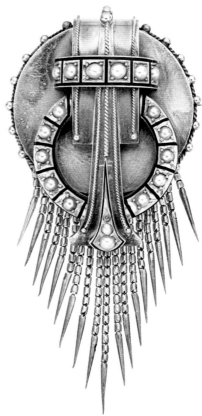

Skinner, Inc.

Whimsical 14k bicolor gold pendant/ brooch, Eric deKolb, circa 1970, designed as an apple in domino, signed, 47.6 dwt, 3 1/8" x 2 5/8". **$2,252**

Skinner, Inc.

Brooch, 14k gold and diamond, set with full-cut diamonds, approximate total weight 2.70 carats, 12.3 dwt, 1 7/8". **$1,800**

Heritage Auctions, Inc.

Multi-stone and gold brooch, circa 1970, designed as a butterfly, highlighted by modified rectangular-shaped citrine measuring 27 x 17.85 x 11.60 mm and weighing approximately 33 carats, enhanced by a myriad of colored gemstones of varying shape and size, such as garnet, peridot, amethyst, citrine and pink tourmaline, set in an open wirework 14k yellow gold frame. **$448**

Heritage Auctions, Inc.

Victorian pearl, enamel and gold pendant-brooch, designed as an elaborate tassel, half-pearls, blue and black enamel applied on 14k yellow gold, retractable bail, pin stem and catch mechanism on reverse, 3" x 1 3/8". **$480**

Heritage Auctions, Inc.

Pair of coral, diamond, emerald, lapis lazuli and gold brooches, circa 1970, each brooch features an oval-shaped coral cabochon measuring 18 x 13 mm, full-cut diamonds weighing approximately 0.60 carat, emerald and lapis lazuli cabochons, set in 18k yellow gold, 1 11/16" x 1 1/2". **$1,526**

Sotheby's

Platinum, gold, sapphire and enamel dress set, Cartier, circa 1920, comprising a pair of cuff links, four buttons, and three studs, set with 11 cabochon sapphires, accented by navy blue enamelwork, cuff links signed Cartier, one button numbered 1379. **$13,750**

Skinner, Inc.

Dress set, 18k gold and onyx, Tiffany & Co., comprising a pair of double cuff links and three shirt studs, each designed as a button, 12 dwt, signed. **$1,800**

Heritage Auctions, Inc.

Gentleman's ruby and gold tie bar, Van Cleef & Arpels, circa 1969, from the Batonnet Collection, features square-shaped rubies weighing approximately 0.35 carat, set in 18k gold, maker's mark for Van Cleef & Arpels, NY, 1/4" x 3/4". **$1,250**

Sotheby's

Dress set, 18k gold, sapphire and diamond, Van Cleef & Arpels, circa 1940, comprising a pair of cuff links and two studs, set with numerous round sapphires, accented by single-cut diamonds weighing approximately .85 carat, gross weight approximately 13 dwts, the cuff links signed Van Cleef & Arpels, with French assay marks, the studs with maker's mark and French assay marks. **$8,125**

Heritage Auctions, Inc.

Diamond and gold dress set, circa 1960, includes one pair of cuff links featuring full-cut diamonds, set in hand engraved 14k gold; together with three matching shirt studs. Cuff links are 1 1/4" x 3/4"; shirt studs are 1 1/8" x 7/16". **$597**

Sotheby's

Pair of platinum, natural pearl and diamond earclips, circa 1920, centered by two pearls measuring approximately 9.1 x 8.8 mm and 9 x 8.7 mm, framed by numerous old mine and single-cut diamonds weighing approximately 6 carats. **$12,500**

Sotheby's

Natural pearl and diamond pendent earrings, circa 1900, each circular-cut diamond suspending a drop-shaped natural pearl measuring approximately 0.4" x 0.4" x 0.6" mm and 0.4" x 0.4" x 0.6", respectively, capped with a foliate surmount millegrain-set with a circular-cut and rose diamonds, screw-back fittings. From the collection of Princess Frances Alice Poniatowska (1901-1989). **$408,530**

Pagoda earrings, circa 1930, chalcedony, coral, marcasite, onyx, each designed as a shaped chalcedony tablet suspended from marcasite pagoda with coral bead accents, cabochon onyx tops, silver mounts, hallmark of Theodor Fahrner. **$3,000 pair**

Jewelry courtesy Didier Antiques London; image by Adam Wide

Dorrie Nossiter garnet and pearl earrings, 1920s, British, 1". **$1,575**

Sotheby's

Natural pearl and diamond pendent ear clips, each suspending a natural drop-shaped pearl, capped with single-cut diamonds, the surmount set with a natural pearl of slightly grey tint and four circular-cut diamonds. **$36,995**

Sotheby's

Pair of gold, ruby, seed pearl, and enamel earclips, Cartier, Paris, circa 1935, the tops designed as lotus flowers accented by 28 ruby beads measuring approximately 4.7 to 2.8 mm and numerous seed pearls measuring approximately 4 to 2.6 mm, suspending articulated fringes comprising clusters of seed pearls and gold segments, the reverses of which are decorated with red, white and green enamel in floral motifs, signed Cartier Paris, with indistinct maker's marks and French assay marks. **$30,000**

Heritage Auctions, Inc.

Diamond and platinum earrings, circa 1950, pear-shaped diamonds weighing approximately 3.10 carats, full-cut diamonds weighing approximately 3.20 carats, set in platinum, completed by posts and omega backs, designed for pierced ears, 1 5/8" x 5/8". **$4,331**

Heritage Auctions, Inc.

Diamond and gold earrings, circa 1960, organic, full-cut diamonds weighing approximately 1.20 carats, set en tremblant in 18k white gold against a textured three-dimensional 18k yellow gold background, omega clips on reverse, designed for non-pierced ears and easily adjusted, 1 1/4" x 1". **$1,045**

Coral and diamond "Rose De Noël" earclips, Van Cleefs & Arpels, France, 1969, round diamonds weighing approximately 1.15 carats, the petals composed of carved white coral, mounted in 18k gold, signed V.C.A., Made in France, numbered 3V487-15, maker's marks, French assay marks. **$23,750**

Heritage Auctions, Inc.

Lapis lazuli and gold earrings, A. Cipullo, circa 1970, lapis lazuli discs set in 18k gold, clip backs, signed A. Cipullo, designed for non-pierced ears, 1" x 1". **$3,883**

Heritage Auctions, Inc.

Ruby, diamond and gold earrings, Van Cleef & Arpels, circa 1960, oval-shaped ruby cabochons weighing approximately 12 carats, full-cut diamonds weighing approximately 10 carats, set in 18k gold, rhodium finish, posts and clip backs, marked Van Cleef & Arpels, NY, reference #39706, gross weight 19.15 grams, designed for pierced ears but easily converted, 1" x 3/4". **$28,680**

Heritage Auctions, Inc.

Citrine and gold earrings, Paloma Picasso, Tiffany & Co., circa 1970, each features an oval-shaped citrine weighing approximately 9.50 carats, bezel set in 18k yellow gold, omega clip back on reverse, marked Paloma Picasso for Tiffany & Co., 15/16" x 13/16". **$1,912**

Heritage Auctions, Inc.

Black onyx and gold earrings, A. Cipullo, circa 1970, square-shaped black onyx tablets set in 18k gold, clip backs, signed A. Cipullo, designed for non-pierced ears, 1" x 1". **$3,585**

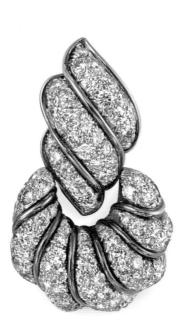

Doyle New York

David Webb earclips, platinum, 18k gold, hoops set with 198 round diamonds weighing approximately 11 carats, flared bombe platinum ribbons lined with slender polished gold bands, signed Webb for David Webb, approximately 19.7 dwt., 1 5/8". **$16,000**

Doyle New York

Pair of gold and diamond hoop earrings, 18k, 272 round diamonds approximately. 8.75 carats, approximately 12 dwt, posts, hinged hoops, 1 3/4" x 3/16", 1 3/8" diameter. **$10,000**

Heritage Auctions, Inc.

Black onyx, frosted rock crystal quartz and gold earrings, Cipullo, Cartier, circa 1973, each button earring features fancy-cut black onyx cabochons bezel set in 18k yellow gold, atop a frosted rock crystal quartz tablet, clip back on reverse, marked A. Cipullo for Aldo Cipullo, Cartier, designed for non-pierced ears, 1 1/8" x 1 1/8". **$4,780**

Heritage Auctions, Inc.

Carnelian and gold earrings, A. Cipullo, Cartier, circa 1974, carnelian tablet, 18k yellow gold knot, clip back on reverse, marked A. Cipullo for Aldo Cipullo and Cartier, designed for non-pierced ears, 1 1/18" x 1 1/8". **$5,078**

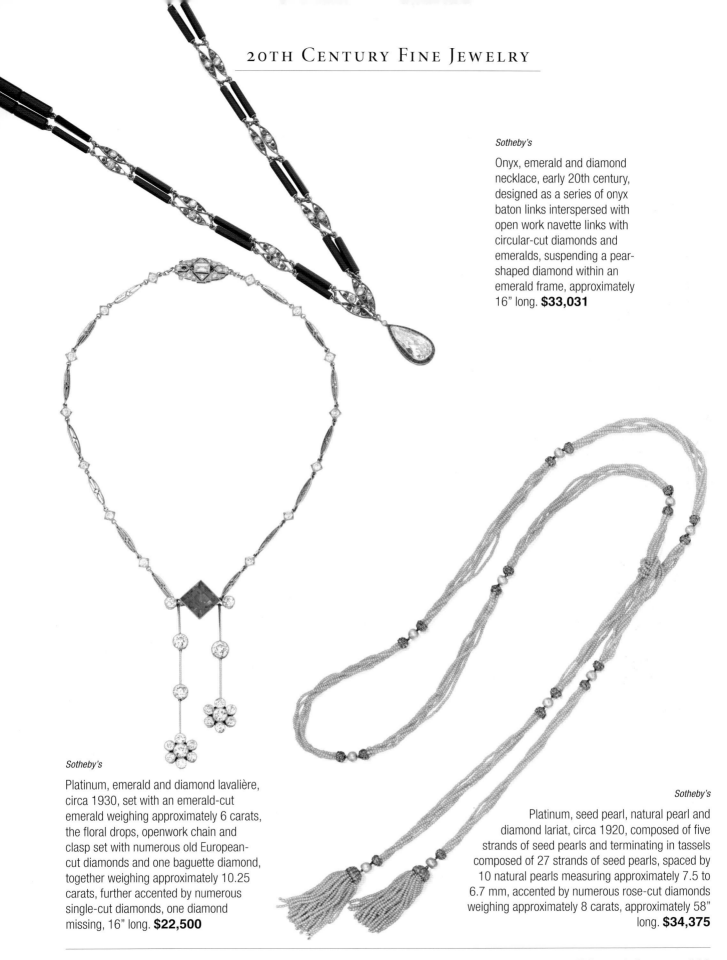

Sotheby's

Onyx, emerald and diamond necklace, early 20th century, designed as a series of onyx baton links interspersed with open work navette links with circular-cut diamonds and emeralds, suspending a pear-shaped diamond within an emerald frame, approximately 16" long. **$33,031**

Sotheby's

Platinum, emerald and diamond lavalière, circa 1930, set with an emerald-cut emerald weighing approximately 6 carats, the floral drops, openwork chain and clasp set with numerous old European-cut diamonds and one baguette diamond, together weighing approximately 10.25 carats, further accented by numerous single-cut diamonds, one diamond missing, 16" long. **$22,500**

Sotheby's

Platinum, seed pearl, natural pearl and diamond lariat, circa 1920, composed of five strands of seed pearls and terminating in tassels composed of 27 strands of seed pearls, spaced by 10 natural pearls measuring approximately 7.5 to 6.7 mm, accented by numerous rose-cut diamonds weighing approximately 8 carats, approximately 58" long. **$34,375**

Sotheby's

Platinum, natural pearl and diamond necklace, Cartier, Paris, circa 1935, graduated single strand composed of 51 natural pearls measuring approximately 11.5 to 5.8 mm, clasp set with old mine- and old European-cut diamonds weighing approximately 1.70 carats, signed Cartier, Paris, numbered 42335, French workshop and French assay marks, 17 1/2" long. **$1,314,500**

Skinner, Inc.

Carnelian and 14k gold pendant-necklace, Walter Lampl, circa 1930s, the pendant carved and pierced to depict a mouse and berries, suspended from ribbed and polished circular links with floral and foliate carnelian tablets, signed WL, 15 1/2", drop is 2 3/4. **$1,541**

Sotheby's

Platinum, emerald and diamond necklace-bracelet combination, France, circa 1930, designed as a meandering vine set with 73 carved emerald leaves, accented by numerous old mine, old European and rose-cut diamonds weighing approximately 9 carats, French assay and maker's mark, necklace is 14 1/2" long and separates into two bracelets 7 1/4" long. **$46,875**

Sotheby's

Platinum and diamond sautoir, circa 1925, supporting a pendant set with one old European-cut diamond weighing approximately .75 carat and one square emerald-cut diamond weighing approximately .65 carat, further set with numerous old European, single-cut, baguette, bullet and marquise-shaped diamonds weighing approximately 17.50 carats, pendant detachable; the necklace composed of openwork links set throughout with old European, single-cut and baguette diamonds weighing approximately 37 carats, 28" long; separates into four bracelets each 7" long. **$146,500**

Sotheby's

Platinum, diamond and ruby necklace, circa 1945, centered by two stylized flowerheads set with two old European-cut diamonds weighing approximately 1.80 carats, further set with numerous round, smaller old European, baguette, marquise and trapeze-shaped diamonds weighing a total of approximately 36 carats, accented by calibré-cut rubies, one ruby missing; accompanied by a white gold brooch fitting allowing the stylized flowerheads to be worn as a double clip-brooch, 15" long. **$36,250**

Heritage Auctions, Inc.

Emerald, diamond and platinum necklace, circa 1950, round and oval-shaped emerald cabochons weighing approximately 76 carats, full-cut diamonds weighing approximately 22.25 carats, baguette-cut diamonds weighing approximately 6.50 carats, marquise-cut diamonds weighing approximately 4.50 carats, all set in platinum, diamond clasp designed as a butterfly, total diamond weight is approximately 33.25 carats, original fitted, velvet-lined box, 15" x 3". **$29,875**

Skinner, Inc.

Diamond and 18k gold necklace, Italy, circa 1950s, designed as a feather motif set with full-cut diamond melee, approximate total weight 7 carats, 57.1 dwt, 14" long. **$14,220**

Skinner, Inc.

Enamel and 14k gold pendant, by noted goldsmith John Paul Miller, circa 1950s, the abstract form with a granulated octopus motif, hidden red and green enamel accents under the body, suspended from a woven black cord, completed by a clasp with granulated starfish motifs, maker's mark, pendant is 2 1/2", cord is 17". **$4,148**

Skinner, Inc.

Caddis worm pendant-brooch 18k gold and enamel, by noted goldsmith John Paul Miller, circa 1950s, the body designed with gold "fragments," reddish-orange enamel highlights, granulation to the eyes, legs, and removable bail, suspended from a woven cord completed by granulated caps, maker's mark, cord is 20" and worm is 2 1/2". Accompanied by original receipt from the Cleveland Museum of Art, 1959. **$11,258**

Skinner, Inc.

Demantoid, 14k rose gold and garnet pendant-necklace, Russia, circa 1940, set with cushion-, pear-, and circular-cut demantoid garnets, synthetic ruby accents, and Greek key motifs, reverse with pinstem; joined to later 10k rose gold chain, hallmarks, 17 1/2", drops are 2 1/2". **$2,963**

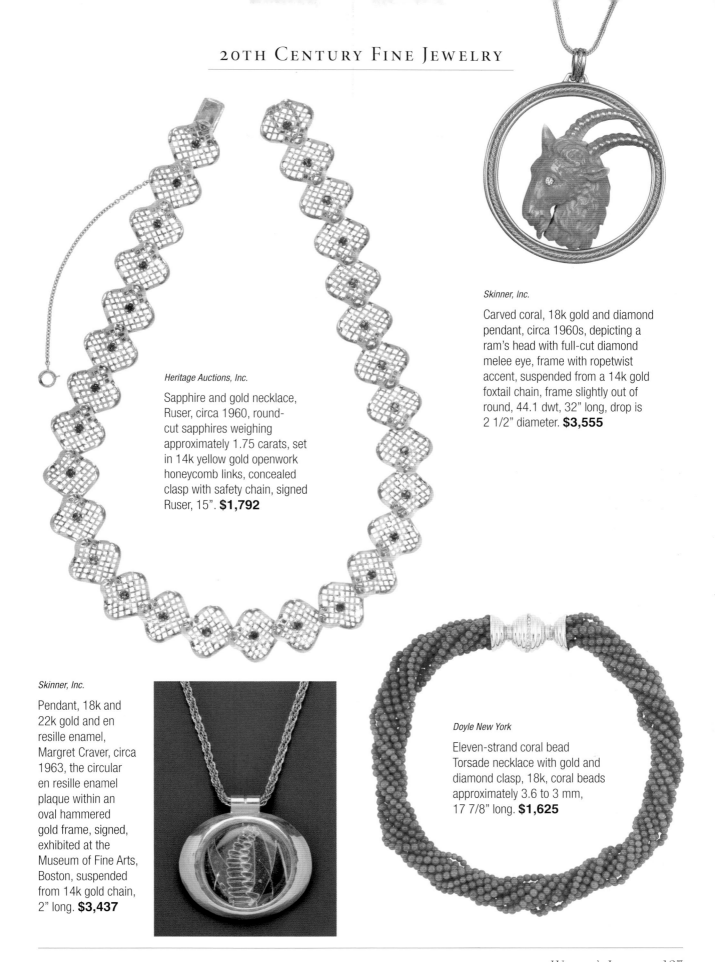

Heritage Auctions, Inc.

Sapphire and gold necklace, Ruser, circa 1960, round-cut sapphires weighing approximately 1.75 carats, set in 14k yellow gold openwork honeycomb links, concealed clasp with safety chain, signed Ruser, 15". **$1,792**

Skinner, Inc.

Carved coral, 18k gold and diamond pendant, circa 1960s, depicting a ram's head with full-cut diamond melee eye, frame with ropetwist accent, suspended from a 14k gold foxtail chain, frame slightly out of round, 44.1 dwt, 32" long, drop is 2 1/2" diameter. **$3,555**

Skinner, Inc.

Pendant, 18k and 22k gold and en resille enamel, Margret Craver, circa 1963, the circular en resille enamel plaque within an oval hammered gold frame, signed, exhibited at the Museum of Fine Arts, Boston, suspended from 14k gold chain, 2" long. **$3,437**

Doyle New York

Eleven-strand coral bead Torsade necklace with gold and diamond clasp, 18k, coral beads approximately 3.6 to 3 mm, 17 7/8" long. **$1,625**

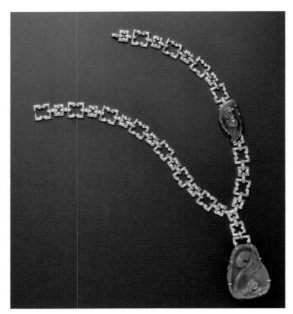

Skinner, Inc.

Jade and 18k gold pendant necklace, Tiffany & Co., circa 1970s, set with Chinese jades, one pendant drop depicting a goldfish with lotus blossom and butterfly motifs, the other a cat, the chain of stylized links, signed Tiffany in script on the clasp, pendant is 4 1/2" long, chain is 23 1/2" long. **$21,600**

Doyle New York

Gold link necklace, Cartier, 18k, pairs of interlocking polished gold oval links, signed Cartier, approximately 65 dwt, 16 5/8". **$10,000**

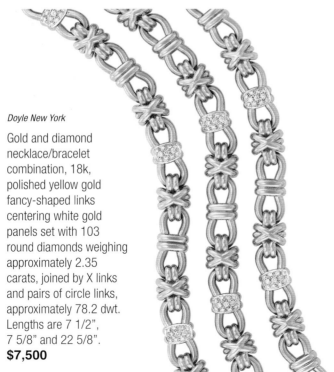

Doyle New York

Gold and diamond necklace/bracelet combination, 18k, polished yellow gold fancy-shaped links centering white gold panels set with 103 round diamonds weighing approximately 2.35 carats, joined by X links and pairs of circle links, approximately 78.2 dwt. Lengths are 7 1/2", 7 5/8" and 22 5/8". **$7,500**

Skinner, Inc.

Sterling silver and enamel pendant, Miye Matsukata, circa 1970s, the polychrome enamel plaque within a hammered silver mount, suspended from snake link chain with hammered tubes and blue glass roundels, signed and dated Miye/MM1975 on the reverse pendant is 2 7/8" long. **$1,896**

Sotheby's

Gold, cabochon emerald and ruby ring, Chanel, circa 1935, cabochon emeralds measuring approximately 12.4 x 9.8 mm and 13 x 9.4 mm, signed Chanel, size 7. **$32,500**

Sotheby's

Rare and important fancy intense yellow diamond and emerald ring, Tiffany & Co., designed by Louis Comfort Tiffany, circa 1915-1920, oval diamond of fancy intense yellow color weighing 11.05 carats, within a gold filigree mounting set with calibré-cut emeralds, foliate pattern engraved inside shank, signed Tiffany & Co., two emeralds missing, size 8. Accompanied by the original silk floral box in the Japonesque style; these boxes were used only for the art jewelry designed by Louis Comfort Tiffany. **$818,500**

Heritage Auctions, Inc.

Diamond and platinum ring, circa 1950, marquise-shaped diamonds weighing approximately 2 carats, tapered baguette-cut diamonds weighing approximately 1.20 carats, single-cut diamonds, set in platinum, total diamond weight is approximately 3.50 carats, size 5 1/2 (sizeable). **$3,000**

Skinner, Inc.

Platinum and diamond ring, Seaman Schepps, circa 1940, bezel-set with an old European-cut diamond weighing approximately 1.10 carats, set with marquise-, old European-, and old single-cut diamonds and cabochon emeralds, signed, size 4 3/4. **$4,800**

Heritage Auctions, Inc.

Retro ruby, diamond, platinum and gold ring, circa 1940, full- and single-cut diamonds weighing approximately 0.50 carat, set in platinum, round-cut rubies measuring 3 mm and weighing approximately 1.80 carats, set in 14k pink gold, 1" x 3/4". **$507**

Heritage Auctions, Inc.

Retro cultured pearl, diamond and platinum ring designed as an oyster shell, circa 1950, cultured pearl measuring 8.50 to 8 mm, full-cut diamonds weighing approximately 1.25 carats, set in platinum. **$836**

Heritage Auctions, Inc.

Ruby, diamond and platinum ring, circa 1950, oval-shaped ruby measuring 8 x 6.30 x 4.80 mm and weighing 2.05 carats, full-cut diamonds weighing approximately 0.50 carat, set in platinum, size 6 1/2 (sizeable). **$2,629**

Heritage Auctions, Inc.

Emerald, diamond and platinum ring, circa 1950, emerald-cut emerald measuring 13 x 12.10 x 7.70 mm and weighing approximately 7.55 carats, full-cut diamonds weighing approximately 3.80 carats, set in platinum, size 4 (sizeable). **$6,875**

Heritage Auctions, Inc.

South Sea-cultured pearl, diamond and platinum ring, circa 1950, pearl measuring 14.40 x 14.20 mm, full and single-cut diamonds weighing approximately 1.25 carats, baguette-cut diamonds weighing approximately 0.80 carat, set in platinum, size 6 (sizeable). **$2,390**

Heritage Auctions, Inc.

Amethyst, diamond and platinum ring, circa 1950, oval-shaped amethyst measuring 18 x 11.50 x 7.50 mm and weighing approximately 8.65 carats, full-cut diamonds weighing approximately 0.95 carat, set in platinum, size 5 1/4 (sizeable). **$3,346**

Heritage Auctions, Inc.

Amethyst, diamond and white gold ring, circa 1950, oval-shaped amethyst measuring 18 x 13 x 8.35 mm and weighing approximately 10.90 carats, European and full-cut diamonds weighing approximately 2.50 carats, set in 14k white gold, size 7 (sizeable). **$1,613**

Heritage Auctions, Inc.

Star sapphire, diamond and platinum ring, circa 1950, round-shaped star sapphire measuring 14.50 x 14 x 6.50 mm and weighing approximately 14.25 carats, marquise-, single- and baguette-cut diamonds weighing approximately 1 carat, set in platinum, size 3 1/4 (sizeable). **$2,100**

Heritage Auctions, Inc.

Star ruby, diamond and platinum ring, circa 1950, oval-shaped star ruby measuring 8.10 x 7 x 3.80 mm and weighing approximately 2.30 carats, single-cut diamonds weighing approximately 0.55 carat, set in platinum, size 6 1/2 (sizeable). **$806**

Heritage Auctions, Inc.

Diamond and platinum ring, circa 1950, full-cut diamonds weighing approximately 2.80 carats, baguette and tapered baguette-cut diamonds weighing approximately 0.75 carat, set in platinum, size 6 1/4. **$3,585**

Heritage Auctions, Inc.

Emerald, diamond and white gold ring, circa 1950, cushion-shaped emerald cabochon measuring 13.50 x 11.40 x 5.20 mm and weighing approximately 6.30 carats, pear-shaped emerald cabochons weighing approximately 0.90 carat, baguette- and tapered baguette-cut diamonds weighing approximately 1.85 carats, marquise-, triangle- and full-cut diamonds weighing approximately 0.55 carat, set in 14k white gold, size 5 3/4 (sizeable). **$1,792**

Heritage Auctions, Inc.

Star sapphire, diamond and platinum ring, circa 1950, round-shaped star sapphire measuring 22.70 x 21.30 x 16.50 mm and weighing approximately 86 carats, European-cut diamonds weighing approximately 3 carats, whistle, baguette, square, half-moon and triangle-shaped diamonds weighing approximately 1.40 carats, set in platinum, total diamond weight is approximately 4.40 carats, size 5 1/2 (sizeable). **$6,572**

Heritage Auctions, Inc.

Jadeite jade, diamond, platinum and gold ring, circa 1960, oval-shaped jadeite jade cabochon measuring 15.25 x 12.60 x 8.70 mm and weighing approximately 14.90 carats, full-cut diamonds weighing approximately 0.50 carat, set in platinum and textured 18k gold, size 6 1/2 (sizeable). **$5,078**

Sotheby's

Coral, 18k gold, emerald, diamond, and enamel ring, David Webb, circa 1975, centered by a baguette emerald weighing .57 carat, flanked by cabochon coral, accented by 36 round diamonds weighing .97 carat and black enamel detailing, unsigned, with box signed David Webb, size 7. **$21,250**

Heritage Auctions, Inc.

Emerald, diamond and platinum ring, circa 1950, emerald-cut emerald measuring 9.65 x 8 x 4.40 mm and weighing approximately 2.50 carats, marquise-cut diamonds weighing approximately 0.60 carat, pear-shaped diamonds weighing approximately 0.35 carat, baguette- and full-cut diamonds weighing approximately 0.45 carat, set in platinum, size 4 3/4 (sizeable). **$1,912**

Heritage Auctions, Inc.

Diamond, ruby and platinum ring, Oscar Heyman Bros., circa 1970, round brilliant-cut diamond measuring 6.10 x 6.10 mm and weighing 0.84 carat, tapered baguette-cut diamonds weighing 1.87 carats, baguette-shaped rubies weighing 2.71 carats, set in platinum, reference # 93023, size 5 1/2 (sizeable). **$10,000**

Heritage Auctions, Inc.

Diamond and gold ring, circa 1960, full-cut diamonds weighing approximately 2.50 carats, set in 14k gold, rhodium finished accents, size 6 1/4 (sizeable). **$1,434**

Doyle New York

Schlumberger band ring, 18k gold, platinum, diamonds, signed Schlumberger, Tiffany, approximately 4 dwt., 3/16". **$1,200**

Sotheby's

Group of gold, moonstone and sapphire jewelry, circa 1945, comprising a pair of earclips and ring by Raymond Yard, and a necklace and bracelet. Necklace set with 28 cabochon moonstones, small round sapphires, mounted in 14k gold, length 16 1/2", signed WAB; the bracelet set with 16 cabochon moonstones, framed by small round sapphires, mounted in 14k gold, length 7 1/2", unsigned; the earclips set with two cabochon moonstones, small round sapphires, framed by scrolling gold ribbons, signed Yard; the ring set with an oval cabochon moonstone, flanked by small round sapphires, also signed Yard, size 6. **$12,500**

Heritage Auctions, Inc.

Retro diamond and gold suite, circa 1940, includes: one brooch featuring full-cut diamonds weighing approximately 1 carat, pavé set in 14k yellow gold with rhodium finished accents, double pinstem and catch mechanism on reverse; matching pair of earrings designed for non-pierced ears, each with a clip back. Total diamond weight is approximately 1.50 carats. Brooch is 2 1/16" x 2 1/16"; earrings are 15/16" x 15/16". **$1,912**

Courtesy Milky Way Jewels; Rocky Day photo

Walter Lampl jadeite brooch and ring set, 1920s, 14k gold, highly polished carved green jadeite imported from China, surrounded by tiny natural seed pearls, finished in 14k gold frame; brooch marked WL 14k; ring marked 14k WL; pin 2", ring 7/8". **$1,125 set**

Sotheby's

Suite of 14k gold and citrine jewelry, the clip brooch by Raymond Yard, circa 1940, the clip-brooch set with a rectangular modified brilliant-cut citrine weighing approximately 350 carats, signed Yard; attached to a necklace designed as a double snake-link chain accented by gold scrolls and a citrine clasp, 14" long; the hinged bracelet set with two large half-moon shaped citrines, internal circumference approximately 7"; the earclips set with emerald-cut citrines within a border of ribbon scrolls. **$56,250**

Sotheby's

Suite of 14k gold, ruby and diamond jewelry, Tiffany & Co., circa 1945, includes: 11 diamonds weighing approximately 0.90 carat, total weight approximately 51 dwts, necklace is 14" long and bracelet is 6 1/2" long. **$7,200**

Heritage Auctions, Inc.

Green beryl and gold suite, Seaman Schepps, circa 1950, from the Bamboo Collection, includes: one pair of earrings designed for non-pierced ears, each featuring a cushion-shaped green beryl, oval-shaped green beryl, cultured pearl, set in 14k yellow gold, clip back on reverse; one brooch featuring a 14k yellow gold bamboo design, flanked by carved green beryl, set in 14k yellow gold, pinstem and catch on reverse. Earrings are 13/16" x 1"; brooch is 1 15/16" x 1 7/8". **$4,780**

Heritage Auctions, Inc.

Turquoise, diamond and gold suite, circa 1950, includes: one clip-brooch featuring an oval-shaped turquoise cabochon, single-cut diamonds, turquoise cabochons, set in 18k yellow gold, double pinstem and catch mechanism on reverse; matching pair of earrings designed for non-pierced ears, each with a clip back on reverse. Clip-brooch is 2 1/4" x 1 3/4"; earrings are 1 3/8" x 1 1/8". **$2,868**

Green glass parure, 1950s, sterling silver and marcasite necklace, bracelet and ring, green molded glass with floral-foliate motif, hallmarked sterling; 15" chain, 7" bracelet. **$150**

Heritage Auctions, Inc.

Emerald, diamond and white gold suite, circa 1950, includes: one brooch featuring emerald-cut emeralds, full- and single-cut diamonds, set in 14k white gold; matching pair of earrings designed for pierced ears but are easily converted. Total emerald weight for the suite is approximately 3.75 carats; total diamond weight for the suite is approximately 1.10 carats. Earrings are 1 1/4" x 5/8"; brooch is 2 1/4" x 3/4". **$2,270**

Sotheby's

Suite of 18k gold, turquoise, sapphire and diamond jewelry, Van Cleef & Arpels, circa 1955, the flexible necklace composed of numerous round turquoise cabochons, accented by floral motifs set with numerous round diamonds weighing approximately 3.70 carats and numerous round sapphires, signed Van Cleef & Arpels, numbered 91.828, internal circumference 15 1/2"; the matching articulated bracelet set with round turquoise cabochons accented by numerous round diamonds weighing approximately 2.25 carats and numerous round sapphires, signed Van Cleef & Arpels, numbered 16305, 7 1/2" long; the earclips of similar design, signed Van Cleef & Arpels, numbered 10896CS. **$104,500**

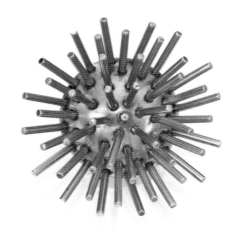

Sotheby's

Pair of 14k gold earclips and matching brooch, Cartier, circa 1960, the sculpted earclips projecting three dimensional gold rays, gross weight approximately 19 dwts, signed Cartier; the brooch of similar design, gross weight approximately 19 dwts, signed Cartier. **$8,750**

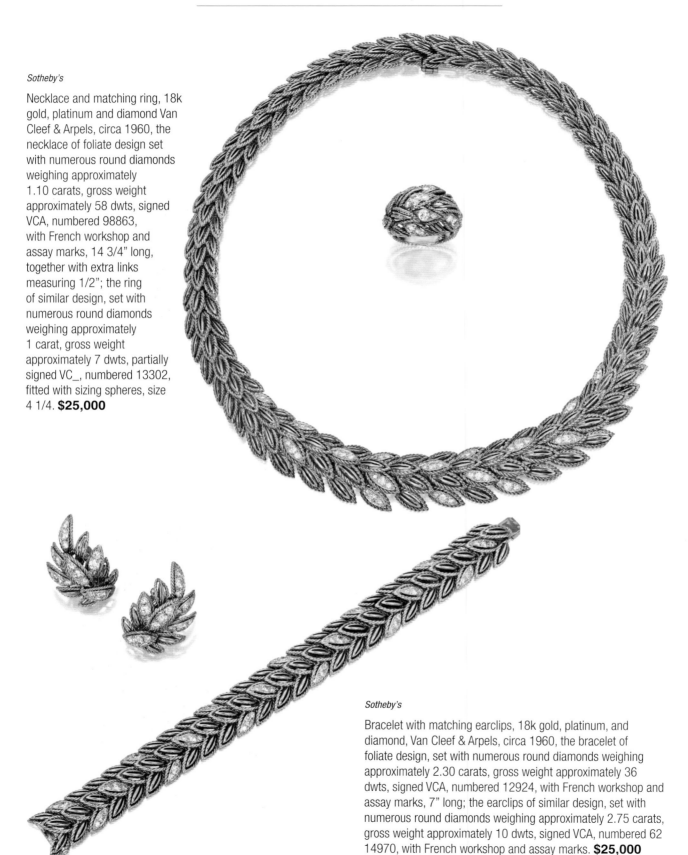

Sotheby's

Necklace and matching ring, 18k gold, platinum and diamond Van Cleef & Arpels, circa 1960, the necklace of foliate design set with numerous round diamonds weighing approximately 1.10 carats, gross weight approximately 58 dwts, signed VCA, numbered 98863, with French workshop and assay marks, 14 3/4" long, together with extra links measuring 1/2"; the ring of similar design, set with numerous round diamonds weighing approximately 1 carat, gross weight approximately 7 dwts, partially signed VC_, numbered 13302, fitted with sizing spheres, size 4 1/4. **$25,000**

Sotheby's

Bracelet with matching earclips, 18k gold, platinum, and diamond, Van Cleef & Arpels, circa 1960, the bracelet of foliate design, set with numerous round diamonds weighing approximately 2.30 carats, gross weight approximately 36 dwts, signed VCA, numbered 12924, with French workshop and assay marks, 7" long; the earclips of similar design, set with numerous round diamonds weighing approximately 2.75 carats, gross weight approximately 10 dwts, signed VCA, numbered 62 14970, with French workshop and assay marks. **$25,000**

Sotheby's

Brooch and matching earclips, platinum, 18k gold, colored stone and diamond, Bulgari, circa 1960, brooch set with four cabochon emeralds and 32 cabochon sapphires, framed by numerous round diamonds weighing approximately 4.50 carats, signed Bulgari, French workshop and assay marks; the earclips set with cabochon emeralds framed by cabochon sapphires and numerous round diamonds weighing approximately 2.60 carats, signed Bulgari, N.Y. From the estate of socialite Brooke Astor. **$31,250**

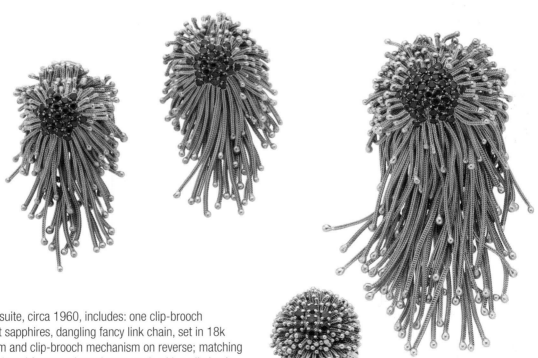

Heritage Auctions, Inc.

Sapphire and gold suite, circa 1960, includes: one clip-brooch featuring round-cut sapphires, dangling fancy link chain, set in 18k yellow gold, pinstem and clip-brooch mechanism on reverse; matching pair of earrings designed for non-pierced ears, each with a clip back on reverse; matching ring. Clip-brooch is 3 1/4" x 1 3/8"; earrings are 2" x 1"; ring is size 5 and sizeable. **$6,453**

Skinner, Inc.

Necklace and bracelet set, 18k gold and diamond, Paloma Picasso, Tiffany & Co., circa 1981, the necklace composed of open links centering one platinum link set with full-cut diamond melee, bracelet en suite, signed, boxed, 44.4 dwt, bracelet is 7" long and necklace is 15 1/4" long. **$3,840**

Sotheby's

Suite of 18k gold, platinum, diamond and onyx jewelry, Van Cleef & Arpels, New York, circa 1970, circular onyx link necklace enhanced with 72 round diamonds weighing approximately 2.45 carats, signed Van Cleef & Arpels N.Y., numbered 42890, pendant detachable, 26 1/2" long; bracelet of similar design set with 42 round diamonds weighing approximately 1.65 carats, signed Van Cleef & Arpels NY, indistinctly numbered _3052, 7 1/2" long; earclips with concentric circles of onyx and gold ropework set with 16 round diamonds weighing approximately .35 carat, signed V.C.&A., numbered 42281, one onyx section missing. From the estate of socialite Brooke Astor. **$68,500**

Sotheby's

Suite of diamond and yellow diamond jewelry, De Grisogono, comprising a necklace, bracelet, and pair of earclips designed as a series of stylized trefoil flowers and leaves, necklace set with 15 pear-shaped rose-cut diamonds weighing approximately 26.80 carats, numerous pavé-set round diamonds weighing approximately 25 carats and numerous pavé-set round diamonds of yellow hue weighing approximately 22.50 carats; bracelet set with nine pear-shaped rose-cut diamonds weighing approximately 13.40 carats, numerous pavé-set diamonds weighing approximately 11.50 carats and pavé-set yellow diamonds weighing approximately 8.75 carats, one diamond missing; earclips set with six pear-shaped rose-cut diamonds weighing approximately 8.75 carats and with numerous pavé-set near colorless and yellow diamonds weighing approximately 8.85 carats, mounted in 18k white and yellow gold; necklace signed de Grisogono, with signed case. Necklace is 16" long; bracelet is 6 1/2" long. **$229,000**

Sotheby's

Group of 18k gold, diamond, onyx and colored stone jewelry, necklace composed of 11 fluted segments of black onyx, accented by numerous round diamonds weighing approximately 1.40 carats, 16 1/4" long; with two interchangeable pendants, the first centered by an oval-shaped blue topaz, framed by numerous round diamonds, within black enamel surrounds; the second pendant centered by a cabochon emerald, framed by numerous round and baguette diamonds within fluted black onyx surrounds; with two rings matching the pendants, the first centered by an emerald-cut blue topaz, accented by round diamonds and applied with black enamel, size 6 1/2; the second ring centered by a cabochon emerald, accented by round and baguette diamonds, within fluted black onyx surrounds, size 6 1/4. **$15,000**

Enamel and 18k gold and bangle bracelet by Tiffany & Co., with a pair of 18k gold and enamel earclips by David Webb, hinged bangle-bracelet of ribbed design applied with alternating segments of green and blue enamel, gross weight approximately 52 dwts, signed Tiffany, internal circumference 7"; the button-shaped earclips applied with green and blue enamel, gross weight approximately 19 dwts, signed Webb. **$10,625**

Pair of earclips and matching ring, 18k gold, peridot, citrine and diamond, earclips set with four buff-topped peridots and eight buff-topped citrines, accented by numerous round diamonds weighing approximately 4.80 carats; the ring of similar design set with two buff-topped peridots and four buff-topped citrines, accented by numerous round diamonds weighing approximately 1.95 carats, size 4. **$6,875**

Sotheby's

Ruby, 18k gold, diamond and yellow sapphire suite, Harry Winston, necklace set at the front with 11 cabochon rubies, each centered by a yellow sapphire, accented throughout with numerous round and pear-shaped diamonds weighing approximately 9.35 carats, 15 1/2" long; the earrings of similar design, the two cabochon rubies centered by a yellow sapphire, set with numerous round diamonds weighing approximately .90 carat; the ring set with a cabochon ruby centered by a yellow sapphire, framed and accented by numerous round diamonds weighing approximately .60 carat, size 6; all pieces with maker's marks for Harry Winston; with signed pouch. **$35,000**

COSTUME JEWELRY

CIRCA 1920-1935

When Coco Chanel (1883-1971) reputedly declared in 1924, "It does not matter if they are real, as long as they look like junk!," costume jewels had already begun to enjoy widespread acceptance by women at all social levels. Both Chanel and her arch-rival, Elsa Schiaparelli, were foremost among Parisian couturiers in designing and promoting the wearing of faux jewelry as an accessory to clothing and as a means of self-expression. Today we call it "making a statement."

Because they were made from non-precious materials, costume jewels gave manufacturers and designers greater freedom to experiment with designs and the opportunity to cater to fashion's whims, trends, and fads. Consequently we see a far greater diversity in costume jewelry of the period compared to fine jewelry.

To be sure, many directly imitative pieces were made, substituting "paste" or rhinestones, and molded or cut glass, for gemstones, and silver or white "pot" metal (tin alloyed with lead) for platinum. Some of these pieces were remarkably well-made. The metal was often rhodium-plated for an even closer resemblance to platinum (rhodium is one of the six metals in the platinum group). Stones were prong- or bead-set; occasionally, millegrained settings were used. At a short distance, one would find it difficult to discern them from the real thing. Verbatim translations of the period style from fine to costume jewelry include flexible and linked plaque bracelets, bead *sautoirs* (sometimes called "flapper beads"), pendant earrings, geometric brooches and pendants, dress clips, and double clip brooches. Coro's version of the double clip brooch, trade named the "Duette," was patented in 1931.

As with fine jewelry, Art Deco costume pieces originated in Europe, where the *Jugendstil*, Bauhaus, Wiener Werkstätte, and Liberty styles had already made a case for modernism, emphasizing design over intrinsically valuable materials. But even in France, where *haute joaillerie* and Cartier reigned, the more adventurous Art Deco artist-designers turned to silver, chrome, glass, lacquer and enamel, and plastics. A separate section on plastic and novelty jewelry starts on P. 246. Some French Deco costume jewelry is of the faux diamond and platinum variety, usually referred to as "French paste," set in silver and extremely well-made. The transitional path of Edwardian to Deco can be followed in these all-white pieces, along the same route as fine jewelry. Similarly styled bracelets, clips, buckles, and brooches in rhinestones and white metal were made in the United States by costume jewelry manufacturers such as Trifari, Krussman and Fishel, later known simply as Trifari (also see section on "Designer/Manufacturer Signed" costume jewelry). Ciner Mfg. Co., in business since 1892, made both fine and costume jewelry. They produced rhinestone and sterling pieces in the French mode during the '20s and '30s. The White Metal Casters' Association made inexpensive rhinestone and pot metal buckles and clips as dress accessories in the '30s.

The French and the Germans also excelled at designing modern-looking jewelry in sterling set with inexpensive gemstones and marcasites, small faceted bits of iron pyrite. Theodor Fahrner, already famous for early 20th century *Jugendstil* designs (as mentioned in the Arts and Crafts section), kept up with fashion by producing fine quality Deco pieces in high-grade silver set with marcasites combined with amazonite, smoky quartz, rock crystal, onyx, carnelian, chrysoprase, lapis, or coral. Other less well-known German manufacturers also made jewelry in this style, most commonly using dyed blue or green chalcedony (imitating chrysoprase) with marcasites and sterling.

Most accounts of fashion history tend to focus on what was original about the 1920s and 1930s, but all was not geometry and streamline. The Victorians did not have a monopoly on revivals; in fact, Victorian fashion and historicism itself were revived beginning in the late '20s and growing in popularity in the '30s and early '40s. Period films and their stars helped set the mood: Mae West in "She Done Him Wrong" (1933), Greta Garbo in "Camille" (1936) and "Conquest" (1937), Bette Davis in "Juarez" (1939), and of course, Vivien Leigh in the immortal "Gone With the Wind" (1939). The clothes and the jewelry (much of the latter created by Eugene Joseff, aka Joseff of Hollywood–see section on "Designer/Manufacturer Signed" costume jewelry) may not have always been authentically of the period portrayed, but they inspired a 1930s trend for softer, more romantic dresses with longer hems, peplums, and puffy sleeves and such Victorian staples as cameos and jet (imitated in glass and plastic), ornate metal filigree, and flower jewelry.

A unique type of collectible jewelry originated in England. However, its primary component, the wings of the Morpho butterfly, came from South America. Several British firms made these pieces, which usually consist of a reverse-painted scene or a white sulfide bas-relief (reminiscent of Wedgwood jasperware) backed with an iridescent blue butterfly wing ground, a domed glass cover, and usually, a sterling silver frame and back. The backs are often marked with a British patent number, granted to Shipton & Co. of Birmingham, England in 1923. Note that the wings can deteriorate or the iridescence flake off if exposed to light, moisture or air, or even excessive movement, especially if the compartments are not air-tight.

The exotic influences of the period that permeated the work of Cartier, Van Cleef and Arpels, et al, found widespread expression in costume jewels as well. The "Egyptomania" instigated by the discovery of King Tutankhamun's treasures and sustained by Hollywood films (e.g., "Cleopatra" in 1934), caused Egyptian motifs to be particularly conspicuous. Enameled silver or gold-plated metal winged scarabs, falcons, vultures, and other motifs were produced in several European countries and the United States, as well as in Egypt itself for export or the tourist trade. The slave bracelet, of enameled metal links set with glass cabochons or molded scarabs, was an extension of the craze. One of the primary sources for Egyptian-themed pieces was Czechoslovakia. Here, the medium was usually glass, but celluloid and metal pieces, or a combination of materials, were also made.

After World War I, Bohemia, long renowned for its glasswork, beads, and garnet jewelry, became part of the new country called Czechoslovakia, created in 1918. In the period between the wars, quantities of glass beads, faceted and molded glass stones and stamped metalwork were produced and exported, some in the form of finished jewelry, some for use in jewelry manufactured in other countries. The center of this production was a town called Gablonz,

now known as Jablonec. Because the country was taken over by the Germans during World War II (exports were curtailed in 1939), the glass and jewelry makers were dispersed to other areas, such as Neugablonz in Germany. Jewelry marked "Czechoslovakia" is easily circa-dated and has become quite sought-after. Prices have risen accordingly.

Czechoslovakia was the source of several types of costume jewelry. Stamped gilt metal filigree necklaces, bracelets, brooches, buckles, clips, earrings, and rings were set with glass cabochons and embellished with enameled foliate motifs, resulting in an ornate look that was more Victorian Revival than Art Deco.

The Deco style was not ignored, however. Geometric-cut pieces of glass resembling gemstones were prong-set in short necklaces and pendent earrings. Glass buckles, clasps, and clips were made in simple modern designs. Small faceted glass stones were often silver-plated to imitate marcasites.

Asian-inspired pieces were made with molded and pierced glass plaques imitating carved jade and carnelian. Glass bead *sautoirs* were another Czech product. Some Czech pieces are marked in difficult-to-read places, like the circumference of a jump ring. Other unmarked pieces are so characteristic of Czech glass and metalwork that they are unmistakable. Still others may have Czech components, but were assembled elsewhere, and may be hard to identify.

Child's bracelet, 1920s, frosted Camphor glass, inset rhinestone crystals, silver filigree links. **$150**

REPRODUCTION ALERT

The same conditions and caveats apply for costume as for fine jewelry, particularly marcasite and silver, which has been reproduced in mass quantities. Again, quality varies widely. Some British and German exports are very well-made. Wholesalers specializing in reproductions advertise in antiques publications and on the Internet.

DESIGNER/MANUFACTURER SIGNED AND OTHER COSTUME JEWELRY

CIRCA 1935-1950

A few years ago, no one would have believed that a brooch made of rhinestones and base metal could be worth more than one made of diamonds and platinum. Up until about 20 years ago, that same old rhinestone brooch probably would have been tossed in a drawer or thrown away.

That was before costume jewelry collectors and price guides entered the picture. Now, it seems that everyone knows and recognizes the "name" pieces–and knows their value, or at least knows better than to throw them away. Costume jewelry was elevated to an even higher level with the opening of an exhibition that toured museums in Europe and the United States from 1991 to 1993, called "Jewels of Fantasy, Costume Jewelry of the 20th Century." The exhibit's accompanying catalog (see "References") has become an important reference resource and a sought-after collectible in its own right, now that it is out of print.

The designer/manufacturer signed section has been divided chronologically, for two reasons. First, to more closely parallel the fine jewelry sections so that the evolution of styles can be compared between precious and non-precious pieces of the same periods. Second, because pre-1950 costume jewelry has a special place in the hearts of some collectors, while post-1950 costume jewelry has its own group of followers. Furthermore, the sheer quantity of what is being collected has grown considerably, and dividing the category at 1950 makes it more manageable.

Expanded though it may be, it is not possible to go into great detail about the many manufacturers and designers whose history and products have already been amply documented by a plethora of entire books on signed and unsigned costume jewelry. New books on the topic in general as well as monographs on specific makers continue to be published. Some of them are better than others. The "References" section in the back of this book list a few of

Crystal balls dress clip, 1950s, multicolor faceted glass orbs in pink, sapphire, topaz, aqua, silver-plated metal, pavé-set rhinestone leaves, unsigned, 2". **$50**

the recommended ones. While these are recommended for the examples, marks, and information they contain, readers should be aware that it is not uncommon to find conflicting information about the same makers in different sources. Furthermore, it is not likely that the true story will ever be known. Most companies did not keep detailed records of their jewelry lines that, at the time they were produced, were thought to be as ephemeral and disposable as the fashions they were meant to complement. Much of the recent research on costume jewelry has of necessity been based on recollections of company executives, designers, and other employees; patent and trademark searches; and advertising and articles in consumer and trade periodicals of the times.

A listing of American costume jewelry manufacturers,

including dates of operation if documented, can be found in an appendix at the back of this book.

Even though much has already been written by others, a few salient points should be made here. The bulk of the "name" jewelry that collectors seek was produced from circa 1935 through the 1960s (1970s costume jewelry is beginning to generate collector interest as well). The few manufacturers who were making costume jewelry before 1935, e.g., Ciner, Coro, Miriam Haskell, Hobé, Napier, Trifari, and designer/couturiers Chanel, Hattie Carnegie, and Schiaparelli, did not consistently mark their pieces, if they signed them at all (the collector terminology for manufacturers' markings is "signed"). Their attributable circa 1920s (and some early 1930s) designs are rare and usually expensive.

Attribution of unsigned pieces and circa-dating of any piece should be backed up by printed evidence, or provenance. Patent numbers found on the backs of pieces assist in circa-dating. Other aspects of a piece, such as style and other elements, may date it later. For example, Coro patented the mechanism for the double clip brooch with Coro's tradename Duette in 1931, when the clips were flat-backed and the motifs were geometric, but figural motif Duettes with double-pronged hinged clips (often called "fur clips") bearing this same patent number were made in the late 1930s and early 1940s.

In 1930, Trifari hired its most celebrated and prolific designer, Alfred Philippe, who designed many now sought-after pieces until 1968. A Frenchman trained in fine jewelry design—he produced designs made by William Scheer for Cartier and Van Cleef & Arpels—Philippe was known for creating molded glass and rhinestone pieces for Trifari, which resembled Cartier's "fruit salad" or "tutti frutti" carved gemstone and diamond jewels from the late 1920s and early 1930s. He was also the apparent designer of many of Trifari's painted enamel pieces of the late 1930s and early 1940s.

However, it should be noted that allegations were made that the inventors/assignees who signed the patent applications, or had them signed by their attorneys, may not have always been the actual designers of the pieces attributed to them. The question of attribution to individual designers is a controversial one that may never be resolved, especially where large manufacturers that employed many designers are concerned. The companies themselves often controlled the ownership of patents and copyrights of designs, which at times were purchased from free-lancers "off the street" (this is known as "work for hire" in copyright parlance.) Many industrial designers who may well deserve credit for their creations worked anonymously. At the time these designs were created, no one could have predicted how important their attribution would become.

During World War II, base metals were restricted for the war effort, as was platinum. Costume jewelry factories were called into service to make munitions and other military equipment. Jewelry production was diminished, but not curtailed. Feelings of patriotism were at an all-time high, and everyone wore jewelry with patriotic themes and/or colors. With the rationing of base metals beginning in mid-1942, sterling silver was used as a substitute. Fewer rhinestones were used because supplies from Czechoslovakia and Austria were cut off, as were simulated ("faux") pearls from Japan. Manufacturers made do with existing stock and with "stones" of Lucite and other plastics. Although base metal restrictions were lifted after the war, some manufacturers continued to use sterling for their higher-end lines until the mid-'50s.

A relatively unknown American manufacturer, Rice-Weiner, made pieces designed by (and signed) McClellan Barclay (1893-1943), who was a well-known artist killed in action during World War II. Founded in 1938, Rice-Weiner also produced jewelry by other designers who worked for the company. The company was the manufacturer of licensed designs inspired by the films of Alexander Korda ("Thief of Bagdad," 1940, and "The Jungle Book," 1942). According to the Brunialtis in *A Tribute to America*, Korda himself had nothing to do with designing these pieces—the marks found on these pieces, "© Alexander Korda" or "Thief of Bagdad Korda ©," refer to the company name "Barclay," which split from Rice-Weiner in 1946, and had nothing to do with the artist McClelland Barclay.

Mid-to-late 1930s and early 1940s Retro Modern costume pieces made of rhinestones and gold-plated or rhodium-plated white metal or sterling silver were often larger in scale than precious stone, gold, and platinum equivalents, but many of the overall designs were quite similar. Some costume jewelry designers, such as Miriam Haskell, also took inspiration from earlier styles, especially during the Victorian Revival of the late 1930s and early 1940s.

Fashion jewelry *forms* also paralleled those of precious jewels. In the '30s and '40s, clips were just as stylish in rhinestones and white metal as they were in diamonds and platinum, moving to gold-plating and colored glass stones as fine jewelry changed to colored gold and gemstones. Gold-plated costume pieces of the late '30s and early '40s were often bicolored rose and yellow to resemble their fine jewelry counterparts.

Although the majority of the jewelry in this section is American-made, two of the genre's most important influences came from Europe, in the persons of designers Gabrielle "Coco" Chanel (1883-1971) and Elsa Schiaparelli (1896-1973). While their influence was felt in the early years of costume jewelry manufacture (see "Costume Jewelry, Circa 1920-1935"), their early pieces, many of which are not signed, are rarely seen today. Chanel closed her business in Paris in 1939 with the advent of World War II, and reopened in 1954, coming out of retirement at the age of 71 and working until she died. It is during this later period that the multicolored glass, faux pearl, and gold-plated metal necklaces, bracelets, brooches, and pendants most familiar to collectors were made.

A huge revelation to rock the costume jewelry-collecting world is documented in the Brunialtis' book, *A Tribute to America*. The authors discovered that costume jewelry marked with the script signature "Chanel" had nothing to do with Coco; it is the mark of the Chanel Novelty Co. of New York, New York, which changed its name to Reinad Novelty Co. The Chanel script mark was in use for only one season, spring 1941 (during the German occupation of France, when Coco Chanel's atelier was closed), which explains the scarcity of pieces so marked.

Elsa Schiaparelli's avant-garde and surrealistic touch is evident in her 1930s jewelry designs, which are usually unsigned. Some late 1930s pieces are signed "schiaparelli"

Miriam Haskell green glass flower brooch with pearl and rhinestone headpins, green and clear chatons, and a green glass leaf, marked Miriam Haskell, 2 1/4" x 1 3/4". **$200-$250**

in lowercase block letters. She opened an office in New York in 1949 and licensed her name for mass production of costume jewelry and accessories made by the David Lisner Co., which was also the authorized American agent and distributor for earlier French-made pieces.

Chanel and Schiaparelli also helped launch the careers of fine jewelry designers Verdura and Schlumberger, both of whom designed costume pieces for their respective employers in the 1930s (see "Fine Jewelry" section).

Some European designs are not signed, but merely marked with country of origin, or in the case of some French jewelry, "DÉPOSÉ" (registered). This mark is not a guarantee of French manufacture—some German makers also used it for their exports to France and England—but if found on a stylistically correct *pate de verre* piece, for example, it offers further evidence of its origin.

Other sought-after designs include circa late 1930s and early 1940s sterling vermeil (gold-plated) or rhodium-plated white metal and painted enamel figural brooches and clips by Marcel Boucher, bearing the mark now known to be a "Phrygian cap" from the French Revolution, not a bird's head; Coro, including sterling and white metal figural Duettes, although demand for these has fallen off a bit; and Corocraft, De Rosa, Eisenberg Original, Hobé, Mazer Bros.,

Pennino, Réja, Staret and Trifari, and well-made unsigned examples. Among these are the now-famous animal "jelly bellies" with clear Lucite centers, most signed Trifari, Coro, or unsigned. Knockoffs and fakes have cooled the jelly belly market considerably. Genuine rarities still command a premium, however.

Vintage 1940s and 1950s Miriam Haskell necklaces, bracelets, and suites continue to have a following, particularly the designer's more elaborate creations. The demand for Haskell increased when a book devoted solely to her jewelry has been published (see "References"). Thanks to author Deanna Farneti Cera's documentation and research, as well as that of collectors/advisors Jane Clarke and Pat Seal, some of Haskell's early unsigned work, designed primarily by Frank Hess, has been identified.

CIRCA 1950-1975

Aside from novelty items covered in the section on plastics, most costume (or fashion) jewelry continued to follow fine jewelry trends until the late '50s, when "fabulous fake" pieces became more exaggerated and glitzier than their fine jewelry counterparts. Hollywood had perhaps even more influence on non-precious jewelry than on fine jewelry. Joseff of Hollywood outfitted many stars with fabulous fakery for their roles in "period" films, and Marilyn Monroe's "diamonds are a girl's best friend" jewels were really rhinestones, as were Audrey Hepburn's "Breakfast at Tiffany's" baubles. It was also a profitable and common practice for manufacturers to produce costume jewels imitating the precious ones worn by the stars, so that even a woman of modest means could afford to emulate her favorite glamour queen.

The use of design patents gradually disappeared after Congress amended the copyright law in 1947, including the notice of copyright and the use of the copyright symbol © on specific works. This made the process of design protection much easier (and of longer duration) than what had been required for design patents. By the mid-1950s, most jewelry manufacturers were adding the copyright symbol to their mark on a piece of jewelry to indicate that the design was copyrighted and protected by law. This explains why design patents are seldom found for costume jewelry after circa 1955.

Concurrent with fine jewelry, the late 1940s and 1950s saw the return of the parure, or suite of necklace, bracelet, earrings, and brooch, or two or three of these. It should be noted that only one or two components of a suite might be marked with a manufacturer's name. If the pieces are separated, identification may prove difficult.

In the 1950s, the crafts movement influenced commercial production of modernist copper and enameled copper designs, notably by Rebajes of New York and Renoir/Matisse of California. Though mass-produced and inexpensive, this copper art jewelry was usually handmade or hand-finished. Frank Rebajes' status has been elevated to that of studio artist, his work having been included in the "Messengers of Modernism" exhibition of studio artists' jewelry. One known German maker is Perli, which specialized in matte enamels with modernistic tendencies.

Some circa 1960s and later pieces by Boucher, Stanley Hagler, Jomaz, Kenneth Jay Lane, Schreiner, and couturiers Christian Dior, Givenchy, Nettie Rosenstein, Yves St. Laurent, Pauline Trigère, as well as Carnegie, Chanel, and Schiaparelli, have a collector following. Sixties and early '70s designs tended toward the large and the dramatic. The more "over the top" it is, the more desirable to collectors.

French designer Robert Goossens is the creator of many "over the top" costume jewels. He began designing costume jewelry for Chanel when she came out of retirement in 1954 (he had already been working for other big-name couturiers).

Schiaparelli's later jewelry was still bold and imaginative, but it lacked the "off-the-wall" look of her earlier work. Chunky suites set with molded iridescent glass stones (sometimes called "watermelon" or "oil-slick") and "aurora borealis" rhinestones (developed by Swarovski in 1955), or large faceted colored glass stones, were mid-1950s Schiaparelli trademarks, signed with her famous script signature. Schiaparelli retired in 1954, but American manufacturers continued producing her designs through the remainder of the decade.

Designer Lyda Coppola (married name Toppo) designed

Lobster brooch, 1940-'42, large claws set en tremblant, gilded base metal, metallic red enamel, crystal rhinestone accents, unsigned but all attributes of Boucher, 4 1/8". **$250+**

pieces for Schiaparelli early in her career. The Italian maker's own company, Coppola e Toppo, was founded in 1946, but her dramatic faceted glass and plastic bead jewelry gained prominence in the 1960s. The company closed in 1986.

Recent collector attention has been given to a circa late 1950s to early 1960s style called "Juliana." The name is derived from a paper hangtag found on some pieces that are unsigned—speculation is that it was made by wholesale jobbers and sold to several different companies. Most often seen are chunky flexible link bracelets or suites of clustered multicolored rhinestones, some with aurora borealis iridescence. Paper tags marked "Gloria" or "Tara" are also sometimes found on this type of costume jewelry. The construction and look are similar.

Jonné is a name found on circa 1950s costume jewelry that bears some resemblance to Miriam Haskell pieces of the same era, including the use of glass beads and "roses

montées" (flat-backed) rhinestones. As is often the case with matched suites of this period, some pieces are not marked.

Ming's of Honolulu, a Hawaiian jeweler in business from circa 1940 to 1999, made jewelry for a niche market with crossover appeal for Hawaiiana collectors as well as jewelry collectors. Its trademark designs were created by founding artist Wook Moon (d. 1989), whose renditions of Hawaiian flora, such as birds of paradise, orchids, hibiscus, and anthuriums, appealed to Hawaiian locals and tourists alike. Most of these were made of carved and dyed ivory and sterling silver. At the height of its production, Ming's maintained shops in cities throughout the mainland, as well as several on the islands. It began closing the mainland stores in the 1960s. Now that the entire business has closed its doors, collector interest in all types of Ming's jewelry has grown.

Gump's of San Francisco was a retailer for sterling designs by Guglielmo Cini (1903-1979), which also found their way to the company's store in Honolulu. According to a source at Gump's, the company's Honolulu location was in business from 1929 to 1950, but the San Francisco store carried Cini jewelry until the mid-1960s.

Today, many collectors and dealers tend to focus on the name of the manufacturer or designer rather than on the jewelry itself. Novice dealers often price a piece high because it is signed, not because of its overall design and craftsmanship. It is true that certain manufacturers and designers have reputations for high-quality production and innovative design, and their names do make an upward difference in price compared to similar unsigned pieces. However, the same caveats apply to this genre of jewelry as to any other: A maker's mark is not a guarantee of quality. Be sure to evaluate a piece on its own merits before you turn it over to look for a mark.

Condition is an especially important factor in costume jewelry because costume pieces are more easily damaged than fine jewelry and are difficult to repair well. Major damage or major repairs lower value considerably. Replaced rhinestones and some wear are acceptable to most collectors, but replating, re-enameling, and soldering often are not. If badly done, the piece is ruined, and even if done well, it may end up not looking right. Proper restoration of a worn or broken piece is a job for a skilled professional who specializes in costume jewelry.

Bracelet, 1938-'42, Russian gold-plated filigree, floral-foliate metal stampings on cast frame, 36 foiled and unfoiled jewel-tone cabochons and jellies plus central large domed fuchsia cabochon and single emerald cabochon bezel-set on box clasp, crescent filigree plaques extending out from central medallion, triple chain strands, possibly unsigned Hobé or Robert but probably Czech, 2 1/2" wide. **$500**

DeLizza & Elster bracelet with blue and black beads that look like seed pods but are called "nugget beads," early 1960s, the set was called "Elegance." **$250-$300**

Cameo bracelet, 1950s, signed "Sterling Original Hand-Wrought Design Rebajes," by Frank Rebajes, sterling "wire wrap" cuff, large central carved MOP oval of anonymous lady in profile, 1 3/4". **$500-$900**

Jomaz bracelet with flawed emerald glass stones and clear navettes and baguettes, signed Jomaz, 7" x 1/2". **$200-$250**

Trifari bracelet with aquamarine glass stones and chaton, tapered baguette and baguette clear stones, marked with the crown Trifari mark, 7 1/2" x 1/2". **$295-$350**

Bracelet, 1930s, unsigned, possibly Trifari, gold-tone metal, large unfoiled emerald cut amethyst center stone, prong set, small clear chatons and red baguettes, safety chain, 6 1/2". **$75-$125**

Butterfly brooch, 1940s, heavy sterling silver, crystal accents, and large, horizontally faceted barrel glass stones in wings; hook and latch construction; signed Eisenberg Original Sterling (twice), 3". **$1,500**

Water lily brooch, 1940s, huge gold-plated flower with tendril, purple-black pearlescent enamel, ruby-rose rhinestones, signed Eisenberg Original, 3". **$500**

Mazer brooch with aquamarine baguettes and square, chaton and baguette clear rhinestones, signed MAZER, 2 3/4" x 1 7/8". **$250-$300**

Floral hat brooch set (earrings not shown), 1940s, gilded sterling silver (vermeil), 3-D, wire trim prong-set with multicolor rhinestones, unsigned other than hallmark but looks like CoroCraft, 2 3/4". **$195 set**

Flower brooch with carved Lucite leaves, 1939-'42, pavé-set crystal chaton, faceted, point-tipped Lucite ball set into tube-like claws on high-quiver spring for lots of movement, unsigned, looks like work of Boucher or Mazer, 4 1/4". **$750+**

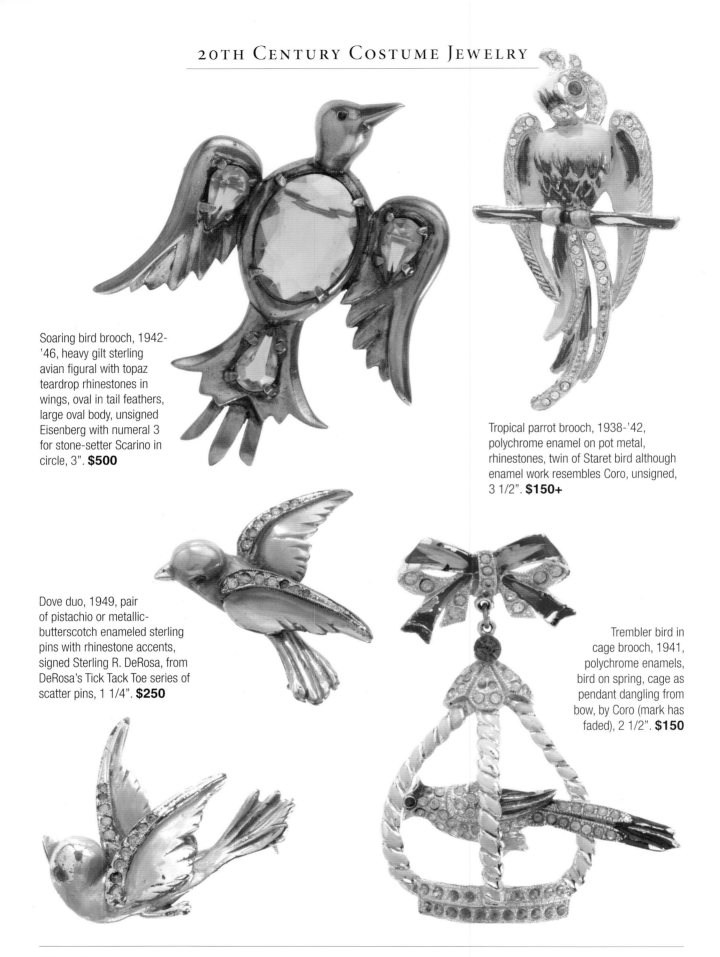

Soaring bird brooch, 1942-'46, heavy gilt sterling avian figural with topaz teardrop rhinestones in wings, oval in tail feathers, large oval body, unsigned Eisenberg with numeral 3 for stone-setter Scarino in circle, 3". **$500**

Tropical parrot brooch, 1938-'42, polychrome enamel on pot metal, rhinestones, twin of Staret bird although enamel work resembles Coro, unsigned, 3 1/2". **$150+**

Dove duo, 1949, pair of pistachio or metallic-butterscotch enameled sterling pins with rhinestone accents, signed Sterling R. DeRosa, from DeRosa's Tick Tack Toe series of scatter pins, 1 1/4". **$250**

Trembler bird in cage brooch, 1941, polychrome enamels, bird on spring, cage as pendant dangling from bow, by Coro (mark has faded), 2 1/2". **$150**

Jewelry courtesy GreatVintageJewelry.com; photo by Veronica McCullough

Vintage peacock pin, 1940-1950s, silver pot metal with glossy peacock-color enamels and faceted marcasites, unsigned, 2 3/8" x 5/8". **$85-$110**

Jewelry courtesy GreatVintageJewelry.com; photo by Veronica McCullough

Heron pin, 1940s, exceptional early silver pot metal figural with white, green, sienna glossy lead enamels, clear and citrine rhinestone accents, unsigned, 2 5/8". **$150**

Pair of geese in flight pin, 1942-'46, highly dimensional, scattered rhinestone accents, sterling silver, unsigned, 3". **$50-$100**

Mechanical pelican pin, 1940-'42, gilded, enameled pot metal, pavé-set rhinestone wing, pushing on head feather plume raises top of beak to reveal one fish, second fish dangles as charm from beak, unsigned, 3". **$500+**

Single-bloom brooch, late 1940s, layered "swedged" (meaning to shape metal using a hammer or crimp), circular arrangement of orchid navettes, clear crystals and pink center rhinestones riveted to gold-plated petals edged with clear rhinestone chaton, unsigned, similar to some Eisenberg-Mazer-Reinad pieces, 2 3/4". **$150+**

Pooch brooch, 1940s, gilded pot metal with 20 emerald-cut amethyst rhinestones, tiny crystal accents, unsigned, 3". **$150**

Brooch, painted, 1950s, molded plastic inset with multicolor rhinestones, riveted to brass die-cut base, probably French, unsigned, 2 7/8". **$50+**

Pheasant pin, 1940s, bronze-toned pot metal, large aquamarine faceted center stone, small sapphire accent stones, tiny clear rhinestone chatons, unsigned, 2 3/4". **$50**

Zany tropical bird pin, 1938-'42, yellow, white, green enamels, gilt pot metal, unsigned, resembles Staret work, 3 1/4". **$150**

Bow-tied sheaf of leaves with simulated blue moonstones, 1930s-'40s, enameled leaves and tie, blue rhinestone accents, looks like a Chanel Novelty piece but pin mechanism French, unsigned, 3 1/4". **$50+**

Pot of flowers pin, 1950s, basket-weave bowl pavé-set with rhinestones, nine flowers set on thin wire stems that move, emerald baguettes invisibly set in one stalk, openwork leaves with emerald rhinestone accents, dimensional, unsigned, 2 1/8". **$50**

Seahorse pin, 1960s, gold-plated stamped metal in layers, plastic beads (turquoise and coral) and fluted coral body, enameled in Coro-like polychrome colors, unsigned, 2 3/8". **$50-$75**

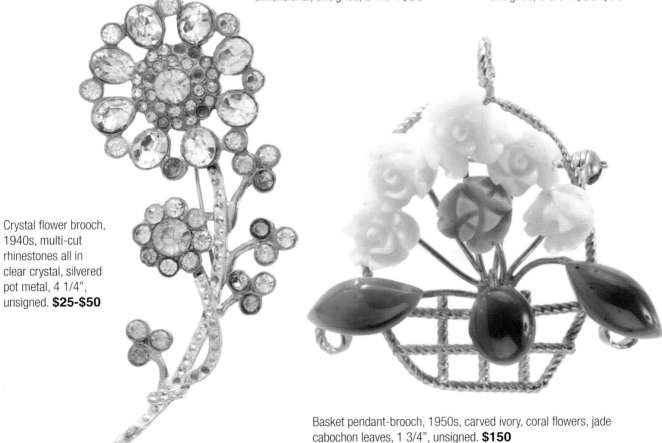

Crystal flower brooch, 1940s, multi-cut rhinestones all in clear crystal, silvered pot metal, 4 1/4", unsigned. **$25-$50**

Basket pendant-brooch, 1950s, carved ivory, coral flowers, jade cabochon leaves, 1 3/4", unsigned. **$150**

Glass dress clip, 1940s, gold-washed metal flowers centered with blue rhinestones set against detailed cast leaves, large faceted crystal glass vase set into prongs; unsigned but has been found signed Mazer and Reinad, 2 3/4". **$250**

Jewelry courtesy GreatVintageJewelry.com; photo by Veronica McCullough

Flower basket pin, silvery pot metal, 1930s thick, heavy urn with rhodium plating, clear and amethyst rhinestones, safety clasp, 3", unsigned, attributed to Reinad. **$110-$155**

Vine floral dress clip, 1950s, gold-plated metal, multicolor rhinestones in four blooms, emerald navette rhinestone leaves, unsigned, 2 1/2". **$25**

Floral dress clip, 1930s, faceted oval orchid rhinestones in enameled pot metal setting, signed Stempa, 2". **$50**

Three-flower in pot enameled fur clip, 1930s, unsigned, 1 3/4". **$25**

Jewelry courtesy Beth Silta; photo by Ross Englund

Schreiner quiver flower pin, 1950s, faux pearls, faceted heart-shaped sapphire rhinestones forming three flower heads; art-glass purple stones as leaves; flower heads sit on tiny sensitive springs and tremble at a hint of air; signed Schreiner. **$150-$200**

Aquamarine arrangement of flowers in enameled white gold basket, 1940s, gilded pot metal, pink centerpiece stones in decorative raised prong settings, unsigned, 3 1/2". **$150+**

Drooping red-hot pokers pin, 1940s, elongated pink-red rounded skinny navettes in gilded sterling (vermeil) vase, wire stems, crystal rhinestone accents add feminine touch, unsigned, 2 3/4". **$150+**

Framed flowers pin, 1930s-1940s, rhinestones and enamel rectangle frames vase of enameled flowers, signed Coro, 2". **$50**

Branched arrangement, 1940s, enameled leaves and flowers in gilded pitcher jardiniere, rhinestone and moonstone accents, from the "Gardenesque Series," rhodium reverse, signed Reja, 2 1/4". **$150-$250**

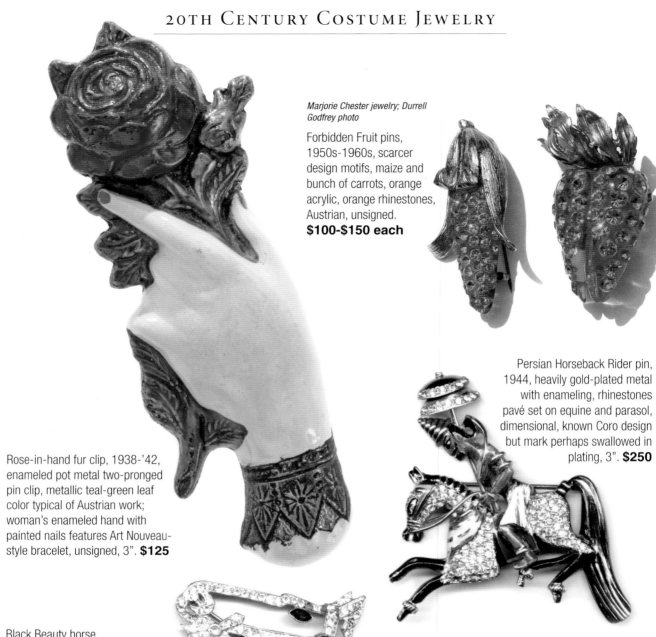

Marjorie Chester jewelry; Durrell Godfrey photo

Forbidden Fruit pins, 1950s-1960s, scarcer design motifs, maize and bunch of carrots, orange acrylic, orange rhinestones, Austrian, unsigned. **$100-$150 each**

Persian Horseback Rider pin, 1944, heavily gold-plated metal with enameling, rhinestones pavé set on equine and parasol, dimensional, known Coro design but mark perhaps swallowed in plating, 3". **$250**

Rose-in-hand fur clip, 1938-'42, enameled pot metal two-pronged pin clip, metallic teal-green leaf color typical of Austrian work; woman's enameled hand with painted nails features Art Nouveau-style bracelet, unsigned, 3". **$125**

Black Beauty horse head fur clip, 1940s, black enamel, silver-plated metal, rhinestone accents and cabochons, unsigned, 2 1/2". **$100.**
Rhinestone horse head, 1940s, open work rhodium metal set with rhinestone brilliants, emerald rhinestone cabochon rosette, ruby navette eye, unsigned, known as a Trifari pin (others in this series signed), 3". **$250**

Trembler knight on steed, 1940s, enameled gold-plated metal, pavé-set rhinestones, 2 1/4". **$150**

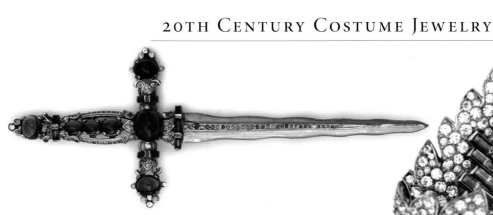

Unsigned Trifari sword pin, 1940s, gold-toned metal with silver-toned metal accents, red, blue, green cabochons, blue and red baguettes, tiny clear rhinestone chatons, 5 1/2". **$250**

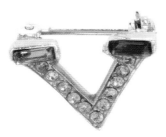

"V" for Victory pin, 1942, red, blue, clear crystal rhinestones, silver-plated metal. **$25**

Fool's Scepter pin clip, 1938-'42, twist-pattern post and articulated leaf-like cap and collar points enameled metallic green, tipped with ruby cabochon beads, post finished with larger glass bead, silvered pot metal, unsigned, sometimes marked Boucher, 2 5/8". **$100-$150**

Signed Trifari leaf pin, 1940s, rhodium-plated, encrusted in small clear chaton rhinestones and overlayed in baguettes, turned leaf edge as though blowing in the wind, 3 3/4". **$500-$700**

Lion pin, unsigned Hattie Carnegie, gold-toned metal, green enameling, plastic face and body, clear and topaz rhinestone chatons, green and sapphire navettes, 2". **$875**

Jewelry courtesy of GreatVintageJewelry.com; photo by Veronica McCullough

Moonstone floral pin, unique vintage floral design in big 3/8" pastel moonstone glass domes and textured pewter metal leaves, signed Czechoslovakia, 2 1/2". **$120-$150**

From left, top to bottom:

Polka-dots tree, multicolor rhinestones on skinny trunk, original 1950-1960s Gem-Craft, signed Craft, 2 5/8". **$100+**

Metallic ornaments tree, original Gem-Craft design, balls dangle and swing from partitions, unsigned, 2 3/4". **$100+**

Teepee trees (bottom left and right), 1960s, original Gem-Craft designs, similar, one with scalloped edges,
the other with more stones, both unsigned, 2 3/4". **$50 each**

Colorful tree (bottom center), 1950s-'60s, brightly hued rhinestones, original vintage design by Alfeo Verrecchia
at Gem-Craft, Austrian coloration, japanned setting, six candles, possibly for Kramer, unsigned, 2 1/4". **$250**

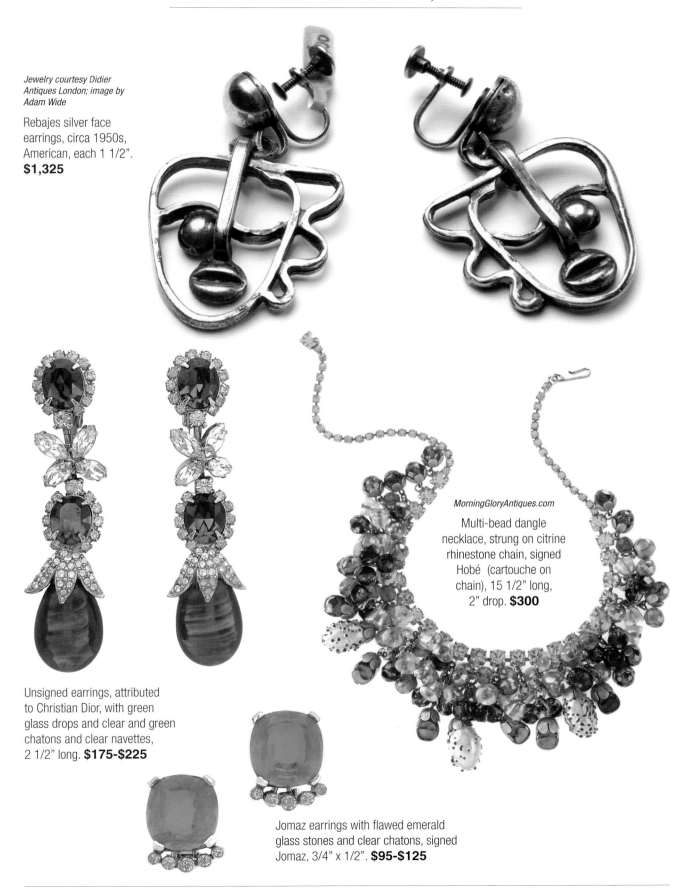

Jewelry courtesy Didier Antiques London; image by Adam Wide

Rebajes silver face earrings, circa 1950s, American, each 1 1/2". **$1,325**

Unsigned earrings, attributed to Christian Dior, with green glass drops and clear and green chatons and clear navettes, 2 1/2" long. **$175-$225**

MorningGloryAntiques.com

Multi-bead dangle necklace, strung on citrine rhinestone chain, signed Hobé (cartouche on chain), 15 1/2" long, 2" drop. **$300**

Jomaz earrings with flawed emerald glass stones and clear chatons, signed Jomaz, 3/4" x 1/2". **$95-$125**

Jomaz necklace with flawed emerald glass stones and clear chatons, signed Jomaz, 14 1/2" x 7/16". **$275-$300**

Jewelry courtesy Addie's Attic; photo by Lisa Brownsen

Simulated jadeite comet set, 1950s, fur clip pin and matching earrings, faux jadeite cabochons and blue gold-specked art-glass navettes, signed Hattie Carnegie, 3 1/2" clip, 1 1/4" earrings. **$179 set**

Doyle New York

Group of costume jewelry of assorted necklaces and a brooch. **$1,500**

Hobe necklace and bracelet set with lavender Lucite beads and white milk glass flower beads, marked Hobe. Necklace is 13 1/2" long with a 3" extender, and bracelet is 7" long. **$125-$175 set**

Doyle New York

Group of costume jewelry, from the top: carved glass leaf and shell pendant-necklace, length adjustable; marcasite pendant-earrings, length adjustable; and a metal, gold-filled, and silver braided choker, signed Dior. **$250**

Doyle New York

Group of costume jewelry, from the top: enamel and leopard bangle, one simulated diamond missing; metal, simulated amethyst and faux diamond necklace, signed Ciner; and Torsade necklace, also signed Ciner. **$96**

Heritage Auctions, Inc.

Pair of earrings and matching pin, signed Miriam Haskell. **$160**

Heritage Auctions, Inc.

Salvatore Ferragamo costume pearl and gilt gold necklace and earrings set, necklace is 26" long. **$203.15**

PORTZLINE COLLECTION OF COSTUME JEWELRY

The photos here and through P. 245 are a small part of the collection of Dr. Thomas Portzline of New York.

Portzline's collection roughly concentrates on pieces from 1937 to 1945 and includes a good representation of all manufacturers and covers a wealth of design, from everyday pieces to masterpieces by Trifari, Boucher, Mazur and Réja, among others.

The Dr. Thomas Portzline Collection was photographed by Carolyn Louise Newhouse.

Enameled ship brooch, rare, signed Trifari, early 1940s, 1 1/2". **$800-$1,000**

Seahorse brooch, unfoiled stones, rare, unsigned Reja, early 1940s, 3 1/2". **$600-$800**

Bee brooch, 1938-'42, enamel and rhinestone pavé work, rare, signed Fenishel, 2 1/2". **$200-$300**

Flower pin, iridescent pink unfoiled stones, rhinestone pavé work, unsigned Reja, rare, early 1940s, 3 1/2". **$500-$700**

Orchid brooch, pink enamel, rare, signed Trifari, early 1940s, 3". **$600-$700**

Lily brooch, pink enamel, rare, signed Reja, early 1940s, 2 1/2". **$200-$300**

Floral brooch, green enamel, large, translucent stones, rare, unsigned DuJay, 1938-'42, 4 1/4". **$800-$1,200**

Flower head brooch, blue enamel, rare, signed Trifari, early 1940s, 3". **$400-$500**

Bluebells brooch, blue enamel, rare, unsigned DuJay, 1938-'42, 2 3/4". **$600-$800**

Twin seahorses brooch, rare, signed Reja, 1940s, 3". **$800-$1,200**

Turtle brooch, large, unfoiled stones, rare, by Ben Meltzer, 1934-'38, 4 1/8". **$2,000+**

Starfish brooch, faceted crystal pavé work and cabochons, rare, unsigned DuJay, 1938-'42, 3 1/4". **$1,200-1,400**

Trembler fish brooch, enamel, rare, unsigned, 1935-'39, 3 1/4". **$250-$350**

Fish brooch, enameled, signed Reja, early 1940s, 3". **$200-$250**

Fish brooch, enamel and simulated coral, rare, signed Leo Glass, early 1940s, 3 1/2". **$400-$600**

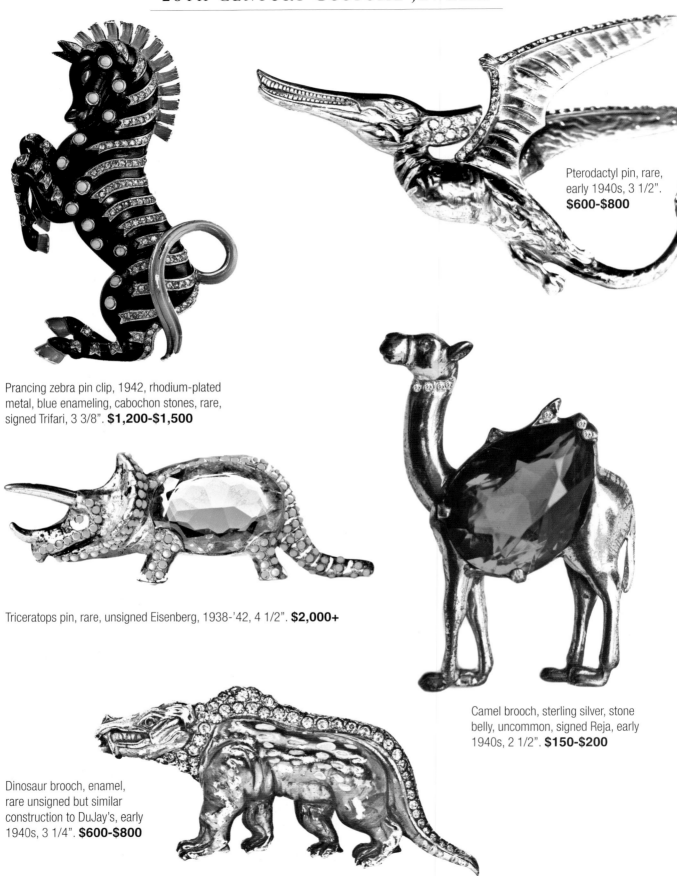

Prancing zebra pin clip, 1942, rhodium-plated metal, blue enameling, cabochon stones, rare, signed Trifari, 3 3/8". **$1,200-$1,500**

Pterodactyl pin, rare, early 1940s, 3 1/2". **$600-$800**

Triceratops pin, rare, unsigned Eisenberg, 1938-'42, 4 1/2". **$2,000+**

Camel brooch, sterling silver, stone belly, uncommon, signed Reja, early 1940s, 2 1/2". **$150-$200**

Dinosaur brooch, enamel, rare unsigned but similar construction to DuJay's, early 1940s, 3 1/4". **$600-$800**

Dancer brooch, sterling silver, signed Nettie Rosenstein, mid-1940s, 2 3/4". **$250-$350**

Grotesque head brooch, rare, signed HC for Hattie Carnegie, early 1940s, 4 1/2". **$500-$600**

Knight in armor brooch, movable mask, trembler shield, rare, unsigned, 1937-'42, 3". **$200-$300**

Mask pin clips, 1940s, gilded base metal, one with fuchsia stones and blue glass leaves, the other with amethyst and sapphire rhinestones and winglike pavé crystal headpiece, both rare, signed Mazer, 2 3/4" and 2 5/8". **$2,000+ pair**

Bird on nest with chicks brooch, enamel, rare, signed with Phrygian cap for Boucher, early 1940s, 3". **$2,000+**

Butterflies-fruit brooch, enamels and unfoiled stones, rare, unsigned DuJay, 1938-'42, 1 3/4". **$800-$1,200**

Butterfly brooch set, sterling silver, enamel, rare, signed Nettie Rosenstein, early 1940s, 3 3/4" pin, 1" clip earrings (not shown). **$600-$800 set**

Butterfly brooch, enameled sterling silver, rare, signed Nettie Rosenstein, 1940s, 3 3/4". **$800-$1,000**

Bird brooch, blue and purple polychrome enamels, large navette crystal belly, kite-shaped crystal tail, rare, signed Mazer, 4 1/8", 1938-'42. **$1,200-$1,400**

Tiger lily brooch, 1938-'42, vibrant enamels, unsigned but with stone setter's mark, rare, attributed to Mazer or Boucher, 3 1/2". **$1,400-$1,600**

Stylized flower brooch, early 1940s, jeweled bloom and pot, aqua and deep topaz, enameled leaves, pavé crystal rhinestone accents, signed Mazer, 2 3/4". **$500-$700**

Pelican pin, rare, signed with Phrygian cap for Boucher, early 1940s, 3 1/2". **$2,000+**

Big bee brooch, 1940s, specialty cut citrine crystals, amethyst rhinestones, pavé-set chaton, enamel, rare, signed Mazer, 2 3/4". **$800-$1,000**

Grasshopper brooch, enamel, rare, signed with Phrygian cap for Boucher, early 1940s, 4". **$2,000+**

Cucumber brooch, enamel, rare, signed with Phrygian cap for Boucher, early 1940s, 4 1/2". **$2,000+**

Raspberries brooch, enamel, rare large size, signed with Phrygian cap for Boucher, early 1940s, 4 1/2". **$1,400-$1,600**

Pineapple pin, enamel, unfoiled stones, very rare, unsigned DuJay, 1938-'42, 3 1/4". **$2,000+**

Grapes pin and earrings set, enamel, signed Reja, early 1940s, pin 3", earrings 3/4". **$250-$300 set**

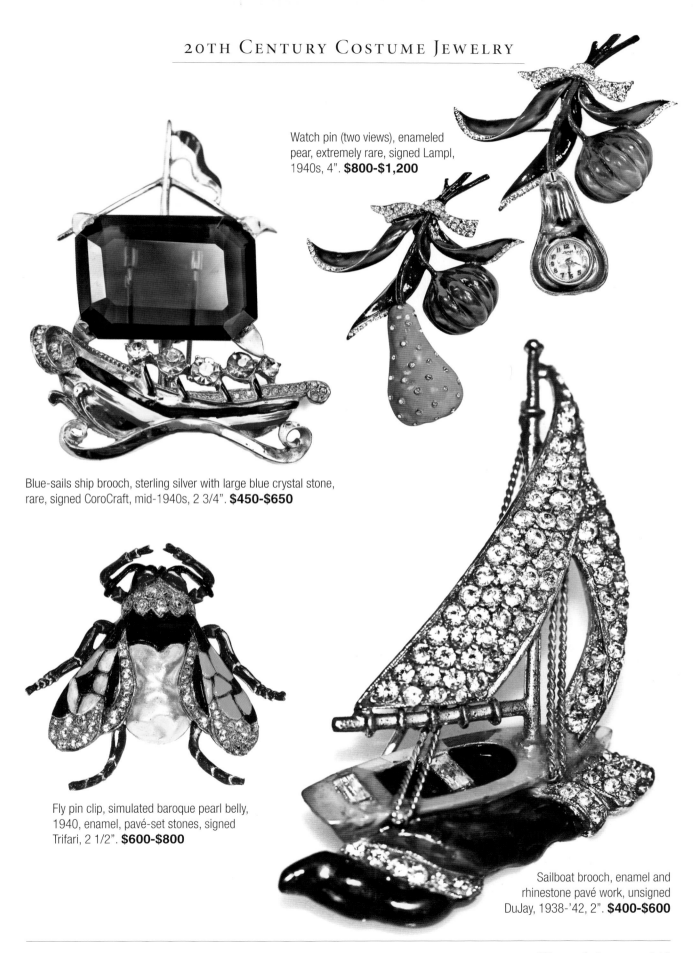

Watch pin (two views), enameled pear, extremely rare, signed Lampl, 1940s, 4". **$800-$1,200**

Blue-sails ship brooch, sterling silver with large blue crystal stone, rare, signed CoroCraft, mid-1940s, 2 3/4". **$450-$650**

Fly pin clip, simulated baroque pearl belly, 1940, enamel, pavé-set stones, signed Trifari, 2 1/2". **$600-$800**

Sailboat brooch, enamel and rhinestone pavé work, unsigned DuJay, 1938-'42, 2". **$400-$600**

PLASTIC AND NOVELTY JEWELRY, CIRCA 1920-1970

In her introduction to the chapter on jewelry in *Art Plastic*, Andrea DiNoto writes, "If one word were needed to summon up the spirit of the twenties and thirties, 'novelty' would do nicely." For the first time, the idea of wearing jewelry for fun caught on.

The ideal material for creating this new type of jewelry was plastic–lightweight, inexpensive, and colorful. Although jewelry had been made from celluloid (the earliest semi-synthetic plastic) as far back as 1875, it was limited in style, made mostly in the form of imitation ivory, coral, amber, and tortoiseshell for naturalistic ornamental and utilitarian pieces (see "Early Celluloid" in Late Victorian section). It was worn primarily by those who could not afford the real thing. It wasn't until the reckless, lighthearted attitude of the flapper came on the scene that we begin to see whimsical and flamboyant items appear, in decidedly unnatural colors.

In the first half of the 20th century, many types of plastic were developed and given trade names by the manufacturers that produced them. Numerous different trade names were given to the same generic substance, as each manufacturer strove for proprietary identification of the material. Over the years, certain names came into generic usage in spite of the fact that they were registered trade names. The three names in most common usage today are celluloid (the word is now seldom capitalized) for pyroxylin-camphor thermoplastic, Bakelite (sometimes written lowercase) for thermosetting phenol formaldehyde resin, and Lucite (seldom lowercase) for thermoplastic polymethacrylates or acrylics. Sometimes these labels are erroneously applied to other related, but not chemically identical, plastics. For example, cellulose acetate (trade name "Lumarith") is often incorrectly called celluloid, and casein plastic, a thermoset (trade name "Galalith"), is commonly confused with Bakelite. Accurately identifying these materials requires a variety of tests, some of which are potentially destructive.

Some collectors believe that a piece of plastic jewelry is collectible and has value because of other factors, such as design and craftsmanship, and that the type of plastic used is of secondary importance. They feel that knowing exactly what a piece is made of is not worth the risks involved in testing. Others consider correct material identification an important part of classifying, circa-dating, and putting a piece in historical context, all of which serves to enhance the value of their collections. The middle ground–the one taken here–is making educated guesses based on non-destructive sensory tests and grouping plastics by generic types–thermoplastics and thermosets–and their related trade names. Although there are now dozens of different plastics on the market, for most collectible jewelry purposes, the ones covered here are celluloid, casein (Galalith), Bakelite, cellulose acetate (Lumarith), and Lucite.

Thermoplastics are those that soften or melt with the application of heat. Once cooled, they again become solid. Thermosets are liquid (resinous) before they are molded or cast, but once they solidify, they remain solid. Thermoplastic scraps can be recycled. Thermosets cannot. All plastics can be classified in one or the other of these two categories.

CELLULOID AND CELLULOSE ACETATE

Celluloid, the first successful semi-synthetic thermoplastic, is part natural fiber, or cellulose. Its generic names, pyroxylin-camphor thermoplastic, sometimes referred to as cellulose nitrate, are clues to its makeup: cellulose fiber mixed with nitric acid (nitrated) to which camphor is added, and subjected to heat. Celluloid was first used as a substitute for natural materials, but its versatility, coupled with imaginative designs and new processes, later yielded a variety of forms. In 1902, a patent was granted for a process of setting rhinestones or metal into celluloid, thereby enhancing its decorative potential. In 1923, a synthetic pearl essence was invented, called "H-scale". It replaced the more expensive fish scale type of pearl essence (the coating on simulated pearls) for celluloid, and was used on toilet articles, decorative accessories, and jewelry.

One of the major drawbacks of celluloid was its flammability, due to the nitrocellulose it contained. In 1927, the Celluloid Corp. introduced Lumarith, its trade name for cellulose acetate, which substituted acetic acid (vinegar) for nitric acid and camphor. Except for its bright colors, in appearance and use cellulose acetate is the same as celluloid, but non-flammable. It is often labeled celluloid, but technically and chemically, this is incorrect. When warmed in hot water, the two materials can be differentiated: Celluloid smells like camphor; cellulose acetate smells like vinegar. (This test should not be used on jewelry set with rhinestones or other materials susceptible to water damage, nor should any piece be immersed in water for more than a few seconds.) The use of cellulose acetate coincided with the development of the injection-molding process, which made mass-production of inexpensive plastic items possible. In the 1960s and '70s, an extensive line of large and small pins, bangles, and stretchy bracelets was made from laminated cellulose acetate by Lea Stein of Paris. These colorful figural and geometric pieces have a large collector following.

Celluloid articles should be stored carefully in a dry and ventilated place. They are subject to disintegration if exposed to extremes of temperature, constant moisture, or corroding metal. Cracks, crystallization, and discoloration are signs of decomposition. Already damaged pieces are contagious and should be kept separate from others.

Much of the foregoing information on celluloid was brought to light by Julie P. Robinson, celluloid historian, who is co-author of a book on collectible celluloid and its inventor, John Wesley Hyatt (see "References"). She obtained copies of U.S. patents and perused the archives of the Celluloid Corp. and other pyroxylin plastics manufacturers, and the Smithsonian Institution.

Hair combs and hatpins were among the earliest items of personal adornment made of celluloid, following fashion's currents at the turn of the century. (Leominster, Massachusetts was a center for hair-comb production, first in natural materials, then plastics.) But when fashions changed, these fell by the wayside. Hatpins shrank to become hat ornaments with a threaded metal pinpoint that was pushed through the hat and secured with a second ornamental "head" (similar to fine jewelry's jabot or *cliquet* pins).

Famous dancer Irene Castle cut her hair in a bob in 1914, prompting thousands of her fans to follow suit, thus signaling the demise of the hair comb. Surprisingly, hair

Image and jewelry courtesy Linda Lombardo and Worn to Perfection, www.rubylane.com

Celluloid pin found with original hangtag, circa 1920s-1930s, marked "Les Creations, Maloupa, Paris, Made in France." **$70**

combs didn't completely disappear when "the bob" became the predominant hairstyle. Large and ornate Spanish-style back combs, often embellished with rhinestones and painted enamel, were still occasionally worn, bound to the head, in the late 1920s, when the tango was all the rage and Spanish lace, fringed shawls, and flounced skirts were part of a dancer's costume.

A more typical '20s head ornament was the headband or bandeau. These, too, were made of rhinestone-studded celluloid. Because the material is flexible, the headbands are adjustable, held by an ornamental celluloid clasp. Today, these are rare finds.

Celluloid bangles, many ivory- or amber-colored but in other colors as well, were worn from wrist to elbow in the fashion made popular by heiress Nancy Cunard. The ones most sought-after today have painted designs and/or geometric patterns of pavé rhinestones set into them. Whimsical figural pins and short chain necklaces with dangling floral or figural motifs were also made of celluloid.

Celluloid (pyroxylin plastics) continued to be used for jewelry well into the 1940s (post-World War II molded figural pieces marked "Occupied Japan" can still be found), but with the development of other less flammable and more easily mass-produced plastics, celluloid fell out of favor. After the Celluloid Corp. became part of Celanese in 1947, U.S. production was discontinued. Japan continued to make pyroxylin items during the 1950s.

BAKELITE AND CASEIN

The first entirely synthesized plastic was invented by Leo H. Baekeland in 1908 (patented 1909). As with many inventions, it was accidental. He was searching for a formula for synthetic shellac, at which he failed miserably. Instead, he came up with "the material of a thousand uses," as the advertisers called it: thermosetting phenol formaldehyde resin. He christened it Bakelite. Other companies started manufacturing similar phenolics and came up with their own trade names, among them: Catalin, Marblette, Durez, and Prystal. Bakelite is the name that has stuck with collectors, although some purists insist upon calling it by the generic name "phenolic" or the trade name "Catalin" (most jewelry made from this material was made by the Catalin Corp.).

Jewelry was not the first of the thousand uses. The Depression created a market for it because it was cheap to manufacture, colorful, and lent itself to a wide range of styles and manufacturing techniques. It gave women a much-needed lift to both their outfits and their spirits. Bakelite was well suited to the chunky, heavy jewelry styles of the '30s. It could be laminated into geometric shapes (polka dots were a popular motif), set with rhinestones, clad or inlaid with metal, carved on a lathe, made into the shapes of animals, fruits, or other realistic figurals. Colorless Bakelite (introduced in 1935 by the Catalin Corp., whose trade name for it was Prystal) was carved on the back side with floral or figural designs. The carving was sometimes enhanced with paint. From the front, the designs look three-dimensional. "Reverse-carved" is today's name for this technique. Over time, the pieces have oxidized to a light amber color, which collectors call "apple juice." Reverse-carved fish and aquarium motifs are particularly desirable.

Bracelets of all types–solid and hinged bangles, link, elastic "stretchies," cuffs, and charm bracelets–brooches, dress clips, shoe clips, buckles, earrings, rings, necklaces, beads, and pendants were all made from Bakelite. Bakelite jewelry and objects have been avidly collected for the past 30 years. Several books and magazine articles have covered the subject quite thoroughly (see "References"). Themed figurals (patriotic, school, sports, animals, people, fruits

Vintage pin, 1940s, deeply carved black Bakelite, unsigned, 3 1/4". **$375**

and vegetables, Mexican motifs, etc.) and multicolored laminated geometrics (especially bangles, solid and hinged) are among today's most sought-after Bakelite items.

Of particular interest to many collectors are designs attributed to Martha Sleeper (1910-1983), an actress-turned-designer whose work has been documented in several books on Bakelite jewelry. Sleeper and her jewelry made headlines in 1938, but after World War II, she went on to other things.

Casein plastic has received relatively little attention compared to Bakelite, the material it is often confused with. Most pieces made of casein plastic generate relatively little collector interest or value, with one exception. Not much plastic jewelry is signed or even attributed, but certain casein plastic pieces were: Auguste Bonaz, whose company is known for its geometric necklaces of the early 1930s, which are now rare and sought-after. According to Ginger Moro in *European Designer Jewelry*, these necklaces were always made of Galalith, the trade name for casein.

LUCITE

Although the German manufacturers Röhm and Haas are credited with being the first to formulate acrylic resin (1928), their trade name for it, Plexiglas, seems to be used mainly in reference to utilitarian and decorative objects. Lucite, introduced by DuPont in 1937, is the trade name most often heard in reference to jewelry.

Lucite is water clear in its original form, but it is often tinted in a wide range of transparent to opaque colors. Molded, tinted and reverse-carved Lucite figural jewelry is nearly as sought-after as its early '40s Bakelite contemporaries. After the war, Bakelite was no longer cost-effective to produce, but Lucite, a thermoplastic, continued to be manufactured and is still in use today. Post-war jewelry forms, however, are quite different from earlier pieces.

Some circa 1940s novelty jewelry was made of Lucite combined with other materials like Bakelite, wood, leather, and metal. "Jelly bellies," one of the hottest items among costume jewelry collectors, have Lucite as the center or "belly" of sterling animal pins. These were made in the '40s by Trifari and other American manufacturers (see "Designer/ Manufacturer Signed Costume Jewelry" section). In the '50s, pearlized Lucite bangles and button earclips, often rhinestone-studded, were popular accessories, as were laminated brooches, bracelets, and earrings encasing flowers or embedded with pastel-dyed shells and glitter. In the 1960s, Lucite was often used in colorless form for chunky rings, necklaces, and bracelets. These were also laminated with colored layers forming reflective stripes.

Sensory tests can reveal a plastic's identity without being destructive. The aforementioned hot water test works for Bakelite, Lucite, and casein as well as celluloid and cellulose acetate. It is not necessary to use any chemical products for testing, some of which do not give consistently positive results and which may be destructive.

As prices of collectible plastics, especially Bakelite, have skyrocketed over the past few years, it is important to remember that plastics, unlike gold and gemstones, are not intrinsically valuable. The material itself is not collectible; what was made from it is. An unimaginative, plain, or downright ugly piece–even though it is "genuine" celluloid, Bakelite, or Lucite–will have little collector interest or value.

Other materials were used concurrently with plastics to produce whimsical novelty articles. In the 1940s, carved wood was a favorite material, alone or in combination with

Jelly parrot pin, Lucite and base metal, 1942, very rare (beware of reproductions), signed Trifari, 4". **$2,000+**

other materials. Western motifs were all the rage in wood as well as plastic, due once again to the movies' influence. Horses' heads are the most prevalent motif.

During wartime shortages, with factories given over to military production and European sources cut off, a kind of "make do" novelty jewelry was made using readily available non-rationed materials to create amusing pieces. Many of these were hand-constructed. Ceramic or plaster composition, felt, yarn, leather, feathers, and sequins were combined to make fashion head brooches, some of them resembling popular movie stars. These have been nicknamed "Victims of Fashion" by collectors. Others had exotic Asian or African faces, some of which were also carved in wood. Wooden heads were also painted with politically incorrect cartoon-like features. The Sears catalog of 1944 advertised "lapel 'pin-ups' in gay hand-painted ceramics"–caricatures of animals and people–with Lucite and yarn details. Once the war was over, this type of jewelry faded into oblivion. In the '50s, "cute" replaced "whimsical," and gold-plated metal and rhinestones were the usual materials of choice.

World War II also gave rise to the popularity of sweetheart jewelry: lockets and lapel pins representing the armed forces worn by wives and girlfriends of soldiers, sailors, and Marines fighting overseas. They often bore the insignia of the different military branches.

Images and jewelry courtesy Linda Lombardo and Worn to Perfection, www.rubylane.com

Art Deco scene pin, circa 1920s-1930s, man and woman seaside, two celluloid layers, colorized background layer, Les Creations Maloupa, Paris, France , 2 1/8". **$90**

Art Deco scene, circa 1920s-1930s, man and woman seaside, two celluloid layers fully colorized, Les Creations Maloupa, Paris, France, 2 1/8". **$125**

Two birds on branches pin, circa 1920s-1930s, single celluloid layer, Les Creations Maloupa, Paris, France, 1 3/4". **$75**

Two birds on branches pin, circa 1920s-1930s, single celluloid layer, colorized, Les Creations Maloupa, Paris, France, 1 3/4". **$85**

Image and jewelry courtesy Linda Lombardo and Worn to Perfection, www.rubylane.com

Venice gondola scene, rare, circa 1920s-1930s, two celluloid layers, fully colorized, Les Creations Maloupa, Paris, France, 1 3/4". **$150**

Images and jewelry courtesy Linda Lombardo and Worn to Perfection, www. rubylane.com

Lovebirds pin, circa 1920s-1930s, colorized, single celluloid layer, "Nous Deux" (We Two) in heart with two brightly colored lovebirds, Les Creations Maloupa, Paris, France, 1 7/8". **$95**

Lovebirds pin, circa 1920s-1930s, original ivory-colored single-layer celluloid, "Nous Deux" (We Two) in heart, Les Creations Maloupa, Paris, France, 1 7/8." **$85**

Ship pin, circa 1920s-1930s, colorized celluloid, three-mast sailing ship, Les Creations Maloupa, Paris, France, 1 3/4". **$80**

Canoe scene celluloid pin, circa 1920s-1930s, Les Creations Maloupa, Paris, France, 1 5/8". **$65**

Cat on roof pin, circa 1920s-1930s, double layer die-cut celluloid in original ivory color, simple openwork gallery, Les Creations Maloupa, Paris, France, 1 5/8". **$70**

Man and flower pins:
Left: head brooch, 1970s, purple-blue galalith plastic, design known as "Cocteau," rare, signed Guillemette l'Hoir Paris, 2". **$500-$1,400**
Right: Floral brooch, 1930s, painted purple celluloid morning glory, c-clasp, 2 1/2". **$25**

Lady and guitar pins:
Left: Lady's head pin signed Lea Stein Paris, made in France, 1970s, 2". **$165**
Right: Heavily carved Lucite guitar pin, 1920s, 4". **$165**

Sotheby's

Bakelite diamond bangle-bracelet, Michele Della Valle, translucent green bangle studded with round diamonds weighing approximately 2.90 carats, mounted in 18k white gold, signed Michele Della Valle, numbered 10927, internal circumference 7 1/2". **$15,000**

Skinner Inc.

Bakelite bracelet, Flamand, Paris, gold tone cuff with green Bakelite and white stone surmount, signed, box inscribed, "Ma petite etoile Gina Taybery(?)" (split to Bakelite), 6" interior circumference. In the 1930s, Flamand made several Bakelite bracelets as promotional devices for films, including one model for Josephine Baker's ZouZou. **$652**

Heritage Auctions, Inc.

Pair of diamond, Bakelite and white gold bangles, feature single-cut diamonds weighing 1.50 carats, set in 18k white gold atop Bakelite, 7" x 3/8". **$4,780**

Heritage Auctions, Inc.

Colored diamond, smoky quartz, Bakelite and gold cuff bracelet, full-cut brown diamonds weighing approximately 2.25 carats, enhanced by pear and rectangular-shaped smoky quartz weighing approximately 3.90 carats, bezel set in 14k gold, inserted into Bakelite, 7" x 1 7/8". **$1,195**

Vintage bangle, 1930s, detailed, highly carved root-beer Bakelite bangle, unusual clasp allows bracelet to open and fit many wrist sizes, rare. **$900**

Private Collection

Rectangular hinged cuff bracelet, 1930s, bronze with hand-carved Bakelite Asian men, French. **$1,500**

Bangle bracelet, 1930s, four-color laminate in Bakelite bangle measuring 7/8" high, unsigned. **$450**

Leafy Bakelite bracelet, 1930s, black with brass trim, hinged so fits larger wrists, leaves each 1 7/8". **$850**

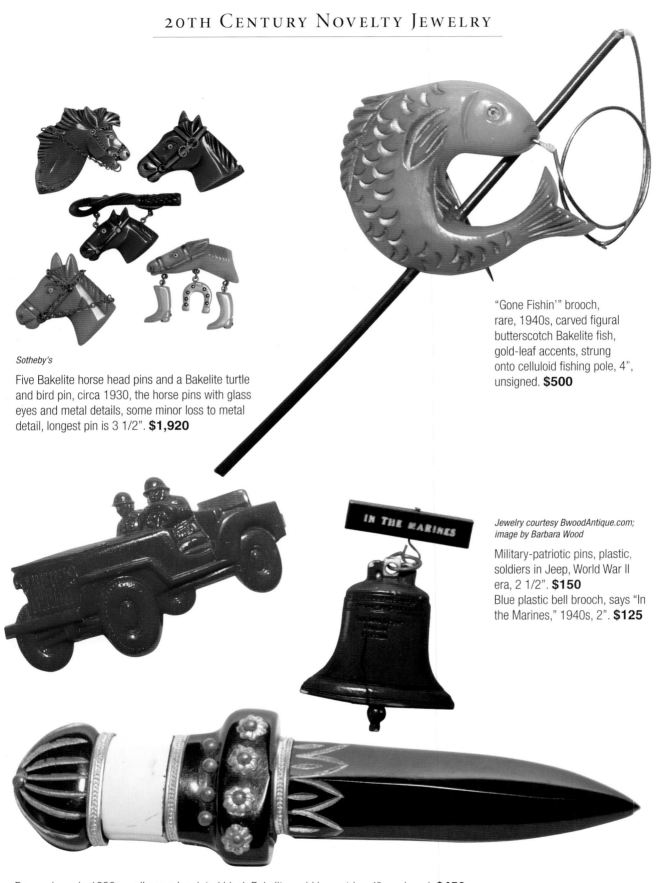

Sotheby's

Five Bakelite horse head pins and a Bakelite turtle and bird pin, circa 1930, the horse pins with glass eyes and metal details, some minor loss to metal detail, longest pin is 3 1/2". **$1,920**

"Gone Fishin'" brooch, rare, 1940s, carved figural butterscotch Bakelite fish, gold-leaf accents, strung onto celluloid fishing pole, 4", unsigned. **$500**

Jewelry courtesy BwoodAntique.com; image by Barbara Wood

Military-patriotic pins, plastic, soldiers in Jeep, World War II era, 2 1/2". **$150**
Blue plastic bell brooch, says "In the Marines," 1940s, 2". **$125**

IN THE MARINES

Dagger brooch, 1930s, well carved, painted black Bakelite, gold brass trim, 4", unsigned. **$450**

Green Bakelite and diamond necklace, Michele Della Valle, composed of translucent green Bakelite beads studded with round diamonds weighing approximately 18.90 carats, mounted in 18k white gold, maker's mark, indistinct numbering, 24" long. **$35,000**

Group of jewelry, Michele Della Valle, comprising an 18k gold, wood and diamond bangle-bracelet of hinged design set with numerous round and baguette diamonds weighing approximately 7.35 carats, internal circumference approximately 7"; pair of Bakelite and 18k two-color gold earrings designed as bows, centered by two coral cabochons framed by black onyx, set throughout with numerous round diamonds weighing approximately 2.75 carats; pair of 18k white gold and Bakelite earrings, set with numerous round diamonds weighing approximately 2.05 carats. All pieces have maker's marks for Michele della Valle, with two signed pouches. **$7,500**

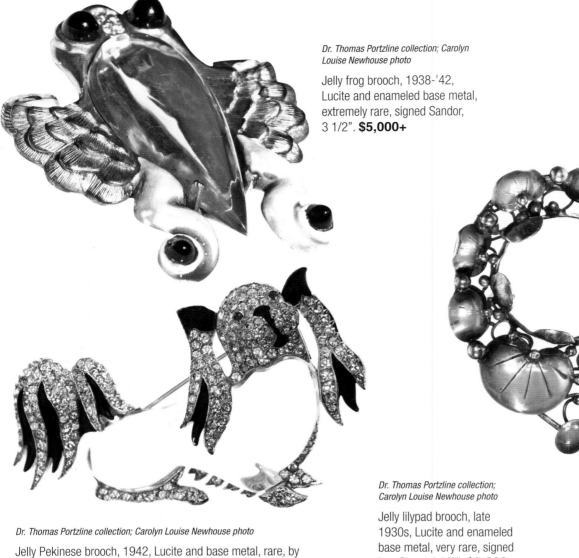

Dr. Thomas Portzline collection; Carolyn Louise Newhouse photo

Jelly frog brooch, 1938-'42, Lucite and enameled base metal, extremely rare, signed Sandor, 3 1/2". **$5,000+**

Dr. Thomas Portzline collection; Carolyn Louise Newhouse photo

Jelly lilypad brooch, late 1930s, Lucite and enameled base metal, very rare, signed Leo Glass, 4 1/8". **$2,000+**

Dr. Thomas Portzline collection; Carolyn Louise Newhouse photo

Jelly Pekinese brooch, 1942, Lucite and base metal, rare, by Trifari, 3 1/8". **$2,000+**

Jewelry courtesy Beth Silta; photo by Ross Englund

Confetti Lucite bracelet, silvery pot metal, clear angled Lucite squares embedded with metallic confetti pieces, signed PAM, 1950s-early '60s. Unusual confetti material often embedded in the plastic. Metallic pieces of various shapes were encased in Lucite, but pieces of shell and mother of pearl were also used. **$35-$75**

Jelly starfish brooch, mid-1940s, Lucite and sterling silver, rare, signed Mosell, 3". **$400-$500**

Jelly elephant brooch, 1942, Lucite and base metal, rare (beware of reproductions), signed Trifari, 3 5/8". **$2,000+**

Jelly larval-like winged insect brooch, 1940s, Lucite and sterling silver, uncommon, signed Jollé, 2 1/2". **$125-$175**

Jelly fish brooch, early 1940s, Lucite and base metal, very rare, signed Calvaire, 4". **$800-$1,200**

Jelly basket brooch, 1948-'49, Lucite and base metal, rare, signed with Phrygian cap for Boucher, 2 1/4". **$350-$450**

Arrow brooch, Lucite and base metal, rare, 1948-'49, signed with Phrygian cap for Boucher, 4". **$300-$450**

Jelly bird head brooch, Lucite, sterling silver, 1938-'42, emerald rhinestones, rare, signed "Sterling Pat Pend, Trifari," 1 7/8". **$800-$1,000**

Jelly eagle brooch, 1943-'44, Lucite and sterling silver, signed "Pat Pend, Trifari," rare, 2". **$500-$600**

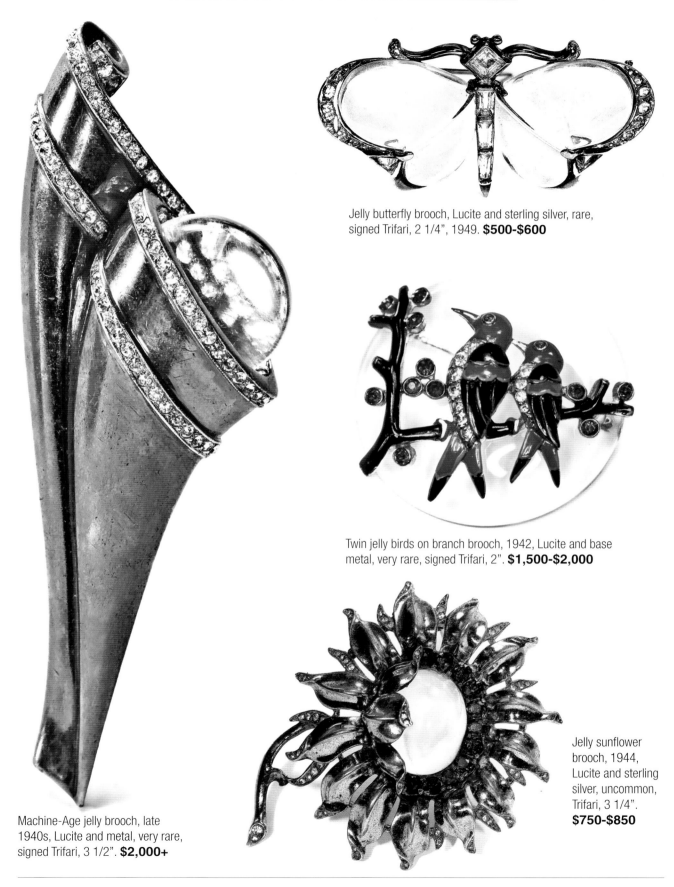

Jelly butterfly brooch, Lucite and sterling silver, rare, signed Trifari, 2 1/4", 1949. **$500-$600**

Twin jelly birds on branch brooch, 1942, Lucite and base metal, very rare, signed Trifari, 2". **$1,500-$2,000**

Jelly sunflower brooch, 1944, Lucite and sterling silver, uncommon, Trifari, 3 1/4". **$750-$850**

Machine-Age jelly brooch, late 1940s, Lucite and metal, very rare, signed Trifari, 3 1/2". **$2,000+**

Jelly shell brooch, 1944-'46, Lucite and sterling silver, uncommon, manufacturer unknown, unsigned, 2 3/8". **$250-$350**

Jelly rose brooch, mid-1940s, Lucite and base metal, signed Trifari, 2 1/2". **$400-$600**

Jelly heart brooch, late 1940s. Lucite and base metal, signed Trifari, 2 1/4". **$250-$350**

Jelly bird-in-cage brooch, 1940s. Lucite and sterling silver, unsigned, 2 3/4". **$75-$100**

Dr. Thomas Portzline collection; Carolyn Louise Newhouse photo

Jelly acorn necklace, mid-1940s, Lucite and metal, rare, signed Mazer, 16". **$800-$1,000**

Jelly lady with fan pin, Lucite and base metal, early 1940s, unsigned, rare, 3 1/2". **$800-$1,200**

Private Collection

Space-themed ray gun novelty pin, silvery aluminum, 1950s, unmarked, movie premium (?), 2". **$25**

Marks on Metals

Marks listed shown larger than actual size

GOLD

Solid karats:

9c/ct (Brit.)	15c/ct (Brit.)
10k	18k or 18c/ct
12k or 12c/ct	20k
14k	22k or 22c/ct

14KP = plumb (exact) [not used until c. 1976]

375 = 9c/ct

583 or 585 = 14k

750 = 18k

Eagle's head (French) = 18k

Eagle's Head

1/20 14k (or 12k) GF = gold-filled

RGP = rolled gold plate

HGE = heavy gold electroplate

PLATINUM

900 Plat - 100 Irid
(alloyed with 10% iridium)

Dog's head (French after 1912)

Dog's Head

SILVER

925 = sterling
(92.5% silver)

British: lion passant = sterling

Lion Passant

Swedish: three crowns =
830 or higher (S after 1912,
oval reserve for imports)

French: boar's head or crab = 800

Austro-Hungarian: dog's or lion's
head = 750 or higher (1866-1937)

Finnish: **813H** = 830; **916H** = 935

800, 825, 830, 850 (European
or continental), **900 standard**
or **coin** (American before 1906)
marked on silver = lower silver content than sterling or 925
(92.5% silver, 7.5% copper)

EPNS = electroplated
nickel silver

German silver, nickel silver =
NO silver content (copper, nickel,
zinc alloy)

Alpaca = copper, zinc, nickel,
2% silver

American Manufacturers' Marks

Newark N.J.

Mark	Manufacturer	Mark	Manufacturer
	ALLING & CO.		LARTER & SONS
	ALLSOPP & ALLSOPP		ENOS RICHARDSON & CO.
	BIPPART, GRISCOM & OSBORN		RIKER BROS.
	CARTER, HOWE (AFTER 1915, GOUGH) & CO.		SLOAN & CO.
	CRANE & THEURER		TAYLOR & CO. (FOR 10K)
	A. J. HEDGES & CO.		UNGER BROS.
	WILLIAM B. KERR & CO.		WHITESIDE & BLANK (HENRY BLANK, CRESARROW)
	KREMENTZ & CO.		WORDLEY, ALLSOPP & BLISS

OTHERS

GEORGE W. SHIEBLER & CO., NEW YORK, N.Y.	TIFFANY & CO., NEW YORK, N.Y.	GORHAM MANUFACTURING, CO., PROVIDENCE, R.I.

20th Century American Costume Jewelry Manufacturers/Designers

ART c. 1950-1980

Avon 1971-present

McClelland Barclay c. 1935-1943

Barclay 1946-c. 1957

Beau (sterling) 1947-present

Bergère 1946-1979

Les Bernard 1962-1996

Bogoff [Spear Novelty Co.] c. 1946-1959?

Boucher 1937-1971 ["Phrygian cap" mark in use 1937-1949]

BSK c. 1948-present [?]

Nadja Buckley c. 1940-1979

Calvaire c. 1920-c. 1960

Hattie Carnegie 1918-1976 [first jewelry 1939]

Castlecliff c. 1918-1977

Alice Caviness 1945-? [Caviness died 1983]

Chanel 1914-1939, 1954-present (most early, some later pieces unmarked)

Chanel Novelty Co. 1941 [Reinad]

Ciner 1892-present [first costume, 1931]

Cini (sterling) 1922-1970, 1993-present

Coro 1901-1979

> *Corocraft (sterling pre-1950) 1933-1979*
>
> *Francois 1938-c. 1960*
>
> *Vendome 1944-1979*
>
> *(Coro, Inc. Canada, to present)*

Sarah Coventry 1949-c. 1984

Danecraft (sterling) 1939-1977

Felch-Wehr Co 1977-present

Deja 1939-1940 [changed to Reja 1941]

Wm de Lillo and Robert Clark 1967-?

DeMario 1945-1965

DeNicola 1957-1970

R.[Ralph] DeRosa 1934-1970

Christian Dior 1948-present [jewelry]

Eisenberg Original c. 1935-1945

> *(sterling 1943-1948)*
>
> *E. (script mark) c. 1942-1945*
>
> *EISENBERG (block letters) c. 1945-1958*
>
> *EISENBERG ice © (block letters) 1970-present*
>
> *(no mark 1958-1970, many pieces not marked 1970-1990)*
>
> *Eisenberg Ice (script) with year 1994 and 2000 (reissued "Classic" series)*

Eisenberg "E" Mark

Emmons 1949-1981

Eugene c. 1950-1960

Florenza c. 1950-1981

Gerry's c. 1950-c. 1996

Givenchy 1952-present

Leo Glass 1928-1957

Stanley Hagler 1953-1996

HAR (Hargo Jewelry Co.) c. 1950-1960

Miriam Haskell 1924-present (most pieces not marked 1924-c. 1947)

Hobé 1927-present [under different ownership]

Hollycraft 1948-1971

Joseff of Hollywood 1938-present

Kramer 1943-c. 1980

Krementz 1866-present [no costume after 1997]

KJL/Kenneth J. Lane 1963-present

Laguna 1944-c. 1980?

Lang (sterling) 1946-1977?

Ledo 1949 c. 1962/Polcini c. 1960-c. 1980?

> *(DBA Leading Jewelry 1911-1948)*

Lisner 1938-c. 1985 [mark; co. founded c. 1904]

Marvella 1911-present

> *(1982-2000: a division of The Monet Group, 2000-present owned by Liz Claiborne)*

Mazer Bros 1923-1951 [mark from 1926]

    Jomaz/Joseph Mazer 1946-81

Ming's of Honolulu c. 1940-1999

Monet 1937-present

    (1989-1994: a subsidiary of Crystal Brands Jewelry Group; 1994-2000: Chase Capital Partners, Lattice Holding, 2000-present, owned by Liz Claiborne)

Napier c. 1922-1999

Original by Robert 1942-1979

    (Fashioncraft Jewelry Co.)

D'Orlan c. 1960-?

Panetta 1945-1995

Pell 1941-present ?

Pennino 1926-1961

Peruzzi c. 1900-present

Rebajes 1932-c. 1967

Regency c. 1950-1970

Reinad c. 1922-c. 1955 [Chanel mark 1941]

Réja 1941-1953

Renoir 1946-1964/ Matisse 1952-1964/Sauteur 1958-1963

Rice-Weiner 1938-1950? (Thief of Bagdad, Korda, McClelland Barclay, c. 1940s)

Nettie Rosenstein c. 1935-1975

Sandor c. 1938-1972

Schiaparelli 1931-1973 (most pre-1949 unmarked)

Schrager c. 1925-c. 1962? (Jonné, c. 1950s)

Schreiner N.Y. 1939-1977

Silson Inc. 1937-c. 1945?

Staret c. 1940-1947

Yves St. Laurent 1959-2002

Tortolani c. 1950-1976, reopened 2002

Trifari 1918-present [mark since 1920, sterling 1942-1947]

    TKF (Trifari, Krussman & Fishel) 1925-1938 (mark used from 1935) (1975-1988: subsidiary of Hallmark; 1988-1994: Crystal Brands; 1994-2000: Chase Capital Partners, Lattice Holding, a division of The Monet Group; purchased by Liz Claiborne, 2000)

Van S Authentics c. 1935-1969

Vogue 1936-c. 1975

Weiss 1942-1971

Whiting & Davis 1876-1991

Wiesner c. 1953-?

WMCA (White Metal Casters' Association) 1930-?

Trifari, Krussman & Fishel

Other Manufacturers: Dates of Operation Unknown

Garman	Juliana	Tara	Joseph Wiesner NY
Gloria	Ramé	Warner	

References:

- Joann Dubbs Ball, *Costume Jewelers, The Golden Age of Design*, Schiffer Publishing, 1990

- Carla Ginelli Brunialti and Roberto Brunialti, *American Costume Jewelry, 1935-50*, Edizioni Gabriele Mazzotta, 1997 (Italian text), and *A Tribute to America, Costume Jewelry 1935-50,* Edita, 2002 (English text)

- Matthew Burkholz and Linda Kaplan, *Copper Art Jewelry, A Different Lustre*, Schiffer Publishing, 1992

- Deanna Farnetti Cera, ed., *Jewels of Fantasy*, Harry N. Abrams, 1992 (out of print)

- Maryanne Dolan, *Collecting Rhinestone & Colored Jewelry*, 4th ed., Krause Publications, 1998

- Harrice Simons Miller, *Official Price Guide to Costume Jewelry*, 3rd ed., House of Collectibles, 2002

- Dorothy Rainwater, *American Jewelry Manufacturers*, Schiffer Publishing, 1988

- Fred Rezazadeh, *Costume Jewelry, A Practical Handbook & Value Guide*, Collector Books, 1998

- Lucille Tempesta, ed., *Vintage Fashion & Costume Jewelry Newsletter*, various quarterly issues

- Back issues of *Vogue* and *Harper's Bazaar* magazines

Basic Hallmark Identification

Hallmarks have been in use in England and France since the 14th century. Most other European countries also use hallmarks. The United States has never used hallmarks per se. Indications of fineness or karat have been required since 1906, but fineness marks were sometimes stamped on silver jewelry in the 19th century ("coin" or "standard" for 900 silver, "sterling" for 925).

Hallmarks are most often found on objects made of precious metals. Jewelry is exempted from hallmarking under certain circumstances. However, when a piece of jewelry is hallmarked, the marks can yield clues to country of origin and, sometimes, date of manufacture, as well as indicate the metal content of the piece. Makers' marks are not strictly considered hallmarks by themselves, although a maker's mark may accompany a hallmark on a piece (see "Glossary" for definition).

Every country has a different system of hallmarking, ranging from simple to complex. The most commonly found marks are discussed here. Others can be found in Tardy's *International Hallmarks on Silver and Poincons d' Or et de Platine* (hallmarks on gold and platinum, French text).

FRENCH HALLMARKS

The French have what is undoubtedly the most complex system of hallmarks in the world, and the most difficult to read. If you can learn to recognize the French marks for gold, silver and platinum, you will have done well. The difficulty lies in the fact that the French never use numbers. Symbols in the form of animals and heads of animals and people, insects, and birds have been used to indicate fineness, place of manufacture, imports and exports. These have changed over the centuries. Tardy's *Hallmarks on Silver*, in English, can help decipher most of these marks and help with understanding the book on gold and platinum marks, which has not been translated from the French.

The most easily recognized and commonly seen French mark is the eagle's head, in use since 1838, indicating 18 karat gold. Assayed French gold is never lower than 18k. The mark can be found on jewelry in any number of places. Look for it on clasps, side edges, galleries, and pin stems as well as on the back surface of a piece.

On French silver jewelry, the most often-seen mark is the boar's head, the mark of the Paris Assay Office, indicating a fineness of 800 or higher on small articles (such as jewelry).

This mark was in use from 1838 to 1961, and since 1962, has also been used by the Paris Assay Office.

After 1838, a maker's mark in a lozenge (diamond shape with four equal sides) was also required on French silver and gold.

From 1829, items made of both gold and silver were stamped with a conjoined boar's and eagle's head.

Platinum was not officially recognized by the French government as a precious metal until 1910, at which time the eagle's head for gold was also used for platinum. In 1912, a special mark for platinum was introduced, a dog's head.

OTHER EUROPEAN HALLMARKS

Many European countries mark silver and gold with numerical fineness marks in thousandths, e.g., 800, 830, 900, 935, etc., for silver; and 333, 500, 585, 750, 875, etc., for gold. Other symbols may be used in combination with these numbers.

Austro-Hungarian items may bear the head of a woman, animal, or bird with a number inside a cartouche or reserve. The most commonly seen mark on silver and silver-gilt jewelry is the dog's head with the number 3 inside a coffin-shaped reserve, indicating 800 silver, in use from 1866-1937.

In Russia, two-digit numbers refer to *zoloniks*, which convert to thousandths, e.g., 56 = 583 (14k), 84 = 875 (silver or 21k gold). Between 1896 and 1908, the national mark was the left profile of a woman's head wearing a diadem ("*kokoshnik*"). From 1908 to 1917, a right-facing profile was used. After the Russian Revolution, the mark was a right-facing worker's profile with a hammer, and the fineness was in thousandths.

Swedish hallmarks after 1912 include a triple crown mark, in a trefoil for local manufacture and in an oval for imports, along with an S in a hexagon for silver indicating 830 or higher. Gold will bear a karat mark in a rectangle. There will also be a date letter and number, a city mark and a maker's mark.

Finnish hallmarks are similar to Swedish. A crown inside a heart indicates local manufacture, a crown in an oval for imports. Place of assay, maker's mark and date letter/number may be added.

BRITISH HALLMARKS

The British system of hallmarking is somewhat complex, but relatively easy to follow once the system is deciphered. British hallmarks include a fineness or purity mark, an assay office mark, a date letter, and usually—but not always—a maker's mark. A royal duty mark was added from 1784 to 1890 (not always found on jewelry of this period). The sequence of marks on a piece is arbitrary.

FINENESS OR PURITY MARKS

On gold, a crown plus the karat (spelled with a "c" in Britain, abbreviated "c" or "ct") was used from 1798 until 1975 (22 ct was marked the same as sterling silver until 1844). In Scotland, a thistle was used instead of the crown. From 1798 to 1854, only gold assayed at 18 and 22 ct was permissible and hallmarked. In 1854, 15, 12, and 9 ct were legalized. The fineness in thousandths was added to these karat marks from 1854 to 1932.

In 1932, 15 and 12 ct were abandoned in favor of 14 ct, which was also marked 585; 9 ct continued to be legal, also marked 375. In 1975, all gold marks were standardized, and the crown mark and the fineness in thousandths became the only marks to be used in addition to place of assay and date letter.

On English silver, the lion *passant* (walking lion) is the symbol for sterling silver (925). Scottish silver before 1975, like gold, bears a thistle mark. A higher silver standard, Britannia silver (958.4), was required to be used for a short period at the end of the 17th century, bearing the figure of Britannia instead of the lion. Britannia silver is still legal but has seldom been used since the reinstatement of the sterling standard in 1720. The lion *passant* was retained in the Hallmarking Act of 1975, but the Scottish thistle was changed to a rampant lion.

PLACE OF ASSAY MARKS:

Assay offices have been located in a number of British cities. The ones still in operation today are in London, Birmingham, Sheffield and Edinburgh. Most jewelry will bear a London, Birmingham, or Chester place of assay mark (the Chester assay office closed in 1962). The mark for London is referred to as a leopard's head (crowned before 1821). The mark for Birmingham is an anchor. Most hallmarks books indicate an upright anchor for silver and a sideways anchor for gold, but this was not strictly adhered to. The mark for Chester is a shield bearing the town's arms, a sword and three sheaves of wheat.

DATE LETTERS:

Each place of assay has its own cycles of hallmarks that include a letter of the alphabet for each year, beginning with the letter A, and continuing through to Z (sometimes the lowercase letter j is omitted, and some cycles end with a letter before Z). The style of the letter and the shape of the reserve or shield background changes with each cycle. A letter can be uppercase or lowercase and of differing typefaces in order to distinguish it from the same letter in an earlier or later cycle.

It is not necessary to memorize these letters. Pocket-sized editions of British hallmarks books make it possible to look up the date letter found on a piece in the field. All that is necessary is to determine the place of assay from its mark and look up the date letter in the tables given for that city. It is important to remember to match the style of letter and shape of its surrounding shield. Occasionally there will be a discrepancy between what is in the books and the mark on the piece, in which case the style of the letter takes precedence over the shape of the shield. With practice, and book in hand, you can learn to read British hallmarks quickly and easily.

PSEUDO HALLMARKS

Because of the association of British sterling with quality, some American manufacturers emulated the British, marking sterling objects and jewelry long before the United States government nationalized the sterling standard in 1906. Not only were British styles and metal quality imitated. Some American maker's marks bear a striking resemblance to British hallmarks. The most well-known of these is the mark of Gorham Manufacturing Co., featuring a walking lion, an anchor and an Old English style capital G, looking very much like a Birmingham hallmark for 1830. Most American maker's marks can be found in Dorothy Rainwater's *American Jewelry Manufacturers*.

Marks References

- John Bly, *Miller's Silver & Sheffield Plate Marks* (English, Continental European, and American), Reed International Books, Ltd., 1993
- Jan Divis, *Guide to Gold Marks of the World* and *Guide to Silver Marks of the World*, English translation reprints, Promotional Reprint Co. Ltd., 1994
- Ian Pickford, ed., *Jackson's Hallmarks*, pocket edition (English, Scottish, Irish silver and gold marks), Antique Collectors' Club, 1991
- Pickford, Ian, ed. *Jackson's Silver and Gold Marks of England*, Antique Collectors' Club, 1989
- Dorothy Rainwater, *American Jewelry Manufacturers*, Schiffer Publishing, 1988
- Tardy, *International Hallmarks on Silver*, Tardy, Paris, 1993; and (French text), Tardy, Paris, 1988
- Seymour B. Wyler, *The Book of Old Silver* (English, European, American), Crown Publishers, 1937 (still in print)

References and Other Sources for Further Information

PART 1: LATE 18TH AND 19TH CENTURY JEWELRY

References (for all of Part 1):

Vivienne Becker, *Antique and Twentieth Century Jewellery*, 2nd ed., N.A.G. Press, 1987 (out of print).

C. Jeanenne Bell, *Answers to Questions About Old Jewelry*, 5th ed., Krause Publications, 1999.

David Bennett and Daniela Mascetti, *Understanding Jewellery*, 2nd ed., Antique Collectors' Club, revised 2000.

Shirley Bury, *Jewellery, 1789-1910, The International Era*, 2 vols., Antique Collectors' Club, 1991 reprinted 1997.

Genevieve E. Cummins and Nerylla D. Taunton, *Chatelaines, Utility to Glorious Extravagance*, Antique Collectors' Club, 1994.

Ginny Redington Dawes & Corinne Davidov, *Victorian Jewelry, Unexplored Treasures*, Abbeville Press, 1991.

Priscilla Harris Dalrymple, *American Victorian Costume in Early Photographs*, Dover, 1991.

Martha G. Fales, *Jewelry in America 1600-1900*, Antique Collectors' Club, 1995.

Margaret Flower, *Victorian Jewellery*, A.S. Barnes & Co., 1951, revised 1967 (out of print), Margaret Flower and Doris Langley-Levy Moore, reprint published by Dover Publications, 2002.

Alison Gernsheim, *Victorian and Edwardian Fashion, A Photographic Survey*, Dover, 1981.

Kristina Harris, *Victorian and Edwardian Fashions for Women*, Schiffer Publishing, 1995

Duncan James, *Antique Jewellery: Its Manufacture, Materials and Design,* Shire Publications, 1998.

Arthur Guy Kaplan, *The Official Identification and Price Guide to Antique Jewelry,* 6th ed., House of Collectibles, 1990 (out of print).

Shena Mason, *Jewellery Making in Birmingham 1750-1995*, Phillimore, 1998.

Clare Phillips, *Jewels and Jewellery*, V & A Publications, 2000 (collection of the Victoria and Albert Museum).

Dorothy Rainwater, *American Jewelry Manufacturers*, Schiffer, 1988.

Diana Scarisbrick, *Jewellery in Britain 1066-1837*, Michael Russell, Publishing Ltd., 2000.

Henri Vever, *French Jewelry in the Nineteenth Century*, English translation of La Bijouterie Francaise au XIXe Siecle (originally published 1906-1908) by Brenda Forman, Ph.D., Antiquorum, 2001 (3 vols.); another translation by Katherine Purcell, Thames & Hudson, 2001 (1 vol., with additional color plates).

Museums: The Victoria and Albert and the British Museums, London. The *Musée des Arts Décoratifs*, Paris, has a collection of jewelry that was pictured in Vever's monumental work (see above). In the United States: the Newark Museum, Newark, N.J., the Toledo Museum of Art, Toledo, Ohio, the Peabody Essex Museum, Salem, Mass., Museum of Fine Arts, Boston, Walters Art Gallery, Baltimore, Md., Cooper-Hewitt Museum, New York, and National Museum of American History, Smithsonian Institution, Washington, D.C., all have some jewelry of the period in their collections. Mount Vernon in Virginia has a collection of Martha Washington's jewelry.

LATE GEORGIAN

References: M.D.S. Lewis, *Antique Paste Jewellery*, Boston Books and Art, 1970 (out of print).

Advisers: Sam Gassman, Daniela Mascetti, Barry Weber.

CUT STEEL, BERLIN IRON, SILESIAN WIRE WORK

References: Anne Clifford, *Cut Steel and Berlin Iron Jewellery*, Adams and Dart, 1971 (out of print).

Exhibition catalog: Derek Ostergard, ed. *Cast Iron From Central Europe, 1800-1850*, The Bard Graduate Center for Studies in the Decorative Arts, 1994 (essay on jewelry by Brigitte Marquardt, many photos of Berlin iron jewelry and wirework).

MEMORIAL, MOURNING, HAIR JEWELRY
References:

Ann Louise Luthi, *Sentimental Jewellery, Antique Jewels of Love and Sorrow*, Shire Publications, 1998.

Ruel Pardee Tolman, *"Human Hair as Pigment,"* Antiques, December, 1925.

Museum: The Mendocino Museum of Mourning in Mendocino, Calif.

Advisers: Lenore Dailey, Carmelita Johnson, Barry Weber.

MINIATURES

References: Robin Jaffee Frank, *Love and Loss: American Portrait and Mourning Miniatures*, Yale University Press, 2000.

Advisers: Elise Misiorowski, Elle Shushan, Barry Weber.

EARLY VICTORIAN (ROMANTIC PERIOD)

References:

The Crystal Palace Exhibition Illustrated Catalogue, reprint of the original Art-Journal publication, Dover, 1970.

Carolyn Goldthorpe, *From Queen to Empress, Victorian Dress 1837-1877*, Metropolitan Museum of Art, New York (exhibition catalog), 1988.

Trade catalogs: *C.D. Peacock*, Chicago, 1912-1914.

Adviser: Sam Gassman.

CORAL

References: see Vivienne Becker, *Antique and Twentieth Century Jewellery*.

HAIRWORK

References: C. Jeanenne Bell, *Collector's Encyclopedia of Hairwork Jewelry*, Collector Books, 1998.

Website: www.hairwork.com, site of Marlys Fladeland

Museum: Leila's Hair Museum, Independence, Mo.

Adviser: Carmelita Johnson.

SCOTTISH JEWELRY

References: see Dawes & Davidov, op. cit.

MID-VICTORIAN (GRAND PERIOD)

Reference: John Loring, Tiffany's 150 Years, Doubleday & Co., 1987, and Tiffany Jewels, Abrams, 1999.

BLACK JEWELRY

References:

Sheryl Gross Shatz, *What's It Made Of?, A Jewelry Materials Identification Guide*, 3rd ed., published by author, 1996.

Sylvia Katz, *Early Plastics*, Shire Publications, Ltd., 1999.

Includes information on vulcanite and other Victorian compositions.

Helen Muller, *Jet Jewellery and Ornaments*, Shire Publications, Ltd., 2001, and *Jet*, Butterworths & Co. Ltd., 1987 (out of print). Both books contain extensive information on jet and its imitations, including history, sources, and identification.

Mike Woshner, *India-Rubber and Gutta-Percha in the Civil War Era*, published by author, 1999 (includes a few jewelry pieces).

Advisers: Colin Williamson (Victorian compositions), Mike Woshner (vulcanite and gutta-percha).

TORTOISESHELL and PIQUE

References: see Becker, op. cit., and Dawes & Davidov, op.cit.

REVIVALIST JEWELRY

Reference: Geoffrey Munn, Castellani and Giuliano, *Revivalist Jewellers of the Nineteenth Century*, Trefoil, 1984 (out of print).

Museum: Some of the ancient jewels that inspired the Castellani can be seen at the British Museum in London (www.thebritishmuseum.ac.uk), which has an extensive collection of Revivalist jewels.

CAMEOS and INTAGLIOS

Reference: Anna M. Miller, *Cameos Old & New*, 3rd edition, Gemstone Press, 2002.

Museums: see Anna Miller's book, above, for information on cameo collections.

Adviser: Anna Miller.

MOSAICS IN JEWELRY

Reference: Jeanette Hanisee Gabriel, *Micromosaics: the Gilbert Collection*, Philip Wilson Publishers, 2000.

Website: www.micromosaics.com

Museum: The Somerset House, London, houses the Gilbert Collection; website: www.somersethouse.org.uk

Advisers: Margot Conté, Laura Hiserote.

MANUFACTURED GOLD, GOLD-FILLED, GOLD-PLATED

References: see Dietz, ed., op. cit., Mason, op. cit.

Museum: Providence Jewelry Museum, Providence, R.I.

Website: www.theassayoffice.co.uk

Late Victorian (Aesthetic Period)

Reference: Lillian Baker, *Baker's Encyclopedia of Hatpins & Hatpin Holders*, Schiffer Publishing, 2000.

EARLY CELLULOID

References:

Mary Bachman, *Collector's Guide to Hair Combs*, Collector Books, 1998.

Sylvia Katz, *Early Plastics*, Shire Publications, Ltd., 1999.

Keith Lauer and Julie P. Robinson, *Celluloid, A Collector's Reference and Value Guide,* Collector Books, 1998.

Website: www.plastiquarian.com, the site of the Plastics Historical Society and the Virtual Plastics Museum.

Advisers: Julie P. Robinson, Belva Green.

SILVER and MIXED METALS

References:

Scott V. Martin, *The Guide to Evaluating Gold & Silver Objects*, SM Publications, 1998.

Janet Zapata and D. Albert Soeffing, "Artistic Wares of George W. Shiebler, Silversmith," in *The Magazine Antiques*, July, 1995.

Periodical: *Silver Magazine*, Website: www.silvermag.com.

Website: www.silvercollecting.com, includes an online encyclopedia of American silver marks.

Advisers: Benjamin Randolph, Janet Zapata.

DIAMONDS and GEM STONES

References:

Dietz, ed., op. cit, Fales, op. cit., Vever, op. cit.

David Federman, "American Diamond Cutting: The Untold Heritage," *Modern Jeweler*, Vol. 84 #1 (January, 1985).

Wm. Revell Phillips and Anatoly S. Talantsev, "Russian Demantoid, Czar of the Garnet Family," *Gems & Gemology*, Summer, 1996.

Museums: Victoria and Albert and the British Museums, London; the Cooper-Hewitt and Metropolitan Museum of Art, New York, and the Smithsonian Institution, Washington, have noteworthy collections.

Advisers: Elise Misiorowski, Peter Shemonsky, Joseph W. Tenhagen.

PART 2:
TURN-OF-THE-CENTURY JEWELRY

References (for all of Part II):

Baker, op. cit., Becker, op. cit., Gernsheim, Op. cit., Harris, op. cit.

Terence Pepper, *High Society, Photographs 1897-1914* (exhibition catalog), National Portrait Gallery, London, 1998.

ARTS and CRAFTS c.1890-1920

References:

Vivienne Becker, *Art Nouveau Jewelry*, Thames & Hudson, 1998.

Malcolm Haslam, *Collector's Style Guide: Arts and Crafts*, Ballantine Books, 1988.

Jo-Ann Burnie Danzker, *Art Nouveau Buckles, 1896-1910,* The Kreuzer Collection, Arnoldsche Art Publishers, 2000 (includes Jugendstil, English, and Danish Arts & Crafts).

Sharon S. Darling, *Chicago Metalsmiths*, Chicago Historical Society, 1977.

Charlotte Gere and Geoffrey C. Munn, *Pre-Raphaelite to Arts and Crafts Jewellery*, Antique Collectors' Club, 1996.

Nancy Impasto, "Paye & Baker Silversmiths," *Silver Magazine*, October 1990.

Elyse Zorn Karlin, *Jewelry & Metalwork in the Arts and Crafts Tradition*, Schiffer Publishing, 1993.

Stephen A. Martin, ed., *Archibald Knox*, Academy Editions, 1995.

Ulrike von Hase-Schmundt et al, *Theodor Fahrner Jewelry, Between Avant-Garde and Tradition*, Schiffer Publishing, 1991.

Janet Zapata, *The Jewelry and Enamels of Louis Comfort Tiffany*, Harry N. Abrams, 1993.

Periodical: *Fine Early 20th Century American Craftsman Silver, Jewelry & Metal* (semiannual catalog with prices), ARK Antiques, Box 3133, New Haven, CT 06515.

Museums: Birmingham Museums and Art Gallery, Birmingham, the Fitzwilliam Museum, Cambridge, and The Victoria and Albert Museum, London, England; The Schmuckmuseum (Jewelry Museum) in Pforzheim, Germany; Museum of Fine Arts, Boston.

Advisers: Rosalie and Aram Berberian (American), Gail Gerretsen, Didier Haspeslagh (British, European), Susan Oakes Peabody, Ramona Tung, Janet Zapata (American).

ART NOUVEAU c. 1895-1910

References:

Vivienne Becker, *Art Nouveau Jewelry*, Thames & Hudson, 1998; and *The Jewellery of René Lalique* (exhibition catalog), Goldsmiths' Company, London, 1987.

Yvonne Brunhammer, ed. *The Jewels of Lalique* (exhibition catalog), Flammarion, 1998.

Danzker, op. cit., Dietz, ed., op. cit., Vever, op. cit.

Dorothy Kamm, *Painted Porcelain Jewelry and Buttons Identification and Value Guide*, Collector Books, 2002.

Museum: The Calouste Gulbenkian Museum in Lisbon, Portugal, houses the René Lalique collection created for its namesake.

Advisers: Ulysses G. Dietz, Dorothy Kamm (porcelain), Elise Misiorowski, Janet Zapata.

BEAUX-ARTS and "NEO-RENAISSANCE" c. 1890-1920
References:

Ulysses G. Dietz and Janet Zapata, "Beaux-arts Jewelry Made in Newark, New Jersey," *The Magazine Antiques,* April, 1997.

Dietz, ed., op. cit.

Ginger Moro, *European Designer Jewelry*, Schiffer Publishing, 1995 (chapter on Hungarian, including "neo-Renaissance" jewelry).

Trade catalog reprint: Daniel Low & Co. *Gold and Silversmiths*, Salem, MA, 1901 (includes designs by Unger Bros. and Wm. B. Kerr), Eden Sterling Co. (www.edensterling.com).

Advisers: Ulysses G. Dietz, Janet Zapata.

EDWARDIAN c. 1890-1920
References:

Bennett and Mascetti, op. cit., Dietz, ed., op. cit.

Franco Cologni and Eric Nussbaum, *Platinum by Cartier, Triumph of the Jewelers' Art*, Harry N. Abrams, 1996 (out of print).

Kenneth Flory, "Suffrage Colors and Alleged Suffrage Jewelry", *Maine Antique Digest*, December, 2003, pp. 30-31B

Elizabeth S. Goring, "Suffragette Jewellery in Britain," *Omnium Gatherum - A Collection of Papers*, The Decorative Arts Society 1850 to the Present, Journal 26 (2002), 84-99.

Hans Nadelhoffer, *Cartier, Jewelers Extraordinary*, Harry N. Abrams, 1984 (out of print).

Penny Proddow and Marion Fasel, *Diamonds, A Century of Spectacular Jewels*, Harry N. Abrams, 1996.

Judy Rudoe, *Cartier, 1900-1939*, Harry N. Abrams, 1997.

Museum: The Virginia Museum of Fine Arts, Richmond, Va., has a sizable collection of Fabergé *objets de vertu* and jewelry.

Adviser: Elise Misiorowski.

PART 3: 20TH CENTURY JEWELRY

FINE JEWELRY c. 1920-1935
References:

Sylvie Raulet, *Art Deco Jewelry*, Rizzoli International, 1985 (out of print), and *Van Cleef & Arpels* (abridged), Universe Publishing, 1998.

Rudoe, op. cit.

Suzanne Tennenbaum and Janet Zapatta, *The Jeweled Menagerie*, Thames & Hudson, 2001.

Museums: *Musée des Arts Décoratifs*, Paris; Toledo Museum of Art, Toledo, Ohio.

Adviser: Peter Shemonsky.

FINE JEWELRY c. 1935-1945
References:

John Culme and Nicholas Rayner, *The Jewels of the Duchess of Windsor*, Vendome Press/Sotheby's London, 1987 (out of print).

Sylvie Raulet, *Jewelry of the 1940s and 1950s,* and *Van Cleef & Arpels*, Rizzoli International, 1987 (both out of print), and *Van Cleef & Arpels* (abridged), Universe Publishing, 1998.

Suzanne Tennenbaum and Janet Zapata, *The Jeweled Menagerie*, Thames & Hudson, 2001.

Adviser: Janet Zapata.

FINE JEWELRY c. 1945-1960
References:

Sylvie Raulet, *Jewelry of the 1940s and 1950s,* Rizzoli International, 1987 (out of print), and *Van Cleef & Arpels,* Rizzoli, 1987 (out of print), and Universe, 1998 (abridged).

Suzanne Tennenbaum and Janet Zapata, *The Jeweled Menagerie*, Thames & Hudson, 2001.

Adviser: Lynne Arkin (Marsh).

FINE JEWELRY c. 1960-1975
References:

Bennett and Mascetti, op. cit.

Daniela Mascetti and Amanda Triossi, *Earrings from Antiquity to the Present*, Rizzoli International, 1990, reprinted 2001; *The Necklace from Antiquity to the Present*, Harry N. Abrams, 1997, and *Bulgari*, Abbeville, 1996.

Penny Proddow and Debra Healy, *American Jewelry*, Rizzoli International, 1987 (out of print); Penny Proddow, Debra Healy and Marion Fasel, *Hollywood Jewels,* Harry N.

Abrams, 1992, reprinted 1996 (out of print).

Penny Proddow and Marion Fasel, *Diamonds, A Century of Spectacular Jewels,* Harry N. Abrams, 1996, and *Bejeweled, Great Designers, Celebrity Style*, Harry N. Abrams, 2001.

Museum: Toledo Museum of Art, Toledo, Ohio.

Advisers: Elise Misiorowski, Amanda Triossi.

COSTUME JEWELRY c. 1920-1935
References:

Deanna Farneti Cera, *Amazing Gems, An Illustrated Guide to the Worlds' Most Dazzling Costume Jewelry,* Harry N. Abrams, 1997; Deanna Farneti Cera, ed., *Jewels of Fantasy, Costume Jewelry of the 20th Century*, Harry N. Abrams, 1992 (out of print).

Sibylle Jargstorf, *Baubles, Buttons and Beads, The Heritage of Bohemia*, Schiffer Publishing, 1993, *Glass in Jewelry, revised ed.,* Schiffer Publishing, 19918 and *Glass Beads from Europe*, Schiffer Publishing, 1995.

Ellie Laubner, *Fashions of the Roaring '20s, with Values*, Schiffer Publishing, 1996 (chapter on jewelry), and *Collectible Fashions of the Turbulent 1930s,* Schiffer Publishing, 2000.

Moro, op. cit.

Penny Proddow, Debra Healy, and Marion Fasel, *Hollywood Jewels*, Harry N. Abrams, 1992.

Ulrike von Hase-Schmundt et al, *Theodor Fahrner Jewelry, Between Avant-Garde and Tradition*, Schiffer Publishing, 1991.

Museums: Glass and Costume Jewelry Museum, Jablonec Nad Nisou, Czech Republic; Providence Jewelry Museum, Providence, R.I.

Adviser: Ellie Laubner.

COSTUME JEWELRY c. 1935-1975
(Designer/Manufacturer Signed and Other)
References:

Carla Genelli Brunialti and Roberto Brunialti, *American Costume Jewelry, 1935-50*, Edizioni Gabriele Mazzotta, 1997 (Italian text), and *A Tribute to America, Costume Jewelry 1935-50,* Edita, 2002 (English text).

Deanna Farneti Cera, *The Jewels of Miriam Haskell,* Antique Collectors' Club, 1997, and Cera, ed., *Jewels of Fantasy.*

Maryanne Dolan, *Collecting Rhinestone & Colored Jewelry*, 4th ed., Krause Publications, 1998 (large section on makers' marks).

Roseann Ettinger, *Popular Jewelry 1840-1940,* Schiffer Publishing, revised ed., 2000, *Forties & Fifties Popular Jewelry*, Schiffer Publishing, 1994, and *Popular Jewelry of the '60s, '70s, and '80s*, Schiffer Publishing, 1997.

Harrice Simons Miller, *Costume Jewelry Identification and Price Guide,* 2nd ed., Avon Books, 1994; 3rd edition (new title: *Official Price Guide to Costume Jewelry*, House of Collectibles), 2002.

Moro, op. cit.

Cherri Simonds, *Collectible Costume Jewelry*, 2nd edition, Collector Books, 2000.

Periodical and Collectors' Club: Vintage Fashion & Costume Jewelry Newsletter/Club, P.O. Box 265, Glen Oaks, NY 11004, e-mail: VFCJ@aol.com, published quarterly, page on Website: www.lizjewel.com (click on "VFCJ Club").

Websites: N & N Vintage Costume Jewelry's site includes a collection of design patents (www.trifari.com), which allows you to view actual patents, including drawings, for many different pieces designed between 1937 and 1956.

Jewelcollect (www.jewelcollect.org) is a forum for an active costume jewelry discussion group, headed by Liz Bryman.

Advisers: Roberto Brunialti, Liz Bryman, Jane Clarke, Neil and Natasha Cuddy, Elayne Glotzer, Amy Milner (Cini), Charles Pinkham, Pat Seal, Sherry Shatz (Ming's), Bobye Syverson (Eisenberg), Lucille Tempesta, Joanne Valentine (Ming's and Gump's).

PLASTICS and OTHER NOVELTY
JEWELRY c. 1920-1970
References:

Matthew L. Burkholz, *The Bakelite Collection*, Schiffer Publishing, 1997.

"Techniques and Materials" (Chapter 8), in Deanna Farneti Cera, ed., *Jewels of Fantasy, Costume Jewelry of the 20th Century*, Harry N. Abrams, 1992 (out of print).

Corinne Davidov and Ginny Redington Dawes, *The Bakelite Jewelry Book*, Abbeville Press, 1988.

Andrea DiNoto, *Art Plastic, Designed for Living*, Abbeville Press, 1984 (out of print).

Keith Lauer and Julie Robinson, *Celluloid, A Collectors' Reference and Value Guide,* Collector Books, 1998.

Moro, op. cit.

Karima Parry, *Bakelite Bangles*, Krause Publications, 1999, and *Bakelite Pins*, Schiffer Publishing, 2001.

Shatz, op. cit.

Website: www.plastiquarian.com, the Virtual Plastics Museum, Website of the Plastics Historical Society.

Advisers: Matt Burkholz (Bakelite), Julie Robinson (celluloid).

SPECIAL THANKS

Apriori Antiques
Aram Berberian
Roberto Brunialti and Carla Ginelli Brunialti
Isabelle "Liz" Bryman
Matthew Burkholz
Steven Cabella
Jane Civins
Jane Clarke
Margot Conté
Jill Crawford
Neil and Natasha Cuddy
Lenore Dailey
Ulysses G. Dietz
Kathy Flood
Samuel C. Gassman
Gail Gerretsen
Elayne Glotzer
Belva Green
Didier Haspeslagh
Bruce Healy

Laura Hiserote
Mary Lee Hu
Svein G. Josefsen
Dorothy Kamm
Patrick Kapty
Ellie Laubner
Keith Lauer
Gail Brett Levine
Karen Lorene
Yvonne Markowitz
Daniela Mascetti
Al Munir Meghji
Shari Watson Miller
Amy Milner
Elise B. Misiorowski
Penny C. Morrill
Ginger Moro
Terrance O'Halloran
Susan Oakes Peabody and John Peabody
B. Lennart Persson

Sigi Pineda
Charles Pinkham
Benjamin Randolph
Fred Rezazadeh
Julie P. Robinson
Marbeth Schon
Patsy Sanders Seal
Sheryl Gross Shatz
Peter Shemonsky
Elle Shushan
Bobye Syverson
Lucille Tempesta
Amanda Triossi
Ramona Tung
Joanne Valentine
Barry Weber
Pamela Y. Wiggins
Colin Williamson
Mike Woshner
Janet Zapata

AUCTION HOUSES

Bonhams & Butterfields
220 San Bruno Ave.
San Francisco, CA 94103
(415) 861-7500
www.bonhams.com

Christie's New York
20 Rockefeller Plaza
New York, NY 10020
www.christies.com

Doyle New York
175 East 87th St.
New York, NY 10128
(212) 427-2730
www.doylenewyork.com

Heritage Auctions, Inc.
3500 Maple Ave., 17th Floor
Dallas, TX 75219-3941
1-800-872-6467
(214) 528-3500
www.ha.com

Skinner, Inc.
357 Main St.
Bolton, MA 01740
(978) 779-6241
www.skinnerinc.com

Sotheby's New York
1334 York Ave.
New York, NY 10021
(212) 606-7000
www.sothebys.com

Glossary

In order for us to understand each other when talking about antique and period jewelry, we must have a common vocabulary. A great many jewelry terms are French. French jewelers were the leaders of the jewelry industry, and so France is where the language of jewelry-making evolved. The terms used there were adopted by English and American jewelers and thus are part of our jewelry vocabulary today. Included in the list below are the most commonly used French jewelry terms, their *approximate* phonetic pronunciation (nasal and glottal sounds are difficult to transcribe) in brackets, and jewelry-related definitions. Words in SMALL CAPS are defined elsewhere in the "Glossary," foreign words are italicized, and approximate phonetic pronunciations appear in brackets.

acrostic jewel a ring, brooch, or other jewel set with a ror or circle of gemstones, the first letter of the name of each stone spelling a word, such as "DEAREST" or "REGARD"

à jour [ah ZHOOR] an open setting which allows light to pass through

aigrette a jeweled hair ornament in the shape of a plume or feather, sometimes with a feather attached

Algerian knot a tubular knot motif, inspired by Algerian cord embroidery

alloy mixture of two or more metals

alpaca yellowish silver-colored metal composed of copper, zinc, nickel, and 2% silver

amber fossilized resin from extinct trees; lightweight and warm to the touch; can be translucent to opaque, imitated in plastics

amphora ancient Greco-Roman two-handled jar or urn with a tapered base, popular mid-Victorian Revivalist motif

annular ring-shaped

arraché eggshell lacquer decoration developed by French artist Jean Dunand

articulated having segments connected by flexible joints or jump rings

assay analytical test to determine metal content

Asscher-cut diamond named after diamond cutter Joseph Asscher, who developed a variation of the step cut in 1902, an octagonal stone (cut-corner square) with 74 facets, small table and high crown

attributed not SIGNED, but considered likely to have been made by a particular person or firm

aurora borealis an iridescent coating applied to faceted glass beads or rhinestones, developed by Swarovski Corp. in 1955

baguette narrow rectangular faceted stone

bail pendant loop finding through which a chain or cord passes

Bakelite trade name for thermosetting phenol formaldehyde resin, first entirely synthesized plastic, patented in 1909 by Leo H. Baekeland

balustered swelled section (as in the posts in a balustrade or railing for a staircase)

bandeau ornamental band worn around the head

bangle rigid circular or oval bracelet

baroque in reference to pearls, having an irregular shape

base metal a non-precious metal

basse-taille [bas TIE yuh] enameling technique: translucent or transparent ENAMEL applied over a decorated (engraved, chased, stamped) metal GROUNDPLATE, similar to *CHAMPLEVÉ*, but with a pattern or design visible through the enamel; when the groundplate has an "engine-turned" pattern, it is known as *GUILLOCHÉ* enamel

baton narrow, stick-shaped

bead set setting in which stones are held in place by beads raised from the surrounding metal

beauty pin small brooch/pin, also called *handy pin, lace pin*

bezel metal band with top edges burnished over to hold a stone in place

biomorphic amoeba-like, organic shape

blackamoor depiction of a dark-skinned man or woman

bloomed gold karat gold that has been treated with nitric acid, causing the alloy to dissipate from the surface, leaving a thin matte surface layer of pure gold (has a frosted appearance)

bog oak fossilized peat; found mainly in 19th century Irish jewelry

bola string tie of braided leather with a decorative slide and ornamental tips, usually silver

bombé having swelled or bulging sides

bookchain chain necklace with folded-over square or rectangular links, often engraved or stamped, popular mid-to-late 19th century

bouquet pin brooch with bowed-out center and a spike mounted on reverse, designed to hold a small flower bouquet

box clasp fastener for bracelets and necklaces, a slotted box into which a V-SPRING catch is inserted

brilliant circular gemstone cut, especially for diamonds, with 58 facets; the *modern brilliant* is a mathematically designed cut published in a treatise by Marcel Tolkowsky in 1919, also called the *American* or *ideal* cut; see also OLD MINE CUT and OLD EUROPEAN CUT

briolette gemstone cut, a three-dimensional faceted pear-shaped drop with small triangular facets

buff top gemstone cut, low cabochon top with a faceted pavilion (portion below the GIRDLE)

bulla ancient neck ornament made of two hinged convex plates, usually circular, suspended from a cord or chain; revived in the mid-Victorian period

bypass bracelet or ring with open ends crossing parallel in front

cable link chain oval links formed of round wire

cabochon unfaceted, domed cut for stones or glass, with a flat base (a *double cabochon* has a convex base)

calibré small faceted gemstones, usually four-sided, cut to fit a setting, often in rows or groups

cameo design carved in relief, often (but not always) from stone or shell with layers of more than one color forming background and foreground; a cameo carved within a concave depression of a gemstone, with the highest part of the design level with the edge of the stone, is called a *chevet* or *chevée, curvette* or *cuvette* (British term: "dished")

cameo *habillé* [ah bee YAY] depicting the head or bust of a person wearing jewelry set with diamonds or other gemstones (literally, "dressed up")

cannetille [kan ne TEE yuh] type of metal ornamentation using thin wires to make a filigree pattern, often in tightly coiled spirals or rosettes, used in the early 19th century

carat unit of weight for gemstones

carbuncle cabochon cut almandite garnet

carré set circular stone set within a square, flat-topped setting

casting molten metal poured or forced into a mold made from a design model

catch closure finding for brooch/pin that holds the pointed end of the pinstem. A *C-catch* is a simple C-shaped hook. See also SAFETY CATCH

celluloid trade name for semi-synthetic pyroxylin-camphor thermoplastic, invented by John Wesley Hyatt in 1868

Celtic knot also known as *entrelac*, an intricate interlaced motif common in ancient Celtic ornamentation, revived by the British Arts and Crafts movement

chamfered having cut or beveled corners

champlevé [chaw le VAY] enameling technique: opaque or translucent ENAMEL fills recesses or depressions that are stamped, etched or engraved into a metal GROUNDPLATE

channel setting row of same-size square or rectangular stones fitted into a continuous metal channel or trough that holds the stones in place

chasing technique of decorating metal from the front, usually by hand, without removing any metal, forming a relief design by raising and indenting

chatelaine ornamental clip worn at the waist from which implements or trinkets are suspended by chains

choker short necklace that fits snugly around the neck

circa within 10 years before or after a given date; literally, "around"

clip type of brooch with a hinged double-pronged mechanism for attaching to clothing, sometimes called a "fur clip" to differentiate from a DRESS CLIP

clipback earring finding for unpierced ear with a hinged clip for clamping earring to ear

cliquet [klee KAY] literally, catch. Type of pin having two ornamental terminals, one at each end of a pinstem, the pointed end having a snap closure or other mechanism for attachment. When worn, the pinstem is invisible. Aka JABOT PIN, SÛRETÉ.

cloisonné [klwah son NAY] enameling technique: a design or pattern is formed of wire soldered onto a GROUNDPLATE, creating cells or *cloisons* that are filled with ENAMEL

collet short tubular band or collar of metal enclosing a stone

compass points (north, south, east, west) to indicate position of stones or design elements: top, bottom, and two sides

costume jewelry made from nonprecious materials, especially since circa 1920

counter-enameled enamel applied to the reverse of a piece for stability

crystal < see LEAD CRYSTAL, ROCK CRYSTAL>

cuff bracelet PENANNULAR rigid bracelet, usually wide with rounded ends

cultured pearl pearl produced by insertion of an irritant (small glass or mother-of-pearl bead) into a mollusk (a *natural* pearl is formed around a foreign particle that occurs in nature)

curb chain twisted oval links forming a chain that lies flat

cushion cut rounded corner square faceted stone

cusped coming to a point, pointed end

cut-down collet or setting method of setting gemstones in a collet or bezel with vertical ribs of metal holding the stone in place

cut steel small faceted steel studs, riveted closely together on a metal backing

damascening decorative technique, the embedding of gold and/or silver wire and/or cutout sheet metal shapes into a blackened iron or steel base (aka "inlaid metal")

demi parure [pah ROOR] two or three matched pieces of jewelry; a partial SUITE

dépose [day poe ZAY] registered (trademark or design) mark found on French items, and on items imported into or exported from France

die rolling repeating design created by rolling thin metal sheets between two steel rollers incised with a pattern

die striking or stamping method of mass production, a relief design produced from a flat sheet of metal with a two-part steel die forming the pattern under pressure

dog collar wide ornamental choker necklace worn tightly around the neck

double clip brooch pair of clips joined with a detachable pinback mechansim

dress clip ornament attached to clothing by means of a hinged clip with a flat back and small prongs on the underside

ebonite <see VULCANITE>

échelle [ay SHELL] literally, ladder. Series of graduated gem-set brooches or dress ornaments (often a bow motif) worn vertically (large to small) down the front of a bodice, 17th-18th centuries

Egyptian faience type of quartz-based glazed ceramic made by the ancient Egyptians

electroplating electrolytic process of depositing a layer of metal over another metal

embossing technique for creating a raised decoration on metal using punches and hammers on the reverse side; also known as REPOUSSÉ work

emerald cut square or rectangular cut stone, square table, chamfered corners, step cut sides

enamel powdered pigmented glass fired onto a metal GROUNDPLATE using a variety of techniques <see *BASSE-TAILLE, CHAMPLEVÉ, CLOISONNÉ, GRISAILLE, LIMOGES, PLIQUE À JOUR, TAILLE D'ÉPARGNE*>

engraving creating a design or pattern on a metal surface with incised lines ; differs from CHASING in that metal is removed with a tool called a graver, or a burin

en esclavage [awn es kla VAJH] literally, enslaved. A necklace or bracelet of identical or graduated plaques joined by swagged chains, usually three or more.

en résille [aw ray ZEE yuh] literally, in a hair-net. A flexible trellis or network, usually of diamonds and platinum, often forming a dog collar or other close-fitting necklace, originated by Cartier, early 20th century.

en tremblant [aw trã BLÃ] brooch or other ornament with a motif (often a flower) mounted on a wire or spring, which trembles with movement of the wearer

equilateral all sides of equal length

estate jewelry previously owned, not necessarily antique, period or vintage

essence d'orient [door ee Ã] (pearl essence) coating used on glass or plastic to imitate pearls, made of fish scales

etching process for creating a design on metal or glass using acids

Etruscan jewelry ancient ornaments from central Italy (western Tuscany), usually of gold, reproduced in the 19th century

extended pinstem extends beyond the body of a brooch/pin; found on some 19th century brooches with C-CATCH closures, used to secure the brooch by weaving back into the clothing

fabrication hand construction using soldered sheet and wire

facet plane cut polished surface of a stone

faux [foe] French: false or fake

faux pearl artificial or imitation pearl, a glass or plastic bead coated with ESSENCE D'ORIENT (pearl essence)

fede ring from the Italian *fede* meaning "faith" or "trust," a ring depicting a pair of clasped hands, often given as a token of affection, dating as far back as the Romans; sometimes the hands are mounted on separate swiveling shanks that open and close, *see* GIMMEL RING

ferronière [fair own ee AIR] literally, blacksmith's wife. A narrow band, usually with a central jewel, worn around the forehead, originally worn in the 15th century, popular circa 1830

fetter chain elongated oval or rectangular links, often combined with short lengths of TRACE, CABLE, or CURB link chain

fibula ancient style brooch, used to close garments, resembles a modern safety pin

filigree metal decoration made of twisted thin wires

findings functional metal parts used in construction and wearing of jewelry: catches, clasps, clips, jump rings, spring rings, etc.

fine jewelry made from PRECIOUS METAL and gemstones

flanged hinge brooch finding, a hinge (called a *joint* by jewelers) with projecting metal sides and a hingepin or internal posts to which pinstem is attached

Florentine finish textured brushed surface created by engraving cross-hatched lines on metal

fob decorative ornament or seal suspended from a watch chain; also, a ribbon or metal band attached to a pocket watch

foiled back thin sheet of metal backing a gemstone or paste, sometimes colored to enhance the appearance of the stone, used in closed-back settings; also, in reference to a RHINESTONE with painted-on metallic backing, as on a mirror, which can be set in an open setting

foliate, foliated any leaf or plant design

forging shaping of metal by heating and hammering

French cut square, mixed cut with a square table turned 45 degrees and triangular crown facets, often used for small accent or CALIBRÈ gemstones

French jet black glass

gadrooned, gadrooning decorative oval beading on a border or edge

gallery strip of metal with a pierced decorative pattern, used for settings

garter motif (French, *jarretière*) a strap with a buckle design

German silver an alloy of nickel, copper, and zinc, also known as NICKEL SILVER

gilding process by which a base metal is plated or coated with a thin layer of gold (called *gilt* metal)

gimmel ring ring with two or more separate shanks that are joined together to form one ring; dating back to the 15th century, often worn as a betrothal ring

girandole [jhee rahn DOLE] literally, chandelier. Brooch or earring in which three pear-shaped drops are suspended from a center stone or motif

girdle widest part of a stone, part usually grasped by the setting; in a BRILLIANT-cut stone, the widest circumference where the crown (upper) and pavilion (lower) facets meet

gold filled mechanical process using heat and pressure to join a layer of gold to a base metal; by law in the United States, the gold layer must be at least 1/20th of the total weight of metal

gold plated layer of gold of less than 1/20th of total weight, can be applied by any process, but often ELECTROPLATED

gold wash very thin coating of gold over base metal

graduated arranged in ascending or descending order of size

granulation ancient decorative technique of applying minute spheres of gold to a gold surface without visible solder, used in ETRUSCAN JEWELRY, a technique approximated by Victorian goldsmiths

grisaille [aw gree SIGH yuh] painted enameling technique, monochromatic, usually in shades of gray and white and/or black

groundplate metal base on which enamels are fired; the method of decoration determines the name given to the technique (see ENAMEL)

guilloché [gee oh SHAY] literally, engine-turned. Machine-engraved decoration on metal, over which translucent enamel is often applied (called *guilloché enamel*)

gypsy setting one-piece mount for a stone that is recessed into the metal with the table (top facet) of the stone level with the metal surface; also called STAR SETTING when lines radiating from the stone are engraved in the metal

hair jewelry ornaments made of, decorated with, or containing human hair

hallmark mark(s) stamped on gold, silver, or platinum indicating fineness or karat; depending on country of origin, hallmarks can also include symbols for place of assay, date of assay (in the form of a letter or letter and number), maker's mark, and importation mark, if applicable

handy pin <see BEAUTY PIN>

Holbeinesque pendant or brooch in the Renaissance style, usually a vertically oriented oval, enameled and gem-set with a pendent drop, named after Renaissance artist Hans Holbein the Younger

intaglio [in TAHL yo] Italian: engraved stone, opposite of a cameo, with a recessed design carved into the surface, common for signet rings and fob seals

invisible setting (*serti invisible*) type of CHANNEL SETTING using specially cut square or rectangular colored gemstones (usually rubies or sapphires) that are notched to slide onto metal tracks and fit closely together in rows; no metal is visible from the front of the piece

jabot pin [zhah BOW] pin with ornamental elements at both ends of a long pinstem that is invisible when worn at the collar (formerly worn on a jabot, a front ruffle on a shirt), see also CLIQUET, SÛRETÉ

japonaiserie decorative motifs in the Japanese style

jarretière [jhar et TYAIR] <see GARTER MOTIF>

japanned black-lacquered metal

jet type of fossilized coal used primarily for mourning jewelry in the 19th century

jump ring round or oval finding for linking or attaching other parts, made of round wire

karat 1/24th of the total weight in a gold alloy, a measure of fineness (24 karats is pure gold)

kidney wire <see SHEPHERD'S HOOK>

lace pin <see BEAUTY PIN>

lavalier, lavaliere, lavallière neckchain suspending a gemstone or small pendant set with gemstones, popularly worn at the turn of the century

lead crystal colorless glass with a high percentage of lead added to enhance clarity and brilliance; resembles and is confused with ROCK CRYSTAL

Limoges [lee MOZH] enameling technique: layers of finely ground colored ENAMEL fired after each application, resulting in an image resembling a painting (without metal borders)

locket two-part pendant or brooch with a hinge and cover, often containing a photo or lock of hair

longchain very long metal chain worn around the neck with the end attached to the bodice, forming a swag, often terminating in a SWIVEL hook for suspending a watch or pendant

lorgnette [lorn YET] pair of spectacles with an attached handle, usually suspended from a neckchain

loupe magnifying lens used by jewelers

lozenge equilateral four-sided shape with corners at compass points; diamond-shaped (as in playing cards)

Lucite DuPont trade name for acrylic thermoplastic

mabé pearl pearl with a flat MOP bottom and rounded top (hollow, filled with epoxy or cement)

manchette [maw SHET] literally, cuff. Bangle bracelet tapering out in the shape of a sleeve cuff

marcasite iron pyrite with a silver luster, cut in small faceted circular stones and often PAVÉ-set in silver or other white metal

marquise cut gemstone cut that is oval or elliptical with pointed ends; the shape is also called NAVETTE

marriage piece put together with two or more components from different sources, not as originally made

married metals creation of a design in contrasting colors of metal (e.g., silver, brass, copper), each metal piece cut out and put together like a jigsaw puzzle to form the design, the edges butted and joined using minimal amounts of solder to form a smooth solid surface (aka "metal mosaic")

melee small cut diamond, under .20 carat

millegrain method of setting stones using a tool around the top edge of a COLLET to form minute beads of metal that hold the stone in place; also a decorative technique

mosaic object or jewel decorated with many small pieces of multicolored stone (called PIETRA DURA) or glass (TESSERAE) inlaid flush into stone or glass to form a design, motif, or scene; often called "*micromosaic*" when the glass tesserae are very small

mother-of-pearl iridescent inside lining of mollusks

mourning jewelry jewelry worn in memory of a deceased loved one, most often black, sometimes containing the hair of the deceased

naja horseshoe- or crescent-shaped silver pendant used in Navajo jewelry, often suspended from a SQUASH BLOSSOM necklace, sometimes set with turquoise or coral

nanny pin brooch with a compartment, usually tubular, for holding sewing needles

navette <see MARQUISE>

neck ring rigid circular metal ornament worn around the neck

négligée [nay glee ZHAY] literally, negligent, careless. A pendant or necklace with two drops suspended unevenly

nickel silver <see GERMAN SILVER>

nicolo variety of onyx with a thin layer of bluish-white over black, from which a cameo or intaglio is carved

niello metallic variation similar to vitreous enameling using a powdered mixture of silver, copper, and lead that is fused by heat into an engraved design in silver, or occasionally gold, creating a grayish-black contrast with the metal ground

old European cut brilliant cut for diamonds with a circular GIRDLE, otherwise similar to OLD MINE CUT; the circular shape, developed circa 1860, was more easily produced with the invention of the power-driven bruting or girdling machine in 1891

old mine cut old style brilliant cut for diamonds, a cushion-shaped stone with a small TABLE, high crown (top facets) and an open or large culet (the small flat facet at the base, virtually eliminated in a modern BRILLIANT)

open back setting setting that permits light to pass through a transparent or translucent stone (same as *À JOUR*)

painted enamel enamel applied in liquid form and baked on at lower temperatures than required for firing powdered enamels; used on costume jewelry

pampille [pahm PEE yuh] articulated row of graduated gemstones or pastes terminating in a tapered pointed drop; grouping of *pampilles* also called *aiguillettes* [ay gwee YET], from *aiguille* (literally, needle)

parure [pah ROOR] complete set or SUITE of jewelry, matching pieces of three or more

paste high lead content glass that has been cut (faceted) to resemble a gemstone; also known as *strass*

pâte de verre literally, glass paste. Molded colored glass used in jewelry, sometimes called poured glass

patina color change on the surface of metal, especially silver, copper, bronze, resulting from age and exposure to the atmosphere; a type of oxidation. Patina may be artificially applied using acids and/or liver of sulphur; color is usually green, brown, or red on copper, brass, or bronze (called *patinated*), greyish-black on silver

pavé [pah VAY] literally, paved. Method of setting many small stones very close together

peacock eye glass glass cabochon or bead with blue and green foiling resembling the center or "eye" of a peacock feather

pebble jewelry Scottish jewelry set with multicolored agates in silver or gold

penannular open-ended ring shape

pendeloque [paw d'LOKE] literally, drop or pendant. Pear-shaped drop earring, suspended from a circular or bow-shaped surmount

pendant (noun) decorative element suspended from a necklace, chain, or cord

pendent (adjective) hanging, suspended

pietra dura literally, hard stone. A type of MOSAIC made of small pieces of stone that form a picture or scenic design, also known as *Florentine mosaic*

pinchbeck alloy of copper and zinc, developed in 1720 by Christopher Pinchbeck; a brass alloy used to imitate gold

piqué [pee KAY] literally, pricked. The inlaying of gold or silver in patterns, usually into tortoiseshell or ivory.

piqué point [pweh] geometric shapes or dots

piqué posé [poe ZAY] floral or ornate patterns of inlay

plaque de cou [plak de KOO] literally, plate of the neck. Central ornamental plaque of a dog collar necklace

plique à jour [pleek ah ZHOOR] enamelling process in which the GROUNDPLATE is removed after firing; the end result resembles stained glass, the translucent enamel framed in metal

polychrome three or more colors, multicolored

pot metal base white metal, tin and lead alloy, greyish in color, used in early 20th century costume jewelry

precious metal gold, platinum, or silver

prong set stones held in place by metal claws or prongs

provenance origin and history of a piece, including its former owners

quatrefoil decorative element having four lobes

regard ring finger ring set with a variety of gemstones, the first letters of which spell "regard" (ruby, emerald, garnet, amethyst, ruby, diamond), see ACROSTIC JEWEL

relief raised or standing out from the background

repoussé [ruh poo SAY] literally, pushed back or out. Raised design in metal. *Repoussage* is a technique of hand-raising a design in metal, working with punches and hammer from the back of the piece

rhinestone faceted colorless or colored glass, cut like a gemstone and usually with a fused metallic backing for light reflection (like silvering a mirror); used in costume jewelry

rivière [ree vee AIR] literally, river or stream. A short necklace of graduated gemstones of the same kind (e.g., diamonds), each stone COLLET-set and linked in a row without further decoration

rock crystal colorless quartz, occurring in nature as a six-sided (hexagonal) crystal

rolled gold thin layer of gold fused over base metal

rondel, rondelle thin disk-shaped metal ornament, sometimes set with rhinestones, strung on a necklace between beads

rose-cut circular gemstone cut with triangular facets coming to a point at the top and a flat back

rose gold gold of a pinkish color (alloyed with copper)

rose montée small, flat-backed circular-cut rhinestones, usually colorless

safety catch brooch finding with a swiveling closure that prevents it from unintentionally opening

safety chain chain attached to a piece of jewelry, which prevents loss if clasp opens

St. Andrew's cross X-shaped motif, Scottish national emblem

sautoir [soTWAHR] very long necklace or strand of beads or pearls, often terminating in a tassel or pendant

saw piercing decorative technique, the creation of an openwork design or pattern by cutting away metal, often used for platinum in the early 20th century

scarab Egyptian symbol of immortality, the *Scarabaeus* beetle, usually carved or molded in stone, clay, or glass

scarf pin, stickpin, tie pin decorative pin with a long pinstem and ornamental top, inserted into a scarf, cravat, or necktie

screwback earring finding for unpierced ear with a screw mechanism for securing earring to ear

seed pearl natural, cultured, or artificial pearl weighing less than one quarter of a grain

sévigné [say veen YAY] bow brooch set with diamonds, worn on the bodice (three or more worn *en échelle*), popular from the 17th century, named after the Marquise de Sévigné (1626-1696), of the court of Louis XIV

sgraffito from the Italian *sgraffiato*, meaning "scratched." Enameling technique: an unfired layer of enamel is scratched through to create a design revealing the layer of enamel or metal underneath

shakudo Japanese alloy of copper with small amount of gold; *shibuichi*, Japanese alloy of copper with silver, tin, and lead or zinc

shank part of a ring that encircles the finger

shepherd's hook, fishhook, kidney wire earring findings for pierced ears, primarily for pendent or drop earrings

shoulder area of a finger ring where the SHANK and BEZEL or head (top) meet

signed marked (engraved, stamped, impressed) with the name, initials, logo, or trademark of the maker, designer, or manufacturer

slave bracelet link bracelet of glass and silver or brass, often enameled; also a bangle worn on the upper arm, popular in the 1920s

slide movable decorative and functional element of a LONGCHAIN, which adjusts its opening; when longchains went out of fashion, collections of slides were strung together and made into bracelets

solder metal alloy used to fuse pieces of metal together with the use of heat; *hard* solder requires high temperatures, is made of an alloy of the same metal being joined, and creates the strongest bond; *soft* or *lead* solder fuses at a lower temperature; it is considered unsuitable (and damaging) for use on PRECIOUS METAL

solitaire mounting of a single stone, usually in a ring

spacer decorative or functional element used to separate pearls or beads

spectacle setting ring of metal around the girdle of a stone, like an eyeglass frame, often used for setting diamonds or other transparent stones linked at intervals on a chain

spring ring type of clasp finding used with a JUMP RING to connect one part to another

sterling silver ALLOY that is 925 parts pure silver and 75 parts copper

stomacher large, usually triangular, bodice ornament, also known as a *corsage ornament* or *devant de corsage*

strass <see PASTE>

stud or post & clutch or nut earring findings for pierced ears

suite several pieces of jewelry similarly designed to be worn together <see also PARURE>

surmount decorative top part of an earring

sûreté [soor TAY] (pin) literally, safety, security. See *CLIQUET.*

swivel type of finding, a hook with a hinged spring closure joined to a swiveling base with a jump ring for attaching watches, PENDANTS, or other items to chains

synthetic gemstone laboratory-created gemstone that is chemically, physically, and optically identical to its natural counterpart; in contrast to an *imitation*, which is only similar in appearance (e.g., purple glass imitating amethyst)

table top facet or surface of a cut stone

taille d'épargne [tie yuh day PARN] literally, saving (economical) cut. Enameling technique: engraved design partially filled with opaque enamel, usually black (also known as *black enamel tracery*)

T-bar clasp closure, usually for chain necklaces, consisting of a T-shaped bar that slips through a circular ring; when the chain is worn, the bar is held in place against the ring

tesserae [TESS er ee] tiny colored glass pieces used in MOSAIC (sometimes called *Roman mosaic*)

Tiffany setting four- or six-prong elevated setting for a solitaire stone introduced by Tiffany & Co. in 1886

torsade multi-strand twisted short necklace, usually beads or pearls; cabled or twisted cord

trace chain chain with oval links of equal size

trefoil decorative element having three lobes

trombone catch two-part sliding tubular closure finding for brooches

tube hinge brooch finding, an elongated tubular hinge (called a *joint* by jewelers) to which a pinstem is attached

v-spring part of a BOX CLASP closure finding in which a wedge-shaped element fits into a metal box

vasiform vase-shaped

vermeil [ver MAY] gold-plated silver, silver gilt

volute spiral, snail shell-shaped

vulcanite vulcanized (hardened) rubber, used for mourning jewelry in the 19th century, also known as EBONITE

watch pin small brooch/pin with a hook at the base of the reverse with its open end up, for suspending a small watch; worn on women's bodices at the turn of the century

white gold alloy of gold with nickel, palladium, or platinum (various formulae) that produces a silver-white color, approximating platinum, for which it is substituted

wirework twisted wire decoration applied to metal ground

yellow gold alloy of gold with silver and copper, most common color of gold

ziggurat stepped triangle or pyramid shape